ETHNICITIES

Ethnicities

Children of Immigrants in America

Edited by
RUBÉN G. RUMBAUT and ALEJANDRO PORTES

UNIVERSITY OF CALIFORNIA PRESS
Berkeley   Los Angeles   London

RUSSELL SAGE FOUNDATION
New York

University of California Press
Berkeley and Los Angeles, California

University of California Press, Ltd.
London, England

Russell Sage Foundation
New York, New York

Ethnicities : children of immigrants in America /
edited by Rubén G. Rumbaut and Alejandro Portes.
    p. cm.
Includes bibliographical references and index.
ISBN 978-0-520-23012-5 (pbk. : alk. paper)
    1. Children of minorities—United States—
Social conditions. 2. Children of immigrants—
United States—Social conditions. 3. Children of
minorities—United States—Family relationships.
4. Children of immigrants—United States—Family
relationships. 5. Minorities—United States—
Social conditions. 6. Immigrants—United States—
Social conditions. 7. Ethnicity—United States.
8. Acculturation—United States. 9. United
States—Emigration and immigration. I. Rumbaut,
Rubén G., 1948– II. Portes, Alejandro, 1944–

E184.A1 E848 2001
305.8′00973—dc21

                      00-048889

Printed in the United States of America
14 13 12 11 10
10 9 8 7 6 5 4

The paper used in this publication meets the
minimum requirements of ANSI/NISO Z39.48-1992
(R 1997) (*Permanence of Paper*). ∞

To the immigrant families and their children
who made this study possible

CONTENTS

TABLES AND FIGURES

Tables

Figures

ACKNOWLEDGMENTS

This book is the product of an unusual experiment. The idea for it emerged as we began work on a companion volume, *Legacies: The Story of the Immigrant Second Generation*. Both are based on the Children of Immigrants Longitudinal Study (CILS), carried out during the 1990s on both coasts of the United States, which followed over 5,200 youths from several dozen nationalities, mostly from Latin America and Asia, through the end of high school. We learned a great deal from our comparative study of their patterns of acculturation, family and school life, language, identity, experiences of discrimination, self-esteem, ambition, and achievement. But we also discovered that every multivariate analysis of CILS results identified nationality or ethnicity as a strong and significant predictor of virtually every adaptation outcome. Just what *ethnicity* meant, however, was not self-evident from those analyses.

What was needed, therefore, was an effort to examine systematically the adaptation patterns and trajectories of children of immigrants *within* key ethnic groups—Mexican, Cuban, Nicaraguan, Filipino, Vietnamese, Haitian, Jamaican, and other West Indian—in the San Diego and Miami/Ft. Lauderdale areas. Our strategy was to bring together a distinguished group of scholars who had specialized in the major immigrant nationalities here under consideration, make available to them the CILS data set, and invite them to combine their expert knowledge of the respective groups with an in-depth analysis of these data. The following chapters are the result of this collective effort. We owe our principal debt to these authors, who worked assiduously to produce insightful, engaging, and creative essays.

The CILS project itself is the product of a decade of work and of the contributions of many people. In San Diego, the study would not have been possible without the exceptional efforts of our research staff, led ably by Linda and Norm Borgen, Kevin Keogan, and Laura Lagunas. We appreciate as well the excellent work of a team of over two dozen interviewers fluent in Spanish, Tagalog, Vietnamese, Cambodian, Lao, Hmong, and other Asian languages representative of the immigrant families that have resettled in the San Diego area. In Miami, our colleague Lisandro Pérez of Florida International University led the fieldwork for the original and follow-up surveys and also contributed a chapter for this volume. His team of field interviewers and coders deserves much of the credit for the success of the project in southern Florida. We are especially grateful to Patricia Fernández-Kelly, who personally conducted many intensive interviews with immigrant parents and also collaborated on another chapter for this book. Much of the CILS data, however, came not from field interviews but from school records. Indeed, the entire project could not have been conducted without the active cooperation and support of the Dade (Miami), Broward (Ft. Lauderdale), and San Diego school systems. We thank the administrators and research staff of each system, and especially the principals and teachers of the dozens of schools that participated in the project, for their indispensable collaboration.

The study has been supported in its successive stages by grants from the Andrew W. Mellon Foundation, the Spencer Foundation, the National Science Foundation, and the Russell Sage Foundation. The Mellon Foundation supported both phases of the project in San Diego as well as exploratory interviews with immigrant parents in the period between surveys; we particularly thank Stephanie Bell-Rose, its former program officer. The Spencer Foundation deserves our gratitude for its strong support of all phases of the project and the sustained encouragement of its staff, in particular its president, Patricia Albjerg Graham. We owe a special debt to the Russell Sage Foundation, whose board adopted the study of the immigrant second generation as one of its research priorities and whose president, Eric Wanner, has given us unfailing support throughout the years. Russell Sage fellowships to the two editors in different years gave decisive momentum to our efforts at conceptualization and data analysis, and another Russell Sage grant made possible an inaugural workshop that convened all the authors of this volume in December 1997 at the foundation's offices in New York City.

The CILS project was originally based at Johns Hopkins University and at San Diego State University and moved subsequently to Princeton University and Michigan State University. We are grateful for the help of our graduate assistants and of the administrative staff of the sociology departments at all four universities. In particular, Barbara McCabe at Princeton collaborated with us in putting the chapters in finished form and coordinating the numerous tasks required to ready the manuscript for production; we thank her for her valuable contribution. We also wish to acknowledge the consistent support and encouragement we have received throughout from Naomi Schneider, our long-term editor at the University of California Press, and Suzanne Nichols, director of publications at the Russell Sage Foundation.

Above all, we are indebted to the over 5,000 children and their immigrant families who are the subjects of this work and to whom it is dedicated. The book will have succeeded if it conveys something of the rich complexity of their lives and the extraordinary diversity of experience that they shared with us over the past decade.

Rubén G. Rumbaut and Alejandro Portes
East Lansing and Princeton
July 2000

Chapter 1

INTRODUCTION
Ethnogenesis: Coming of Age in Immigrant America

Rubén G. Rumbaut and Alejandro Portes

> "Being American means that you feel like you're the norm," one of my
> friends tells me. [But] in a splintered society, what does one assimilate
> to? . . . I want to figure out, more urgently than before, where I belong
> in this America that's made up of so many subAmericas.
>
> **Eva Hoffman, *Lost in Translation* (1989: 202)**

The new immigration to the United States—notably from Asia, Latin
America, and the Caribbean, with smaller but growing components
from Europe, Africa, and the Middle East—is unprecedented in its diversity of color and class and cultural origins. Over the past few
decades, it has been changing fundamentally the racial and ethnic composition and stratification of the American population as well as the social meanings of race and ethnicity and of American identity. In the
process, in familiar as well as surprising ways, the immigrants and their
children are themselves being transformed into the newest Americans.
Over time and generations, their intermarriages and other intermin-
glings may produce complex new ethnic formations and identities, even
as the process of "becoming American" has come to include the adoption or rejection of such officially constructed panethnic labels as "Hispanic" and "Asian/Pacific Islander," which lump together scores of nationalities into one-size-fits-all minority-group categories—much as the
oldest minorities, "Indians" and "Negroes," were first defined as a single entity from the outside (see Petersen 1980). The U.S. Census Bureau
continues to divide Americans into distinct racial groups, as it has variously done since the first census of 1790, but for the first time the 2000

1

census abandoned its binary notion of race and allowed multiple choices that can yield as many as 63 different racial types, further exposing the arbitrary character of rigid racial categorization and of the dubious projections that are made on the basis of such categories.

Indeed, immigration, race, and ethnicity have again become the stuff of front-page news. Increasingly, newspapers throughout the United States, especially in major urban centers where large immigrant communities have sprouted, have focused attention (often tinged with an accompanying sense of alarm) on the manifold impact of immigration on their cities' and states' ethnic composition and status hierarchies and on the perennial question of what it means to be—and to become—an American. Here is a recent sampler from California, Florida, and New York:

> Within the first few minutes of the new year, the future of Orange County could be heard in the cries of newborns. The first boy and first girl of 2000 in California were born to immigrant couples—one from Cambodia, one from Mexico. The parents of the boy, Nearyroth Lach and Bonrith Peou, fled their native Cambodia after Pol Pot came to power and [they] settled near family and friends in Santa Ana, where they are now creating a new second generation; they gave their newborn an American name—James. The girl was named Anayeli de Jesús Dector. Her parents, from Puebla and Veracruz, came to the U.S. in the 1990s looking for a better future, and hope for the same for their daughter: "To be a good student and to go to the university." —Kate Folmar and Scott Martelle, "The New Faces of Orange County's Future" (2000: A-1)

> Demographic change in California is occurring so fast that by next year, no single ethnic group will comprise a majority of the state's population, according to forecasts in a new state report. The researchers predict that California's white population will fall to 50% next year—the lowest since the Gold Rush—continuing a decades-long downward slide. In 1970, whites accounted for 77% of California's residents. As the percentage of whites decreases, the burgeoning Latino population will account for almost a third of the state's 34 million people in 2000. By 2021, Latinos are expected to be California's largest ethnic group, at about 40%. —Armando Acuña, "California and the West" (1999: A-1)

> Does a Latino identity even exist? Do Cuban blacks really have much in common with Anglo-Argentines or Mayan Indians from Guatemala? What sort of common bond is there between Honduras and El Salvador, who once went to war over a soccer match? Costa Ricans detest their neighbors so much that they've refused to sign a treaty that permits movement between Central American countries without visas. When Puerto Ricans, Mexicans and Cubans living in the United States were surveyed in 1992 about whether they preferred to be called "Latino" or "Hispanic," they overwhelmingly answered: Puerto Rican, Mexican and Cuban. —Glenn Garvin, "Latin America" (2000: A-1)

The re-Cubanization of Miami-Dade County is now in full swing. And nothing at century's end seems likely to check it. Fed by an unabating stream of newcomers from the island, Miami in the 21st Century will become even more Cuban in flavor and fact than it is already . . . and it will also become more diverse: more Haitian, more Jamaican, more Nicaraguan, even more Russian. Like it is now, only more so. This is no paradox. It's how U.S. immigration works. The overwhelming numerical disadvantage of non-Hispanics in Miami-Dade, on the other hand, will continue to grow. White non-Hispanics and native-born blacks, in particular, could find themselves increasingly overwhelmed, culturally and perhaps even economically. In the near term, though, no other place in America will look or feel quite like Miami-Dade, one of the few U.S. metropolitan areas where an immigrant group makes up not just the largest ethnic group, but more and more of the economic and political establishment.   —Andrés Viglucci, "Ethnic Make-Over of South Florida Likely to Intensify" (2000: A-1)

Sachin and Purvi Shah arrived with their infant daughter at Newark International Airport on a crisp day in February as the newest of immigrants from Barooda, India. But instead of heading to Flushing or Jackson Heights, they drove . . . [to] an affluent township, some 40 miles from New York City. All told, it took an hour for the Shahs to achieve what earlier immigrants often could not claim for decades, even generations: middle-class comfort and prosperity in suburban America. By leapfrogging to the most desirable suburbs, many Asian immigrants are upending stereotypes about new immigrants' being poor and invisible, tethered to ethnic neighborhoods, desperate to wriggle out of the city. Instead, these newcomers are younger and more economically diverse, equipped with graduate degrees and work visas, gifted in science and technology.   —David W. Chen, "Asian Middle Class Alters a Rural Enclave" (1999: A-1)

In the Old World, there was one way of life, or 2, maybe 10. Here there are dozens, hundreds, all jammed in together, cheek by jowl, especially in the dizzying cities. Everywhere has a somewhere else just around the corner. We newish Americans leapfrog from world to world, reinventing ourselves en route. We perform our college selves, our waitress selves, our dot-com selves, our parent selves, our downtown selves, our Muslim, Greek, Hindi, South African selves. Even into the second or third generation, we speak different languages—more languages, often, than we know we know. We sport different names. . . . We wonder who we are—what does it mean to be Irish-American, Cuban-American, Armenian-American?—and are amazed to discover that others wonder, too. Indeed, nothing seems more typically American than to obsess about identity. Can so many people truly be so greatly confused? We feel very much a part of the contemporary gestalt. Yet two or three generations later, we still may not be insiders.   —Gish Jen, "The Making of a Newly American Mind" (2000)

American Ethnicity, Old and New

The ethnic groups that make up the population of the United States were forged, along with peculiarly American ideologies of race, in the process of its national expansion. Their unequal modes of incorporation reflect fundamentally different starting points, contexts of reception, and attendant definitions of the situation. This ethnogenesis—the construction and evolution of American ethnicity—has taken shape over many generations, molded by the European conquest of indigenous and enslaved peoples and by massive waves of migration from all over the world. Thus, immigration as well as enslavement, annexation, and conquest were the originating processes by which American ethnicities were formed and through which, over time, the United States was transformed into one of the world's most ethnically diverse societies.

A legacy of that history is that a deeply entrenched divide came to mark what is euphemistically referred to as "race and ethnic relations" in American social science: a "color line" that W. E. B. DuBois, in *The Souls of Black Folk,* prophesied would be "the problem of the twentieth century . . . the relation of the darker to the lighter races of men in Asia and Africa, in America and the islands of the sea" ([1903] 1989: 10). That color line has historically defined the boundary between two broad modes of ethnic incorporation into American social life: one epitomized by assimilation, the master process that purports to explain how it came to be that the descendants of tens of millions of European immigrants from heterogeneous national and cultural origins were absorbed into the mainstream of white society, their identities eventually becoming largely symbolic and fading into a "twilight of ethnicity" (Gans 1979; Alba 1985; Waters 1990; see also Glazer and Moynihan 1970); and another largely resistant to such absorption into the majority regardless of level of acculturation or socioeconomic attainment, characterized instead by persistently high social distances in intergroup relations and discrimination (Massey and Denton 1993; Pedraza and Rumbaut 1996).

For example, in *The Social Systems of American Ethnic Groups,* perhaps the definitive statement on the subject near midcentury, W. Lloyd Warner and Leo Srole (1945) describe the progressive advance of eight European-origin immigrant groups in the major status hierarchies of "Yankee City," explicitly linking upward social mobility to assimilation, which they saw as determined largely by the degree of ethnocultural (religion and language) and above all racial difference from the dominant group. While racial groups were subordinated through caste restrictions on residential, occupational, associational, and marital choice, the clash of ethnic groups with the dominant institutions of the host society was not much of a contest, particularly among the young. The industrial economy, the polity, the public school, popular culture, and the American family system all undercut and absorbed ethnicity in various ways so that even when "the ethnic parent tries to orient the child to an ethnic past . . . the child often insists on being more American than Americans" (1945: 284). And for the upwardly mobile, with socioeconomic success came intermarriage and the further dilution of ethnicity.

Our conventional models of immigrant acculturation and ethnic self-identification processes largely derive from the historical experience of those (and earlier) European immigrants and their descendants. Indeed, it is hard to imagine that barely three decades before Warner and Srole's authoritative portrayal, the large-scale new immigration of allegedly unassimilable southern and eastern Europeans—Italians, Poles, Greeks, Russian Jews, and many others—had occasioned vitriolic public denunciations and widespread fears about the "mongrelization of the race," culminating in forced Americanization campaigns and the passage of the restrictionist national-origins quota laws of the 1920s (see Higham 1955). By 1965, the prevailing view of the matter was framed succinctly by Vladimir Nahirny and Joshua Fishman: "The erosion of ethnicity and ethnic identity experienced by most (but not all) American ethnic groups takes place in the course of three generations. . . . Ethnic heritage, including the ethnic mother tongue, usually ceases to play any viable role in the life of the third generation" (1996: 266).

But today a new era of mass immigration—and hence of ethnogenesis—now overwhelmingly non-European in composition, is again raising familiar doubts about the assimilability of the newcomers and alarms that they might become consigned to a vast multiethnic underclass, on the other side of a new twenty-first-century color line. It is also raising serious questions about the applicability of explanatory models developed in connection with the experience of European ethnics, despite the fact that today's immigrants are being incorporated in a more complex, post-civil-rights context characterized more by ethnic revivals and identity politics than by forced Americanization campaigns. Indeed, while assimilation may still represent the master process in the study of today's immigrants, it is a process subject to too many contingencies and affected by too many variables to render the image of a relatively uniform and straightforward path convincing.

Instead, the present second generation of children of immigrants is better defined as undergoing a process of segmented assimilation in which outcomes vary across immigrant minorities and in which rapid integration and acceptance into the American mainstream represent just one possible alternative. Why this is so—and how it is that different groups may come to assimilate into different sectors of American society—is a complex story that hinges on a number of factors, among which the following can be considered decisive: (1) the history of the immigrant first generation, including the human capital brought by immigrant parents and the context of their reception; (2) the differential pace of acculturation among parents and children, including the development of language gaps between them, and its bearing on normative integration and family cohesiveness; (3) the cultural and economic barriers confronted by second-generation youth in their quest for successful adaptation; and (4) the family and community resources for confronting these barriers (Portes and Rumbaut 1996, 2001).

These factors combine in ways that magnify the relative social advantages or disadvantages of particular immigrant groups as they make their way in America, and mold both the character of parent-child relations within immigrant families and the adaptive experiences and trajectories of their children. For example, by far the most-educated *and* the least-educated groups in the United States today are immigrants, a reflection of polar-opposite types of migrations embedded in very different historical contexts. They come as state-sponsored refugees or through regular immigration channels or without legal authorization. The undocumented tend to consist disproportionately of manual laborers, whose legal vulnerability makes them more economically exploitable and likely to be concentrated in central cities; their children, in turn, attend schools where they are exposed disproportionately to peer groups involved with youth gangs and intergroup violence. Professionals enter under the occupational preferences of U.S. law and are also typically found among the first waves of refugee flows; they are more likely to become naturalized citizens and, usually within the first generation, homeowners in the suburbs. Internal characteristics, including the structure and cohesiveness of their families, interact in complex but patterned ways with external contexts of reception—government policies and programs, the state of the economy in the areas where they settle, employer preferences in local labor markets, the extent of racial discrimination and nativist hostility, the strength of existing ethnic communities—to form the conditions within which immigrant children adapt, react, and assimilate into different segments of American society.

The chapters in this book examine the patterns and paradoxes of incorporation of youths of diverse national origins—Mexican, Cuban, Nicaraguan, Filipino, Vietnamese, Haitian, Jamaican, and other West Indian—coming of age in immigrant families on both coasts of the United States.

From Immigrants to Ethnics

As reflected in the excerpts from the news stories cited previously, new American ethnic groups are forming more quickly than ever before. This outcome is now due entirely to international migration and the ethnogenic processes set off in its wake, which, as noted earlier, is once more accompanied by the official construction of panethnic categories such as "Asian" and "Hispanic" into which newcomers from many different countries and cultures are classified. The emerging ethnic groups of the United States in the twenty-first century will be the children and grandchildren of today's immigrants. Their numbers and diversity will ensure that the process will have a profound societal impact, although it is too early to draw firm conclusions from the forms of social and economic adaptation experienced by this still young population or to predict with accuracy their probable trajectories of incorporation.

Nonetheless, four decades into a new era of mass immigration, it is now a commonplace to note that the United States is in the midst of its most profound demographic transformation in a century. As Table 1.1 shows, the immigrant-stock population of the United States in 1997 numbered approximately 55 million people—that is, persons who were either foreign-born (nearly 27 million) or U.S.-born children of immigrants (28 million)—and they represented slightly more than one-fifth (20.5 percent) of the total U.S. population. This figure can be confidently expected to grow rapidly through ongoing immigration and natural increase (Rumbaut 1998).[1]

To be sure, the current *proportions* fall well short of those that obtained during the last era of mass immigration a century ago. During the period from 1880 to 1930, as Table 1.1 makes clear, the foreign-stock population consistently comprised about one-third of the national total (peaking at 35.3 percent in the 1910 census), with the foreign-born share reaching nearly 15 percent of the total in 1890 and

TABLE 1.1 DECENNIAL TRENDS, 1890–1998, IN THE U.S. FOREIGN-BORN AND FOREIGN-STOCK POPULATION AND IN LEGAL IMMIGRATION BY REGION OF ORIGIN

	U.S. Census Bureau Data: Foreign-Born and Foreign-Stock Population				Immigration and Naturalization Service Data: Legal Immigration by Decade and Region of Last Residence				
Census Year	Foreign-Born[1] N (millions)	Percent of Total U.S. Population	Foreign-Stock[2] N (millions)	Percent of Total U.S. Population	Decade	Immigrants N (thousands)	Europe, Canada (%)	Latin America (%)	Asia (%)
1890	9.2	14.8	20.8	33.2	1881–1890	5,247	97.8	0.6	1.3
1900	10.4	13.6	26.0	34.3	1891–1900	3,688	96.5	1.0	2.0
1910	13.4	14.7	32.5	35.3	1901–1910	8,795	93.9	2.1	3.7
1920	14.0	13.2	36.7	34.7	1911–1920	5,736	88.3	7.0	4.3
1930	14.3	11.6	40.3	32.8	1921–1930	4,107	82.5	14.4	2.7
1940	11.7	8.8	na	na	1931–1940	528	86.3	9.7	3.1
1950	10.4	6.9	na	na	1941–1950	1,035	76.6	14.9	3.6
1960	9.7	5.5	34.1	19.0	1951–1960	2,515	67.8	22.2	6.1
1970	9.6	4.7	33.6	16.5	1961–1970	3,322	46.3	38.6	12.9
1980	14.1	6.2	na	na	1971–1980	4,493	21.6	40.3	35.3
1990	19.8	7.9	na	na	1981–1990	7,338[3]	12.5	47.1	37.3
1997	26.8	9.7	54.7	20.5	1991–1998	7,605[4]	14.8	50.4	30.1

SOURCE: U.S. Census Bureau 1992, Tables 1, 5–6, 45; U.S. Census Bureau 1999, Figure 8-1; U.S. Immigration and Naturalization Service, Tables 1–2.

[1] Data on nativity from decennial censuses, 1890–1990, and from the Current Population Survey for 1997. Since the 1890 census, persons born in a foreign country but with at least one parent who was a U.S. citizen have been redefined as *native* rather than *foreign born*. Persons residing in the United States who were born (or whose parents were born) in any "outlying areas" of the United States are also classified as natives. These have included Puerto Rico since 1900 and others at different times; for example, persons born in the Philippines were classified as native in 1900–1940 and as foreign born in 1950 (after independence in 1946) and since.

[2] The *foreign stock* population is defined as the sum of the foreign-born population (the first generation) and the native population with at least one foreign-born parent (the second generation). The question on nativity or birthplace of parents was asked in censuses from 1870 to 1970 bur dropped from the 1980 and 1990 and 2000 censuses. The question has been asked in the (March) Current Population Surveys annually since 1994.

[3] Data include 1,359,186 formerly undocumented immigrants who had resided in the United States since 1982 and whose status was legalized in fiscal years 1989 and 1990 under the amnesty provisions of the Immigration Reform and Control Act (IRCA) of 1986.

[4] Data include another 1,329,209 formerly undocumented immigrants, mostly special agricultural workers, whose status was adjusted to permanent resident under IRCA in fiscal years 1991 and since. Virtually all IRCA legalizations were completed by 1993.

again in 1910. This compares to 7.9 percent in 1990 and 9.7 percent in 1997. In that earlier period, it was not only the sheer size of the immigration flows but also the sharp shift in their national origins, from northwestern to southern and eastern European countries, that heightened nativist fears. Today's immigration is likewise large in volume and marked by an even sharper shift in its composition: While the proportion of immigrants arriving during 1880–1900 came overwhelmingly from Europe (97 percent), the proportion of European immigrants arriving during 1980–1998 plummeted to just over 10 percent of the total number of legal admissions. By 1997, of the 27 million foreign born—already the largest immigrant population in history—fully 90 percent arrived after 1960. Of these post-1960 immigrants, the majority (52 percent) came from Latin America and the Caribbean. Nearly a third (29 percent) came from Asia and the Middle East. The Filipinos, Chinese, and Indochinese alone accounted for 15 percent of the total, or as much as all of those born in Europe and Canada combined. By 1999, the number of their U.S.-born children—the new second generation—had surpassed the prior record set up by children of earlier European immigrants.

As in the past, today's newcomers are heavily concentrated in certain areas of settlement. Fully one-third of the country's immigrant-stock population resides in California, and another third resides in Florida, Texas, and New York/New Jersey, with the ethnic concentrations being still denser within metropolitan areas in this handful of states. By 1997, 62 percent of the Los Angeles area's 9.5 million people were of immigrant stock, as were 54 percent of New York City's, 43 percent of San Diego's, and 72 percent of Miami's (Rumbaut 1998). But unlike the last great waves of European immigration, which were halted by the passage of restrictive legislation in the 1920s and especially by the back-to-back global cataclysms of the Great Depression and World War II, the current flows show no sign of abating. On the contrary, inasmuch as immigration is a network-driven phenomenon and the United States remains the premier destination for a world on the move, the likelihood is that it will continue indefinitely. This has immense implications for the future of American society—and of the ethnic composition of its population.

The increasing size and concentration of this population, added to its diverse national and socioeconomic origins, makes its intergenerational evolution central to the future of the country. Yet while the rapid growth of immigration over the last few decades has led to a mushrooming research literature and an intensified public debate about the new immigrants' impact on American society, much less noticed has been the fact that a new generation of Americans raised in immigrant families is coming of age. Over time, its members will decisively shape the character of their ethnic communities and their chances for success or failure (see Portes 1996; Portes and Rumbaut 1996, 2001; Rumbaut and Cornelius 1995).

Hence, the long-term effects of contemporary immigration will hinge more on the trajectories of these youths than on the fate of their parents. For all intents and purposes, the children of today's immigrants—a generation oriented not to their parents' immigrant pasts but to their own American futures—are here to stay and, as such, form the most lasting consequence of this mass movement. Whether this new ethnic mosaic revitalizes the nation or exacerbates its social problems depends on the forms of social and economic adaptation experienced by this still young population. Some of the ethnic groups created by the new immigration are in a clearly upward path, moving into society's mainstream in record time and enriching it in the process with their culture and energies. Others, on the contrary, seem poised for a path of blocked aspirations and downward mobility, reproducing the plight of today's impoverished domestic minorities. Indeed, this is what is meant by the concept of segmented assimilation introduced previously; its clarification and the analysis of its determinants represent a core agenda for the study of the immigrant second generation. In a scenario of pervasive downward mobility, the size of American cities' problems may increase concomitantly, the only change being that the participants may come from new ethnic quarters. Were this outcome to become dominant among the second generation, a new "rainbow underclass"—and an attendant color line—would be the prospect facing urban America by the middle of the next century. That, of course, remains an open empirical question.

The Children of Immigrants Longitudinal Study

The chapters that follow aim to provide a close empirical look at some of the principal new ethnicities being formed in the United States today. More specifically, they examine the results of the Children of Immigrants Longitudinal Study (CILS), a multifaceted investigation of the educational performance and social, cultural, and psychological adaptation of children of immigrants. CILS is the largest study of its kind to date in the United States. A number of publications based on CILS have provided comparative analyses of diverse aspects of the adaptation of these youths—for example, of their patterns of linguistic acculturation, ethnic identity, well-being, and educational aspirations and achievement—but none had yet focused attention on the experience of particular national minorities.[2] Notably, however, every multivariate analysis of CILS results to date has identified nationality or ethnicity as a strong and significant predictor of virtually every adaptation outcome (see especially Portes and Rumbaut 2001).

What is needed, therefore, is an effort to probe systematically and in depth the adaptation patterns and trajectories of concrete ethnic groups. Our strategy was to bring together a group of scholars who had specialized in each of the major immigrant nationalities under consideration, make available to them the CILS data set, and invite them to combine their expertise on the respective groups with an in-depth analysis of these data. The following chapters are the result of this collective effort.[3]

Since late 1991, the CILS project has followed the progress of a sizable sample of teenage youths representing 77 nationalities in two key areas of immigrant settlement in the United States: southern California (San Diego) and southern Florida (Miami and Fort Lauderdale). The original survey, conducted in Spring 1992 (T1), interviewed 5,262 students enrolled in the eighth and ninth grades in schools of the San Diego Unified School District ($N = 2,420$) and of the Dade and Broward County Unified School Districts ($N = 2,296$ and 339, respectively, with another 207 enrolled in private bilingual schools in the Miami area). The sample was drawn in the junior high grades, a level at which dropout rates are still relatively rare, to avoid the potential bias of differential dropout rates between ethnic groups at the senior high school level. For purposes of the study, students were eligible to enter the sample if they were U.S. born but had at least one foreign-born parent or if they themselves were foreign born and had come to the U.S. at an early age (before age 12). The resulting sample is evenly balanced between males and females and between foreign-born and U.S.-born children of immigrants—that is, respectively, between the 1.5 generation and the second generation.

Three years later, in 1995–1996 (T2), a second survey of the same group of children was conducted—this time supplemented by separate, in-depth interviews with a large sample of their parents. The purpose of this follow-up effort, which succeeded in reinterviewing 82 percent of the baseline sample, was to ascertain changes over time in their family situation, school achievement, educational and occupational aspirations, language use and preferences, ethnic identities, experiences and expectations of discrimination, and psychosocial adjustment. By this time the youths, who were originally interviewed in junior high school when most were 14 or 15 years old, had reached the final year of senior high school and were beginning their transitions to adulthood, firming up plans for their future as well as their outlooks on the surrounding society.

To highlight the differences between the communities where the CILS study took place (the study began during the 1991–1992 school year), a socioeconomic profile is sketched in Table 1.2 comparing 1990 census data for the population of the city of San Diego—the jurisdiction covered by the San Diego Unified School District—with that for the metropolitan area of Miami-Dade (covered by the Dade County Unified School District, where most of the southern Florida survey was carried out). Data for the total U.S. population is provided for comparative purposes.

San Diego's school district is the nation's eighth largest, with 133,000 students enrolled K–12 (in 1991–1992), drawn from the city's (1990) population of 1.1 million, the sixth-largest city in the nation. The Dade County Unified School District is the fourth largest in the country, with over 300,000 students enrolled K–12, since it draws from the much larger metropolitan Miami-Dade area. The socioeconomic profiles in Table 1.2 characterize the populations whose children were enrolled in the two main school districts from which the CILS samples were drawn. Compared to Miami-Dade (and other large cities and school districts in the country), San Diego's is a comparatively more affluent, better-educated, still primarily non-Hispanic white population, with a four-to-one ratio of professionals to laborers in its labor force, in contrast to a ratio of less than two-to-one for the Miami metropolitan area.

Nearly half (45.4 percent) of the Miami area's population was foreign born in 1990—highest among American metropolitan areas—compared to 20.9 percent of San Diego's and only 7.9 percent for the United States as a whole. Hispanics in metro Miami, who are mostly of Cuban and other Caribbean Basin origin, comprised about half (49.2 percent) of its total population, compared to a one-fifth share (20.1

TABLE 1.2   THE CILS SITES: PROFILES FOR
SAN DIEGO, MIAMI, AND THE UNITED STATES

Social and Economic Characteristics	City of San Diego	Metro Miami (Dade County)	United States
N	1,110,549	1,914,689	248,709,873
% Non-Hispanic white	58.8	30.1	75.8
% Hispanic	20.1	49.2	8.8
% Black	9.3	20.7	12.0
% Asian	11.8	1.3	2.9
% Foreign born	20.9	45.4	7.9
% Non-English speakers	29.2	57.6	13.8
% High school graduates	82.3	65.0	75.2
% College degree	29.8	18.8	20.3
% Unemployment rate	6.2	7.7	6.3
% Professionals, managers	32.5	24.6	26.4
% Laborers, fabricators	8.8	13.6	14.9
% Poverty rate (persons)	13.4	18.0	13.1
% Poverty rate (families)	9.7	14.2	10.0

SOURCE: U.S. Bureau of the Census 1993.

percent) in San Diego, where they are overwhelmingly of Mexican origin. San Diego's Asian-origin population (11.8 percent), composed preponderantly of Filipinos and southeast Asians, is well above the equivalent proportion of the U.S. population (less than 3 percent) and the even smaller proportion found in the Miami metropolitan area. These figures are mirrored in the ethnic composition of the student bodies of the respective school systems—and in the CILS sample.

As broken down in Table 1.3, the principal nationalities represented in the San Diego component of the study are Mexican, Filipino, and Vietnamese as well as smaller groups from Asia (Laotian, Cambodian, Chinese, Japanese, Korean, and Indian) and Latin America. In the southern Florida sample, the principal nationality groups consisted of Cubans, Nicaraguans, Haitians, Jamaicans, and others from Latin America and the Caribbean (Colombians, Dominicans, Trinidadians, and many others from Central and South America). These groups are representative of the principal types of contemporary immigration to the United States, including immigrant laborers, professionals, entrepreneurs, and political refugees with sharply contrasting migration histories and contexts of exit and of reception (Pedraza and Rumbaut 1996; Portes and Rumbaut 1996; Rumbaut 1994b). The principal na-

TABLE 1.3   THE CILS SAMPLE: NATIONAL
ORIGIN OF RESPONDENTS BY LOCATION IN
FLORIDA OR CALIFORNIA

Location of CILS Sample

National Origin	Southern Florida (N)	Southern California (N)	Total Sample (N)
Mexico	28	727	755
Cuba	1,224	2	1,226
Nicaragua	340	4	344
Other Latin America	634	63	697
Haiti	177	1	178
Jamaica, West Indies	253	19	272
Philippines	11	808	819
Vietnam	8	362	370
Other Asia	47	428	475
All other countries	120	6	126
TOTAL	2,842	2,420	5,262

tionalities represented in the CILS sample, which are the specific subject of the following chapters, are briefly depicted in the following list.

1. Mexicans constitute by far the largest legal and illegal immigrant population in the United States. Indeed, they are part of the largest, longest, and most sustained labor migration in the history of the nation. San Diego, situated along the Mexican border, has long been a major recipient of Mexican immigration. The 1990 census showed that among adults over 25, Mexican immigrants had the lowest educational levels of any major U.S. ethnic group, native or foreign born.

2. Since the 1960s, Filipinos have constituted the second-largest immigrant population in the country, and they are the largest Asian-origin immigrant group in California and in the nation. Many have come as professionals (nurses most conspicuously) and through military connections (especially the U.S. Navy). The 1990 census showed that Filipino immigrants have the lowest poverty rate of any sizable ethnic group in the United States.

3. Cubans form the third-largest contemporary immigrant nationality in the United States, becoming internally diversified over time. Cuban refugee migration has not been continuous but has

taken place in a series of spurts—from the huge first waves of
political exiles of the early 1960s to the so-called freedom flights
of 1965–1973, the Mariel boatlift of 1980, and the *balseros*
(rafters) of the 1990s. Over half of the total Cuban population
in the country is concentrated in southern Florida, building a
dense and highly visible ethnic enclave that has been dubbed
"Havana USA" (see García 1996; Portes and Stepick 1993).
Miami has also been the primary settlement site for another sizable group of Latin American exiles—the Nicaraguans—who
came largely during the 1980s but who, unlike the earlier waves
of Cubans, did not meet with a similarly positive reception and
were mostly left in ambiguous legal statuses.

4. Since the end of the Indochina War in 1975, refugees from Vietnam, Cambodia, and Laos have formed the largest refugee population in the United States—indeed, they came as part of the
largest refugee resettlement program in American history (see
Rumbaut 1996). The 1990 census found the highest poverty and
welfare dependency rates in the country among Laotians and
Cambodians (many of whom were survivors of the so-called
killing fields of the late 1970s). The most recent Current Population Surveys (CPSs) show that the Vietnamese are now the country's fifth-largest foreign-born population, following Mexicans,
Filipinos, Cubans, and Chinese (from China, Hong Kong, and
Taiwan).

5. Haitians and Jamaicans (as well as Trinidadians and smaller
groups of English-speaking West Indians), who are concentrated
in the New York and southern Florida areas, are not only
among the top recent immigrant groups in terms of size but also
form the two largest groups of black immigrants in the United
States. Despite the many differences between Haitians and West
Indians in their class and cultural backgrounds and migration
histories, their children's experiences of incorporation have commonly underscored the persistent salience of racial prejudice and
discrimination in American society (Stepick 1997; Waters 1999).

Although the 27 million immigrants living in the United States in
1997 came from over 150 different countries, about 40 percent came
from only four: Mexico, the Philippines, Cuba, and Vietnam. Children
of immigrants from those same four countries make up 60 percent of
our study's sample (see Table 1.3). The chapters that follow focus on

these four nationalities as well as on the contrasting experiences of Nicaraguans, Haitians, and West Indians who have settled in significant numbers in southern Florida. To provide a general perspective on these specific national stories, Chapter 2 reviews recent census data on the new second generation and on its principal patterns of settlement and adaptation. The analyses of individual nationalities in Chapters 3 to 9 flesh out this demographic overview with an in-depth look at the migration histories and contexts of exit and incorporation of each group as well as their respective effects on immigrant families and children. In the concluding chapter we take stock of the principal findings reported in the analyses of particular groups and reflect on their implications for theory and policy in the forging of a new America.

Notes

1. Leif Jensen's estimates in the following chapter put the immigrant-stock population at over 56 million as of 1997, including a second-generation estimate of 30 million.

2. For published results to date, see Fernández-Kelly and Schauffler 1996; Pérez 1996; Portes 1995, 1996; Portes and Hao 1998; Portes and MacLeod 1996a, 1996b, 1999; Portes and Rumbaut 1996, 2001; Portes and Schauffler 1996; Portes and Zhou 1993; Rumbaut 1994a, 1995, 1997, 1998, 1999a, 1999b, 2000.

3. During the course of this effort, the authors met at conferences in December 1997 and June 1998 held at the Russell Sage Foundation and Princeton University, respectively.

References

Acuña, Armando. 1999. California and the West: Changes in state's ethnic balance are accelerating. *Los Angeles Times,* October 20, p. A-1.

Alba, Richard D. 1985. *Italian Americans: Into the twilight of ethnicity.* Englewood Cliffs, N.J.: Prentice Hall.

Chen, David W. 1999. Asian middle class alters a rural enclave. *The New York Times,* December 27, p. A-1.

DuBois, W. E. B. [1903] 1989. *The souls of black folk.* Reprint, New York: Bantam.

Fernández-Kelly, M. Patricia, and Richard Schauffler. 1996. "Divided fates: Immigrant children and the new assimilation." In *The New Second Generation,* edited by Alejandro Portes. New York: Russell Sage Foundation.

Folmar, Kate, and Scott Martelle. 2000. The new faces of Orange County's future: Reflecting changing demographics, immigrants give birth to year's 1st babies. *Los Angeles Times,* January 2, p. A-1.

Gans, Herbert J. 1979. Symbolic ethnicity: The future of ethnic groups and cultures in America. *Ethnic and Racial Studies* 2 (January), pp. 1–20.

García, María Cristina. 1996. *Havana USA: Cuban exiles and Cuban Americans in South Florida, 1959–1994.* Berkeley: University of California Press.

Garvin, Glenn. 2000. Latin America: The main source of immigrants to the United States. *The Miami Herald,* January 2, p. A-1.

Glazer, Nathan, and Daniel Patrick Moynihan. [1963] 1970. *Beyond the melting pot: The Negroes, Puerto Ricans, Jews, Italians, and Irish of New York City.* Reprint, Cambridge, Mass.: MIT Press.

Higham, John. 1955. *Strangers in the land: Patterns of American nativism, 1896–1925.* New Brunswick, N.J.: Rutgers University Press.

Hoffman, Eva. 1989. *Lost in translation: A life in a new language.* New York: Penguin.

Jen, Gish. 2000. The making of a newly American mind. *The New York Times Magazine,* May 7.

Massey, Douglas S., and Nancy A. Denton. 1993. *American apartheid: Segregation and the making of the underclass.* Cambridge, Mass.: Harvard University Press.

Nahirny, Vladimir C., and Joshua A. Fishman. [1965] 1996. "American immigrant groups: Ethnic identification and the problem of generations." In *Theories of Ethnicity: A Classical Reader,* edited by Werner Sollors. Reprint, New York: New York University Press.

Pedraza, Silvia, and Rubén G. Rumbaut, eds. 1996. *Origins and destinies: Immigration, race, and ethnicity in America.* Belmont, Calif.: Wadsworth.

Pérez, Lisandro. 1996. "The households of children of immigrants in South Florida: An exploratory study of extended family arrangements." In *The New Second Generation,* edited by Alejandro Portes. New York: Russell Sage Foundation.

Petersen, William. 1980. "Concepts of ethnicity." In *Harvard Encyclopedia of American Ethnic Groups,* edited by Stephan Thernstrom, Ann Orlov, and Oscar Handlin. Cambridge, Mass.: Harvard University Press.

Portes, Alejandro. 1995. "Children of immigrants: Segmented assimilation and its determinants." In *The economic sociology of immigration: Essays on networks, ethnicity, and entrepreneurship,* edited by Alejandro Portes. New York: Russell Sage Foundation.

———, ed. 1996. *The new second generation.* New York: Russell Sage Foundation.

Portes, Alejandro, and Lingxin Hao. 1998. E pluribus unum: Bilingualism and loss of language in the second generation. *Sociology of Education* 71 (October), pp. 269–294.

Portes, Alejandro, and Dag MacLeod. 1996a. Educational progress of children of immigrants: The roles of class, ethnicity, and a school context. *Sociology of Education* 69 (October), pp. 255–275.

_____. 1996b. What shall I call myself? Hispanic identity formation in the second generation. *Ethnic and Racial Studies* 19 (July), pp. 523–547.

_____. 1999. Educating the second-generation: Determinants of academic achievement among children of immigrants in the United States. *Journal of Ethnic and Migration Studies* 25 (July), pp. 373–396.

Portes, Alejandro, and Rubén G. Rumbaut. 1996. *Immigrant America: A portrait.* 2d ed. Berkeley: University of California Press.

_____. 2001. *Legacies: The story of the immigrant second generation.* Berkeley and New York: University of California Press and Russell Sage Foundation.

Portes, Alejandro, and Richard Schauffler. 1996. "Language and the second generation: Bilingualism yesterday and today." In *The New Second Generation,* edited by Alejandro Portes. New York: Russell Sage Foundation.

Portes, Alejandro, and Alex Stepick. 1993. *City on the edge: The transformation of Miami.* Berkeley: University of California Press.

Portes, Alejandro, and Min Zhou. 1993. The new second generation: Segmented assimilation and its variants. *Annals of the American Academy of Political and Social Sciences* 530 (November), pp. 74–96.

Rumbaut, Rubén G. 1994a. The crucible within: Ethnic identity, self-esteem, and segmented assimilation among children of immigrants. *International Migration Review* 28, no. 4 (Winter), pp. 748–794.

_____. 1994b. Origins and destinies: Immigration to the United States since World War II. *Sociological Forum* 9, no. 4 (December), pp. 583–621.

_____. 1995. "The new Californians: Comparative research findings on the educational progress of immigrant children." In *California's immigrant children: Theory, research and implications for educational policy,* edited by Rubén G. Rumbaut and Wayne A. Cornelius. La Jolla, Calif.: Center for U.S.-Mexican Studies, University of California, San Diego.

_____. 1996. "A legacy of war: Refugees from Vietnam, Laos, and Cambodia." In *Origins and destinies: Immigration, race, and ethnicity in America,* edited by Silvia Pedraza and Rubén G. Rumbaut. Belmont, Calif.: Wadsworth.

_____. 1997. "Ties that bind: Immigration and immigrant families in the United States." In *Immigration and the family: Research and policy on U.S. immigrants,* edited by Alan Booth, Ann C. Crouter, and Nancy S. Landale. Mahwah, N.J.: Lawrence Erlbaum Associates.

_____. 1998. Coming of age in immigrant America. *Research Perspectives on Migration* 1 (6), pp. 1–14.

_____. 1999a. "Assimilation and its discontents: Ironies and paradoxes." In *The Handbook of International Migration: The American Experience,* edited by Charles Hirschman, Josh DeWind, and Philip Kasinitz. New York: Russell Sage Foundation.

_____. 1999b. "Passages to adulthood: The adaptation of children of immigrants in southern California." In *Children of immigrants: Health, adjustment, and public assistance,* edited by Donald J. Hernández. Washington, D.C.: National Academy Press.

_____. 2000. "Profiles in resilience: Educational achievement and ambition among children of immigrants in southern California." In *Resilience across contexts: Family, work, culture, and community,* edited by Ronald Taylor. Mahwah, N.J.: Lawrence Erlbaum Associates.

Rumbaut, Rubén G, and Wayne A. Cornelius, eds. 1995. *California's immigrant children: Theory, research and implications for educational policy.* La Jolla, Calif.: Center for U.S.-Mexican Studies, University of California, San Diego.

Stepick, Alex. 1997. *Pride against prejudice: Haitians in the United States.* Boston: Allyn and Bacon.

U.S. Census Bureau. 1992. *Statistical abstracts of the United States.* 112th ed. Washington, D.C.: U.S. Department of Commerce.

———. 1993. *1990 Census of population, United States: Social and economic characteristics,* 1990 CP-2-1. Washington, D.C.: U.S. Department of Commerce.

———. 1999. *Profile of the foreign-born population in the United States: 1997.* Current Population Reports, P23-195. Washington, D.C.: U.S. Department of Commerce.

U.S. Immigration and Naturalization Service. 1991–1999. *Statistical yearbooks, 1990–1998.* Washington, D.C.: U.S. Department of Justice.

Viglucci, Andrés. 2000. Ethnic make-over of South Florida likely to intensify. *The Miami Herald,* January 2, p. A-1.

Warner, W. Lloyd, and Leo Srole. 1945. *The social systems of American ethnic groups.* New Haven, Conn.: Yale University Press.

Waters, Mary C. 1990. *Ethnic options: Choosing identities in America.* Berkeley: University of California Press.

———. 1999. *Black identities: West Indian immigrant dreams and American realities.* Cambridge, Mass., and New York: Harvard University Press and Russell Sage Foundation.

Chapter 2

THE DEMOGRAPHIC DIVERSITY
OF IMMIGRANTS AND THEIR CHILDREN

Leif Jensen

Americans have always been ambivalent about immigration (Martin and Midgley 1994). We pride ourselves on being a nation of immigrants and a haven for the "tired and poor," but we are apprehensive about the social and economic implications of mass immigration and have long since sought to turn away those likely to become public charges (Jensen 1989). In many ways the concerns of today are little different from those heard a hundred years ago. At that time, as the immigrants' countries of origin had shifted decidedly from northwestern Europe to poorer southern and eastern Europe, public and political worries focused on the penury of many new arrivals and on the prospects for the assimilation of groups that differed in language, ethnicity, and appearance (Simon 1985). Since the 1960s we have been in the midst of another sustained wave of immigration, characterized again by a shift toward poorer countries of origin (Latin American and Asian) that are sending newcomers who are phenotypically and linguistically different from the predominant native-born population (Martin and Midgley 1994). Now decades old, the impact—both positive and negative—of this latest "new immigration" has again been at the center of heated debate.

While the circumstances of the new immigrants themselves are well documented, the experiences and fortunes of their children have only more recently begun to be explored. This new concern is important since the children of immigrants make up a sizable and rapidly growing component of the U.S. population. Estimates from recent Current Population Surveys (CPSs) place the number of native-born children under age 18 who have one or more foreign-born parents—the second generation—at 11.5 million, an increase of 13.9 percent over their number just four years earlier in 1994 (10.1 million) (U.S Census Bureau 1994, 1997). By contrast, native-born children of native-born parents—the third and higher generations—grew by merely 0.4 percent to 57.1 million. Along with children who are themselves foreign born—the first generation—there are some 14.2 million first- and second-generation children in the United States today. They represent about 5 percent of all Americans and 20 percent of all children. In no small measure, they also represent the future of this country (Portes 1996). The prospects and problems faced by the new second generation have clear implications for the ultimate consequences of recent waves of immigration to the United States (Jasso and Rosenzweig 1990). A new report on immigrant families by the National Academy of Sciences puts it this way: "As the predominantly white baby-boom generation reaches retirement age, it will depend increasingly for *its* economic support on the productivity, health, and civic participation of adults who grew up in minority immigrant families. Indeed, the *long-term* consequences of contemporary immigration for the American economy and society will hinge more on the future prospects of children in immigrant families than on the fate of their parents" (Hernandez and Charney 1998: 2; first emphasis added, second emphasis in original).

While an assessment of these consequences is important, it is equally critical to recognize the heterogeneity of today's immigrants. As the chapters in this volume attest, immigrant children are coming of age in America amidst an extraordinary diversity in origins and circumstances. Recognition of the striking differences across immigrant groups in their backgrounds, experiences, and outcomes has prompted the search for alternatives to conventional straight-line models of assimilation and, indeed, was a driving force behind the Children of Immigrants Longitudinal Study (CILS). The CILS data explored in this book were tailored to provide rich answers to cutting-edge questions about adaptation and assimilation among the children of immigrants.

The purpose of this chapter is to place the following analyses of the CILS data within a national-level context. This is done is two ways. First, to paint a broad aggregate portrait, I document the demographic and economic characteristics of the first, second, and third and higher generations (hereafter, third generation) as a whole. Second, to contextualize each individual analysis and to capture the circumstances of these groups relative to one another, I provide statistical profiles for the country-of-origin groups that are the focus of the chapters to follow and for selected additional groups that have significant immigration streams. These profiles describe individuals according to place of residence, demographic characteristics, headship structure, poverty and income packaging, education and labor force outcomes, and health status and health insurance coverage.

Data and Measures

As researchers have turned their attention to the circumstances of the children of immigrants, they have been challenged by a lack of survey data that allow a full appraisal. Most nationally representative survey data sets are either not large enough to reliably describe relatively small populations or suffer from other limitations. For example, while much has been learned from analyses of the vast public-use files of the U.S. Census (Jensen and Chitose 1994; Oropesa and Landale 1997), only those second-generation individuals still residing with their immigrant parents can be identified and analyzed because the census long-form questionnaire does not ask about the nativity of parents.

The U.S. CPS is a monthly survey of the civilian noninstitutional population of the United States that contains data on roughly 50,000 households and the 130,000 individuals residing within them (U.S. Census Bureau 1994, 1995, 1996, 1997). As the principal source of government data on employment and unemployment, in any given month the CPS includes important labor force status and demographic indicators. The March CPS, or annual demographic file, contains additional information on work experience, income, and migration and since 1994 has included items on the place of birth of each individual's mother and father. The latter feature provides the opportunity to examine the native-born children of foreign-born parents, regardless of whether those children still reside with their parents. As such, the

March CPS now allows for a more thorough assessment of the circumstances of the second generation and for a comparison with the first and third generations.

I analyze CPS data from those March surveys that were conducted in 1994, 1995, 1996, and 1997. To maximize the number of cases available for analysis, I concatenated these data files and analyzed them simultaneously. However, because of the unique sample design of the CPS, doing so required that I delete some cases from the analysis. The CPS is based on a rotating sample of households such that up to half the households interviewed in any two consecutive March surveys are the same. Because of the lack of observational independence this entails, I delete nonindependent households from my analysis. Because the U.S. Census Bureau drew an entirely new CPS sample between 1995 and 1996, I analyze all cases from those two years. However, I delete those households in the 1994 survey that were reinterviewed in 1995 as well as those in the 1997 survey that had been interviewed in 1996.[1] By analyzing multiple surveys in this way, I essentially compare immigrant generations as of the mid-1990s.

To meet the twin goals of describing immigrant generations in the aggregate and by country of origin, I use two highly similar nativity breakdowns. For the aggregate portrait, the first generation consists of foreign-born individuals—excluding those born abroad of American parents and those born in Puerto Rico and other U.S. protectorates, whom I define as native born. Statistics are presented for the first generation in total and by whether individuals are naturalized citizens or noncitizens. The second generation consists of those who are native born and who have at least one foreign-born parent (again, where those born in U.S. protectorates are considered native and not foreign born). The second generation is then subdivided into those who have two foreign-born parents versus only one. Finally, the third generation comprises those who are native born and have native-born parents.[2] Data are presented for the third generation as a whole and, within that generation, for non-Hispanic whites and all others separately.[3]

Country-of-origin-specific (hereafter, country-specific) portraits are provided for first- and second-generation individuals with origins in the following countries or country groups. The sending countries featured in this volume include Mexico, Cuba, Nicaragua, Haiti, Jamaica (and other English-speaking Caribbean nations identified in the CPS),[4] the Philippines and Vietnam. Selected additional origin countries include Laos and Cambodia combined, China (mainland China and Taiwan combined), Korea (South and North combined), India, El Salvador, and the Dominican Republic.[5] For the country-specific portraits, the first-generation consists of those who were born in a given country (again, subdivided into citizens and noncitizens), while those in the second generation have at least one parent born in that country. The second generation is broken down further into those who have only one parent born in that country (the other being native born) and those who have both parents born in that country.[6]

In 1997 there were an estimated 30 million second-generation individuals in the United States, representing approximately 11 percent of the civilian noninstitutional population (Table 2.1). The second generation was about evenly split between those who had only one foreign-born parent and those who had two (14.3 versus 15.7 million). The estimated number of foreign-born individuals is 26.3 million, with noncitizens outnumbering citizens by almost two to one. These estimates are based on 131,854 individual records from the 1997 CPS.[7] Combining the 1994–1997 March CPSs, with nonindependent cases deleted as described previously yields about 48,000 and 41,000 second- and first-generation cases, respectively, for the aggregate analyses that follow. The country-specific N's in the second panel of Table 2.1 underscore the predominance of those of Mexican origin in the first and second generation. Of all individuals with origins in one or more of the countries considered here, about 62 percent and 51 percent of second- and first-generation individuals have origins in Mexico. Salvadorans, Filipinos, Cubans, and Dominicans also contribute substantial numbers of cases to the analysis of the second generation, and these countries, along with Vietnam, India, Jamaica, and Korea, are amply represented among the foreign born. While most groups have sufficient CPS cases to sustain meaningful analysis, some caution is warranted, particularly for second-generation Chinese, Nicaraguans, Haitians, and Laotians/Cambodians.[8]

A Statistical Portrait of Immigrants and Their Children

Place of Residence

Like their predecessors of a century ago, the new immigrants have tended to settle in urban and coastal locales. Regionally, about 65 percent of the first generation and 61 percent of the second live in the

TABLE 2.1 POPULATION ESTIMATES AND WEIGHTED
NUMBERS OF CASES AVAILABLE FOR ANALYSIS

	Native-Born Individuals				At Least One Foreign-Born Parent			Foreign-Born Individuals		
	Native-Born Parents									
	Total	White	Other	Total	Only One	Both	Total	Citizens	Noncitizens
1997									
Total population estimate (millions)	210.6	167.8	42.8	30.0	14.3	15.7	26.3	9.2	17.1
Weighted N (thousands)[1]	104.7	83.5	21.2	14.4	6.9	7.5	12.7	4.5	8.3
1994–1997 Combined[2] Weighted N (thousands)[1]	336.9	268.5	68.4	48.0	22.7	25.4	40.6	13.0	27.6

At Least One
Foreign-Born Parent

Country-Specific Description: Weighted[2] Numbers of Cases, 1994–1997 Combined

	Total	Only One	Both	Total	Citizens	Noncitizens
Major sending countries of immigration						
Mexico	11,254	4,028	6,584	11,510	1,536	9,974
Cuba	904	330	179	1,392	680	711
Nicaragua	224	57	91	431	72	359
El Salvador	1,299	692	370	1,146	165	981
Dominican Republic	828	155	419	924	208	716
Haiti	356	50	261	597	145	452
Jamaica	579	253	238	934	349	585
Phillipines	1,191	486	626	1,773	950	823
China (s)	181	26	139	457	237	220
Korea (s)	365	169	188	857	311	546
Vietnam	426	155	240	986	402	584
Laos/Cambodia	363	32	252	559	161	398
India	429	90	271	952	341	611

SOURCE: U.S. Census Bureau 1994, 1995, 1996, 1997.
[1]Weighted by the March supplement weight divided by the mean of the March supplement weight to yield weighted N approximately equal to sample size.
[2]Not including those 1994 households that were reinterviewed in 1995 and those 1997 households that were interviewed in 1996.

northeastern or western states. This compares to only 36 percent of the third generation (64 percent of whom live in the South or Midwest). The bicoastal residential dispersion of immigrant generations also can be seen when refining the geographic focus to state of residence. The top five states of residence for the second generation are California (24.6 percent), New York (10.6 percent), Texas (8.8 percent), Florida (7.0 percent), and Illinois (4.9 percent). The state distribution of the foreign born themselves is similar, though even more concentrated on the East and West coasts. For the first generation, the top five states are California (33.2 percent), New York (12.9 percent), Florida (9.2 percent), Texas (8.7 percent), and New Jersey (4.7 percent). Together, 60.5 percent of the second generation and 73.2 percent of the first live in one of these six states, which compares with less than one-third (32.6 percent) of the third generation.

Besides their distribution across states, also noteworthy is their concentration within states. After all, to a degree the large number of immigrants and their children in states such as California and New York simply reflects the tendency for Americans in general to be found in high-population states. Are there smaller states that nonetheless have a comparatively high concentration of first- and second-generation individuals? Ranked in this way, a somewhat different picture emerges. Outstanding again, however, is California, where 25.5 percent of the population is foreign born and 22.4 percent is second generation. California is the only state where close to half (47.9 percent) of the population consists of the foreign born or their native-born offspring. There is little wonder why California is perennially at the center of the storm in immigration debates. The top five states by second-generation concentration are California (22.4 percent), Hawaii (22.6 percent), Rhode Island (20.6 percent), Connecticut (17.9 percent), and New York (17.2 percent). The top five states by first-generation concentration are California (25.5 percent), New York (17.6 percent), Florida (16.0 percent), New Jersey (14.9 percent), and Arizona (12.0 percent).

The United States has long been a predominantly urban society, but this is particularly true for the foreign born. Immigrants and their children are more likely than the third generation to live in metropolitan (metro) areas generally and in the central cities of metro areas in particular (Table 2.2). Almost all (94.1 percent) foreign-born individuals live in the central cities or suburbs of metro America, and nearly 9 in 10 (89.1 percent) of second-generation individuals do so. Proportionately fewer (75.5 percent) of the third generation live in metro areas. Looking

TABLE 2.2 METROPOLITAN RESIDENCE BY NATIVITY STATUS

| | Native-Born Individuals | | | | | | Foreign-Born Individuals | | |
| | Native-Born Parents | | | At Least One Foreign-Born Parent | | | | | |
	Total (%)	White (%)	Other (%)	Total (%)	Only One (%)	Both (%)	Total (%)	Citizens (%)	Noncitizens (%)
Metropolitan	75.5	73.5	83.4	89.1	85.8	92.1	94.1	93.8	94.3
Central city	(21.7)	(16.1)	(43.4)	(30.6)	(25.2)	(35.5)	(42.6)	(36.2)	(45.7)
Noncentral city	(38.4)	(41.3)	(27.0)	(46.0)	(45.8)	(46.3)	(43.1)	(48.7)	(40.5)
Not identifiable	(16.1)	(16.8)	(13.3)	(12.8)	(15.3)	(10.5)	(8.6)	(9.2)	(8.3)
Nonmetropolitan	23.9	25.8	16.3	10.6	3.8	7.7	5.7	5.9	5.5
Not identifiable	0.7	0.7	0.3	0.3	0.4	0.3	0.2	0.3	0.2
Country-Specific Description: Percentage Residing in Central Cities of Metro Areas[1]									
Major sending countries of immigration									
Mexico				43.9	39.4	46.1	48.1	45.8	48.5
Cuba				28.4	25.6	27.2	37.8	30.8	44.4
Nicaragua				37.7	31.3	37.6	50.4	32.1	54.2
El Salvador				39.5	28.8	53.4	52.1	43.6	53.5
Dominican Republic				70.9	63.0	83.4	80.5	74.6	82.2
Haiti				45.9	—[2]	50.6	52.6	53.2	52.4
Jamaica				56.3	51.5	63.1	61.7	61.0	62.1
Philippines				41.3	32.1	48.7	43.9	43.0	44.9
China (s)				32.4	—[2]	31.7	35.8	28.6	44.2
Korea (s)				40.2	34.2	42.6	42.8	32.9	48.2
Vietnam				43.7	47.2	40.3	48.8	41.9	53.4
Laos/Cambodia				65.5	—[2]	73.9	69.8	43.7	82.1
India				40.2	39.2	42.5	38.6	30.6	43.3

SOURCE: U.S. Census Bureau 1994, 1995, 1996, 1997.
[1] Among those who are identified (not missing) on the central-city identifier.
[2] Data not shown; calculation based on fewer than 50 cases.

within metro areas, the first generation, noncitizens especially, is more likely than the second generation to live in central cities. Indeed, among those metro residents who are identifiable on the central-city variable,[9] the percentage residing *outside* central cities exceeds (in relative terms) the percentage residing within by 1.2, 50.3, and 77.0 percent, respectively, for first-, second-, and third-generation individuals. The point is that immigrants themselves are especially likely to live in metro areas, central cities in particular, and that the second and, even more so, the third generations are less highly urban in residence. A question for the future is whether America's newest immigrants will move into less urban locales within or across generations or continue to prefer the city much like third-generation minorities.[10]

Specific country-of-origin groups do not differ much in their propensity to live in metro areas; they are all overwhelmingly likely to do so (data not shown).[11] However, the groups portrayed in the chapters to follow differ strikingly with respect to central-city residence. Among the second generation, much less than one-third of all Cubans live in central cities (28.4 percent), a reflection perhaps of the economic success of the so-called golden exile—the comparatively privileged earliest waves of Cuban refugees. By contrast, over half of all Jamaicans and other anglophone Caribbeans (56.3 percent) and close to two-thirds of Laotians/Cambodians (65.5 percent) reside in central cities. Among the other origin groups, the Dominican second generation stands out for its tendency to live in the inner city (70.9 percent). A similar pattern of residential diversity across these country-of-origin groups is seen among the foreign born themselves.[12] Almost without exception they are more likely than their second-generation counterparts to reside in the central city. But the same cross-country differences are seen with Jamaicans, Laotians/Cambodians, and Dominicans standing out for their inner-city residence and with Cubans, Filipinos, Chinese, Koreans, and Indians having comparatively large shares living in the suburbs of metro areas.

That suburban residence is partly a function of economic success should mean that these same groups show signs of comparative privilege in other respects as well. One such characteristic is tenure status— whether one's home is owned or rented (Table 2.3). The first, second, and third generations become progressively more likely to own their homes (with or without a mortgage) and less likely to rent. At the extreme, only 38.1 percent of foreign-born noncitizens are living in owner-occupied housing, which compares with 65.5 percent of the second

TABLE 2.3 HOUSING TENURE STATUS BY NATIVITY STATUS

| | Native-Born Individuals | | | | | | Foreign-Born Individuals | | |
| | Native-Born Parents | | | At Least One Foreign-Born Parent | | | | | |
	Total (%)	White (%)	Other (%)	Total (%)	Only One (%)	Both (%)	Total (%)	Citizens (%)	Noncitizens (%)
Home is owned or being bought	69.8	74.8	50.4	65.5	68.6	62.7	48.0	69.1	38.1
Renting	28.5	23.6	47.7	33.1	30.0	35.9	50.4	29.6	60.2
No cash rent	1.7	1.7	1.9	1.4	1.5	1.4	1.5	1.3	1.6

Country-Specific Description: Percentage Living in Owner-Occupied Housing

Major sending countries of immigration	Total (%)	Only One (%)	Both (%)	Total (%)	Citizens (%)	Noncitizens (%)
Mexico	51.9	58.4	48.5	36.4	62.5	32.4
Cuba	66.1	66.6	69.3	57.9	71.6	44.9
Nicaragua	45.7	45.2	49.7	26.6	53.7	21.1
El Salvador	48.5	59.9	32.1	26.9	45.5	23.8
Dominican Republic	30.3	31.9	17.7	15.6	31.7	11.0
Haiti	50.2	50.4	49.8	41.2	56.3	36.4
Jamaica	50.0	44.6	52.0	53.5	65.5	46.4
Philippines	70.6	62.7	75.3	63.3	74.7	50.1
China (s)	78.7	—[1]	80.6	66.2	86.9	43.9
Korea (s)	59.7	65.7	55.4	44.1	67.8	30.6
Vietnam	62.8	51.3	66.7	46.8	70.2	30.6
Laos/Cambodia	41.5	37.5	30.9	37.2	65.3	25.8
India	72.6	76.4	73.0	55.1	73.5	44.9

SOURCE: U.S. Census Bureau 1994, 1995, 1996, 1997.
[1]Data not shown; calculation based on fewer than 50 cases.

generation and 69.8 percent of the third. Among the third generation, whites are far more likely to own than nonwhites (74.8 and 50.4 percent, respectively). In fact, of the groups considered, only immigrant noncitizens have lower rates of home ownership than third-generation minorities, and the latter are disadvantaged compared to the second generation. This pattern is seen repeatedly in the analyses to follow.

Among first- or second-generation individuals from the countries this book profiles, Cubans and Filipinos have the highest rates of home ownership. The rate for children of Vietnamese immigrants also is high (62.8 percent), especially considering the much lower rate among Vietnamese immigrants themselves (46.8 percent). At the other end of the spectrum, first- and second-generation Nicaraguans and Laotians/Cambodians have a comparatively low prevalence of home ownership. Among the other important sending countries, the Chinese and Indians are far more likely to live in owner-occupied housing than are Salvadorans or Dominicans.

Demographic Characteristics

In this section I describe immigrant generations along an array of demographic characteristics including age, race and ethnicity, marital status (among adults), and the presence of parents (among children).[13] First, age distributions differ somewhat across the immigrant generations, with the second generation having a comparatively large elderly population, the first generation having proportionately fewer children and elders and more young-adults, and the third generation having an age distribution closer to that of the nation as a whole (data not shown). Moreover, within the first generation, citizens have more middle-aged and elderly adults, while noncitizens have proportionately more children. To a certain degree these age differences, and particularly the fact that 17.4 percent of the second generation is aged 65 or more (versus 9.5 percent and 11.4 percent, respectively, for the first and third generations), needs to be borne in mind when interpreting some of the following results.

Immigrant generations differ in predictable ways by race and ethnicity (data not shown). I used a five-category race/ethnicity variable consisting of Latin Americans and non–Latin American whites, blacks, Asians, and others. Reflecting the well-known shift in the country-of-origin composition of immigrants, compared with the third generation, the second and first generations are progressively less white and more

Latin American and Asian. Eight of 10 (79.7 percent) third-generation individuals are white, which compares with somewhat more than half (55.5 percent) of second- and about one-quarter (25.1 percent) of first-generation individuals. About one-third (32.1 percent) of the second generation is Latin American, and 8.0 percent is Asian. Among the foreign born themselves, these shares increase to 47.8 and 20.5 percent, respectively. Within the first generation, citizens are much more likely to be white than noncitizens (39.6 percent versus 18.3 percent), and within the second generation, those with only one foreign-born parent are more likely to be white than those with two (67.6 percent and 44.7 percent). Both of these differences need to be kept in mind as I document other inequalities between these groups in the following sections.

In terms of marital status, second- and third-generation adults have remarkably similar distributions. About 57 percent are married; about 20 percent are widowed, separated, or divorced; and about 23 percent have never been married. The profile of the foreign born also is similar, though proportionately more have never been married and fewer are widowed, separated, or divorced.

An important correlate of the social and economic well-being of children is the presence of both parents in the household. At first blush the data in Table 2.4 suggest a disadvantage for the third generation in this regard. At 68.1 percent, they are less likely than second-generation (73.6 percent) or first-generation (74.7 percent) children to be living with both parents, and they are correspondingly more likely to be living in father-absent families. While this may be true overall, the advantage of first- and second-generation children is largely due to the very low percentage of third-generation *minority* children who are living with both parents (39.3 percent). First- and second-generation children are actually slightly *less* likely than third-generation whites to be living with both parents.

Differences in presence of parents by country of origin suggest a somewhat different constellation of advantage and disadvantage when compared with previous tables. Of the groups featured in this volume, the most advantaged in terms of the likelihood of living with both parents are the Filipinos, Laotians/Cambodians, and Vietnamese. This advantage is welcome for Laotians/Cambodians and Vietnamese, who tend to be somewhat disadvantaged along other indicators. On the other hand, first- and second-generation Haitian and Jamaican children have a comparatively low percentage living with both parents. Three of the other country-specific groups—Chinese, Korean, and Indian children—

TABLE 2.4 PRESENCE OF PARENTS AMONG FAMILY MEMBERS UNDER AGE 18 BY NATIVITY STATUS

	Native-Born Individuals						Foreign-Born Individuals		
	Native-Born Parents			At Least One Foreign-Born Parent					
	Total (%)	White (%)	Other (%)	Total (%)	Only One (%)	Both (%)	Total (%)	Citizens (%)	Noncitizens (%)
Both parents present	68.1	77.9	39.3	73.6	71.2	75.5	74.7	77.2	74.0
Mother only present	24.7	16.6	48.5	21.2	23.0	19.7	19.1	16.7	19.7
Father only present	3.9	3.6	4.8	2.8	3.4	2.3	3.5	3.8	3.4
Neither parent present	3.3	1.9	7.4	2.4	2.4	2.4	2.8	2.4	2.9
Country-Specific Description: Percentage of Children Residing with Both Parents									
Major sending countries of immigration									
Mexico				72.6	67.3	74.7	75.6	69.8	75.9
Cuba				72.3	71.5	68.7	—[1]	—[1]	—[1]
Nicaragua				69.2	—[1]	66.7	—[1]	—[1]	57.5
El Salvador				64.5	57.7	70.2	63.8	—[1]	60.8
Dominican Republic				50.2	42.3	35.2	41.6	—[1]	41.9
Haiti				58.3	—[1]	61.8	48.0	—[1]	45.2
Jamaica				56.2	41.9	59.0	53.5	—[1]	52.2
Philippines				81.1	77.2	83.7	80.0	83.2	78.5
China (s)				90.1	—[1]	91.9	74.7	—[1]	—[1]
Korea (s)				90.3	89.0	91.8	85.4	92.0	80.4
Vietnam				79.8	66.0	85.1	71.1	—[1]	73.2
Laos/Cambodia				77.0	—[1]	79.7	91.1	—[1]	96.8
India				93.8	—[1]	98.1	88.3	—[1]	89.0

SOURCE: U.S. Census Bureau 1994, 1995, 1996, 1997.
[1]Data not shown; calculation based on fewer than 50 cases.

have among the highest rates of living with both parents of all groups considered, while children from the Dominican Republic have the lowest prevalence of living with both parents.

Household Economic Status

The rancor over immigration and immigration policy has always been substantially driven by economic concerns, notably the worry that immigrants are poor and a drain on social welfare coffers. At the same time, economic improvement across immigrant generations is central to lore concerning their assimilation. Here I address these issues by describing immigrant generations according to their poverty status and income packaging.

There is striking variation in poverty across the groups considered here. The top panel of Table 2.5 shows poverty rates for all individuals and for children separately, using both the 100 percent poverty thresholds ("official poverty") as well as 50 percent of these thresholds ("deep poverty"). The pattern for all individuals and children is the same. Focusing on children, over one-third (34.2 percent) of foreign-born children are poor, which compares with 28.7 percent of second-generation children and one-fifth of third-generation children (20.0 percent)—suggesting improvement across immigrant generations. However, there is important variation within the immigrant generations as well. Among foreign-born children, noncitizens are far more likely to be poor than citizens (39.2 versus 14.7 percent). Among the second generation, children with two foreign-born parents are much more likely to be poor than those with one foreign-born and one native-born parent (34.4 versus 21.6 percent). And among the third generation, Latin American and other nonwhite children are far more likely to be poor than those who are non-Hispanic white (42.0 versus 12.4 percent). Indeed, the deep poverty rate for third-generation minority children (22.0 percent) far exceeds that for foreign-born noncitizen children (16.0 percent). The latter comparison testifies to the stark reality that assimilation in America occurs within a society that is highly stratified by race and ethnicity, even among those whose roots in this country go back generations.

Differences in child poverty rates by country of origin also underscore the highly divergent economic circumstances faced by children. While fewer than 1 in 10 second-generation Filipino children are poor (7.5 percent), over half (54.2 percent) of all Laotian/Cambodian

TABLE 2.5 TOTAL POVERTY RATES AND CHILD POVERTY RATES BY NATIVITY STATUS

| | Native-Born Individuals | | | | | | Foreign-Born Individuals | | |
| | Native-Born Parents | | | At Least One Foreign-Born Parent | | | | | |
	Total (%)	White (%)	Other (%)	Total (%)	Only One (%)	Both (%)	Total (%)	Citizens (%)	Noncitizens (%)
Total poverty rates									
100 percent threshold	13.5	9.7	28.2	16.3	13.0	19.2	22.1	11.1	27.2
50 percent threshold	5.6	3.7	13.2	6.1	5.2	7.0	8.5	4.0	10.6
Child poverty rates									
100 percent threshold	20.0	12.4	42.0	28.7	21.6	34.4	34.2	14.7	39.2
50 percent threshold	9.6	5.3	22.0	10.9	8.8	12.7	13.8	5.6	16.0
Country-Specific Description: Percentage of Children in Poverty (100 Percent Threshold)									
Major sending countries of immigration									
Mexico				42.4	37.0	45.7	58.6	35.9	59.9
Cuba				21.1	16.5	22.9	—[1]	—[1]	—[1]
Nicaragua				28.5	—[1]	29.8	35.0	—[1]	35.5
El Salvador				34.0	28.3	41.0	33.2	—[1]	32.8
Dominican Republic				49.0	43.4	57.7	54.0	—[1]	57.1
Haiti				41.9	—[1]	43.5	52.1	—[1]	53.5
Jamaica				28.0	31.9	32.1	33.6	—[1]	35.2
Philippines				7.5	12.8	5.1	3.4	4.1	3.1
China (s)				3.2	—[1]	2.8	—[1]	—[1]	—[1]
Korea (s)				7.9	5.3	9.9	12.3	0.0	21.7
Vietnam				23.8	25.7	25.1	56.8	—[1]	57.6
Laos/Cambodia				54.2	—[1]	54.3	52.5	—[1]	54.2
India				7.3	—[1]	5.5	15.8	—[1]	18.4

SOURCE: U.S. Census Bureau 1994, 1995, 1996, 1997.
[1]Data not shown; calculation based on fewer than 50 cases.

children have family incomes that are below the official poverty line. Second-generation Cubans are again comparatively advantaged relative to the other groups considered in this book, with a child poverty rate of 21.1 percent, as are children of Vietnamese immigrants (23.8 percent). Second-generation Mexicans and Haitians are relatively disadvantaged, with child poverty rates of 42.4 and 41.9 percent, respectively. Finally, it is important to recognize that the improvement in child poverty rates across immigrant generations noted above holds for several country-specific groups. Most notably, poverty rates for Vietnamese-origin children drop from 56.8 percent for the first generation to 23.8 percent for the second.

That immigrants and their children are more likely to be poor, and that certain immigrant groups have especially high poverty rates, is unsettling to some in view of implications for use of means-tested cash transfers. Table 2.6 shows how immigrant generations differ in their pattern of reliance on three sources of income—wages and salaries, public assistance, and all other sources combined. I have chosen to examine household rather than family income under the assumption that income tends to be shared among all household members. To measure "income packaging," the cells in Table 2.6 indicate the mean percentage of household income that obtains from these three broad sources.[14] For first-, second-, and third-generation individuals, the clear majority of all household income comes in the form of wages and salaries. Those in the second generation have proportionately less from this source (65.2 percent) and more from other sources (30.0 percent), a reflection of the greater numbers of elders in this group who rely on Social Security and retirement benefits.

Despite the fact that immigrants and their children are appreciably more likely to be poor than the third generation, their reliance on public assistance is only slightly greater. Indeed, the next panel of Table 2.6 confirms that among the poor, first-, second-, and third-generation individuals are in households with progressively heavier reliance on public assistance and lighter reliance on earnings. For example, on average 60.9 percent of the household income of poor first-generation individuals comes from wages and salaries and only 18.7 percent from public assistance. Among the second generation, the corresponding figures are 50.0 percent for wages and salaries and 23.8 percent for welfare, while for the third generation they are 41.9 and 26.1 percent, respectively. The point is, the immigrant poor seem to rely less on transfers and more on earnings than do the native poor.

TABLE 2.6   INCOME PACKAGING BY NATIVITY STATUS

	Native-Born Individuals						Foreign-Born Individuals		
	Native-Born Parents			At Least One Foreign-Born Parent					
	Total	White	Other	Total	Only One	Both	Total	Citizens	Noncitizens
All individuals			Average Percentage of Household Income by Source[1]						
Wages and salaries	70.0	70.9	66.2	65.2	67.6	63.1	74.0	69.4	76.2
Public assistance	4.3	2.3	12.1	4.8	3.9	3.9	5.5	3.1	6.6
Other	25.7	26.8	21.7	30.0	28.5	33.0	20.5	27.5	17.2
Poor individuals									
Wages and salaries	41.9	44.4	38.5	50.0	46.8	51.4	60.9	44.9	63.9
Public assistance	26.1	17.7	37.0	23.8	24.3	23.5	18.7	20.1	18.5
Other	32.0	37.9	24.5	26.2	28.9	25.0	20.4	35.0	17.6
Country-Specific Description: Average Percentage of Income from Earnings and Public Assistance (Poor Individuals)									
Major sending countries of immigration									
Mexico Wages and salaries				61.8	54.4	64.9	76.5	60.3	77.9
Public assistance				26.7	24.7	18.6	9.8	13.0	9.5
Cuba Wages and salaries				39.1	—[2]	27.5	30.9	15.7	35.9
Public assistance				34.9	—[2]	34.7	31.8	18.2	36.3
Nicaragua Wages and salaries				53.6	—[2]	—[2]	77.8	80.6	80.6
Public assistance				26.6	—[2]	—[2]	11.9	—[2]	10.2
El Salvador Wages and salaries				55.6	40.8	66.3	76.1	—[2]	77.6
Public assistance				24.7	28.1	21.0	14.3	—[2]	12.9
Dominican Republic Wages and salaries				34.0	20.8	25.5	38.7	28.5	40.5
Public assistance				51.2	65.8	60.1	42.1	49.9	40.8

Haiti	Wages and salaries	64.5	—[2]	69.7	76.8	—[2]	79.0
	Public assistance	14.9	—[2]	14.6	6.1	—[2]	7.5
Jamaica	Wages and salaries	36.0	34.0	—[2]	54.9	—[2]	60.9
	Public assistance	45.0	51.8	—[2]	18.4	—[2]	16.6
Philippines	Wages and salaries	67.4	—[2]	—[2]	59.3	—[2]	—[2]
	Public assistance	13.1	—[2]	—[2]	7.0	—[2]	—[2]
China (s)	Wages and salaries	—[2]	—[2]	—[2]	—[2]	—[2]	—[2]
	Public assistance	—[2]	—[2]	—[2]	—[2]	—[2]	—[2]
Korea (s)	Wages and salaries	—[2]	—[2]	—[2]	57.2	—[2]	58.6
	Public assistance	—[2]	—[2]	—[2]	12.0	—[2]	10.4
Vietnam	Wages and salaries	35.7	—[2]	—[2]	45.1	—[2]	44.7
	Public assistance	48.4	—[2]	—[2]	40.5	—[2]	44.3
Laos/Cambodia	Wages and salaries	15.9	—[2]	13.0	14.7	—[2]	14.9
	Public assistance	77.6	—[2]	83.7	74.6	—[2]	77.0
India	Wages and salaries	—[2]	—[2]	—[2]	68.8	—[2]	77.0
	Public assistance	—[2]	—[2]	—[2]	3.3	—[2]	0.2

SOURCE: U.S. Census Bureau 1994, 1995, 1996, 1997.
[1]Among those with positive income from a given source.
[2]Data not shown; calculation based on fewer than 50 cases.

There is considerable heterogeneity across country-of-origin groups in income packaging among poor individuals. The bottom panels of Table 2.6 suggest that among the first- and second-generation poor, Mexican, Haitian, Nicaraguan, Filipino, and Salvadoran individuals are in households that rely rather heavily on earnings and not so much on public assistance. By contrast, the Cuban, Laotian/Cambodian, Vietnamese, and Dominican poor are in households with greater reliance on welfare and less on earnings. The heavy reliance on public assistance among most of the latter groups may reflect the aftermath of refugee resettlement packages that included liberal welfare provisions. Remarkably, these data suggest that on average close to three-quarters of the income of the Laotian/Cambodian poor is from public assistance. Finally, as was seen in the aggregate portrait in the first panel, the country-specific data suggest a pattern of overall increase in welfare receipt among later immigrant generations. Jamaicans are exemplary. While 54.9 and 18.4 percent of household income was from earnings and welfare, respectively, among the Jamaican second-generation poor, the percent from wages and salaries drops to 36.0 percent, while that from welfare increases to 45.0 percent. However, such increases must be viewed against the fact that many of these groups—Jamaicans included—also show declining poverty rates between the first and second generations.

Education and Labor Force Status

Education is of clear importance for economic success in the United States, and school performance is central to many of the CILS analyses to follow. Table 2.7 shows how individuals aged 24 and older are distributed across a four-category education variable. There is little question that adults without a high school education fare poorly in the U.S. labor market, and first- and second-generation adults are disadvantaged in this regard. While nearly one-third (32.6 percent) of the first generation lacks a high school degree, only one-sixth (16.5 percent) of third generation adults do. Second-generation adults fall between these extremes (20.7 percent). As was seen previously for poverty, there are stark differences within immigrant generations in high school completion, with clear advantages going to citizens over noncitizens within the first generation; those with only one foreign-born parent versus those with two within the second; and non-Hispanic whites over minorities within the third. At the high end of the education hierarchy, the story is considerably different. There is virtually no difference between first-, second-, and third-generation adults in rates of four-year college completion—about 23 percent of all three groups have a baccalaureate degree or better. However, within the immigrant generations the same inequalities are seen, with higher college completion rates enjoyed by first-generation citizens, those with only one foreign-born parent in the second generation, and third-generation whites.

The country-specific differences in educational attainment are glaring. Among immigrant adults themselves, Mexicans, Cambodians/Laotians, Salvadorans, and Dominicans stand out for their comparatively low educational attainment. For example, only 3.7 percent of Mexican-born adults have a college degree; 69.8 percent do not have so much as a high school degree. In sharp contrast, those born in the non-refugee-sending Asian countries have very high educational attainment. Among Filipino immigrants, 44.8 percent have a college degree, and only 12.0 percent have not completed high school. Thus, their educational attainment—like that of the Chinese, Koreans, and Indians—far exceeds the attainment of third-generation whites. Finally, there is some evidence of improvement in educational attainment between first and second generations for Mexicans, Cubans, Jamaicans, Salvadorans, and Dominicans. For example, while 19.4 percent of Cuban-born adults have a college degree or better, 32.2 percent of second-generation Cuban adults have a college degree.

These educational disparities translate directly into inequalities in labor market outcomes. Table 2.8 shows the distribution of workers across four broad occupational categories: professional, executive, administrative, and managerial; technical, sales, and clerical; service occupations; and operatives and laborers. Compared to second- and third-generation workers, the foreign born themselves are less likely to be found in higher-status professional occupations and more likely to occupy lower-status laborer jobs. Again, noncitizens among the foreign born and minorities among the third generation are especially disadvantaged in their occupational attainment. The country-specific portrait suggests that among the first generation, the most disadvantaged workers in terms of occupational attainment include Mexicans, Nicaraguans, Laotians/Cambodians, Salvadorans, and Dominicans. On the other hand, Cubans, Jamaicans, Filipinos, Chinese, Koreans, and Indians are more likely to have professional occupations and less likely to have laborer positions.

TABLE 2.7 EDUCATION OF INDIVIDUALS AGED 24 AND OLDER BY NATIVITY STATUS

| | Native-Born Individuals | | | | | | Foreign-Born Individuals | | |
| | Native-Born Parents | | | At Least One Foreign-Born Parent | | | | | |
	Total (%)	White (%)	Other (%)	Total (%)	Only One (%)	Both (%)	Total (%)	Citizens (%)	Noncitizens (%)
Less than high school	16.5	14.4	26.0	20.7	16.3	24.8	32.6	21.8	39.2
High school	35.2	35.3	34.9	31.3	31.5	31.2	25.0	27.5	23.5
Some college	25.4	25.6	24.3	24.1	26.0	22.3	18.9	23.1	16.4
Bachelor's degree or more	23.0	24.7	14.8	23.9	26.2	21.7	23.5	27.7	20.9

Country-Specific Description: Percentage with Less Than High School (HS) and Bachelor's Degree or More

Major sending countries of immigration

				Total (%)	Only (%) One	Both (%)	Total (%)	Citizens (%)	Noncitizens (%)
Mexico	Less than HS			36.9	33.2	41.9	69.8	55.9	72.6
	Bachelor's or more			10.6	11.1	10.0	3.7	6.3	3.2
Cuba	Less than HS			12.4	18.2	10.2	38.3	22.9	55.4
	Bachelor's or more			33.2	32.2	34.8	19.4	28.2	9.6
Nicaragua	Less than HS			—¹	—¹	—¹	39.6	—¹	44.1
	Bachelor's or more			—¹	—¹	—¹	14.1	—¹	12.1
El Salvador	Less than HS			25.1	24.7	—¹	60.5	34.3	65.5
	Bachelor's or more			18.8	18.9	—¹	5.3	14.6	3.6
Dominican Republic	Less than HS			19.2	—¹	—¹	54.9	42.0	60.2
	Bachelor's or more			16.6	—¹	—¹	8.2	14.5	5.5
Haiti	Less than HS			—¹	—¹	—¹	35.5	20.4	41.0
	Bachelor's or more			—¹	—¹	—¹	12.6	19.7	10.0

Jamaica	Less than HS	13.8	—	—	20.7	13.1	27.1
	Bachelor's or more	26.3	—	—	18.0	23.2	13.5
Philippines	Less than HS	7.8	8.2	8.4	12.0	7.3	18.1
	Bachelor's or more	38.0	38.0	42.8	44.8	45.1	44.4
China (s)	Less than HS	—	—	—	4.4	2.4	6.9
	Bachelor's or more	—	—	—	64.3	64.2	64.3
Korea (s)	Less than HS	—	—	—	9.6	4.6	12.5
	Bachelor's or more	—	—	—	44.4	47.6	42.6
Vietnam	Less than HS	—	—	—	30.8	12.2	48.2
	Bachelor's or more	—	—	—	15.3	24.8	6.5
Laos/Cambodia	Less than HS	33.5	—	—	45.3	22.4	57.9
	Bachelor's or more	4.4	—	—	12.3	28.4	3.4
India	Less than HS	—	—	—	9.4	5.8	11.7
	Bachelor's or more	—	—	—	62.5	67.6	59.4

SOURCE: U.S. Census Bureau 1994, 1995, 1996, 1997.
[1]Data not shown; calculation based on fewer than 50 cases.

TABLE 2.8 OCCUPATIONS OF EMPLOYED INDIVIDUALS BY NATIVITY STATUS

| | Native-Born Individuals | | | | | | Foreign-Born Individuals | | |
| | Native-Born Parents | | | At Least One Foreign-Born Parent | | | | | |
	Total (%)	White (%)	Other (%)	Total (%)	Only One (%)	Both (%)	Total (%)	Citizens (%)	Noncitizens (%)
Professional, executive, administrative, managerial	27.4	29.1	19.4	28.9	30.2	27.5	22.9	29.5	19.3
Technical, sales, clerical	30.4	30.6	29.4	30.6	31.5	29.7	25.3	29.7	23.0
Service occupations	24.7	23.7	29.6	24.4	23.6	25.2	28.9	25.1	31.0
Operatives and laborers	17.5	16.6	21.6	16.1	14.8	17.6	22.9	15.7	26.8

Country-Specific Description: Percentage Professional, Etc., and Operative/Laborer

Major sending countries of immigration				Total (%)	Only One (%)	Both (%)	Total (%)	Citizens (%)	Noncitizens (%)
Mexico	Professional, etc.			16.5	18.4	14.2	5.1	11.7	4.0
	Operative/laborer			22.0	22.2	22.0	45.9	35.0	47.8
Cuba	Professional, etc.			30.7	28.4	31.9	23.3	34.1	11.1
	Operative/laborer			8.4	13.3	5.9	19.5	12.5	27.3
Nicaragua	Professional, etc.			28.4	—[1]	—[1]	7.2	8.8	6.8
	Operative/laborer			16.1	—[1]	—[1]	24.3	11.0	27.7
El Salvador	Professional, etc.			26.4	28.2	—[1]	6.1	14.1	4.8
	Operative/laborer			18.7	17.4	—[1]	28.5	19.5	30.1
Dominican Republic	Professional, etc.			19.0	—[1]	17.4	9.5	21.4	4.8
	Operative/laborer			13.5	—[1]	12.2	34.7	22.2	39.6

Jamaica	Professional, etc.	28.3	40.2	14.1	24.7	37.7	16.5
	Operative/laborer	9.7	8.8	13.6	12.1	8.4	14.4
Philippines	Professional, etc.	30.2	33.0	28.2	28.5	31.1	24.9
	Operative/laborer	12.1	13.3	8.1	14.3	12.6	16.6
China (s)	Professional, etc.	—	—	—	47.9	50.5	43.1
	Operative/laborer	—	—	—	3.0	2.8	3.4
Korea (s)	Professional, etc.	25.0	—	—	28.3	35.2	23.1
	Operative/laborer	4.8	—	—	10.1	8.6	11.2
Vietnam	Professional, etc.	17.5	15.2	—	12.9	21.2	2.7
	Operative/laborer	39.7	38.4	—	28.5	17.9	41.7
Laos/Cambodia	Professional, etc.	—	—	—	14.7	19.1	10.6
	Operative/laborer	—	—	—	32.4	19.5	44.8
India	Professional, etc.	37.1	—	—	48.8	54.6	45.0
	Operative/laborer	9.2	—	—	12.1	11.7	12.4

SOURCE: U.S. Census Bureau 1994, 1995, 1996, 1997.
[1]Data not shown; calculation based on fewer than 50 cases.

While occupation provides one indicator of labor force status, it is relevant only for those who actually have a job. To round out this appraisal of labor force circumstances, I document the underemployment of immigrant groups (Zhou 1993). *Underemployment* goes beyond the conventional measure of unemployment (being out of a job and actively looking for work) by also including those who would like to work but have given up trying to find a job (discouraged workers), those who are working part time only because they cannot get full-time hours (involuntary part time), and those who are working full time but whose wages are insufficient to bring them over 125 percent of the poverty line for individuals (working poor) (Clogg 1979; Hauser 1974).

Table 2.9 suggests there is little difference between second- and third-generation workers in their prevalence of underemployment; about 19 percent of both groups are underemployed (that is, they fall in any of the underemployment categories). First-generation workers are more likely to be underemployed, but this is solely because of the rather high prevalence of underemployment among foreign-born noncitizens (29.3 percent). The country-specific comparisons tell a now-familiar story of diversity by country of origin. Mexican, Haitian, Nicaraguan, Salvadoran, and Dominican immigrant workers have comparatively high rates of underemployment, while Filipinos, Chinese, and Indians have lower underemployment rates. Interestingly, given assorted signals of disadvantage in earlier tables, Vietnamese and Laotian/Cambodian immigrant workers do not have particularly high underemployment rates.

Health Status and Health Insurance Coverage

Health issues have always been near the top of the national policy agenda. In the final tables I assess whether there are differences in health status and health insurance coverage across these immigrant status groups. While the CPS has long included items that monitor health insurance coverage, since 1996 subjective health data also have been obtained. Respondents were asked to appraise their own health and that of household members, using a five-category ordinal scale ranging from excellent to poor. Few meaningful differences are seen across immigrant generations in their propensity to be in subjectively poor or fair health (Table 2.10). However, first- and second-generation individuals are somewhat less likely to rate their health as excellent. This is in line with results from the National Health Interview Survey suggesting that first- and second-generation parents are less likely than others to say

TABLE 2.9 UNDEREMPLOYMENT BY NATIVITY STATUS

| | Native-Born Individuals | | | | | | Foreign-Born Individuals | | |
| | Native-Born Parents | | | At Least One Foreign-Born Parent | | | | | |
	Total (%)	White (%)	Other (%)	Total (%)	Only One (%)	Both (%)	Total (%)	Citizens (%)	Noncitizens (%)
Adequately employed	80.6	82.1	73.6	80.4	81.1	79.6	73.9	79.9	70.7
Underemployed	19.4	17.9	26.4	19.6	18.9	20.4	26.1	20.1	29.3
Unemployed/ discouraged	4.8	3.9	9.5	5.3	4.8	5.8	7.0	5.5	7.8
Low hours	7.5	7.3	8.4	7.8	7.5	8.1	9.3	7.4	10.4
Low income	7.1	6.8	8.6	6.6	6.6	6.5	9.7	7.2	11.1
Country-Specific Description: Percentage Underemployed									
Major sending countries of immigration									
Mexico				30.0	29.7	30.5	37.3	28.0	39.4
Cuba				17.3	11.8	13.2	23.4	15.7	32.2
Nicaragua				29.8	—¹	—¹	32.7	20.7	35.7
El Salvador				21.2	20.3	—¹	40.2	24.7	42.9
Dominican Republic				37.6	—¹	36.8	35.5	21.7	40.8
Haiti				29.7	—¹	—¹	35.9	31.3	37.7
Jamaica				25.4	14.7	—¹	25.8	26.2	29.6
Philippines				20.0	19.8	20.0	15.4	11.8	20.4
China (s)				—¹	—¹	—¹	13.3	11.4	16.7
Korea (s)				19.2	—¹	—¹	20.3	12.4	26.1
Vietnam				34.7	35.9	—¹	20.7	13.9	28.8
Laos/Cambodia				—¹	—¹	—¹	21.5	11.4	31.5
India				12.1	—¹	—¹	18.9	16.2	20.7

SOURCE: U.S. Census Bureau 1994, 1995, 1996, 1997.
¹Data not shown; calculation based on fewer than 50 cases.

TABLE 2.10 SUBJECTIVE HEALTH BY NATIVITY STATUS

	Native-Born Individuals			At Least One Foreign-Born Parent			Foreign-Born Individuals		
	Total (%)	White (%)	Other (%)	Total (%)	Only One (%)	Both (%)	Total (%)	Citizens (%)	Noncitizens (%)
Excellent	36.2	37.9	29.3	31.9	35.2	29.0	31.0	31.8	30.6
Very good	30.1	30.4	29.2	29.8	29.8	29.8	30.3	29.8	30.5
Good	22.0	20.8	26.4	25.2	22.9	27.3	27.9	26.5	28.7
Fair	8.0	7.4	10.2	8.8	8.3	9.2	7.4	8.1	7.0
Poor	3.8	3.5	4.9	4.2	3.6	4.7	3.4	3.8	3.2

Country-Specific Description: Percentage in Excellent and Fair/Poor Subjective Health

Major sending countries of immigration

		At Least One Foreign-Born Parent			Foreign-Born Individuals		
		Total (%)	Only One (%)	Both (%)	Total (%)	Citizens (%)	Noncitizens (%)
Mexico	Excellent	31.0	33.1	29.1	24.6	21.6	25.1
	Fair/poor	9.0	10.5	8.4	11.6	18.0	10.6
Cuba	Excellent	44.7	50.1	47.3	21.5	23.9	18.9
	Fair/poor	4.0	5.2	3.0	22.7	16.3	29.5
Nicaragua	Excellent	36.8	—¹	—¹	28.9	—¹	27.6
	Fair/poor	5.8	—¹	—¹	7.1	—¹	7.4
El Salvador	Excellent	37.0	37.9	38.8	28.5	32.4	27.7
	Fair/poor	9.2	12.8	5.3	11.7	12.1	11.5
Dominican Republic	Excellent	27.9	28.8	23.7	18.4	20.6	17.5
	Fair/poor	8.2	11.5	7.5	16.0	18.1	15.2
Jamaica	Excellent	40.4	35.5	42.3	28.8	30.5	27.6
	Fair/poor	6.0	7.5	3.4	10.1	13.4	8.1

Haiti	Excellent	37.6	—¹	41.1	20.3	16.5	21.8
	Fair/poor	5.8	—¹	4.3	12.5	15.8	14.5
Philippines	Excellent	43.0	41.1	43.3	28.6	31.5	25.5
	Fair/poor	4.5	3.6	5.4	11.5	12.8	10.1
China (s)	Excellent	47.7	—¹	51.8	34.2	32.9	36.1
	Fair/poor	2.4	—¹	1.9	3.2	3.3	2.9
Korea (s)	Excellent	36.5	44.4	31.0	29.2	33.0	27.0
	Fair/poor	2.8	3.7	2.2	12.9	12.2	13.3
Vietnam	Excellent	42.7	31.1	48.4	24.3	29.6	19.8
	Fair/poor	6.3	5.7	6.1	17.0	11.0	21.8
Laos/Cambodia	Excellent	25.2	—¹	28.7	23.6	33.9	19.6
	Fair/poor	6.7	—¹	4.1	22.3	11.9	26.3
India	Excellent	54.7	—¹	61.0	38.4	36.3	40.0
	Fair/poor	0.1	—¹	0.1	9.1	12.9	7.0

SOURCE: U.S. Census Bureau 1994, 1995, 1996, 1997.
¹Data not shown; calculation based on fewer than 50 cases.

their children are in excellent health (Hernandez and Charney 1998: 74–75).

In general, the country-specific data indicate that economically disadvantaged groups tend to have somewhat poor subjective health. Among second-generation individuals, Mexicans, Laotian/Cambodians, and Dominicans have comparatively low proportions reported to be in excellent health, while their Cuban, Filipino, Vietnamese, Chinese, and Indian counterparts have high proportions in excellent health. For all of these country-of-origin groups, foreign-born individuals have poorer subjective health than do second-generation individuals. Immigrant Cubans and Laotians/Cambodians, noncitizens in particular, have quite high percentages that are reported to be in fair or poor health. Respectively 29.5 and 26.3 percent of Cuban-born and Laotian/Cambodian-born noncitizens are stated to be in fair or poor health.

Clearly, caution is warranted given differences in the way that such subjective health categories might be interpreted. Nonetheless, these results are suggestive of some health disadvantages among certain groups of immigrants and their offspring. More concrete are the disadvantages in health insurance coverage captured in Table 2.11. Third-, second-, and first-generation adults are progressively more likely to lack health insurance coverage. At the extreme, 37.1 percent of foreign-born noncitizen adults lack coverage. Even more alarming is the very high prevalence of noncoverage among children; 31.8, 45.3, and 55.3 percent of third-, second-, and first-generation children, respectively, lack health insurance. Among second-generation children, Mexicans, Laotians/Cambodians, Salvadorans, and Dominicans are especially vulnerable given their high prevalence of noncoverage.

Conclusion

The demographic and socioeconomic circumstances of immigrants are highly diverse. I sought to capture this diversity by offering a national-level comparison of first-, second-, and third-generation Americans as a whole and by sketching country-specific profiles for the groups spotlighted in the following chapters and other key sending countries. Here I summarize the most salient patterns, focusing in turn on the aggregate immigrant generation comparisons and the country-specific profiles.

Even in the aggregate, the first, second, and third generations differ sharply from one another. Immigrants and their children are marked by their highly urban character and residential concentration in the East and West. Immigrants also are on less secure economic footing than other Americans. With high proportions that lack a high school degree, it is little surprise that the first generation also is challenged by lower occupational status, higher underemployment, higher poverty and child poverty rates, and a high proportion that lacks health insurance coverage. The circumstances of foreign-born *noncitizens* are particularly stark in all these respects, underscoring their acute vulnerability. While less severe, many of these disadvantages also are seen among the second generation.

In broadest terms, the correspondence between deeper generational roots in this country, on the one hand, and declining residential concentration in central cities, increasing home ownership, decreasing poverty and child poverty, and increasing educational attainment, on the other, is consistent with linear images of success across immigrant generations. While these differences are real, at best they only partly reflect economic assimilation. The data I analyze here are cross-sectional. As such, apparent improvements in child poverty and other outcomes may partly be an artifact of changes in the qualities of immigrant cohorts. Nonetheless, to the extent they do capture assimilation, it is noteworthy that not all of the changes across immigrant generations are necessarily positive. There was mild evidence, for example, that first-, second-, and third-generation children become *decreasingly* likely to live with both of their parents. I also found that first-, second-, and third-generation poor individuals come to rely *more* heavily on public assistance as an economic survival strategy. A provocative and highly speculative implication is that more so than natives, immigrants eschew welfare, but their children and grandchildren progressively lose this aversion.

The sizable differences I found between citizens and noncitizens within the first generation and between whites and nonwhites within the third highlight the heterogeneity that is masked by using gross categories like *first, second,* and *third generation.* The diversity of immigrants is even more apparent in the country-specific profiles. Taken together, these statistical vignettes strongly underscore the important reality that the children considered in the chapters to follow are beginning their journey in American society under sharply different circumstances. Across the wide array of indicators I have used here, the country-specific analyses consistently show a pattern of advantage for some groups and disadvantage for others. Whether measured in terms of labor force status, poverty, or lack of health insurance, the country-of-origin groups that were consistently disadvantaged included Mexicans, Laotians/

TABLE 2.11 LACK OF HEALTH INSURANCE COVERAGE
OF ADULTS AND CHILDREN BY NATIVITY STATUS

| | Native-Born Individuals | | | | | | Foreign-Born Individuals | | |
| | Native-Born Parents | | | At Least One Foreign-Born Parent | | | | | |
	Total (%)	White (%)	Other (%)	Total (%)	Only One (%)	Both (%)	Total (%)	Citizens (%)	Noncitizens (%)
Percentage without health insurance coverage									
Adults	14.5	12.8	21.8	16.4	15.3	17.4	30.4	17.9	37.1
Children	31.8	23.3	56.3	45.3	34.5	53.8	55.3	30.6	61.1
Country-Specific Description: Percentage of Adults and Children without Health Insurance Coverage									
Major sending countries of immigration									
Mexico Adults				29.0	26.7	31.4	52.5	35.5	55.4
Mexico Children				66.0	55.7	70.8	78.9	73.0	79.2
Cuba Adults				16.9	14.7	19.7	19.4	12.2	26.5
Cuba Children				35.9	23.8	43.5	—[1]	—[1]	—[1]
Nicaragua Adults				17.9	—[1]	—[1]	49.6	25.8	55.0
Nicaragua Children				67.3	—[1]	70.0	—[1]	—[1]	—[1]
El Salvador Adults				17.0	15.8	26.9	53.4	29.7	57.5
El Salvador Children				59.0	46.9	66.5	81.9	—[1]	84.6
Dominican Republic Adults				32.8	40.1	30.7	36.8	25.7	40.2
Dominican Republic Children				70.0	66.6	76.7	77.2	—[1]	79.7
Haiti Adults				32.4	—[1]	44.1	39.0	17.8	46.3
Haiti Children				52.7	—[1]	52.8	75.9	—[1]	—[1]

Jamaica	Adults	20.1	16.5	22.3	26.3	17.3
	Children	41.0	47.8	42.5	64.9	—¹
Philippines	Adults	17.5	17.0	17.3	18.3	11.2
	Children	18.4	23.7	15.7	31.7	—¹
China (s)	Adults	20.4	—¹	19.0	24.0	22.3
	Children	21.9	—¹	22.2	—¹	—¹
Korea (s)	Adults	26.0	19.8	33.9	42.0	24.3
	Children	45.3	39.3	48.7	34.8	—¹
Vietnam	Adults	29.1	29.5	—¹	27.2	25.8
	Children	38.3	35.8	41.8	61.6	—¹
Laos/Cambodia	Adults	12.1	—¹	—¹	14.0	9.8
	Children	60.5	—¹	64.4	—¹	—¹
India	Adults	12.1	12.5	2.5	23.6	12.4
	Children	23.0	—¹	18.5	32.8	—¹

SOURCE: U.S. Census Bureau 1994, 1995, 1996, 1997.
¹Data not shown; calculation based on fewer than 50 cases.

Cambodians, Haitians, Nicaraguans, Salvadorans, and Dominicans. By comparison, Filipinos and, to a lesser extent, Cubans (particularly second generation) were consistently advantaged relative to the other groups portrayed in this volume. They were usually joined by the Chinese, Koreans, and Indians in their comparative advantage. The country-specific data also provided some evidence of improvement between generations. For example, the educational attainment of several groups (Mexicans, Cubans, Jamaicans, Salvadorans, and Dominicans) was substantially greater for second- than first-generation adults.

While the CPS holds some promise as a source of data on immigrants and their children, it will always be hampered by a somewhat limited sample size that precludes analyses of very small groups. The CPS also lacks many of the questions needed to explore new debates about immigrant assimilation and adaptation, and its cross-sectional design necessarily precludes longitudinal examination of real cohorts of immigrant youngsters as they make their way in American society. The CILS data, which are analyzed in the chapters that follow, were specifically designed to capture these processes.

Notes

Computational support for this research was provided by the Population Research Institute at the Pennsylvania State University, which has core support from the National Institute on Child Health and Human Development (P30 HD28263–01). I thank Jason P. Schachter for assistance with computer programming. I also thank the editors and authors of this volume for their helpful comments on a previous version of this chapter. As always, I am responsible for any errors that remain.

1. A small number of variables were not available in 1995, while a couple of questions, such as those covering subjective health, were not asked until 1996. In these cases I analyzed all of the 1996 data and that part of the 1997 sample that had not been interviewed in 1996.

2. While I refer to these groups as the *first*, *second*, and *third generation*, it must be cautioned that not all those in the first generation are truly immigrants. Many foreign-born individuals, such as students and others, are residing in the United States only temporarily with little intention or prospect of staying permanently.

3. This breakdown of the third generation into non-Hispanic whites versus others (essentially racial and ethnic minorities) is done in part to provide a fairer comparison to the second and first generations who themselves are disproportionally nonwhite and/or Latin American (Hernandez and Charney 1998).

4. Because many of these countries were identified only after 1994, I use only the 1995–1997 CPSs for these portraits. In addition to Jamaica, these nations include: the Bahamas, Barbados, the Dominican Republic, Grenada, and Trinidad and Tobago.

5. Separate Laotian and Cambodian profiles—each based on a comparatively low number of cases—indicated the groups were highly similar to one another. Accordingly, I combined these two groups.

6. This breakdown thus eliminates the circumstance, rare for most country-of-origin groups considered here, where a native-born person has two foreign-born parents who were born in different countries. These results are available on request.

7. All analyses are weighted by the population weight (i.e., March supplement weight) divided by the mean of that weight to yield a weighted N approximately equal to sample size. The public-use version of the 1994 CPS used here had incorrect March supplement weights. I employ corrected weights which were merged with the original 1994 data.

8. In the tables, data are not shown in circumstances when a percentage or mean is based on fewer than 50 cases.

9. To protect the confidentiality of CPS respondents, anywhere from 8.3 to 16.8 percent of these nativity groups are not identified on the central-city variable.

10. The CPS contains several indicators of internal migration. I found few noteworthy differences between immigrant generations in their propensity to move from one year to the next. These results are not reported here but are available on request.

11. Among the second generation, the percentage residing in metro areas ranged from 89.3 percent (Mexico) to 99.6 percent (China). The corresponding range for the first generation was 89.8 percent (Mexico) to 99.6 (Dominican Republic). The somewhat higher prevalence of nonmetro residence among Mexicans partly reflects their greater propensity to be employed in agriculture.

12. To a degree, this similarity is accounted for by the fact that many in the second generation are still residing with their first-generation parents and would thus have the same household and residential characteristics.

13. To save space, only the results for presence of parents are presented in tabular form. Tables for age, race and ethnicity, marital status, and household size are available on request.

14. The mean percentage of household income from a given source is a function of both the propensity of households to receive it and the amount received among those that do. Data on percent receiving and mean receipt are not shown but are available from the author.

References

Clogg, Clifford. C. 1979. *Measuring underemployment: Demographic indicators for the United States.* New York: Academic Press.

Hauser, Phillip. M. 1974. The measurement of labour utilization. *Malayan Economic Review* 19 (1), pp. 1–17.

Hernandez, Donald J., and Evan Charney, eds. 1998. *From generation to generation: The health and well-being of children in immigrant families.* Washington, D.C.: National Academy Press.

Jasso, G., and M. R. Rosenzweig. 1990. *The new chosen people: Immigrants to the United States.* New York: Russell Sage Foundation.

Jensen, Leif. 1989. *The new immigration: Implications for poverty and public assistance utilization, 1960–1980.* New York: Greenwood Press.

Jensen, Leif, and Yoshimi Chitose. 1994. Today's second generation: Evidence from the 1990 U.S. Census. *International Migration Review* 28 (Winter), pp. 714–735.

Martin, Philip, and Elizabeth Midgley. 1994. Immigration to the United States: Journey to an uncertain destination. *Population Bulletin* 49 (2), pp. 1–47.

Oropesa, R. S., and Nancy S. Landale. 1997. In search of the new second generation: Alternative strategies for identifying second generation children and understanding their acquisition of English. *Sociological Perspectives* 40 (3), pp. 429–455.

Portes, Alejandro. 1996. "Introduction: Immigration and its aftermath." In *The new second generation,* edited by Alejandro Portes. New York: Russell Sage Foundation.

Schmidley, A. Dianne, and J. Gregory Robinson. 1998. How well does the Current Population Survey measure the foreign-born population of the United States? Technical working paper no. 22, Population Division, U.S. Bureau of the Census, Washington, D.C.

Simon, Rita J. 1985. *Public opinion and the immigrant: Print media coverage, 1880–1980.* Lexington, Mass.: Lexington Books.

U.S. Census Bureau. 1994. Current population survey, March. Machine-readable data file. Washington, D.C.: U.S. Census Bureau.

———. 1995. Current population survey, March. Machine-readable data file. Washington, D.C.: U.S. Census Bureau.

———. 1996. Current population survey, March. Machine-readable data file. Washington, D.C.: U.S. Census Bureau.

———. 1997. Current population survey, March. Machine-readable data file. Washington, D.C.: U.S. Census Bureau.

Zhou, Min. 1993. Underemployment and economic disparities among minority groups. *Population Research and Policy Review* 12 139–157.

Chapter 3

MEXICAN AMERICANS
A Second Generation at Risk

David E. López and Ricardo D. Stanton-Salazar

The Mexican-American "new" second generation shares many points in common with the other cases included in this volume. Its members display much the same complex pattern of partial acculturation and ambivalent ethnic identity that is typical of other new second-generation youth. They are socially defined as nonwhite, though race is for them a source of confusion and ambivalence. They feel caught between, on the one hand, the demands of their parents, who are struggling to build new lives in the United States, and, on the other hand, their own struggles to combat what they perceive as a hostile environment and their need to construct a new identity that will allow them to face that environment with confidence. Yet in other ways the Mexican-American case stands apart. They and their parents lack many of the resources that have allowed other recent groups of newcomers to the United States to thrive. On average, adult immigrants have only a few years of schooling, limited urban job skills, and little or no knowledge of English. Immigrant Mexican communities are by no means disorganized in the old-fashioned sociological sense of the term; two-parent households and high levels of labor force participation are the norm. However, in comparison with certain other immigrant communities, they lack the web of organizations and social practices that have allowed specific groups to utilize traditional culture to help children achieve (see Gibson and Ogbu

57

1991). A rather large proportion of children of Mexican immigrants do poorly in school, and their occupational prospects are bleak (Valencia 1991). U.S.-born children, increasingly disconnected from the forward-looking immigrant outlook of their Mexican-born cousins, are even further at risk (Buriel 1984; Stanton-Salazar 2001b). The socioeconomic disadvantages and dismal school performance of the Mexican-origin second generation are particularly striking in California, where other contemporary immigrant groups are notable for just the opposite.

If Mexican-origin youth were just another in the vast array of new second-generation groups, there would be only modest cause for concern regarding their below-average achievement and future prospects. It would be nice if all of America's ethnic groups and all their children were, as in Lake Wobegone, above average; in the real world, some have to fall below the mean. But in California and the Southwest, *Mexicanos* and their children are not just another immigrant-based ethnic group. They are instead by far the largest minority and are rapidly becoming the single-largest ethnic group, destined to outnumber whites sometime in this century. Among California's schoolchildren, Mexican Americans already constitute the single-largest ethnic group, and four out of five are the children of immigrants. Mexican-American youth are also much more likely to be in blue-collar/working-poor families than whites, Asians, or even African Americans. It would be no exaggeration, therefore, to say that the Mexican-origin second generation is on its way to becoming the single-largest segment of California's population when it is broken down along the three dimensions of ethnicity, generation, and class.

In this chapter we tell the story of the new Mexican-origin second generation, drawing from the Children of Immigrants Longitudinal Study (CILS) surveys of Mexican-American youth in San Diego, U.S. Census data, and other related research. As concerned as we are with understanding the challenges facing second-generation adolescents growing up and the vagaries of their ethnic identity, our primary goal is to understand the trajectory of socioeconomic adaptation and advancement for this rapidly growing segment of the population. Our focus is on California, because the Mexican-American CILS sample comes from San Diego and because immigration and settlement, and the children that result from it, have a greater impact in California than in the rest of the United States. We begin with a discussion of the unique importance of the Mexican case and some of the difficulties involved in comparing it with other new second-generation groups. We next provide a description of the San Diego Mexican-origin community and of the sample of Mexican-origin schoolchildren in San Diego that provided much of our data. In the fourth section we turn to the thorny question of race and perceived discrimination among Mexican Americans, which we consider to be a key issue that is usually oversimplified. The final section reviews the socioeconomic status and accomplishments of second-generation Mexican Americans, from the school and labor force accomplishments of an earlier second generation through the school performance of second-generation youth in San Diego and California today.

The Unique Importance of the Mexican Case

In addition to poverty and sheer numbers, the Mexican-American case is distinctive for its historical depth and its unique combination of racial ambiguity and negative stereotypes. Today's is by no means the first Mexican-American second generation. The very roots of California and the Southwest are, of course, Mexican, and Mexicans have continuously inhabited the region for hundreds of years, though they were both politically and numerically overwhelmed by Anglos after 1850. In the early part of the twentieth century, a constellation of tiny traditional Mexican/Hispanic communities were dwarfed by migration from Mexico, a migration that produced its own second generation, which came of age 40 years ago. Indeed, a discernible third generation (U.S.-born grandchildren of immigrants) was coming of age when large-scale immigration began again in the 1960s. In 1960 two-thirds of the Latino children in California were third or later generation; today two-thirds are the children of immigrants, the new second generation. In 1960 the average age of the Latino second generation was 25; today it is 10.[1]

The preexisting Mexican-American community serves as an important part of the context of reception for new immigrants, but beyond this, such a context is key to understanding today's second generation for two more specific reasons. First, the social and economic attainments of preceding generations provide a rough guide to the fate of today's second generation and perhaps of tomorrow's third. Second, the status of the preexisting Mexican-American population inevitably determines the expectations and stereotypes that others apply to this new generation of Mexicans in the United States.

Another important difference from other immigrant groups today is racial ambiguity and the persistent negative stereotypes attached to being Mexican in America: By official statistics Mexicans and other Latinos are white, black, Asian, or Native American, but in practice *Latino* and especially *Mexican* serve as quasi-racial terms. However ambiguous race may be on the individual level for Mexican Americans, on the group level Mexicans have a history of stigmatization, economic exploitation, and racial exclusion in California and the Southwest (Gutiérrez 1995). Just as Mexican immigrants early in the twentieth century inherited the traditional status of Mexicans in the United States, so today's immigrants and their children are inheriting the inner and outer burdens of Mexican "color" as it developed throughout the twentieth century (Donato, Menchaca, and Valencia 1991). We believe that these four distinctive characteristics—disproportionate poverty, group size, historical depth, and racist stereotypes—interact to create special barriers to upward mobility for Mexican-American youth in such a way that their school performance and socioeconomic trajectories cannot be explained by the analysis of individual characteristics.

Thirty years ago, in their massive study *The Mexican-American People,* Grebler, Moore, and Guzmán (1970) argued that the future of Mexican Americans might go in either of two directions: They might proceed along a somewhat delayed path of assimilation and increased economic equity, like Italians and other Euro-American ethnic groups, or they might share the castelike fate of African Americans. The answer was to be found in the future, as third- and fourth-generation Mexican Americans became the majority of the group's population. Grebler and his associates, or anyone else for that matter, did not foresee the great revival of immigration that has taken place in the past 35 years. *The Mexican-American People* appeared just as the old second generation was hitting their peak earning years and their children were moving into young adulthood. As we shall see in the following sections, their mixed success, under economic conditions generally considered better than today's, does not support optimism about the economic future of the emerging new second generation.

Much of our description and analysis revolves around the question of low academic achievement and its long-term consequences for Mexican Americans and for California. We believe that this is one of the gravest policy questions facing the state and the Mexican-American/ Latino community at the dawn of the millennium. But in the historical context of immigration to the United States, it is not a particularly interesting *sociological* question. We are not shocked and amazed about dismal academic performance by the children of Polish peasants and

Italian farm laborers a century ago. Why expect the children of Mexican *campesinos* to do any differently?

In some ways, the Mexican example reflects the *normal* run of things in American immigration history: The children of immigrants get the minimal education offered by their new homeland and find jobs somewhere between the dirty work their parents did and the careers of more privileged groups. In other important ways, however, the history of incorporation of *Mexicanos* is categorically different from the cycle of assimilation experienced by white ethnics. When the burdens of historical segregation, economic exploitation, and enduring racial stereotypes are added to their socioeconomic disadvantages, then low Mexican-American achievement levels become significantly more comprehensible.

Why, then, is there such concern for explaining this low achievement? We see three reasons: First, today's Mexican-American second generation happens to be growing up alongside the truly unusual Asian-American second-generation groups—among whom we find many poor children doing well in school—and Mexican-American children are inevitably compared unfavorably with them. Even if achievement differences between Asians and Latinos could be explained by statistically controlling socioeconomic factors (and it appears that they cannot), the general public cares little for multivariate analysis and focuses on the group differences, not their causes; people are inclined to only see racial/ethnic differences, while the stratifying and exclusionary mechanisms of class are rendered obscure. Second, the previous conditions that facilitated second- and then third-generation mobility in the past, particularly the availability of good, unionized manual-labor jobs that do not require high levels of formal education, simply do not exist today. We now live in a service-oriented economy, with an increasingly bifurcated job market. These are sociological platitudes, of course, but what is not always made clear is that this structural change is really a problem only for those groups entering the U.S. job market *at the social bottom,* and Mexicans are the only large immigrant group that does so at the present time. Third, there is substantial evidence that the older Mexican-American third generation did not experience the same levels of upward mobility and social assimilation as those experienced by Italians and other European ethnics but rather appears stuck near the bottom, along with African Americans (Grebler, Moore, and Guzman 1970; Ortiz 1996). As with African Americans, a small middle-class segment is doing just fine, but a substantial portion seems to be left behind, albeit not in quite the dire straits of the so-called black urban underclass. This suggests that today's Mexican-American second generation may not serve as a traditional transition between their parents and their fully integrated and assimilated children but may rather represent the transition from a permanently disadvantaged minority to a permanently disadvantaged majority in California and the Southwest.

Although we stress the uniqueness of the Mexican-American case, we believe that it fits neatly within the general "segmented assimilation" theoretical framework of the CILS project that frames the potential for success in terms of background resources, labor market conditions and fit, and the general political/social context of reception (Portes and Rumbaut 2001: ch. 3). The Mexican-American case demonstrates the importance of cultural and material capital, or rather their absence. Today, as throughout the twentieth century, labor market conditions have played an important role in both attracting Mexican labor and in determining the social destinies of Mexican Americans raised in the United States. Even more so does it underline the importance of the cultural as well as material dimensions of the context of reception into which immigrants arrive, which in turn sets the stage for the world in which their children grow up. In the case of Mexican Americans, this includes expectations based on historically rooted racial stereotypes and institutional treatments that are more complex than white attitudes and social practices toward African Americans or Asians but no less consequential.

San Diego: Setting and Sample

San Diego County has the third-largest concentration of Latinos in California, following greater Los Angeles and the San Francisco Bay area. According to the 1990 census, one in five residents in the county was of Latino origin, totaling a bit more than a half a million people. About 86 percent of these Latino residents are of Mexican origin. While San Diego has only about half the Latino proportion of the greater Los Angeles area and only about 6 or 7 percent of the state's total Latino population, its Mexican-origin population is similar to that of the entire state in both history and socioeconomic makeup.

San Diego County has historically served as the principal gateway for migration from Mexico and Latin America into the United States. In fact, the San Diego–Tijuana border is recognized as the busiest international border in the world. The cities of San Diego and Tijuana, whose

downtown centers are only 19 miles from each other, together constitute one of the major trading and industrial centers of the Pacific Rim.
The San Diego–Tijuana region is also one of the principal population
and industrial centers along the U.S.-Mexican border. San Diego's
Mexican-origin population grew rapidly as a result of emigrants fleeing
the economic and political turmoil of the Mexican Revolution. The city
and smaller municipalities stretching to the border have well-established Mexican/Chicano neighborhoods; most are of low and modest
income, but some are traditional middle-class areas established by better-off segments of the community (including some well-off entrepreneurial families from Tijuana).

Despite—or perhaps because—of its proximity to Mexico, San
Diego has never been a place where Mexican Americans have felt particularly welcome, and the white elite and electorate have managed to
keep them marginalized economically and politically throughout the
twentieth century. The resurgence of immigration from Mexico has
increased white/Mexican tensions. The gradual and proportional decrease in white blue-collar workers and in white children in the public
school system, together with downward mobility of white middle-class
families in the 1980s, has led to the kind of scapegoating reminiscent of
the depression years. It is along the border just south of San Diego that
homeowner groups flooded crossing areas with their car headlights—
not to aid migrants but rather to force the border patrol to arrest them.
It is also noteworthy that before becoming the most notoriously anti-
immigrant governor in California's recent history, Pete Wilson was the
mayor of San Diego.

It is quite paradoxical, then, that San Diego's economy is increasingly dependent upon Latino workers, as is the case in other major California cities. Latino labor participation in the county jumped from 13
percent in 1980 to 20 percent in 1990 and will probably surpass 25
percent by the year 2000. While the 1980s saw Latinos heavily concentrated in the manufacturing sector, in the 1990s Latinos were more
likely to be involved in the construction, trade, and services industries.
As in the state as a whole, the Latino workforce in San Diego is increasingly composed of immigrants, most of whom have only a few
years of schooling and poor English skills. The Latino population in the
county is also substantially younger than the region's total population.
While the median age for the general population was 30.9 in 1990, for
Latinos it was 24.3 years. Latinos also accounted for 29 percent of the

region's population under 5 years of age and 29 percent of the school-age population (ages 5–17).

The growing presence of Latino youth is most marked within the public school system, where demographic shifts have been remarkable. In 1977, white students constituted 71 percent of the county's student enrollment (ages 5–17); by 1989, this percentage had decreased to 54 percent, and by the time of the last CILS in 1996, whites constituted less than 50 percent of the K–12 population. Latino students, representing by far the largest segment of the new majority, constituted about 27 percent of the county's student body. This is somewhat less than the statewide Latino presence (40 percent) and much less than the overwhelming Latino presence in Los Angeles and other highly impacted municipalities.

Latinos are a large and rapidly growing part of San Diego's public schools, but they are still a numerical minority. They are also linguistically diverse: Forty-three percent of the Latino student body in San Diego in 1990 was classified as limited English proficient (LEP), with a bit less than one-third classified as a bilingual yet fluent English proficient (FEP). Another 28 percent are classified as English dominant. The school system has had to respond to this growing presence; for example, in 1990, San Diego County employed 875 teachers with bilingual credentials, yet this number accounted only for a bit less than half of the region's need for bilingual and credentialed educators (United Way of San Diego 1991).

Table 3.1 provides a demographic sketch of the CILS San Diego Mexican-American sample. Seven hundred and twenty-seven Mexican-American youth were interviewed in 1992, and researchers were able to reinterview 578 in 1995–1996. This 80 percent reinterview rate is quite good by survey research standards, though it is the lowest of all the ethnic group samples in San Diego. All statistics given here apply only to the remaining 578 cases.

At first glance the sample appears to have considerable generational diversity, with 61 percent U.S. born and 39 percent born in Mexico. However, in reality there is little sociological diversity here: Seventy-nine percent have been in the United States all their lives or at least since the age of 5, and most of the remaining one-fifth arrived between the ages of 6 and 12. Sampling criteria of necessity limit the degree to which respondents might legitimately be considered immigrants. Only those who had already been in the United States for several years before 1992 were eligible, so even most of the 11 percent who did arrive after the age of 10

TABLE 3.1 NATIVITY, LANGUAGE PROFICIENCY,
AND SOCIOECONOMIC STATUS OF THE CILS
MEXICAN-AMERICAN SAN DIEGO SAMPLE IN 1995

	N	Percentage
Nativity		
U.S. born	354	61
1.75 generation	104	18
1.5 generation	59	10
1.25 generation	61	11
TOTAL	578	100
Language proficiency		
Effective bilingual	129	25
English dominant	166	32
Spanish dominant	217	42
TOTAL	512	100
Parental SES and family characteristics		
Father has some college		15
Mother has some college		11
Fathers' occupation		
Upper white collar	10	2
Lower white collar	43	10
Low-wage service worker	166	38
Blue collar	218	50
TOTAL	437	100
Own home		43
In two-parent household		60
Percent in households of four or less		36

SOURCE: 1995 CILS San Diego Survey.
NOTE: 1.75 generation = foreign born, arrived in the United States before age 5. 1.5 generation = arrived between the ages of 6 and 10. 1.25 generation = arrived between the ages of 11 and 15.

were only 11 or 12 when they entered the country. This is, after all, a study of the second generation, children growing up in the United States.

Certainly it makes little sense to distinguish between the native born and those who arrived before the age of 5. Those who arrive between the ages of 6 and 12 are progressively more subject to the set of potential advantages and disadvantages associated with growing up *Mexicano* in Mexico as opposed to growing up Mexican in southern California. Many of these students come with a number of years in Mexican schools and usually exhibit a secure identity as Mexicans, good literacy and language skills, and a solid knowledge of Mexican society. Even with acculturation, they don't easily assimilate into the peer societies of the U.S.-born. Furthermore, while U.S.-born students and recent immigrants both have immigrant parents, these two groups of parents are often in very different positions. Parents of U.S.-born adolescents, for example, have had many more years to learn about their racialized and stigmatized position in the United States, perceptions that might serve to depress the educational expectations for their acculturated children (see Gibson and Ogbu 1991). There are presumably some advantages to growing up north of the border: Families are likely to be more economically secure, and English skills are likely to be better.

The relatively small number of recent immigrant youth in our CILS sample, however, renders nativity and length of residence inappropriate as key independent variables. Furthermore, age at immigration is particularly difficult to interpret since, of course, it is so correlated with the length of time that one's parents have been in the United States, which is a major determinant of economic advancement for adult immigrants.

Wherever they are born, most children of immigrants to the United States begin life speaking their ethnic mother tongue but then progressively adopt English. A certain percentage of this group lose their propensity and ability to speak the language of their parents. It has been well documented that this linguistic shift is slower for Mexican-American youth today than it is for the children of Asian immigrants, but the difference is one of degree, and it is difficult to say if Spanish is being maintained more tenaciously than European immigrant languages early in the twentieth century. That said, the vitality of Spanish as a used language in San Diego and southern California generally is incontrovertible: Immigrants, who make up half the work force in many industries, often speak Spanish as their only language; their children are mostly bilingual, with varying degrees of competence in each language, and a significant minority of the Mexican-American/Latino third generation continues to use Spanish if only as an interactional symbol of ethnic solidarity (López 1996; Portes and Hao 1998).

The high school students in San Diego in our sample all speak English to some degree, and over half reported that they speak it very well. As the children of Mexican immigrants, almost all speak Spanish to some degree (the principal exceptions being those with one or more parents who do not speak Spanish regularly), and two-thirds said that they speak it very well. However in 1995, 78 percent of the U.S. born and 63 percent of the Mexico born declared that they preferred to speak English, marking substantial increases from 1992 for both groups. High as these rates are, they are lower than the Asian sub-groups also included in the San Diego survey.

All reports on language preference, use, and ability are intrinsically fuzzy measures, but there is no question that this is a population under-going linguistic change. Only time will tell if this second generation will choose to pass Spanish on to their children, but the results of this study, which are well supported by other research, strongly suggest that this is a population undergoing transitional bilingualism. On the other hand, a solid majority of them do report that they can speak Spanish very well, suggesting that at least the potential for language maintenance is present. The Latino youth scene in California, and specifically southern California, is largely defined by children and youth growing up in the United States with immigrant parents and strong continuing ties to Mexico. They, as well as many "native of native" Latino children, grow up in barrios where the cultural and linguistic milieu is characterized by the clash and constant negotiation between youth subcultures and Mexican/Latino immigrant culture, between the forces of youth iden-tity formation and the nostalgic re-creations of immigrant adults. Over the last 15 years, however, the apparent Mexicanization of barrios across the state has served to infuse a new Mexicanist ethnic identity into contemporary Mexican-American youth culture, which we believe will continue to be supportive of the Spanish language. Past studies of language shift, then, may not be good guides to the future of Spanish in California.

As with generation and language, this sample of Mexican-American youth is also quite homogeneous with respect to their parents' economic status. Data about their parents' education and jobs that are filtered through the eyes of adolescents is certain to be only approximate, but it does seem to roughly correspond with what we know of the educational and occupational profile of Mexican immigrants. Only 11 to 15 percent of the parents are reported to have any college education at all, and the median of schooling was about eight years. A minuscule 2 percent of their fathers had better white-collar jobs (i.e., managerial/professional/technical), and a bare 10 percent had white-collar working-class jobs (e.g., sales and clerical). The vast majority were classified as low-wage service workers or blue-collar workers. The mothers who were in the workforce followed much the same pattern. But, of course, immigrants have tradi-tionally done the dirty work and, as emphasized previously, Mexican immigrants follow the classic immigrant pattern much more than Asian immigrants today.

As Hayes-Bautista, Schink, and Chapa (1988) have emphasized, economic success and assimilation for Mexican immigrants is found not through education, the professions, or even extraordinary rates of entrepreneurship but rather through stable families acting collectively to achieve economic goals. In this sample, this is reflected in rates of two-parent households and home ownership that are high in comparison to African Americans or to Puerto Ricans in the East though lower than average for the other immigrant groups. Family size, here represented by the percent in smaller families, is close to the norm for other groups included in the study, as are labor force participation rates, which are somewhat below average. Perhaps the most significant measure is the remarkable increase in home ownership in the brief three years separating the two surveys: up 20 percent for households of U.S.-born children and a remarkable 50 percent for the households of immigrant children.

In sum, data from the San Diego survey reflect other studies of Mexican immigrant households: In comparison with African Americans and Puerto Ricans, levels of two-parent families, home ownership, evidence of familial cooperation, and other "positive" characteristics are comparatively high, but they do not stand out when compared with other immigrant groups. Put another way, there is no evidence that the social and cultural characteristics of Mexican immigrant households give them an advantage when compared with other immigrants, and therefore there is no reason to believe that they can compensate for the economic and educational disadvantages typical of Mexican immigrant households.

Adolescence is typically a time of identity confusion and shift along the dimensions of ethnicity, gender, and social status. Understandably, ethnic identity is particularly salient to these children of immigrants. In 1992 the most popular terms of identity were panethnic (*Latino, Hispanic, Chicano*): 45 percent for the U.S. born and 51 percent for those born in Mexico. In 1992 and 1995, 40 percent of the U.S. born labeled themselves as Mexican-American, but only 12 to 15 percent of those born in Mexico used this term at either point in time; their preferred identity was Latino/Hispanic in 1992, but by 1995 they had largely abandoned these panethnic terms in favor of some variant of the straightforward term *Mexican*. Only 2 percent of the U.S. born and none of the immigrants had adopted nonethnic terms such as *American* in 1992 or 1995.

When identity in 1992 is cross-classified with identity in 1995, the picture gets even more complex. In Table 3.2 we have combined the

TABLE 3.2 ETHNIC IDENTITY AND IDENTITY CHANGE AMONG
THE SAN DIEGO MEXICAN-AMERICAN SECOND-GENERATION SAMPLE

Preferred Identity in 1995

Preferred Identity in 1992	Hispanic/ Latino	Chicano	Mexican	Mexican American	Other	Total
Hispanic/Latino	48	4	88	33	4	177 (32%)
Chicano	13	21	27	29	2	92 (17%)
Mexican	14	1	69	15	4	103 (18%)
Mexican American	23	8	51	75	10	167 (30%)
Other	2	6	2	7	6	17 (3%)
TOTAL	100 (18%)	34 (6%)	237 (42%)	159 (29%)	26 (4%)	556 (100%)

two nativity groups and separated the term *Chicano* from the panethnic terms, since we believe it is better seen as a nationalistic political identity. Table 3.2 shows that the principal shift has been from panethnic terms to *Mexican* and, to a lesser degree, to *Mexican American.* Those previously using the term *Chicano* also shifted substantially to these categories. In contrast, those who identified as Mexican or Mexican-American in 1992 tended to stick with these terms. There is also a substantial and somewhat puzzling decline in the use of the term *Chicano,* a self-identifier that expressed the political aspirations of second- and third-generation youth in the 1970s. Those abandoning the term moved in all directions, to *Mexican, Mexican American,* and *Hispanic,* suggesting a plain drop in the term's popularity rather than any meaningful shift.

It is probably unwise to attribute too much meaning to these shifts. They are, after all, only changes over a three-year period in answers given by adolescents. On the other hand, those particular three years are probably more significant historically (and politically) than developmentally. It was precisely during this time that anti-immigrant sentiments bubbled and boiled over in California, as reflected in the bitter campaign over Proposition 187, which, though framed as a denial of rights to illegal immigrants, was widely interpreted as an attack on all Mexicans in the United States, legal or illegal. Locally in San Diego County, school boards and city councils debated what to do about "the children of illegals" in schools and hospitals, and white citizen groups wore down their car batteries shining headlights along the border. In this context, a nationalistic reaffirmation of identity is hardly surprising.

Will these identity changes have lasting consequences? We have no way of knowing to what degree these findings might mirror similar changes in other parts of California and the Southwest or the degree to which they reflect developmental as opposed to historical changes. Portes and MacLeod (1996), analyzing the 1992 CILS survey results, found that panethnic identity (including Chicano as well as Hispanic and Latino) was actually identified with lower socioeconomic status (SES) and lower levels of assimilation and self-esteem. Given the changes from 1992 to 1995, it is not surprising that we did not find a similar pattern within the Mexican-American sample in 1995. *Mexican* is the clear favorite among the Mexico-born children, but, after all, they are Mexicans. Mexico is a fervently patriotic and nationalistic society, and Mexicans are apparently increasingly willing to express these feelings even when they live in southern California, as demonstrated on

Mexican national holidays and when Mexican soccer teams play in the United States. But on the other hand, among the U.S. born, *Mexican American* continues to be the single most popular term, followed by *Latino/Hispanic*. This suggests that specifically Mexican identity wanes among the second generation, and it is logical to expect it to be even weaker among the third. On the other hand, it is worth pointing out that over 98 percent of the sample chose *some* form of Mexican/Latino identity; at least among second-generation adolescents there is no evidence that ethnic distinctiveness is being obliterated by acculturation.

In sum, the San Diego sample would seem to well represent the Mexican-American second generation in general, in terms of both social and cultural makeup. There is relatively little socioeconomic or linguistic diversity and a strong identity with the terms *Mexican* and *Mexican American*. The clear tendency over time and generationally from immigrants to the native born is an increasing preference for English and a tendency to express their Mexican identity in "hyphenated-American" form. We turn now to the confusing but essential question of race and Mexican Americans, which we believe is at the crux of the dilemma of understanding the present and future place of the Mexican-American new second generation and, indeed, of all Mexican Americans.

The Mexican "Race": Ambivalence, Ambiguity, and Perceived Discrimination

The major students of European assimilation and its discontents in American life and their critics have all emphasized the disjunction between the typical Euro-American experience and that of racially distinct groups, by which they principally meant African Americans but with less certainty included Asians and Latinos as well. In their recent work, Alba and Nee (1997) are skeptical about the significance of non-whiteness per se as a barrier to assimilation and success in America, as indeed they would have to be in the face of the evidence: Asian immigrant groups today demonstrate cultural and economic assimilation more rapid than Europeans a century ago, and their rates of social assimilation more closely approximate the European experience than the exclusion that faced all nonwhites 50 years ago and that still is the norm for African Americans. Middle-class black anglophone Caribbeans seem to outpace native African Americans, though poor black Puerto Ricans are among the most marginalized "immigrants" in

the continental United States. Clearly, the variety of incorporation experiences among nonwhite groups demands that we look at other factors, just as segmented assimilation theory insists.

What about Mexicans, specifically? In the popular press, Mexicans
are sometimes depicted as just another ethnic group on the path toward
assimilation. Some Chicano activists are equally certain that Mexican
Americans are uniformly an oppressed racial group. The U.S. Census
Bureau has never known what to make of Mexicans. Variously identified by mother tongue and surname in the past, in the last three decennial censuses they have been identified through a distinct "Hispanic Origin" question, separate from the question on race with which Latinos
must identify themselves as white, black, or Asian. If they insist on writing in something like *Mexicano,* it is recoded as *white.* This results in
two separate definitions of the nation's white population: all classified
as white on the race question and the "real" white population, which
the Census Bureau awkwardly but revealingly refers to as "non-
Hispanic whites." One can write in *Mexican* on the ancestry question,
but only Europeans and miscellaneous other whites are included in publications based on this ethnic definer; Mexicans and other Latinos are
relegated to separate publications and tables, just like blacks and Asians.

It is perhaps unfair to chide the Census Bureau, since race among
Mexican Americans *is* confusing. Race is both a variable and a constant
for Mexican Americans. Those who fit the mestizo/Indian phenotype,
who "look Mexican," cannot escape racial stereotyping any more than
African Americans, though the stigma is usually not so severe. The sizable minority that looks essentially Euro-American has at least the potential to pass as individuals, but to the degree that they continue to be
identified as Mexicans, they are subject to much the same treatment as
their darker brothers and sisters.

The very acceptance of white Mexicans holds within it the key to
continuing resentment about racism and the internalization of self-
deprecation, even among those Mexican Americans who have personally experienced little direct racism: The experience of being told that
one does not "look Mexican" or having friends say things like "I
thought you were Spanish" with good intentions might lead an individual lacking in ethnic pride to hide his Mexicanness, but it also has the
effect of reinforcing negative stereotypes. When even a well-meaning
individual uses the term *Mexican* or *Latino* in opposition to *white,* she
is explicitly categorizing them as nonwhite, with all the negative bag-
gage that that implies in Anglo-American mainstream culture.

We argue that a special burden of the new Mexican-American second generation is that they inherit this preexisting stigma, and it is reinforced by their own life experiences. Their parents, struggling to *ganar la vida,* are probably less affected by U.S. anti-Mexican attitudes, though we believe that they do convey the contradictory message about race that they bring from Mexico. Portes and Bach (1985: 282, 333) argued that in a sense, a heightened awareness of discrimination can be seen as an indicator of increased participation in and understanding of American society. In other words, when children learn what it means to be Mexican in California, they are undergoing precisely what Gordon (1964) meant by "acculturation": They are learning, though not necessarily internalizing and certainly not benefiting from, the norms of the dominant society. The severe poverty of their parents reinforces the castelike status of being Mexican, both in their eyes and in the eyes of others. We believe that it helps explain otherwise puzzling findings regarding identity and perceived discrimination, to which we now turn.

As Rumbaut (1996: 123) has pointed out, coming to grips with discrimination and prejudice can be much more psychologically damaging for children and adolescents than for adults. The degree of damage depends on individual factors as well as on the strength of family and community networks, but when the available support comes from disaffected peer groups rather than families, the result can be a general rejection of schooling and other "white" institutions and goals (Fordham and Ogbu 1986; Sánchez and Fernández 1993). The resulting oppositional subculture is an important, if ultimately destructive, form of segmented assimilation (Suárez-Orozco 1991; Portes and Zhou 1993). As Rumbaut (1997) points out, there can be a great diversity of adaptive responses within the same community, depending on individual as well as social heterogeneity. Putting aside the individual factors, which do not concern us here, it follows that the comparatively low level of social heterogeneity in the Mexican-American San Diego sample would lead us to expect comparatively little heterogeneity in adaptive responses among them.

Table 3.3 presents the rates of perceived discrimination among San Diego Mexican-American youth, divided according to language proficiency and use. We chose this dimension of internal variation because it came closest to yielding distinct cultural subgroups. Perhaps the most striking finding is the degree to which perceptions of discrimination and racial conflict are pronounced across all three groups. Even among the Spanish dominant, who are generally the most recently arrived from

TABLE 3.3   PERCEPTIONS OF DISCRIMINATION
BY LANGUAGE DOMINANCE AMONG THE
SAN DIEGO MEXICAN-AMERICAN SECOND-
GENERATION SAMPLE

	Spanish Dominant	Bilingual	English Dominant
There is racial discrimination in America: percent agree or strongly agree	88	83	90
has personally experienced discrimination	67	63	69
There is much conflict between races in America: percent agree or strongly agree	87	78	88

SOURCE: 1995 CILS San Diego Survey.

Mexico, 88 percent agreed that there is racial discrimination in America, and 67 percent report having personally experienced it. The rates of agreement on these two measures are similar for the other two groups, with a slight tendency for the more bilingual to have slightly lower perceptions and experiences of discrimination. All three groups also agree that there is considerable racial conflict in America with, again, rates of agreement increasing with assimilation. When the sample is divided by gender (omitted from Table 3.3), there is a very slight tendency for boys to perceive higher levels of racial conflict and discrimination.

Studies show that individual minority-group members "consistently rate discrimination directed at their group as a whole substantially higher than discrimination aimed at themselves, personally, as a member of that group" (Ruggiero and Taylor 1997: 375). Ruggiero and Taylor explain that "by minimizing the discrimination that confronts them, minority group members may be able to maintain [self-esteem as well as] the perception of control over personal outcomes in their lives" (375). This pattern is reflected in our data: Respondents were substantially more likely to acknowledge structural discrimination than to acknowledge personal discrimination. Yet two-thirds of our respondents were, in fact, willing to acknowledge personal discrimination, and further analysis shows that 54 percent of those who had reported no personal discrimination at T1 (1992) now reported they had such experiences in the follow-up survey. Here, our highly bilingual respondents appeared the least willing to acknowledge personal discrimination, although the majority did perceive it.

In spite of the hypotheses proposed by this research, our findings on perceived discrimination do not seem to capture and sustain any particular pattern. For example, other measures of perceived structural discrimination in the CILS data do not show the kind of consensus seen in the first measure of perceived structural discrimination. When presented with a statement claiming that nonwhites (i.e., minorities) enjoy equal opportunities to get ahead, only 46 percent (at T2) disagreed to some degree—a sizable percentage but not the majority. In fact, only 16 percent disagreed a lot with this statement (i.e., had strong perceptions of inequality). We suspect that much of the research on minority youth, which traditionally has been carried out among African Americans, with some studies including Chicanos and Puerto Ricans as well, has only limited applicability to understanding today's second-generation youth, particularly Asians, Mexicans, and others who live in intergenerational ethnic communities that sustain conflicting and contradictory norms and sentiments (Stanton-Salazar 1997).

Such contradictory sentiments emerged in a separate study carried out by the second author in a large urban high school in southern California.[2] On the one hand, strong evidence that Mexican-American students feel discriminated against did emerge. Two-thirds agreed that Latino students suffer prejudice and discrimination in schools at the hands of teachers and staff, and only 14 percent disagreed. On the other hand, the same sample generally agreed that Latino students did have an equal opportunity to achieve at school (compared with other ethnic/racial groups).

Ambivalent feelings and contradictory perceptions may be emblematic of Mexican-origin adolescents at this time, particularly in the current absence of any strong social justice movement in the Southwest that would concretize and validate young people's penetrations into the reality of racial discrimination in the United States. These contradictory perceptions may be interpreted in a way consonant with Ruggiero and Taylor's discussion (1997) of the research on perceived control and motivation. By maintaining contradictory perceptions regarding racial inequities in educational opportunity, these youth may be able to sustain the belief that although discrimination exists at the system level and although prejudice may be prevalent at their school (e.g., among teachers and counselors), they as individuals do have sufficient reason and opportunity to persist in their academic endeavors. To believe otherwise might very well undermine their motivation to stay in school. In the absence of a sociological discourse that would heighten academic motivation while acknowledging discrimination in the environment, these youth opt to downplay their personal vulnerability to discriminatory institutional forces.

This conundrum, we believe, is aggravated by the historical individualism that pervades every aspect of high schools' institutional culture (Stanton-Salazar 1997; McQuillan 1998; Fine 1991). Utilitarian individualism can operate to bring disorder to students' emerging insights into the social and racial order around them (see Fine 1991). The result is often ambivalence and forms of contradictory consciousness that require downplaying personal victimization to sustain some degree of academic motivation.

Support for this thesis emerged in the study by Stanton-Salazar (2001b), where most students similarly provided mixed, contradictory, or ambivalent perceptions and attitudes regarding racial discrimination and school achievement. Although students generally acknowledged the existence of societal racism and were usually able to cite examples in their or their family's lives where they encountered prejudice and discrimination, such incriminations were often tempered with accounts of how Mexicans often create their own problems. One young woman, Rosa, in her last year in high school, tells of having a job interview over the phone and then coming in and feeling that the manager looked surprised to see that see was Mexican. "I guess they heard me over the phone, and I guess I sounded kind of white. Once I got to the store, I saw there was only white girls working there. Well, they never called me back." Later, Rosa states that differential access to information about educational and occupational opportunities is something Mexicans in the U.S. must frequently contend with: "We don't get enough information about things." Yet her analysis ultimately reverts to a victim-blaming perspective: "We don't know what's going on, and we don't bother to find out. And a lot of us are too lazy. We're not trying hard enough. We're not all lazy, but we just don't try hard enough."

Clearly, perceptions of individual and institutional racism are bound up in complex ways with the experience of being the teenage child of immigrants in America today. While acknowledging discrimination, Mexican-American second-generation youth seem less willing to attribute all their problems to racism and seem to evince a strong ethic of self-reliance and rugged individualism, no matter how inappropriate it may be to the world in which they live. The scourge of ideological individualism is seen perhaps most clearly in the help-seeking and help-giving practices of urban schools. In his investigation of the social support networks of Mexican-origin high school youth, Stanton-Salazar (2001b) found that while teachers and counselors professed a commitment to do whatever possible to provide a sound education to their students, the school site was not governed by clearly articulated help-giving and help-seeking norms and values typically embodied in cooperative contexts. The result was that students turned inward to cope with the distresses rooted in precarious life circumstances (e.g., family economic circumstances, parental separation or divorce, anxiety over possible unplanned pregnancy) and plummeting academic performance. The communitarian ideal, also partly manifested in terms of students acting as skillful providers of support to other students (emotional as well as academic), was similarly not an intrinsic feature of the organizational culture in spite of the fact that the school was officially undergoing restructuring.

Educational Aspirations and Achievement

Aspirations

Educational aspirations and expectations, as well as the role of significant others in shaping these orientations, are understood as a principal link between socioeconomic background and eventual attainment in adulthood (Duncan, Featherman, and Duncan 1972; Wilson and Portes 1975). Since aspirations have been theoretically tied to the encouragement and moral support of parents and of other significant members of a young person's social network, they have also played an important role in accounting for those minority youth from low-SES communities who do experience academic success and educational mobility (Velez 1989). Kao and Tienda (1995), examining a large national sample of eighth graders, found that relative to the children of U.S.-born parents, the children of immigrants had higher educational aspirations. Most telling were the pronounced hopes of immigrant parents, expressing aspirations for their children that even exceeded those of the children themselves.

The Mexican-origin youth in our San Diego CILS sample reported uniformly high educational aspirations for themselves, as shown in Table 3.4; for example, 67 percent of the U.S. born aspired to complete college. Aspirations varied little by gender, though girls' were modestly higher; multivariate analysis yielded no clear pattern of determinants in

TABLE 3.4   EDUCATIONAL ASPIRATIONS
AMONG MEXICAN-AMERICAN YOUTH IN
SAN DIEGO IN 1995

	College (%)	Advanced Degree (%)	Total Higher Education (%)
Foreign born	31	26	57
U.S. born	44	23	67

SOURCE: 1995 CILS San Diego Survey.

this sample.[3] Students' high aspirations may have to do with widely shared perceptions that the market for good jobs is fiercely competitive and that a college degree is now a prerequisite merely to enter the competition (Carnoy and Levin 1985). These are perceptions believed to be widely shared across social classes and ethnic groups. Nonetheless, these aspirations are highly optimistic; in fact, when students were asked what level of schooling they realistically expected, rates were markedly lower, though still unrealistic, given that only 10 to 20 percent of this sample will probably finish college. Occupational aspirations were equally unrealistic (60 percent hoped to have professional or managerial jobs). The disjunction between educational aspirations and expectations suggests that Mexican-origin youth may be aware of the depressed probabilities of their actually achieving their aspirations. Perceptions of discrimination, and of the lack of economic means, may have something to do with these disjunctions. In the San Diego study, other ethnic groups reported even higher aspirations.

Supporting the findings reported by Kao and Tienda (1995), the CILS data show Mexican immigrant parents either reporting higher educational expectations than their children or at least sharing the same expectations. Significantly more than two-thirds of mothers, or 71 percent, expected that their child would attend two or more years of college. Of this college-minded parent group, 68 percent expected college completion. About one in five parents surveyed expected their child to receive postgraduate training. Only 12 percent of parents surveyed reported expecting their child (the one surveyed) to receive some sort of vocational training.

The importance that Mexican immigrant parents place on higher education is also reflected in the survey and qualitative research by the second author (Stanton-Salazar 2001b). He found that adolescents had a strong sense of the unequivocal value their parents placed on education, but it was also clear that immigrant parents typically had only vague ideas about the many steps entailed in preparing for and completing a college education. One female adolescent, in the U.S. since infancy, expresses sentiments reflective of so many other adolescent children of immigrants:

> I think that most parents of Mexican origin, they push you along, they tell you for the millionth time that you've gotta work hard so that you can do something they never did; or, you know, just climb the social ladder like they never did and never will.

Parents repeatedly told tales of hardship and sacrifice, including their own lack of educational opportunities and their determination that their children would succeed. They were relentless in their exhortations. One mother expressed her sentiments in the following way:

> I am someone who washes toilets, who cleans houses, who takes the most strenuous and difficult jobs, all because I didn't study. . . . I wanted to be successful, hoping that my children would be something . . . not for my own benefit, but for their benefit so that they wouldn't have to kill themselves like me. . . . I don't want that to happen to them, that's why I want them to study.

Such appeals and stories of hardships are only part of the strategy used by Mexican parents to motivate their children. In spite of their lack of knowledge about the intricacies of the educational system, the data from both the San Diego CILS survey and Stanton-Salazar's fieldwork show that most parents do speak with their children about schoolwork and the importance of studying. From the CILS data, we see that 77 percent of mothers reported speaking to their child regularly about school. Only a few parents admitted to rarely speaking to their child concerning academic and school matters (6 percent). Similarly, about 93 percent reported talking to their child about their educational future, at least occasionally.

Parents also worried about the negative influences on their children at school. From the CILS survey we see that Mexican parents appear a bit more likely to worry about such influences, relative to the average reported by parents from the Caribbean and from Latin America (76.2 percent versus 67.6 percent). Only Asian parents reported a higher average (93.9 percent "worried"—Vietnamese, Lao/Hmong/Cambodian, and Chinese combined).

Although Mexican parents do stress the importance of education, immigrant family processes often militate in the opposite direction.

Stanton-Salazar (2001b), for example, found that many immigrant parents gradually shift their attention to younger children while expecting their adolescent to share in family-related responsibilities (childcare, housework, brokering for parents). Given that adolescent children know about the inner machinery of the school system in ways that their parents never will, they are also generally expected to manage, and take responsibility for, their own school and academic affairs. Yet at critical moments, the frustrations of going at it alone becomes quite distressful for many adolescents. They wish their immigrant parents could better understand how challenging school can be. As one young woman put it: "God, they don't really see or understand how hard it is to do all the work to get good grades. They react based on what little they see, and not on what the kid has really accomplished. It pisses me off!"

The children of immigrants often speak of the split between the world of school and their world at home (see also Phelan, Davidson, and Yu 1998). Many learn to accept this split, embracing a sense of independence that leaves little room for sharing their academic world with her parents. The young woman quoted previously conveys this split in the following way:

> They try to get involved, but I tell them, I consider it to be part of my personal life. Since I was young, they really haven't had much involvement with my school work. So in a sense I have grown accustomed to it and I don't get them involved.

In sum, educational success is valued by Mexican-origin children and their immigrant parents, but the scarcity of educational resources that parents bring to the table means that in many cases they are not able to translate those values into effective institutional support for their children, especially as they confront the difficult years of adolescence. Though we lack the data to support it, we are certain that Mexican immigrant parents stress education much more than immigrants from Poland or Italy 80 years ago, if only because higher education was much less pervasive in those days. The tragedy is that exhortation alone will not move today's Mexican-American second generation into the middle class.

Achievement

Examining the dynamics of class and race operating within immigrant families helps us understand low achievement among the Mexican-American second generation. It is, alas, the pattern established by earlier generations of Mexican Americans in the United States, including the third generation that was coming of age when the research was being done for *The Mexican American People* (Grebler, Moore, and Guzmán 1970). The evidence is compelling that the previous second and third generations were not faring well in school or the workplace, even before the return of large-scale immigration. Grebler and his associates, utilizing 1960 census data and the surveys from Los Angeles and San Antonio that they had carried out in 1965, concluded that second-generation Mexican Americans were doing better occupationally than their parents but not nearly so well as European Americans of the same generation. Other studies that included but did not focus on Latinos, including Blau and Duncan's pathbreaking *The American Occupational Structure* (1967), reached much the same conclusions. So did subsequent studies focused on Latinos, such as Bean and Tienda's analysis (1986) of the 1980 census and Ortiz's analysis (1996) of the 1990 census. All these studies document disparities in education, in occupational status net of education, and in income attainment net of occupation and education. The continuing effect of educational disadvantage is by far the greatest factor explaining low occupational and income attainment among Mexican Americans. What is even more striking is the small difference between second- and third-generation Latino achievements in education and subsequent attainments. Whereas historically for European ethnic groups the step up from second to third generation was as significant as the step up from first to second, for Mexican Americans the change was insignificant.

Another useful study focusing on immigrant children but including explicit comparisons with the native born comes from the Rand Corporation (Vernez and Abrahamse 1996). In that study, based on data from 1980–1986, the authors conclude that across all major ethnic groups there is a substantial positive effect on both aspirations and actual achievement of being an immigrant or child of an immigrant. The immigrant/native aspiration gap is particularly marked among Latinos. However, as a group, immigrant Latino children were found to have the least preparation and the lowest college attendance rates. They note that much but not all of the difference between Latino and other immigrant children is statistically explained by the poverty and poor educational backgrounds of the parents, such that the positive immigrant effect is overwhelmed by these factors among Latino children.

These studies provide a valuable context for understanding the school performance of Mexican-American second-generation youth in San Diego. We begin with an overview of the indicators of school success among Mexican-American second-generation youth in San Diego in comparison with other groups in the San Diego CILS study. Table 3.5 contains the grade point average (GPA) and test score data collected in both the 1992 and 1995 surveys. Most Asian subgroups scored nearly a full grade point above Mexican-American students; Mexican-American test scores on the increasingly familiar Stanford Nine tests of reading and math in San Diego were about half that of other second-generation students.[4] Of the Asian subgroups, only the Hmong have scores comparable to Mexican Americans; however, even their GPAs are substantially better. Controlling for parental educational and occupational differences only slightly reduces the gap between Mexican American and other groups (Portes and MacLeod 1996).

Perhaps most distressing is the small proportion of Mexican Americans labeled as gifted. This designation is based on test scores and a number of other objective and subjective criteria. Since the foreign-born students generally had markedly lower reading scores, few ended up labeled as gifted; for example, only 1 percent of Cambodians made it. In contrast, 35 percent of Chinese-American children were on the school's gifted list. One can argue that being labeled gifted is an inherently unfair, subjective, and even racist process, but that is beside the point: In the end, such judgments by teachers are what determine the fate of students in school.

Is this pattern of substantially lower Mexican-American achievement in contrast to other second-generation groups in San Diego reflective of a general pattern? Table 3.6 suggests that it is, at least for California. This table reports two crucial measures of school achievement: Scholastic Aptitude Test (SAT) scores and University of California (UC) eligibility rates. SAT examinations are typically taken by a relatively high-achieving subset of students, within or across ethnic groups. Nevertheless, ethnic differences in average SAT scores are regularly found. In the latest round in California, Latino and black test takers lagged behind whites and Asians by 144 to 211 points, roughly enough to be the difference between the 30th and 60th percentile.[5] SAT scores are, of course, highly associated with social class and the quality of education one has been afforded, but even if ethnic differences could be explained

TABLE 3.5   SELECTED INDICATORS OF
STUDENT ACHIEVEMENT BY ETHNICITY IN THE
SAN DIEGO SAMPLE

	Mexican	Vietnamese	Filipino	Chinese	Hmong
GPA T1	2.24	3.03	2.93	3.44	2.95
GPA T2	2.25	3.02	2.86	3.64	2.65
Reading[1]	26	38	52	68	16
Math[1]	31	59	60	63	31
Percent gifted	6	16	22	35	0

SOURCE: 1992 and 1995 CILS San Diego Surveys.
[1]National percentiles in Stanford Achievement Test.

TABLE 3.6   INDICATORS OF ACHIEVEMENT
AMONG SCHOOL CHILDREN IN CALIFORNIA,
BY ETHNICITY

	State Avg.	Latino	White	Asian	Black
SAT Scores for California 1996					
Verbal	497	442	532	488	433
Math	516	452	540	550	428
TOTAL	1,013	894	1,072	1,038	861
UC Eligibility 1996					
UC eligible	21	8	27	44	7
Percent of UC eligible	100	14	56	28	2

SOURCE: California Post-Secondary Education Commission 1997; Smith 1998.

away by background factors (and the evidence is that they cannot be entirely), the social consequences of these differences will not disappear.

The bottom section of Table 3.6 gives UC eligibility rates by ethnicity as well as the ethnic composition of those who are potentially eligible for UC. Only about half will actually attend UC, but most of the rest will complete other four-year colleges; hence, this is a good measure of the state's future elite. By this measure, 44 percent of Asian graduates are headed for the state's elite, compared with 8 percent of Latino graduates. Since over 90 percent of recent Asian high school graduates and 80 percent of Latinos are the children of immigrants, these data suggest that inequality in the second generation will be massive, mirroring the gap between their parents. The bottom line in Table 3.6 represents the composition of the state's academic elite (top 20 percent): Half are white, 28 percent are Asian, 14 percent are Latino, and only 2 percent are black. We believe that these figures are a rough but accurate guide to the ethnic composition of the top quarter of the state's occupational structure in the next 25 years.[6]

What about the determinants of GPA within the Mexican-American sample? As shown in Table 3.5, senior GPA for Mexican-American students did not differ significantly by country of birth. The dropout rate among the Mexican-American sample from T1 to T2 is somewhat higher than for other groups, and, of course, it is the poor achievers who are more likely to drop out, though the average GPA for Mexican Americans remained the same. As is generally the case, there is an association with gender, with girls doing somewhat better than boys. In Table 3.7 we report both the zero-order correlations and the coefficients resulting from a multivariate analysis, controlling for an array of logically relevant background, household, and individual factors. As is to be expected in a data set with generally low levels of correlation, there are mostly minor differences between zero-order and partial coefficients. When other factors are controlled, the relation between GPA and self-esteem actually strengthens a bit, while the relation between GPA and doing homework is attenuated, though it is still strong. Parents' education and SES play no role, but reports that friends or teachers help with homework are very strongly associated with GPA and are the only factors significant at the .001 level.

What to make of all this? First of all, most levels of association reported here are modest and marginally significant if at all, and the amount of variance explained, measured by R^2, is a modest .06 to .20, depending on the number of variables in the equation. Whatever factors explain GPA, they are not well captured by this study. It is hardly startling that GPA is strongly correlated with self-esteem and the amount of homework that students do. The strong association with getting help with homework (which is in part a measure of actually doing homework) suggests that the implied support networks are essential for academic success. That is, those few Mexican-American students who are lucky enough to have helping networks, whether par-

TABLE 3.7   MULTIVARIATE ANALYSIS OF THE
CORRELATES OF GPA AMONG MEXICAN-
AMERICAN STUDENTS IN SAN DIEGO, 1995

With GPA:	Zero-Order Correlation	Partial Coefficient	$p > t$
Being female	.17	.18	.04
Mother's education	−.08	−.02	.04
Father's occupation	.00	.00	.33
Two-parent household	.08	.12	.18
Amount of homework	.27	.15	.00
Family cohesion	.13	.06	.18
Self-esteem	.17	.27	.01
Parents help with homework[1]		.27	.00
Teacher helps with homework[1]		.35	.00
Friend helps with homework[1]		.37	.00

[1]Each "helps with homework" variable is entered as a dummy variable, with "no one" the omitted reference category.

ents, friends, or teachers, are the ones who are making it. Having parents sufficiently well educated to be able to help with homework is one but apparently not the only path to success.

Conclusion

As we suggested at the beginning of this chapter, perhaps the greatest misfortune of the Mexican-American new second generation is in its timing: Large-scale labor immigration from Mexico began again after a hiatus of 35 years just as the immigration of generally well-educated middle- and upper-middle-class Asians began for the first time. The only other large-scale migration from Latin America (until Central Americans began to come in large numbers in the mid-1980s) was that of the Cuban middle and upper classes fleeing Castro's communism. Cubans, like the Vietnamese after them, were able to parlay their class resources and refugee status into substantial success, built in large part on an enclave economy. Most Asian groups did not have the advantages of being refugees from communism, but they did not need them; their individual and community resources have facilitated their integration into the U.S. economy and set the stage for a very advantageous context of assimilation for their children. Mexican and most Central

American immigrants and their children share few of these advantages, and many come with the added burden of irregular legal status. Most also must struggle with the well-established negative stereotypes based on a long history of white-Mexican relations and on the experience and prior treatment of the Mexican Americans already present in the United States.

Mexican and Central American immigrants play a well-defined if controversial role in the American economy. They do the dirty work in virtually all industries in California and the Southwest, and they are increasingly filling these roles throughout the country. Their children, the second generation, may well outnumber immigrant Latinos in the workforce within a decade or two. But it is not at all clear what economic role they will play. Certainly they will be dissatisfied with and will reject the poorly paid dirty work done by their fathers and mothers. On the evidence from San Diego and California generally, they will lose out to whites and Asians in the competition for the good jobs to which they and their parents aspire. Inevitably, they will occupy some middle status between the largely white and Asian middle and upper classes and the dirty work that fresh waves of poor immigrants will eagerly embrace. This is not a pretty picture; indeed, if decent jobs in the middle are not there, it could turn out to be positively ugly. But in the absence of some miraculous change in the social dynamics associated with growing up Mexican in the United States, it seems starkly inevitable.

Notes

1. The 1960 figures come from U.S. Bureau of the Census (1963: 2–20); current estimates were derived from the 1996–1998 Current Population Survey's public use samples. Other Latin Americans came to the United States before 1960, but in much smaller numbers and in nothing like the concentrated immigration from Mexico between 1900 and 1930. In the nineteenth and early twentieth centuries, substantial numbers of Chinese and then Japanese workers arrived in California, but both these streams of immigration were cut off abruptly as a result of racist legislation. Japanese-American history has in fact been written in terms of first, second, and third generations, but there was no significant resurgence of Japanese immigration after 1965. The temporal origins of the pre-1965 Chinese-American population are spread out over 100 years, from the California Gold Rush to the fall of Nationalist China, and their history is not easily written in neat generational terms. Among today's significant immigrant groups, only Filipinos might be considered to have had a discernible second generation in the past, and their case is complicated by the highly unbal-

anced sex ratios (the absence of Filipina women) among earlier immigrant workers. All of these generalizations are meant to apply to the continental United States; the ethnic history of Hawaii is, of course, radically different.

2. Stanton-Salazar 2001. All quotations on pages 75–80 are from interviews conducted by the author for this project in the late 1990s.

3. Much more research is needed to clarify the complex influence of gender on aspirations and expectations. There is some evidence that boys receive greater pressure or encouragement to pursue further education in order to secure job security and to eventually support a family (Ramos and Sanchez 1995). Other studies (e.g., Hout and Morgan 1975), however, maintain that minority adolescent girls are less affected by male peer subcultures, where norms often exist against doing well in the classroom (see also Ogbu 1991). According to this position, ethnic/racial minority girls are more willing to adopt the student role necessary for conventional classroom learning. Certainly, gender roles have changed considerably in the last 20 years, as has the economy, where women today are well positioned across the occupational structure and much better represented in the professions (Baca Zinn and Eitzen 1999). Still, gender forces may still be operative, particularly in the choice of career. One study of college Mexican-origin freshmen (Arbona and Novy 1991) showed that Mexican-origin women were more likely to select service occupations, while Mexican-origin men were more likely to expect to enter higher-prestige occupations, including the fields of research and business.

4. These are nationally normed tests. A group score of 38 means that the average score for that group is at the 38th percentile nationally. These tests were administered to the San Diego samples only in 1992. As a rule, test scores decline for cohorts of poor youth over time. In the past two years, California schools have administered statewide the same Stanford Nine test used in the first CILS survey in 1992. Statewide results will parallel the sharp ethnic differences found in San Diego.

5. These data come from the author's analysis of data that appeared in Smith 1998.

6. Of course, no perfect correlation exists between schooling and occupation, but the relation is strong: In the California workforce, 70 percent of college graduates have upper-white-collar jobs, while 68 percent of those without a high school education are laborers, factory workers, or lower service workers. These correlations hold across ethnic lines (from analysis of the 1996 Current Population Survey's public use sample).

References

Alba, Richard, and Victor Nee. 1997. Rethinking assimilation theory for a new era of immigration. *International Migration Review* 31 (4), pp. 826–874.

Arbona, C., and D. Novy. 1991. Career aspirations and expectations of black, Mexican American and white students. *Career Development Quarterly* 39 (3), pp. 231–239.

Baca Zinn, Maxine, and D. Stanley Eitzen. 1999. *Diversity in families.* 5th ed. New York: Longman.

Bean, Frank, and Marta Tienda. 1986. *The Hispanic-origin population of the United States.* New York: Russell Sage Foundation.

Blau, Peter, and Otis Dudley Duncan. 1967. *The American occupational structure.* New York: John Wiley & Sons.

Buriel, Raymond. 1984. "Integration within traditional Mexican American culture and sociocultural adjustment." In *Chicano psychology,* edited by J. L. Martínez and R. Mendoza. New York: Academic Press.

California Post-Secondary Education Commission. 1997. *Eligibility of California's 1996 high school graduates for admission to the state's public universities.* Sacramento: December 1997.

Carnoy, Martin, and Henry M. Levin. 1985. *Schooling and work in the democratic state.* Stanford, Calif.: Stanford University Press.

Donato, Rubén, Martha Menchaca, and Richard R. Valencia. 1991. "Segregation, desegregation and the integration of Chicano students: Problems and prospects." In *Chicano school failure and success: Research and policy agendas for the 1990s,* edited by Richard R. Valencia. New York: Falmer Press.

Duncan, Otis Dudley, David Featherman, and Beverly Duncan. 1972. *Socioeconomic background and achievement.* New York: Seminar Press.

Fine, Michelle. 1991. *Framing drop-outs: Notes on the politics of an urban public high school.* Albany: State University of New York.

Fordham, S., and John U. Ogbu. 1986. Black students' school success: Coping with the burden of "acting white." *The Urban Review* 18 (3), pp. 176–206.

Gibson, Margaret A., and John U. Ogbu. 1991. *Minority status & schooling: A comparative study of immigrant and involuntary minorities.* New York: Garland Press.

Gordon, Milton. 1964. *Assimilation in American life.* New York: Oxford University Press.

Grebler, Leo, Joan Moore, and Ralph Guzman. 1970. *The Mexican-American people.* New York: The Free Press.

Gutierrez, David G. 1995. *Walls and mirrors: Mexican Americans, Mexican immigrants and the politics of ethnicity.* Berkeley: University of California Press.

Hayes-Bautista, David, Werner O. Schink, and Jorge Chapa. 1988. *The burden of support: Young Latinos in an aging society.* Stanford, Calif.: Stanford University Press.

Hout, Michael, and William R. Morgan. 1975. Race and sex variations in the cause of the expected attainment of high school seniors. *American Journal of Sociology* 81 (2), pp. 365–394.

Kao, G., and M. Tienda. 1995. Optimism and achievement: The educational performance of immigrant youth. *Social Science Quarterly,* 76 (1), no. 1–19.

López, David. 1996. "Language: Diversity and assimilation." In *Ethnic Los Angeles,* edited by Roger Waldinger and Mehdi Bozorgmehr. New York: Russell Sage Foundation.

McQuillan, Patrick J. 1998. *Educational opportunity in an urban American high school: A cultural analysis.* Albany: State University of New York.

Ogbu, John U. 1991. "Low school performance as an adaptation: The case of blacks in Stockton, California." In *Minority status and schooling: A comparative study of immigrant and involuntary minorities,* edited by Margaret A. Gibson and John U. Ogbu. New York: Garland Press.

Ortiz, Vilma. 1996. "The Mexican-origin population: Permanent working class or emerging middle class?" In *Ethnic Los Angeles,* edited by Roger Waldinger and Mehdi Bozorgmehr. New York: Russell Sage Foundation.

Phelan, Patricia, Ann Locke Davidson, and Hanh Cao Yu. 1998. *Adolescents' worlds: Negotiating family, peers and school.* New York: Teachers College Press.

Portes, Alejandro, and Robert L. Bach. 1985. *Latin journey: Cuban and Mexican immigrants in the United States.* Berkeley: University of California Press.

Portes, Alejandro, and Lingxin Hao. 1998. E pluribus unum: Bilingualism and loss of language in the second generation. *Sociology of Education* 71 (October), pp. 269–294.

Portes, Alejandro, and Dag MacLeod. 1996. What shall I call myself? Hispanic identity formation in the second generation. *Ethnic and Racial Studies,* 19 (3), pp. 523–547.

Portes, Alejandro, and Rubén G. Rumbaut. 2001. *Legacies: The story of the new second generation.* Berkeley and New York: University of California Press and Russell Sage Foundation.

Portes, Alejandro, and Min Zhou. 1993. The new second generation: Segmented assimilation and its variants. *The Annals of the American Academy of Political and Social Science* 530 (November), pp. 74–96.

Ramos, L., and A. R. Sánchez. 1995. Mexican-American high school students: Educational aspirations. *Journal of Multicultural Counseling and Development* 23 (4), pp. 212–221.

Ruggiero, K. M., and D. M. Taylor. 1997. Why minority group members perceive or do not perceive the discrimination that confronts them: The role of self-esteem and perceived control. *Journal of Personality and Social Psychology* 72 (2), pp. 373–389.

Rumbaut, Rubén G. 1996. "The crucible within: Ethnic identity, self-esteem, and segmented assimilation among children of immigrants." In *The new second generation,* edited by Alejandro Portes. New York: Russell Sage Foundation.

Rumbaut, Rubén G. 1997. Passages to adulthood: The adaptation of children of immigrants in southern California. Report to the Russell Sage Foundation Board of Trustees.

Sánchez, Juan and David Fernández. 1993. Acculturative stress among Hispanics: A bidimensional model of ethnic identification. *Journal of Applied Social Psychology* 23 (8), pp. 654–668.

Smith, Doug. 1998. SAT scores rise slightly for L.A. high schools. Los Angeles Times, September 2, p. B3.

Stanton-Salazar, Ricardo D. 1997. A social capital framework for understanding the socialization of racial minority children and youth. *Harvard Educational Review* 67 (1), pp. 1–40.

Stanton-Salazar, Ricardo D. 2001a."The development of coping strategies among urban Latino youth: A focus on network orientation and help-seeking behavior." In *Latino adolescents: A critical approach to diversity,* edited by Martha Montero-Sieburth and Francisco A. Villaruel. New York: Garland Press.

Stanton-Salazar, Ricardo D. 2001b. *Manufacturing hope & despair: The school and kin support networks of U.S.-Mexican youth.* New York: Teachers College Press.

Suárez-Orozco, Marcelo. 1991. "Immigrant adaptation to schooling: A Hispanic case." In *Minority status and schooling: A comparative study of immigrant and involuntary minorities,* edited by Margaret A. Gibson and John U. Ogbu. New York: Garland Press.

United Way of San Diego. 1991. *Herencia y futuro: Latino future.* San Diego: December.

U.S. Bureau of the Census. 1963. Persons of Spanish surname. *Census of population: 1960. Subject reports.* PC(2)-1B. Washington, D.C.: U.S. Government Printing Office.

Valencia, Richard R., ed. 1991. *Chicano school failure and success: Research and policy agendas for the 1990s.* New York: Falmer Press.

Velez, W. 1989. High school attribution among Hispanic and non-Hispanic white youths. *Sociology of Education* 62 (2), pp. 119–133.

Vernez, Georges, and Alan Abrahamse. 1996. *How immigrants fare in the U.S. education.* Santa Monica, California: Rand Corporation.

Wilson, Kenneth L., and Alejandro Portes. 1975. The educational attainment process: Results from a national sample. *American Journal of Sociology* 81 (2), pp. 343–362.

Chapter 4

GROWING UP IN CUBAN MIAMI
Immigration, the Enclave, and New Generations

Lisandro Pérez

Children of Cuban origin represent the largest single ethnonational group in the Children of Immigrants Longitudinal Study (CILS). A total of 1,242 of the CILS respondents in 1992 (T1) had at least one parent born in Cuba. The Cuban plurality in CILS was an unavoidable consequence of selecting southern Florida as one of the two sites for the study. The nearly three-quarters of a million persons of Cuban birth or descent who live in greater Miami are indisputably the largest single ethnic group in the area and account for the largest concentration of Cubans in the United States. Three of every five Cuban Americans live there.

The Cuban-born population of the United States numbers 879,000, representing one of the most sizable nationality groups among America's immigrants. Those who consider themselves of Cuban origin or descent (including those born in Cuba) are estimated at more than 1.2 million (U.S. Bureau of the Census 1996–1997). There is a well-founded perception that Cubans represent a fairly exceptional case among U.S. immigrants arriving in the second half of this century. This is not to deny that Cubans have a number of commonalities with other immigrant groups. But it is in the Cubans' unique combination of characteristics that rests the case for their exceptionality.

Those unique sets of characteristics can analytically be placed under two broad headings: (1) the migration process from Cuba and (2) the process of incorporation into U.S. society.

Migration from Cuba: The Cold War Faucet

Although there is a long history of Cuban migration to the United States, the bulk of the country's current Cuban population has its origins in the revolutionary process initiated in 1959. At the core of that process was Cuba's radical transformation into a country with a centrally planned economy with no private industry and a government organized along Marxist-Leninist principles, with close ties and dependence upon the Soviet Union. Such a transformation resulted in conflict that was most intense in the early 1960s but that has lasted to this day. It is a conflict that originated over competing economic, political, and ideological systems and inextricably combined an internal class struggle with an international cold war confrontation. In that conflict, both the U.S. government and various sectors of Cuban society, especially the elites, virtually all of which went into exile, have shared a strong interest in overthrowing the Cuban government and have cooperated in a number of ways toward that end.[1]

The most visible and recurring manifestation of that conflict has been emigration. The waves of migration from the island since 1960 have all taken place within that enduring climate of hostility and international confrontation. Although those waves have differed a great deal from each other in their specific conditions and characteristics, they have all been the result of an international conflict that has utilized migration as a political tool. Consequently, the analogy usually employed to depict migration streams, that of a constant ebb and flow, is of little use to describe the Cuban case. Rather, Cuban migration has been more akin to the flow from a water faucet: abruptly turned off and on at the will of those in power in Havana and Washington in response to political considerations. A climate of hostility and the absence of normal relations between the two countries, combined with the geographic fact that Cuba is an island, have made migration difficult and generally unavailable except when the two governments, unilaterally or bilaterally, decide to provide the means for migration to occur. The timing, length, intensity, and characteristics of each wave are largely consequences of the conditions under which the migration from Cuba to the United States is allowed to take place.

There have been four major migration waves to the United States from Cuba since the rise of the present Cuban government in 1959.[2] Three of them are clearly visible in Figure 4.1, which shows the number of Cubans arriving in the United States each year from 1959 to 1995 (the last year that comparable data are available from the Immigration and Naturalization Service [INS]).[3]

The first wave spanned the years from 1959 to October 1962 and amounted to about 200,000 persons. The U.S. government facilitated their entry by granting them refugee status, allowing them in the country without the restrictions imposed on most other nationality groups.[4] A program was established to assist in the resettlement and economic adjustment of the arrivals. In this initial wave, the displaced elite were disproportionately represented among the migrants. Many of those alienated from the revolutionary process were especially fearful of the implications of the political changes for their children. Consequently, families of upper socioeconomic status with children under 18 years of age are overrepresented in this wave.[5]

The second wave started in the Fall of 1965 when the Cuban government opened a port and allowed persons from the United States to go to Cuba to pick up relatives who wanted to leave the country. Some 5,000 persons left from the port of Camarioca before the United States and Cuba halted the boatlift and agreed to an orderly airlift, also called the "freedom flights," which started in December 1965 and lasted until 1973. The twice-daily flights brought 260,500 persons, making it the largest of all the waves, although it was much less intense than the others, taking place over eight years. The airlift allowed the Cuban government to pick and choose from among a large pool of applicants for a departure permit. Males of military age were excluded, and the government expedited the applications of the elderly.

The third wave took place in 1980, when the pressures for emigration once again caused the Cuban government to open a port for unrestricted emigration. The port was Mariel, giving the name to the boatlift that lasted for six months and that brought, in a manner uncontrolled by the United States, more than 125,000 Cubans into the country. It was not as large as the previous waves, but it took place in less than a year.

The Mariel exodus was a disorganized migration on vessels that went to Cuba from Florida to pick up relatives of persons already re-

Figure 4.1.   Cubans Arriving in the United States, 1959–1995

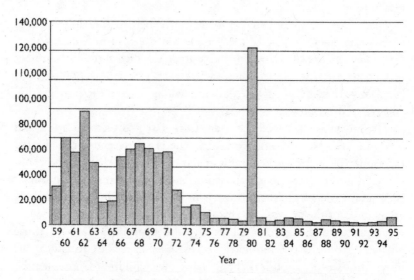

SOURCE: *Statistical Yearbook of the Immigration and Naturalization Service*, passim.
NOTES: Actual new arrivals per year. The figure for 1959 represents only the arrivals from January 1 to June 30. From 1960 to 1976, the fiscal year ends on June 30. Starting in 1977, the fiscal year ends on September 30. Figures have been adjusted accordingly.

siding in the United States. More than relatives boarded the boats, however, and the result was a wave that is perhaps the closest to being representative of the Cuban population. It included, for the first time, sizable representation from Cuba's lower socioeconomic sectors and its nonwhite population.

Throughout the rest of the 1980s and the early 1990s, there was a lull in migration from Cuba. Only about 2,000 persons were being admitted by the United States each year. In August 1994, responding to a rise in unauthorized departures, the Cuban government announced it would not detain anyone trying to leave Cuba in a raft or other vessel. As a result, nearly 37,000 Cubans were rescued by the U.S. Coast Guard in a one-month period. Despite having occurred in 1994, this fourth wave does not appear in Figure 4.1. The bulk of the arrivals were detained for more than a year in camps at the U.S. naval base in Guantánamo and were not admitted into the United States until 1996. As a result of the so-called 1994 rafter crisis, the United States agreed to admit at least 20,000 Cubans a year through the normal visa process.

Incorporation into U.S. Society:
The Golden Exile and the Golden Enclave

Recognizing that the initial wave from revolutionary Cuba drew disproportionately from the elite sectors of Cuban society, the early literature on Cubans in the United States focused a great deal on the issue of economic adjustment, analyzing the exceptional manner in which Cubans were able to achieve a rapid process of incorporation, exhibiting relatively high levels of occupational achievement. The explanation for this Cuban success story almost invariably rested on human capital factors: Those alienated from the revolutionary process during the early 1960s possessed a complex of skills, aspirations, attitudes, and experiences that gave them a relative advantage over most other U.S. immigrant groups in the process of economic adjustment.[6] Portes (1969) argued that the refugees' educational and occupational characteristics, combined with a middle-class ethic that was not too dissimilar to that of the dominant sectors of the host society, made possible what he called the "Golden Exile" of U.S. Cubans.

By the late 1970s, however, it became evident that the trends in Cuban immigration had started shifting away from the Golden Exile model. The representation of persons drawn from somewhat lower socioeconomic sectors of Cuban society grew among U.S. Cubans (Amaro and Portes 1972; Portes, Clark, and Bach 1977). The Mariel boatlift, as noted earlier, accentuated that trend (Díaz-Briquets and Pérez 1981).

Despite the decline in the human capital factors that had led to the Golden Exile, Cubans continued to maintain an economic edge over other immigrant groups. During the mid-1980s, the search was on for alternative explanations of the Cuban success story that did not rest exclusively on the selectivity of the migration. Pedraza-Bailey (1985) argued for the role played by the federal assistance programs intended to encourage and facilitate Cuban immigration that remained in effect until the mid-1970s. Pérez (1986b) suggested that at the household level, a contributing factor was the family organization of U.S. Cubans, which favored upward mobility through a large number of workers per family, high rates of female labor force participation, low fertility, and a high incidence of the economically functional three-generation family.

Another explanation for the Cubans' continued economic success gathered substantial support and has since become a principal conceptual framework for the analysis of the structural incorporation of not just Cubans but other immigrant groups as well. First advanced by

Portes and Bach (1985), it is referred to as the *enclave approach*. Viewing Cuban Miami as the foremost U.S. example of a true ethnic enclave, Portes and Bach defined such an enclave as "a distinctive economic formation, characterized by the spatial concentration of immigrants who organize a variety of enterprises to serve their own ethnic market and the general population" (203). The basis of the enclave is a broad range of highly differentiated entrepreneurial activity. Cuban Miami's substantial entrepreneurial base was established largely by those Cuban immigrants arriving during the first wave, in the early 1960s, who possessed the complex of skills and attitudes that eventually made possible their entry into various means of self-employment (Portes 1987; Portes and Stepick 1993).

The wide range of sales and services, including professional services, available within the community makes possible its institutional completeness, which tends to insulate the immigrant from the usual processes of the segmented labor market (Pérez 1992). In Miami, recent Cuban immigrants may enter the U.S. labor market through the large number of firms that are owned and operated by members of their own group who arrived earlier. While compensation may not be higher in the enclave, ethnic bonds provide for informal networks of support that facilitate the learning of new skills and the overall process of economic adjustment, blurring the different effects of the primary and secondary labor markets. It is argued that these positive implications of the enclave for economic adjustment have sustained a relatively successful incorporation in the United States beyond the initial advantage provided by the socioeconomic selectivity of the earlier waves.

Clearly, then, Cubans in the United States combine a set of unique characteristics among America's immigrant groups: first, a migration process embedded in a perennial international confrontation and an internal class conflict, with distinct and contrasting waves of migration to the United States; and second, a successful process of incorporation into the United States, initially abetted by a selective process of migration and subsequently reinforced by the creation of a strong ethnic enclave.

New Generations in Cuban Miami: Conceptual Considerations

The unique combination of forces that shaped the migration and incorporation processes of Cuban Americans has special implications for the analysis of the CILS data on the new generations growing up in Cuban Miami. We know quite a bit about how those processes have affected the adaptation of their parents to a new society, but what about their children?

The migration process, divided into distinct waves by the previously mentioned cold war faucet, requires that the analysis of the CILS data take a special look at the internal differences within the sample in terms of the parents' arrival date. Although all of the Cuban children in the sample, by definition, have in common *where* their parents were born, they vary according to *when* their parents arrived in this country. Given the contrasting sociodemographic and economic characteristics of the various waves, there are distinct "vintages" of Cubans according to date of arrival. The expectation is that the results of the outcome variables among the children will be affected by an intergenerational persistence of the socioeconomic differences between the waves of arrival of the parents' generation.

Since the purpose here, as in the other chapters in this book, is to discern the implications of growing up in specific ethnonational contexts, it is important to recognize that at least with the Cuban case, it is even more difficult than with other groups to generalize about the context in which these children grew up. Or, to put it in simpler terms, in the United States there are Cubans and there are Cubans. Furthermore, the waves vary sharply according to the specific conditions under which the faucet was opened and shut, and not, as in many other immigrant groups, as a simple function of length of residence in the United States. The analysis in this chapter, therefore, pays careful attention to differentiating the results by wave of arrival of the parents.

In terms of the process of incorporation, one of the most salient issues centers around the implications of the enclave for the second generation. As noted earlier, the dynamics of the enclave make it golden for the immigrants, facilitating their incorporation into the U.S. labor market through ethnic networks and in a familiar language and culture. But those are first-generation dynamics. What does the enclave mean for the adjustment of the children of immigrants?

The CILS data on Cubans provides one of the first opportunities to examine that question. In the first place, the Cuban community in Miami represents the truest example of an ethnic enclave. Indeed, it was in the study of Cuban Miami that the entire construct was first developed. In addition, the Cubans make up one of the oldest groups in CILS (in terms of their history in the United States) as well as the largest, providing some rich analytical opportunities within a single ethnonational category.

What does the existing body of knowledge lead us to expect regarding the enclave and the second generation as we approach the CILS data? In *Latin Journey,* Portes and Bach (1985) had data only on the immigrant generation. However, noting the historical experience of the Japanese and the Jews, two groups that before World War II had achieved economic prominence through land or business ownership and by effectively using ethnic networks, they observed that "progress made by the immigrants was then consolidated into educational and occupational mobility, within and outside the ethnic enclave, by later generations" (346).

The expectation that the Golden Enclave could be a Golden Springboard for the second generation was articulated by Portes (1995) in his analysis of the process of segmented assimilation, using data from the first (1992) wave of CILS interviews. He focused on the role of community social resources in facilitating the immigrant parents' agenda of upward mobility for their children, successfully "fending off" the threat of downward assimilation. Those community resources, or social capital, were most developed in those groups in which "immigrant solidarity is grounded in a common cultural memory and the replication of home country institutions" (1995: 258), which leads to greater density of social networks. That greater density and multiplexity of social ties increases the parents' social control as well as the availability of social capital that can be marshaled to lower the probability of downward mobility for the second generation.

The Cuban enclave in Miami represents the prime example of an immigrant community whose institutional development maximizes that social capital. In fact, Portes specifically refers to one fairly unique feature of Cuban Miami that in many ways represents the ultimate expression in the creation of community resources favorable to intergenerational upward mobility: the establishment of a network of private schools. Either secular or religious, the "enrollment in these schools insulates Cuban American children from contact with downtrodden groups as well as from outside discrimination (Portes 1995: 264). Portes and Rumbaut (1996: 254) expand on this point: "A central aspect of the development of this ethnic enclave was the growth of a system of bilingual private schools. Children of middle-class refugees attending these schools are effectively insulated both from outside discrimination and from inner-city influence. Staffed mostly by other first-generation immigrants, the schools reinforce the values and outlooks of parents, blocking any possibility of role reversal."

In approaching the CILS data on Cubans, therefore, the existing literature would lead us to expect that the enclave exerts a positive influence on its children, placing community resources at their disposal and consequently facilitating upward mobility. We would also expect that the enclave, with its insularity and its density of social networks, reinforces a group's common cultural memory, facilitating the intergenerational transmission of the group's cultural traits and identity.

Since private schools have been identified as a prime vehicle for the implementation of the community's social capital, it is imperative that the analysis look at the differential impact of the type of school attended on the outcome variables. Only a minority of Cuban children actually attend private schools. Those in public schools are in a variety of school settings, from mostly white suburban schools to mostly Latino suburban schools, inner-city Latino schools, and even predominantly black schools. The CILS data permit an intragroup analysis of the differential effect of a variety of school settings on the children's outcome variables.

In summary, therefore, the relevant body of literature points to the importance, in the Cuban case, of looking at both wave of arrival and type of school attended. With the former, the expectation is that the second generation will exhibit characteristics that reflect the widely contrasting profiles of the waves of arrival of the parental generation, with those arriving earlier having a distinct advantage, not primarily because of length of residence in the United States but because of the socioeconomic selectivity of the emigration. Overall, the enclave can be expected to favor intergenerational transmission of the group's cultural traits and to have a favorable impact on the aspirations and achievement of Cuban children, particularly on those attending the type of schools in which the social capital of the community can be most effectively implemented and made available to the second generation.

As we shall see, the findings do not reinforce all of these expectations, especially in the area of academic achievement. The analysis uncovered an achievement paradox that brings into question the assumption that the relative success of the first generation will be extended to their children.

The Characteristics of the CILS Cuban-Origin Respondents

As indicated earlier, a total of 1,242 CILS respondents interviewed in 1992 (T1) had at least one parent (either sex) born in Cuba. In 960 (77.3 percent) of those cases, both parents were Cuban born. A total of 331 of the children in the sample were themselves born in Cuba (in all of those cases, both parents were also Cuban born). Only 24 of the 911 children not born in Cuba were not born in the United States. But of the 282 children who had only one parent born in Cuba, the other parent was slightly more likely (54 percent) to have been born in a third country rather than in the United States. The non-Cuban parent was also more likely to be the father but only by a narrow margin: 52 to 48 percent. The largest single nativity category in the subsample of Cubans was children born in the United States but with both parents born in Cuba (621, or exactly 50 percent).

Among the 1,242 CILS respondents of Cuban origin, males have a numerical advantage, accounting for 52.7 percent of the total. The number reinterviewed in 1995 (T2) was 982 (79.1 percent).

Figure 4.2 presents the distribution of the Cuban CILS sample according to the date of arrival of the parents, grouped into six distinct time periods.[7] There is representation from each arrival period in the sample. Considering that the CILS data are drawn from a specific age cohort, the distribution of the CILS sample by arrival periods is surprisingly close to the same distribution from the total 1990 U.S. Cuban-born population. The differences between the two distributions are exactly what we would expect given the characteristics of the CILS sample, that is, a population born between 1975 and 1978. The largest group, the airlift arrivals, are underrepresented in CILS, for, as noted earlier, that migration overrepresented the elderly. The wave of the early exiles (1960–1964), on the other hand, included a large number of families with children who by the mid-1970s had reached reproductive ages and had children eligible for inclusion in CILS. At the other end of the graph, those CILS respondents whose parents arrived shortly before, during, and after Mariel are all Cuban born themselves. The graph shows that there are two major generations of Cubans in CILS, and neither of them can be regarded, strictly speaking, as a second generation. Those born in Cuba and who arrived as children since 1979 are more accurately defined as a 1.5 generation, while those whose parents came in the early waves are likely, given the time elapsed, to be the U.S.-born children of those who arrived from Cuba as children, making that group of CILS respondents members of a 2.5 generation.

Type of school attended in 1992 by the CILS Cuban-origin respondents is shown in Table 4.1. The category with the largest number of respondents, "mostly Latino suburban," is composed of the public

Figure 4.2. Comparison of the Percent Distributions of Cuban-Born Persons in the 1990 U.S. Census with Cuban-Born Parents of CILS Respondents, by Year of Arrival

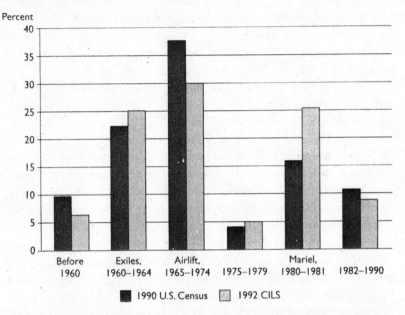

SOURCE: Figures from the 1990 Census were compiled and computed from the U.S. Bureau of the Census, Public-Use Microdata Sample, 1990 U.S. Census of Population.

NOTES: CILS Cuban-origin respondents are those with at least one Cuban-born parent (N = 1,242 in 1992). In this chart, N = 893, for it includes only those respondents with information on the Cuban parents' year of arrival.

TABLE 4.1 PERCENT DISTRIBUTION OF CILS CUBAN-ORIGIN RESPONDENTS, BY TYPE OF SCHOOL ATTENDED IN 1992

	Percentage
Total	100.0
Private, predominantly Cuban	14.9
Mostly white suburban	16.1
Mostly Latino suburban	36.1
Little Havana and Hialeah	28.6
Predominantly black	4.3

NOTE: Cuban-origin respondents are those with at least one foreign-born parent (N = 1,242 in 1992).

schools located in what is known as the West Dade area, a suburban area of Dade County that is predominantly Latino and Cuban. "Little Havana and Hialeah" brings together those schools that are located within the two largest incorporated areas of greater Miami: the cities of Miami and Hialeah. This category is roughly equivalent to a predominantly Latino inner-city grouping, but this term is avoided because it is of questionable applicability to Hialeah.[8]

The most important question regarding the representativeness of this sample centers on the number of respondents in private schools. Interviews were conducted in two predominantly Cuban schools in Dade County, established and managed by Cuban immigrants. The respondents from those schools amount to 14.9 percent of the sample. It is not possible to obtain an exact figure of the total enrollment of Cuban-origin students in all religious and secular private schools in greater Miami, largely because while schools may keep figures on student characteristics by broad racial/ethnic categories, they do not do so by specific nationalities. But by combining data from the 1990 U.S. Census, the Dade County Public Schools, and the Archdiocese of Miami, it is possible to estimate that between 17 and no more than 20 percent of all Cuban-origin students in greater Miami attend private schools (Lisandro Pérez, memorandum to Rubén Rumbaut and Alejandro Portes, April 23, 1998). The sample is therefore not far off the mark, especially if one considers that conceptually the parameter is not precisely all private schools but those that can be regarded as enclave private schools.

There is one additional observation regarding private school enrollment, one that bears on the question of Cuban exceptionality. It is not likely that one can find a contemporary U.S. immigrant community in which nearly one-fifth of its children are enrolled in private schools, especially private schools established and administered by members of the group.[9]

It was noted earlier that these two principal independent variables, wave of arrival and type of school, are heavily influenced by socioeconomic factors. It is therefore to be expected that they are interrelated. Figure 4.3 shows that relationship. The shifts in type of school attended from the exile wave to the more recent waves are dramatic. Very few of the children of the earlier exiles attend public schools in Little Havana and Hialeah, but those schools have more than half of the children whose parents arrived in or after 1980. Similarly, the percent in private schools diminishes markedly across the table from the high of about one-third of the children of the early exiles.

Figure 4.3.   Type of School Attended in 1992, by Parents' Wave of Arrival, CILS Cuban-Origin Respondents

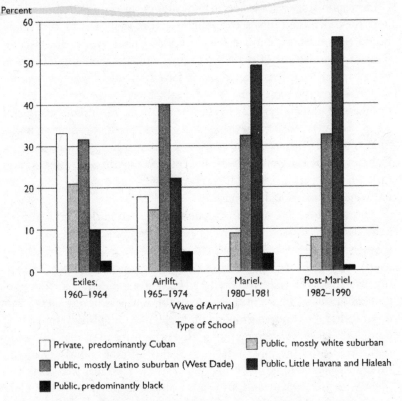

NOTES: Cuban-origin respondents are those with at least one Cuban-born parent (N = 1,242). In this chart, N = 793, for it includes only those respondents with information on the Cuban parent's year of arrival.
Percentages add to 100 within each arrival cluster.

Findings: Bivariate Analysis

The presentation of findings from the CILS survey covers the following outcome variables: ethnic self-identification, perceptions of discrimination and of U.S. society, language, and aspirations and achievement. Because of the conceptual importance attributed to parents' wave of arrival and type of school attended as independent variables, the results are first examined through bivariate tabulations of those independent variables with the outcome variables. Multivariate analysis is then used to examine further the salient issues identified by these bivariate results.

Ethnic Self-Identification

CILS respondents were asked to indicate, in an open-ended question, how they identified themselves. Slightly more than half of all Cuban-origin respondents identified themselves as Cuban American. In comparison with the rest of the CILS sample, Cubans were more likely in 1992 to identify as hyphenated Americans than any other major ethnonational group in the sample. Three years later, they were second only to Filipinos in identifying as hyphenated Americans. In both 1992 and 1995, however, Cubans ranked lowest of all major ethnonational groups in the percent that identified as unhyphenated nationals (e.g., Cubans). Furthermore, they were also more likely than any other group (in both time periods) to identify as American, the opposite pole of the unhyphenated-national response.

Those findings are not surprising when viewed in the context of the analysis by Portes and MacLeod (1996) of the results of the first CILS survey. They argued that groups that are more advantaged and had lengthier stays in the United States exhibit a greater tendency to identify as American. That may well be the best explanation for the phenomenon, since Cubans fit that description. But it is nevertheless paradoxical that the children growing up in the most highly developed U.S. immigrant enclave, a community with mechanisms of insulation and of reinforcement of the cultural traits brought from the country of origin, should be the children most likely to eschew the label that identifies them with that origin and also be most prone to embrace the plain American identity.

Ethnic self-identification in 1995, by parents' wave of arrival, is shown in Figure 4.4. There is a sharp and complementary contrast between the children of those arriving in the earlier wave and those arriving since Mariel in the tendency to identify, on the one hand, as American and, in the opposite direction, as Cuban. Cuban American is the most popular label for all arrival categories, although less so among more recent arrivals, given their strong tendency toward a plain Cuban identity.

Given the relationship between wave of arrival and type of school, Figure 4.5 shows the expected pattern in terms of the self-identification of the respondents in various school types. It is noteworthy that although the mostly Latino suburban, Little Havana and Hialeah, and private schools all have very high densities of Cubans, the latter have a much higher percentage of those identifying as plain American, point-

Figure 4.4. Ethnic Self-Identification in 1992, by Parents' Wave of Arrival, CILS Cuban-Origin Respondents

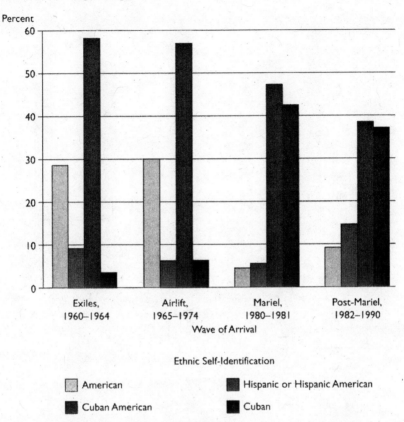

Ethnic Self-Identification

American

Cuban American

Hispanic or Hispanic American

Cuban

NOTES: Cuban-origin respondents are those with at least one Cuban-born parent (N = 1,242). In this chart, N = 763, for it includes only those respondents with information on the Cuban parent's year of arrival. It also excludes 24 respondents who in 1992 identified with various labels other than the four in this chart.
Percentages add to 100 within each arrival cluster.

ing to the primacy of the explanation, advanced by Portes and MacLeod (1996), that more advantaged groups with lengthier periods of residence in the United States are more likely to embrace that label.

An important dimension of the analysis of ethnic self-identification merits additional scrutiny, that is, changes between the first and follow-up surveys. Figure 4.6 is a double graph intended to show in d̶e̶t̶a̶i̶l̶ changes between the two time periods. Focusing first on the to̶p̶

Figure 4.5.   Ethnic Self-Identification, by Type of School Attended, CILS
Cuban-Origin Respondents, 1992

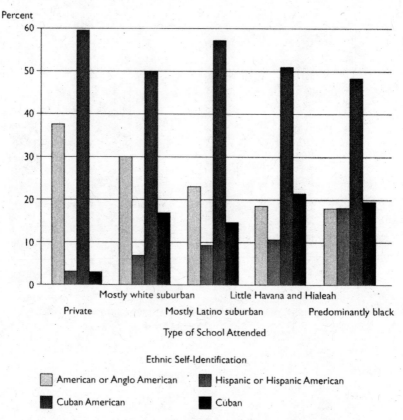

Percent

Type of School Attended

Ethnic Self-Identification

☐ American or Anglo American   ■ Hispanic or Hispanic American

■ Cuban American   ■ Cuban

NOTES: Cuban-origin respondents are those with at least one Cuban-born parent
(N = 1,242). In this chart, N = 1,176, for it excludes respondents who in 1992 identified with various labels other than the four in this chart. The private schools are predominantly Cuban. Except for the category labeled as "private," all other school types
are public. Percentages add to 100 within each school-type cluster.

the graph and on the length of the bars, it verifies the relative standings of
the various labels, with Cuban American by far the largest category, followed by American. As Portes and MacLeod (1996) noted in looking at
the first survey, Cubans were not likely in 1992 to identify as Hispanics.

Three years later, however, there is a different story. The shadings of
the bars in the top part of the graph indicate how the respondents in each
of the 1992 categories identified in 1995. It is evident that the American

Figure 4.6. Ethnic Self-Identification of the Cuban-Origin Respondents, CILS Sample, 1992 and 1995

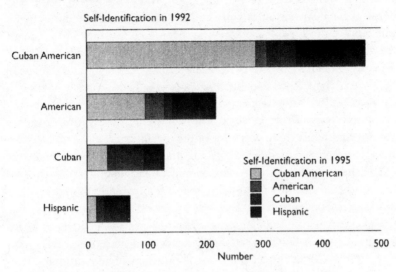

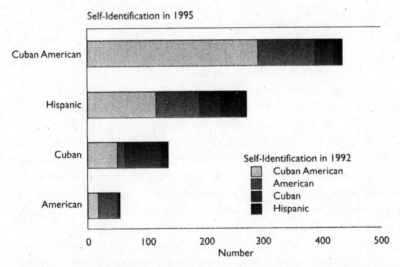

NOTES: Cuban-origin respondents are those with at least one Cuban-born parent (N = 1,242). In this chart, N = 925. Only those respondents interviewed in both 1992 and 1995 are included. Also excluded here are 38 respondents who in 1992 identified with various labels other than the four in this chart.

label is the biggest loser, while the biggest gainer was Hispanic. That is confirmed in the bottom part of the graph, where the length of the bars represent the distribution in 1995 and the shadings indicate how the respondents in those 1995 categories had identified in 1992. The Hispanic and American labels switched places in the three years. The former grew primarily though switchovers from the Cuban-American and American categories. The Cuban-American label retained its primacy because it also acquired many of the former Americans, a label that was used by relatively few respondents in 1995. One additional observation from the graph is that while there was a lot of movement from 1992 to 1995 between the Cuban-American, Hispanic, and American labels, there was little exchange between the American and Cuban identifiers. As the two poles of the self-identity continuum, they are apparently too far apart to exchange respondents in the three years between the surveys.

The overwhelming tendency of second-generation Cubans to abandon the American label in late adolescence was shared by every other group in the CILS sample. But what about the Cubans' dramatic shift toward the Hispanic category? While some groups shifted to such an identity in the follow-up survey, others moved away from it. The Cubans were among the groups in which the shift toward a panethnic label was most dramatic. The explanation for this shift is elusive. Rumbaut (1996), examining the same data for the groups in the CILS San Diego sample, noted the opposite for Mexicans, that is, away from Hispanic, in comparison with most Asian nationalities (toward Asian). His preliminary explanations rested on the impact of political events in California in the period between the two CILS surveys. Comparable events did not take place in Florida to influence the shifts in self-identity among the Cubans. There is little space here to attempt an answer to this question. But it is clearly an important one, especially given the observation by Portes and MacLeod (1996) and also by Rumbaut (1996) that in early adolescence, Cubans largely rejected the Hispanic label. The question takes on even greater importance in light of the finding by Portes and MacLeod that the "adoption of a Hispanic identity is not associated with a positive adaptation profile, but with several dimensions of disadvantage" (1996: 541).

Perceptions of Discrimination

Our respondents were asked if they had ever felt discriminated against. Of all the groups in CILS, Cubans are by far the group least likely to re-

Figure 4.7.   Percentage Who Reported Experiencing Discrimination, by Parents' Wave of Arrival, Cuban-Origin Respondents, 1992 and 1995

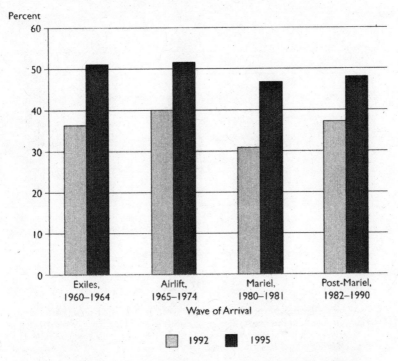

NOTES: Cuban-origin respondents are those with at least one Cuban-born parent (N = 1,242 in 1992). In this chart, N = 646, for it includes only those respondents with information on the Cuban parent's year of arrival who were reinterviewed in 1995.

port discrimination. Although the Cubans greatly increased their perception of discrimination between surveys, in the follow-up they were still reporting the lowest proportion: Half of Cuban respondents indicated they had never felt discriminated against. This is a result consistent with both the relative advantage of Cubans and the completeness and insularity of the enclave.

When perceptions of discrimination are viewed by wave of arrival (Figure 4.7), it is evident that there are few differences between these categories. All seem to have equally low percentages reporting discrimination (most below 50 percent). Interestingly, those in the Mariel category are the least likely to report discrimination of all the arrival waves.

Figure 4.8. Percentage Who Reported Experiencing Discrimination, by Type
of School Attended, CILS Cuban-Origin Respondents, 1992 and 1995

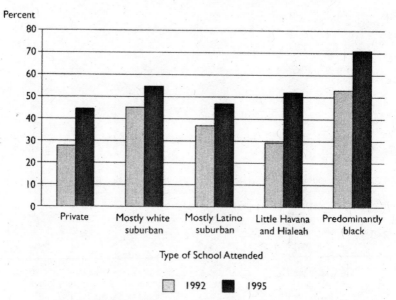

NOTES: Cuban-origin respondents are those with at least one Cuban-born parent
(N = 1,242 in 1992). In this chart, N = 979, for it includes only those reinterviewed in
1995. The private schools are predominantly Cuban. Except for the category labeled as
"private," all other school types are public.

This appears paradoxical, given that Mariel refugees received the most
negative reception, vilified and stereotyped by the press and popular
opinion and even by other Cubans (Portes and Stepick 1993). This finding is explainable by the strong tendency of Mariel refugees and their
children to be deeply ensconced in the Cuban enclave. These second-
generation youths attend mostly Cuban schools and are, therefore, the
beneficiaries of the enclave's capacity to shield its members from discrimination by the host society.

The insulating effects of the enclave are also evident in Figure 4.8,
which presents the extent of perceived discrimination by type of school
attended. In both 1992 and 1995, students in mostly white and predominantly black schools, especially the latter, are more likely to report
discrimination than those in schools in which Cubans represent a plurality.

Figure 4.9.   Percentage Who Preferred English, by Parents' Wave of Arrival, CILS Cuban-Origin Respondents, 1992 and 1995

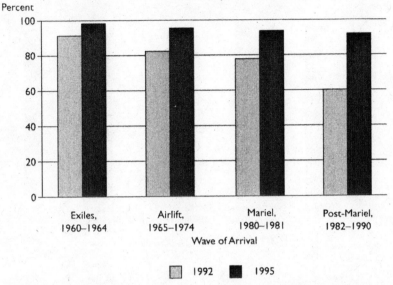

NOTES: Cuban-origin respondents are those with at least one Cuban-born parent ($N = 1,242$ in 1992). In this chart, $N = 648$, for it includes only those respondents with information on the Cuban parent's year of arrival who were reinterviewed in 1995.

Language

The CILS data address three dimensions of the respondents' language use: English proficiency, language preference, and foreign language proficiency. Generally, Cubans did not represent an exceptional case in comparison with other groups in the sample.[10] English language proficiency and preference for English are relatively high and increased between surveys, with predictable differences according to length of U.S. residence.

Figure 4.9 shows that by 1995 and across all arrival categories, more than 90 percent of Cuban respondents preferred to speak English. Even among the most recent arrivals, 60 percent already expressed a preference for English in 1992, a percentage that increased to 90 percent three years later. The same overwhelming preference for English can be observed across the different school types, as shown in Figure 4.10.

Figure 4.10.   Percentage Who Preferred English, by Type of School Attended, CILS Cuban-Origin Respondents, 1992 and 1995

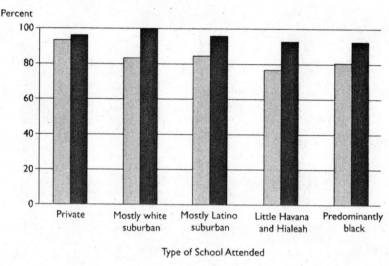

NOTES: Cuban-origin respondents are those with at least one Cuban-born parent (N = 1,242 in 1992). In this chart, N = 982, for it includes only those reinterviewed in 1995. The private schools are predominantly Cuban. Except for the category labeled as "private," all other school types are public.

Proficiency in Spanish shows the expected relationship with wave of arrival, as Figure 4.11 indicates. The percent reporting that they speak Spanish "very well" is noticeably higher among those in the most recent arrival wave. Interestingly, the other arrival categories report improvements in Spanish language proficiency from 1992 to 1995, especially the children of the early exiles. That observation is likely to be the result of the most salient language-related finding in the Cuban-origin sample, namely, the role of private schools in enhancing foreign language proficiency, shown in Figure 4.12. Looking first at the 1992 columns, it is interesting that students in private, predominantly Cuban schools defied the expectation that they should have forgotten Spanish, given that the bulk of them are members of the 2.5 generation, children of children who arrived during the earliest wave. Nevertheless, the percentage of private school students that reported speaking Spanish well is exceeded only by Cubans in the schools of Little Havana and Hialeah, who are mostly recent arrivals.

Figure 4.11.   Percentage Who Reported Speaking a Foreign Language
Very Well, by Parents' Wave of Arrival, CILS Cuban-Origin Respondents,
1992 and 1995

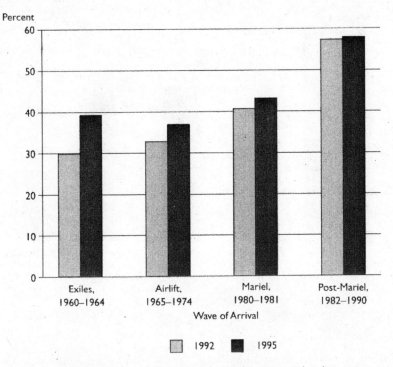

NOTES: Cuban-origin respondents are those with least one Cuban-born parent
($N = 1,242$ in 1992). In this chart, $N = 648$, for it includes only those respondents
with information on the Cuban parent's year of arrival who were reinterviewed in
1995.

By 1995, however, a dramatic shift had taken place. The percentage
of students in private schools reporting that they spoke Spanish very
well rose significantly, while the percentages for those in schools in Little Havana and Hialeah and in mostly white and black schools either remained constant or dropped. The improvement in foreign language proficiency in the private schools can be attributed to their concerted effort
to offer a curriculum that enhances Spanish language skills. The two private schools in the sample, consistent with the ethos of the enclave, require instruction in the Spanish language throughout the senior high
school years. While they are not properly bilingual schools because the
language of instruction for all academic subjects is English, students are

Figure 4.12.   Percentage Who Reported Speaking a Foreign Language Very Well, by Type of School Attended, CILS Cuban-Origin Respondents, 1992 and 1995

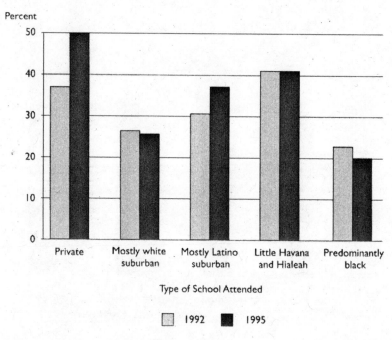

NOTES: Cuban-origin respondents are those with at least one Cuban-born parent (N = 1,242 in 1992). In this chart, N = 982, for it includes only those reinterviewed in 1995. The private schools are predominantly Cuban. Except for the category labeled as "private," all other school types are public.

given Spanish language classes as part of their curriculum and according to their level of proficiency, eventually placing the more advanced in classes in Spanish literature and grammar. Proficiency in Spanish is further supported by strong Spanish-related extracurricular activities, such as a large and active Spanish Club, Spanish cultural school fairs, and writing contests in Spanish. One school's social science course, required of all seniors, is Latin American History (taught in English).

It is important to highlight this finding, given the ease with which children of all immigrant nationalities tend to rapidly and irretrievably lose skills in their parents' language, to their detriment and to the detriment of the society at large. The experience of these private schools shows that offering students formal instruction in the language that they speak at home goes a long way toward enhancing their skills and arresting the usual

Figure 4.13.   Percentage Who Aspired to Earn an Advanced Degree, by Parents' Wave of Arrival, CILS Cuban-Origin Respondents, 1992 and 1995

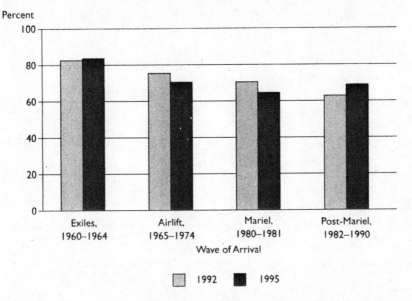

NOTES: Cuban-origin respondents are those with at least one Cuban-born parent ($N = 1,242$ in 1992). In this chart, $N = 644$, for it includes only those respondents with information on the Cuban parent's year of arrival who were reinterviewed in 1995. An advanced degree is any postgraduate degree.

downward slide in their ability to use their parents' native language. It is not an effort that takes place at the expense of English. The same private school students who reported such a dramatic rise in their Spanish language abilities also increased both their English language skills and their preference for English. By 1995, 95.3 percent expressed an unequivocal preference for English as the language of everyday communication.

Aspirations and Achievement

Overall, Cuban children have comparatively high aspirations, among the highest of all nationalities in the sample. In 1992, nearly 94 percent aspired to earn a college degree, and 70 percent had goals for a postgraduate degree. This is not surprising, given both the relative advantage of the first generation as a whole and the resources that the enclave can marshal to prevent downward assimilation.

Figure 4.13 presents the numbers who aspired to an advanced (postgraduate) degree, by parents' wave of arrival. Generally, aspirations in-

Figure 4.14.   Percentage Who Aspired to Earn an Advanced Degree, by Type of School Attended, CILS Cuban-Origin Respondents, 1992 and 1995

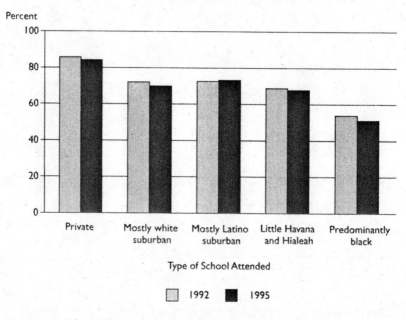

Percent

NOTES: Cuban-origin respondents are those with at least one Cuban-born parent (N = 1,242 in 1992). In this chart, N = 975, for it includes only those reinterviewed in 1995. The private schools are predominantly Cuban. Except for the category labeled as "private," all other school types are public. An advanced degree is any postgraduate degree.

crease with the age of the arrival wave, and they decrease across surveys, arguably a result of students adjusting their aspirations to the realities that they face in the late high school years. The only deviation from this pattern is the increase in aspirations among the most recent post-Mariel arrivals, for whom a greater period of U.S. residence has led to a rise in their educational goals. Viewing aspirations by type of school (Figure 4.14) yields the expected results, with private schools and predominantly black schools representing opposite categories in terms of ambition for the future.

Given the high ambitions of Cuban-origin respondents, findings regarding achievement are both surprising and paradoxical. Table 4.2 shows the mean GPA (weighted) and the incidence of dropping out for each arrival wave and type of school attended. Looking first at GPA, note that the overall Cuban GPA, as well as the GPAs for virtually all

TABLE 4.2   MEASURES OF EDUCATIONAL
ACHIEVEMENT, BY PARENTS' WAVE OF ARRIVAL
AND TYPE OF SCHOOL ATTENDED, CILS CUBAN-
ORIGIN RESPONDENTS

	Latest Available Mean GPA (weighted)	Percentage Who Had Dropped Out of School by 1996
All CILS respondents	2.46	7.3
All Cuban-origin respondents	2.19	10.2
Parents' wave of arrival		
Exiles, 1960–1964	2.49	10.7
Airlift, 1965–1974	2.27	8.5
Mariel, 1980–1981	2.00	9.1
Post-Mariel, 1982–1990	2.22	9.2
Type of school attended		
Private	2.64	—[1]
Mostly white suburban	2.41	7.7
Mostly Latino suburban	2.07	11.2
Little Havana and Hialeah	2.07	9.3
Predominantly black	2.04	16.3

[1] Data on private school attrition are omitted because they are not comparable with public school dropout data.

arrival categories, are well below the total CILS sample GPA (the Cuban figures include students in private schools). Even the group with the highest mean GPA, the children of the early exiles, exhibits a figure below 2.5. Mean GPA by type of school attended shows that only the Cubans in private schools exceed the overall CILS mean and only the students in mostly white suburban schools approach it. The mean for students in the other three school types barely exceeds 2.0.

Turning to dropout rates, the results are still more startling. Cubans have the highest dropout rates of all the nationalities in CILS, the only group with school attrition rates in double digits. It should be noted that private school students are excluded from the analysis because of the lack of comparability in the concept of dropping out between public and private schools. Even so, the results are nothing short of remarkable, given what we would expect from the children of an advantaged group who are supported by a strong enclave.

Looking at dropout rates by parents' wave of arrival, it is worth noting that the group with the highest mean GPA and the longest period of

U.S. residence (the 2.5 generation) should also be the one with the highest dropout rate. The other arrival waves do not show a linear relationship with length of U.S. residence. Note the widely contrasting dropout rates between Cuban-origin respondents and the total CILS sample. In the absence of data on private schools, the students in mostly white suburban schools have the lowest dropout rates, while Cuban students in predominantly black schools have by far the highest.

Since the data on grades and dropout rates are provided by the respective school districts, is there any confirmation of these findings directly from the CILS data? The variable most consistently related to school achievement is time spent on homework in both surveys. Results of that variable show that Cubans report spending the least amount of time on homework of all national groups in the sample at both times. Because of their importance, these findings deserve further scrutiny through multivariate analysis, along with other salient results from bivariate relationships in this section.

Findings: Multivariate Analysis

Although a number of bivariate results merit a further analysis, space constraints make it necessary to limit multivariate analysis to the most perplexing and significant finding: the achievement paradox. Given the earlier discussion about the Golden Exile and the Golden Enclave, there is every expectation that such favorable migration and reception contexts would translate into successful academic outcomes for the Cuban second generation. Instead, our Cuban-origin respondents have below-average grades and the highest dropout rate in the sample.

In this section, 1995–1996 GPA and the incidence of dropping out (school attrition) are dependent variables in multiple regression models employing first-survey predictors. Each model has two types of predictors. In addition to demographic, socioeconomic, attitudinal, language, and behavioral factors, the model contains a number of dummy variables designed to measure the effect of the variables that have been emphasized throughout this chapter: wave of arrival and type of school attended.

Figure 4.15 presents standardized regression coefficients (beta weights) for the model, with GPA as the dependent variable. The value of the betas is given by the length of the bar, positive or negative. The level of significance is given by the shading of the bar. Not surprisingly,

Figure 4.15. Predictors (1992) of GPA by 1995–1996, CILS Cuban-Origin Respondents

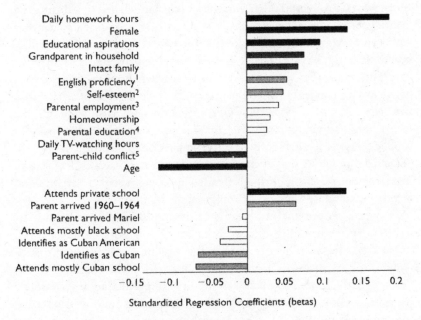

TI (1992) Predictors

Standardized Regression Coefficients (betas)

Levels of Significance

p < .0001   p < .01   p < .10   not significant

NOTES:
[1]Mean of 4-item scale (self-reported ability to speak, understand, read and write English), scored 1 to 4.
[2]Mean of the 10-item Rosenberg self-esteem scale, scored 1 to 4.
[3]Three-item index of parents' labor force participation (0 = both parents not employed; 2 = both parents employed).
[4]Five-item index of parents' educational level (2 = both parents not high school graduates; 6 = both parents college graduates).
[5]Mean of 3-item scale, scored 1 to 4.

daily homework hours, being female, and educational aspirations showed strong positive associations with GPA. Household characteristics (intact family and presence of grandparents) are also positively related (at the .01 level). TV-watching and parent-child conflict, among others, exert a predictable negative influence. Interestingly, the set of variables that center on parents' socioeconomic status (employment, homeownership, and education) were not significantly related to school achievement.

Overall, the arrival and school variables showed weaker relationships with GPA. Net of other variables in the model, arriving during the Mariel period was not significantly related to GPA, despite the fact that children of Mariel entrants exhibited the lowest GPA in Table 4.2. On the other hand, having arrived in the early exile wave had a slight positive impact (at the .10 level). As shown earlier, however, this arrival wave has a high degree of collinearity with the only type of school that strongly and positively predicts GPA: private school enrollment. On the other hand, attending a mostly Cuban school (a variable that includes public schools) has a slightly negative impact on GPA (at the .10 level). This result suggests that enclave private schools positively affect school performance primarily through their socioeconomic characteristics and academic standards and not through ethnic homogeneity.

Figure 4.16 presents the results of the model applied to school attrition. Since dropping out is coded higher, a positive association means that the variable operates in the direction of increasing the incidence of attrition. At a glance it is clear, from the shadings of the bars, that the model is much less effective in predicting school desertion than GPA. With the exception of having unemployed parents, the model is not helpful in explaining the incidence of dropping out among Cubans.

Obviously, further investigation is needed to understand the dynamics of academic achievement among children of Cuban immigrants in Miami. Two tentative and complementary explanations suggest themselves, both within the context of the earlier conceptual discussion.[11] One is that Cubans are the most advantaged, oldest, and hence acculturated group in CILS and that, as a result, their school behavior and achievement begin to resemble that of the students with native-born parents. In other words, Cubans are moving away from the model of academic achievement that characterizes most immigrant children and starting to follow the mainstream American pattern in which aspirations remain high, as does confidence that resources will be available for upward mobility without extraordinary academic effort. It is suggestive, for example, that dropout rates by wave of arrival show that children of the earliest (and most successful) wave have the highest percentage of all arrival categories. In this interpretive framework, assimilation would be bad for academic achievement, a pattern that Rumbaut identifies as one of the main "paradoxes of assimilation" (1997: 498).

Figure 4.16.   Predictors (1992) of School Attrition before High School Graduation, CILS Cuban-Origin Respondents

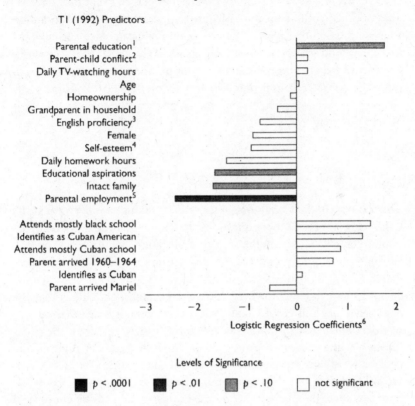

TI (1992) Predictors

Parental education[1]
Parent-child conflict[2]
Daily TV-watching hours
Age
Homeownership
Grandparent in household
English proficiency[3]
Female
Self-esteem[4]
Daily homework hours
Educational aspirations
Intact family
Parental employment[5]

Attends mostly black school
Identifies as Cuban American
Attends mostly Cuban school
Parent arrived 1960–1964
Identifies as Cuban
Parent arrived Mariel

Logistic Regression Coefficients[6]

Levels of Significance

■ $p < .0001$ ■ $p < .01$ ■ $p < .10$ ☐ not significant

NOTES:
[1]Five-item index of parents' educational level (2 = both parents not high school graduates; 6 = both parents college graduates).
[2]Mean of 3-item scale, scored 1 to 4.
[3]Mean of 4-item scale (self-reported ability to speak, understand, read, and write English), scored 1 to 4.
[4]Mean of the 10-item Rosenberg self-esteem scale, scored 1 to 4.
[5]Three-item index of parents' labor force participation (0 = both parents not employed; 2 = both parents employed).
[6]So as to facilitate comparisons among variables, the actual figure plotted is the ratio of the coefficient to its standard error.

The second possible interpretation is complementary with the first but pays closer attention to the dynamics of the enclave. The confidence of second-generation Cubans to succeed without extraordinary effort is rooted in their position as the dominant immigrant group in the Miami area, with control over the resources necessary for upward mobility.

Those resources, especially the availability of employment within the enclave, may make it possible for children to perceive that they have viable options to the educational route as means for upward mobility. The enclave, in other words, may function not as a golden springboard for the second generation but as a basic safety net. Further work by Portes and Rumbaut on this achievement paradox suggests that the explanation for the phenomenon rests heavily on the impact of time of arrival from Cuba. As such, it supports the prominence given to that variable in this chapter.

Conclusion

This analysis of the Cuban-origin sample, by taking a wide swath at the CILS data, has raised more questions than it has answered. Two in particular come to mind: (1) the shift to a Hispanic identity from the first to the second survey and (2) the disappointing and unexpected academic performance of these students.

Two major points, however, have been established. One is that the experience of children of Cuban immigrants cannot be viewed outside of the context that their parents created. For these children, the peculiarities of the migration process from Cuba and the dynamics of the enclave in Miami represent the "world of their fathers," to use Irving Howe's phrase, and that world must be the starting point of any attempt to solve the puzzles encountered in the analysis. The conceptual framework presented at the start of this chapter and the dynamics of the enclave represent the primary source for hypotheses to interpret the CILS data on the Cuban-origin children.

The second point is that the basis for the CILS study was a sound one: The adaptation process of the children of immigrants may be quite different from that of their first-generation parents. That is certainly true, for example, in the case of academic achievement. The enclave may have very different implications for the second generation than for the first. If the CILS data on Cubans force us to reexamine our assumptions about the adjustment process of children of immigrants, that would be appropriate. After all, it was precisely the Cuban exceptionality in its mode of incorporation—the enclave—that reformulated a great deal of what we know about immigrant adjustment. The offspring of that enclave may well do the same for our body of knowledge on the incorporation process, and the future, of children of immigrants in the entire nation.

Notes

The author acknowledges the comments of his CILS colleagues, Alejandro Portes and Rubén G. Rumbaut. His work on this chapter was made possible by the generous support of the Russell Sage Foundation, where the author spent the 1997–1998 year as a visiting scholar.

1. The bibliography on the process of revolutionary change in Cuba is extensive. For three of the best works, see Domínguez 1978; Pérez-Stable 1993; Paterson 1994.

2. For more extensive analyses of the history of migration from Cuba to the United States since 1959, see Masud-Piloto 1995; Pedraza 1996; Pérez 1986a.

3. Although data for more recent years is already available from the INS, those are data on persons admitted into the United States. Admissions may include persons who were already in the United States with a temporary visa and had their status "adjusted" formally, admitting them as immigrants. The data in Figure 4.1 are for arrivals, a more accurate measure of migration flows, especially in the Cuban case. As of this writing, the data on arrivals was not yet available for years after 1995.

4. For a detailed analysis of the welcome that Cubans have received in the United States, see Masud-Piloto 1995.

5. One of the earliest studies of Cuban migration to the United States after 1959 focused precisely on the process of disaffection from the revolution and its implications for the migration of much of Cuba's elite. See Fagen, Brody, and O'Leary 1968; O'Leary 1966. There was even an entire program to send unaccompanied children to the United States under the care of the Catholic Church. See Triay 1995.

6. See, for example, Rogg 1974; Rogg and Cooney 1980; Newman 1978; Borjas 1982.

7. As noted in the chart, it was not possible to ascertain parents' year of arrival for all respondents in the sample. For those cases in which only one parent is Cuban born, the chart shows, when available, only the year of arrival of the Cuban parent. In cases where both parents are Cuban born but arrived in different periods, allocation of the case was made to the period of arrival of the parent who arrived earliest. In charts subsequent to this one, data are presented only for those periods of arrival that can properly be considered waves, omitting the migration period prior to 1960 and the 1975–1979 arrivals. Not only are those two relatively small, but they also very heterogeneous, especially with respect to the conditions of migration.

8. Hialeah is an incorporated area in the northwest area of greater Miami. It has a high concentration of Cuban-born persons, especially recent

arrivals, and therefore has the ethnic homogeneity of many inner-city areas. On the other hand, it is a working-class (lower-middle- to low-SES) bedroom community.

9. A critical factor in the establishment of what can be regarded as Cuban enclave schools in Miami was the transplantation of religious educational institutions from Cuba as a result of the church-state conflict that arose in the early years of the revolution. For an analysis of that process and its consequences for the Cuban community in Miami, see Pérez 1994.

10. For analyses of the T1 CILS data on language, see Portes and Schauffler 1996; Rumbaut 1996.

11. I wish to acknowledge that these interpretations emerged from discussions with my CILS colleagues, Rubén Rumbaut and Alejandro Portes.

References

Amaro, Nelson, and Alejandro Portes. 1972. Una sociología del exilio: situación de los grupos cubanos en Estados Unidos. *Aportes* 23 (January), pp. 6–24.

Borjas, George J. 1982. The earnings of male Hispanic immigrants in the United States. *Industrial and Labor Relations Review* 35, no. 3 (April), pp. 343–353.

Díaz-Briquets, Sergio, and Lisandro Pérez. 1981. Cuba: The demography of revolution. *Population Reference Bureau Bulletin Series* 32 (1), pp. 1–41.

Domínguez, Jorge I. 1978. *Cuba: Order and revolution.* Cambridge, Mass.: Harvard University Press.

Fagen, Richard R., Richard A. Brody, and Thomas J. O'Leary. 1968. *Cubans in exile: Disaffection and the revolution.* Stanford, Calif.: Stanford University Press.

Masud-Piloto, Felix. 1995. *From welcomed exiles to illegal immigrants: Cuban Migration to the U.S., 1959–1995.* Lanham, Md.: Rowman and Littlefield.

Newman, M. J. 1978. A profile of Hispanics in the U.S. work force. *Monthly Labor Review* 101 (12), pp. 3–14.

O'Leary, Thomas J. 1966. Cubans in exile: Political attitudes and political participation. Ph.D. diss., Stanford University.

Paterson, Thomas G. 1994. *Contesting Castro: The United States and the triumph of the Cuban Revolution.* New York: Oxford University Press.

Pedraza, Silvia. 1996. "Cuba's refugees: Manifold migrations." In *Origins and destinies: Immigration, race, and ethnicity in America,* edited by Silvia Pedraza and Rubén G. Rumbaut. Belmont, Calif.: Wadsworth.

Pedraza-Bailey, Silvia. 1985. *Political and economic migrants in America: Cubans and Mexicans.* Austin: University of Texas Press.

Pérez, Lisandro. 1986a. Cubans in the United States. *The Annals of the American Academy of Political and Social Science* 487 (September), pp. 126–137.

———. 1986b. Immigrant adjustment and family organization: The Cuban success story reexamined. *International Migration Review* 20 (Spring), pp. 4–20.

————. 1992. "Cuban Miami." In *Miami now! Immigration, ethnicity, and social change,* edited by Guillermo J. Grenier and Alex Stepick III. Gainesville: University Press of Florida.

————. 1994. "Cuban Catholics in the United States." In *Puerto Rican and Cuban Catholics in the U.S., 1900–1965,* edited by Jay P. Dolan and Jaime R. Vidal. Notre Dame, Ind.: University of Notre Dame Press.

Pérez-Stable, Marifeli. 1993. *The Cuban revolution: Origins, course, and legacy.* New York: Oxford University Press.

Portes, Alejandro. 1969. Dilemmas of a Golden Exile: Integration of Cuban refugee families in Milwaukee. *American Sociological Review* 34 (August), pp. 505–518.

————. 1987. The social origins of the Cuban enclave economy in Miami. *Sociological Perspectives* 30 (October), pp. 340–371.

————. 1995. "Children of immigrants: Segmented assimilation and its determinants." In *The economic sociology of immigration: Essays on networks, ethnicity, and entrepreneurship,* edited by Alejandro Portes. New York: Russell Sage Foundation.

Portes, Alejandro, and Robert L. Bach. 1985. *Latin journey: Cuban and Mexican immigrants in the United States.* Berkeley: University of California Press.

Portes, Alejandro, Juan M. Clark, and Robert L. Bach. 1977. The new wave: A statistical profile of recent Cuban exiles to the United States. *Cuban Studies/Estudios Cubanos* 7, no. 1 (January), pp. 1–32.

Portes, Alejandro, and Dag MacLeod. 1996. What shall I call myself? Hispanic identity formation in the second generation. *Ethnic and Racial Studies* 19, no. 3 (July), pp. 523–547.

Portes, Alejandro, and Rubén G. Rumbaut. 1996. *Immigrant America: A portrait.* Berkeley: University of California Press.

Portes, Alejandro, and Richard Schauffler. 1996. "Language and the second generation: Bilingualism yesterday and today." In *The new second generation,* edited by Alejandro Portes. New York: Russell Sage Foundation.

Portes, Alejandro, and Alex Stepick. 1993. *City on the edge: The transformation of Miami.* Berkeley: University of California Press..

Rogg, Eleanor Meyer. 1974. *The assimilation of Cuban exiles: The role of community and class.* New York: Aberdeen Press.

Rogg, Eleanor Meyer, and Rosemary Santana Cooney. 1980. *Adaptation and adjustment of Cubans: West New York, New Jersey.* New York: Hispanic Research Center, Fordham University.

Rumbaut, Rubén G. 1996. "The crucible within: Ethnic identity, self-esteem, and segmented assimilation among children of immigrants." In *The new second generation,* edited by Alejandro Portes. New York: Russell Sage Foundation.

————. 1997. Paradoxes (and orthodoxies) of assimilation. *Sociological Perspectives* 40, no. 3 (1997), p. 498.

Triay, Victor Andrés. 1995. The flight from Never-Never Land: A history of Pedro Pan and the Cuban children's program. Ph.D. diss., Florida State University.

U.S. Bureau of the Census. 1996–1997. Current Population Surveys (combined), public-use microdata sample. Washington, D.C.: U.S. Census Bureau.

Chapter 5

NICARAGUANS
Voices Lost, Voices Found

Patricia Fernández-Kelly and Sara Curran

Some 280,000 Nicaraguans currently live in the United States.[1] Their story is brief but instructive. Fleeing political and economic upheaval in the wake of the Sandinista Revolution, they saw themselves as freedom fighters deserving a reception similar to that bestowed upon Cubans after Fidel Castro's ascent to power. Yet their avowals of political persecution and petitions of legal residence were consistently rejected at the federal, state, and local levels. As a result, the most singular aspect of the Nicaraguan diaspora was the rupture of a collective voice. Instead of exiles, Nicaraguans became illegal aliens. Without external support for their shared narrative, they fell into a sort of vacuum, their protestations muffled by a chilly din.

Several factors contributed to that outcome. Ironic and most important was timing. While Cuba had been a central piece in the confrontation between the Soviet Union and the United States in the 1960s, Nicaragua was, two decades later, a small country of little strategic consequence. Solidarity with the disaffected presented potential advantages to hardly anyone. Attitudes toward migration, always ambivalent in southern Florida, had hardened after the 1980 Mariel boatlift. Finally, numbers were small; Nicaraguans had not been preceded in migration by large flows of conationals. Eighty-one percent of those now living in the United States were born in their country of origin; two-

127

thirds arrived between 1980 and 1990 (U.S. Immigration and Naturalization Service 1993).

In Miami, where their dramatic experience unfolded in sharpest detail, Nicaraguans became second only to Cubans as a foreign-born group, and it is against a Cuban backdrop that their story acquires full meaning. Facing hostility is part of the immigrant fare; breaking the law, a risk worth taking in the pursuit of a better life. Nevertheless, Nicaraguans saw themselves as more than seekers of economic advantage. Their anticommunism was consistent with the preaching of the country to which they fled for protection. When they were rebuffed, the ensuing sense of betrayal was deeply traumatic, the contrast with the Cuban experience almost too harrowing for words.

The rejection of Nicaraguan definitions about the causes of their migration had sensible effects. Without endorsement for their motives, they had few elements to forge a cohesive community. As a result, they splintered. Uncertain legal status limited economic and educational alternatives, but more importantly, it undermined the capacity of parents to retain authority over, and demand compliance from, their children. This, too, was fraught with irony. Most Nicaraguans had arrived in Miami with their families. It was, in fact, for the sake of the children that they had undertaken the hazardous journey in the first place.

They came from sizable cities such as Managua, Masaya, and Rivas and were thus familiar with urban mores. Many boasted a middle-class bearing, a fair complexion, and a proper education. In their country they had been professionals, clerks, and technical workers. Now they faced an uncertain future. While they pleaded their cases, some depended on temporary work permits, and others disappeared in the morass of unregulated employment. Without prospects for real progress, they accepted menial jobs—their past experience and credentials made irrelevant by circumstance.

Besieged by threats of deportation, Nicaraguans crowded in the same Miami neighborhoods adjacent to Eight Street, *Calle Ocho*, that had been occupied, made famous, and then left behind by Cubans. Unable to buy homes, they rented and waited. They waited for their plight to be recognized, for policy to soften, for immigration authorities to change their minds. In the meantime, their children grew up in environments characterized by the dearth of resources and in relative isolation from mainstream institutions. This, too, had a major impact upon their prospects for assimilation. Little over a decade after their arrival, Nicaraguan youngsters were already showing symptoms of decline—a social darkening of sorts. But the trend was not uniform; among those whose families had been able to obtain legal residence, the outlook was promising. The division between legal and undocumented Nicaraguans underscores the significance of state policy as facilitator or deterrent of assimilation (Portes and Rumbaut 1997).

In this chapter, we consider the case of Nicaraguan migrants in the United States as an ideal type reflecting distinctive forces and outcomes in areas of destination. We claim that, contrary to accounts that privilege culture to explain variations in immigrant adaptation, it is the context of reception that determines the kinds of adjustments newcomers must make to survive. It is true that immigrants rely upon norms and understandings learned in their home countries to make their way in unfamiliar and hostile environments. But the extent to which those shared understandings are transformed into behaviors depends mostly upon the material, human, and symbolic resources at hand in their adoptive country. In our analysis we thus rely upon a critical distinction between social processes and assets of various kinds. We argue in favor of a dynamic definition of ethnicity that simultaneously highlights the narratives accounting for a shared experience and the material context in which those accounts are deployed (Fernández-Kelly 1995).

Our reasoning can be summarized as follows: There is a gradual progression between migration and ethnicity. When crossing borders, individuals tend to identify in terms of place or nationality but are seen by others in destination areas as constituents of unfamiliar, often disdained, groups. Continued stigma and exclusion contribute to the formation of bounded identities (Portes and Zhou 1993). Thus, the extent to which newcomers assimilate or become members of ethnic minorities depends on their capacity to prosper economically and achieve acceptance in the larger society. To become a true citizen, images of ethnicity must be cast off.

In the United States, the national differences between Cubans and Nicaraguans are obliterated by their common designation as Hispanics. Yet that term has a distinct meaning for each of the two groups. Cuban exiles, whose economic success has been amply documented, tend to repudiate the stigmatizing tag. At first, Nicaraguan youngsters did the opposite: They adopted *Hispanic* as a way to escape the negative stereotypes imposed on their national origin. The passage of time, however, ushered a surprising new development. As more became ̶ ̶ discrimination, they privileged *Nicaraguan* as a self-defi̶ tance and defense. The term is thus emerging not as a si̶

tion of point of provenance but as a marker of minority status in their new country. To explain this critical shift in identity is one of our main objectives.

Our chapter is divided into five parts. First we discuss the origins and characteristics of Nicaraguan migrants. The second section contains information about the context of reception and its effects on settlement and adaptation. That is followed by an explanation of the effects that early experiences after migration are having on Nicaraguan children. In the fourth section we give attention to the ways in which second-generation Nicaraguans are redefining their collective identity. The conclusion summarizes key findings and highlights their bearing on present theories of immigrant adaptation across generations.

Who Are They and Why Did They Come?

A sense of devotion to children melded with a common political purpose united Nicaraguans as they fled their country. The Sandinista Revolution of the 1980s forced many to reassess options and take drastic steps. Almost without exception, discontented Nicaraguans saw their anticommunist struggle as a matter of agreement with U.S. policy. That was true for Carmela Miranda. Poised and fashionably dressed, she held strong views about the motives that had led her and her family to leave the city of Rivas in 1982:

> [Back in Nicaragua] we had a Cuban neighbor who explained the way Communism changed things. . . . We were afraid the Sandinistas would turn our children around. . . . I was a teacher and saw the way things were after the Revolution. The literacy program was not really about educating the masses but about altering their consciousness and their minds, and our future consisted of our three children. That's why we left. We were fighting for their lives.[2]

First, the Mirandas moved to Washington, D.C., where they survived by cleaning houses. Later, fearing deportation, they went to Miami, chasing a job offered by an acquaintance. Although Mrs. Miranda had been a teacher, in the United States she worked as a maid for a large hotel. With the passage of time many of her hopes faded and she acquired a nervous affliction, but she felt it had all been worthwhile, considering what she had left behind.

At fifty-two, Luis Gómez had a similar story to tell. He was no youngster when he arrived in the United States illegally by swimming with his three children in tow across the U.S.-Mexico border—the two younger ones bobbing atop the tire of a truck. The journey— more than 3,000 hazardous miles—had taken him from Managua to Guatemala City, Tapachula, Mexico City, and finally Reynosa. There he had contracted a *coyote,* or smuggler, to help with the border crossing. In that alone he had spent more than $1,000, a considerable sum for someone who had lost most of his assets to the Sandinista Revolution. He had reached McAllen, Texas, only to be apprehended by the immigration authorities and then released on his own recognizance. He had later joined his sister in Miami and tried to keep a low profile while seeking asylum. Although his application was denied, he received a work permit. For 13 years, he had toiled without respite.

Before migrating, Mr. Gómez had owned his own hauling business, but his political involvement had landed him in jail several times. As a trucker in Miami, he earned, on the average, $500 a week. Almost without help (his wife had left him long ago), he had raised two daughters and bought a modest home. In 1995, when he was interviewed for this study, he had few regrets other than the premature death of his older son.

The two cases just outlined are typical of the conditions surrounding early Nicaraguan migration. Exodus was preceded by political turmoil, but arrival was marked by high expectations. Their experience, hopes upon arrival, and realities of their reception situate Nicaraguan immigrants uniquely in relation to other immigrant groups. To illustrate this proposition, we compare Nicaraguan immigrant parents with parents in other immigrant groups in Table 5.1.[3] More than 80 percent arrived in the 1980s and thus constitute the latest arrivals among those represented in our sample. Their short period of residence is also related to relatively low levels of citizenship as compared with other immigrants.

Nicaraguans show slightly higher levels of marital stability and educational attainment than other groups. Overall, they are more likely to be married and less likely to be divorced or separated. Fathers are twice as likely to have college degrees. Mothers tend to have some college education. Perhaps even more important is the comparatively high representation of Nicaraguans who held professional or white-collar jobs in their country of origin. Fathers were more than three times as likely as other immigrants to have been professionals before arriving in the United States.

Terms of reception were also different for Nicaraguans by comparison with other groups. Although most had as many relatives in Miami

TABLE 5.1 BACKGROUND CHARACTERISTICS OF NICARAGUAN PARENTS AND OTHER PARENTS IN THE CILS SOUTH FLORIDA SAMPLE

	Father's Characteristics		Mother's Characteristics	
	Nicaraguan (%)	Other (%)	Nicaraguan (%)	Other (%)
Year of arrival[1]				
Before 1960	0.0	7.7	0.8	3.6
1960–69	0.0	32.8	0.0	31.2
1970–79	17.9	25.5	18.2	33.5
1980–89	82.1	34.0	81.1	31.7
U.S. citizen[1]				
Yes	12.5	66.8	11.4	60.8
Marital status[1]				
Married	92.9	90.0	67.4	67.3
Cohabiting	0.0	1.5	1.5	1.1
Divorced/separated	7.1	5.0	18.2	25.7
Widowed	0.0	3.1	4.5	3.7
Educational attainment[1]				
Less than high school	7.1	12.0	18.9	15.0
High school graduate	5.4	20.5	14.4	24.4
Vocational/technical	3.6	18.9	21.2	24.9
Some college	19.6	16.6	25.0	19.5
College or more	64.3	32.0	20.4	16.3
Occupation in place of origin[1]				
Professional	70.9	23.6	32.8	14.6
White collar	10.9	8.0	30.5	12.5
Blue collar/service	14.5	22.4	4.6	8.7
No job	3.6	46.0	32.1	64.1
Relatives living in U.S. upon arrival[1]				
No relatives	19.6	24.7	23.5	25.2
1–2 relatives	35.7	28.2	31.1	27.9
3–9 relatives	16.1	30.1	23.5	26.0
10 or more relatives	28.6	17.0	22.0	20.8
Amount of help received from relatives[1]				
None	26.8	21.6	22.0	16.7
A little	28.6	17.8	18.2	17.2
A lot	25.0	35.9	35.6	40.3
Friends living in U.S. upon arrival[1]				
None	19.6	24.7	55.0	38.6
1–2 friends	35.7	28.2	9.3	10.6
3–9 friends	16.1	30.1	18.0	22.7
10 or more friends	28.6	17.0	17.7	28.0
Amount of help received from friends[1]				
None	30.4	17.8	27.3	16.3
A little	14.3	13.9	15.1	12.8
A lot	17.9	15.1	18.9	15.1
Number of cases N = 1,123	N = 56	N = 259	N = 132	N = 615
% of total sample 100%	5.0	23.1	11.7	54.8

[1]Significant differences between Nicaraguans and others (chi-square p-value ≤ .05)
NOTE: Percent distributions within columns.

as other immigrants, a majority claimed to have received little or no help from them. Friendship networks were smaller by comparison with other groups, and Nicaraguans reported fewer instances in which friends or acquaintances provided help. As discussed later in this chapter, the absence of support from relatives and friends in the early stages of migration had discernible effects on the character of Nicaraguan settlement.[4]

How Were They Received and with What Results?

Luis Gómez, whose journey we sketched earlier, believed he had achieved most of his goals in Miami. Still, feelings of disappointment plagued him more than a decade after his first arrival:

> We came . . . because of our opposition to a Communist government. The Sandinistas took everything we had, even our dignity. And so, naturally, we looked for refuge in the United States, the richest, most democratic country in the world. But . . . [U.S. authorities] slammed the door in our face, [they saw us as] greedy nobodies looking to take advantage. They never cared about our struggle.

Thus, the cause of Mr. Gómez's distress was not the ordeal of relocation but the absence of validation of the reasons that had led him to migrate. He was not alone in his frustration. In contrast to other groups—Mexicans, for example—who leave their countries prompted primarily by want, Nicaraguans' motives were political. To endure illegality, in their case, was more than inconvenient; it was a blow to their sense of virtue.

Illegal status combined with linguistic limitations to exacerbate feelings of inadequacy. This was especially vexing for women who saw themselves as advocates for their children. Thirty-nine-year-old Norma Rentería had arrived in Miami in 1985. Since then she had worked without papers, in constant fear of deportation.

Before migrating, Norma had completed high school and studied some accounting. She had also worked as a secretary. In 1993 she was helping her husband, Eddie, clean offices. She also sewed at home, at piece rate, for a Nicaraguan contractor. A thousand hems, at 10 cents each, easily netted Norma $100 a day, but the supply of work was irregular. With five children in the house, she spent very little time doing anything other than work. Most debilitating was the absence of respect:

> We have felt very humiliated in this country. When we get sick, we have no place to go because we are not here legally. When we come into contact with

Figure 5.1. Language Use and Preference among Nicaraguan Parents and Other Immigrant Parents

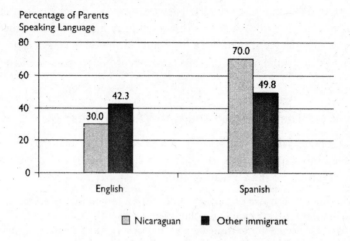

Percentage of Parents
Speaking Language

Legend: ☐ Nicaraguan   ■ Other immigrant

people who are better educated, they make us feel inferior. . . . I don't speak English fluently but I can understand what people say when they sneer and make offensive remarks. I was enrolled at Miami-Dade [Community College] for three years trying to learn English . . . then I had to stop because my children needed care. But because I can't speak English well, I can't help them with their homework.

The factors that facilitate or hinder adjustment in areas of destination—the mode of reception—converge with collective endowments to influence outcomes, even across generations (Ogbu 1991). Here we focus upon language ability, socioeconomic status (as measured by income, work, and employment), assistance received during the first year of residence in the United States, perceptions of discrimination, and perceptions of social support.

Figure 5.1 presents results for language ability and preference, two influential factors in adaptation processes (Portes and Hao 1998). Nicaraguan parents are much more likely to speak Spanish at home than other immigrant parents in southern Florida. They also have significantly lower self-reported knowledge of English (as measured by the average sum of a four-point scale across four items: reading, writing, comprehension, and speaking). On average, Nicaraguan parents reported that their English ability is limited (average score = 2.57),

TABLE 5.2   EMPLOYMENT ADAPTATION AND
INCORPORATION OF NICARAGUAN AND OTHER
SOUTHERN FLORIDA PARENTS

Parent's Characteristics

	Nicaraguan (%)	Other (%)	Total (%)	Sample Size
Father's work status				
Employed full time	84.5	84.0	84.1	314
Employed part time	6.9	4.7	5.1	
Unemployed and looking	5.2	4.7	4.8	
Unemployed or keeping house	0.0	0.8	0.6	
Other	3.4	5.9	5.4	
Mother's work status				
Employed full time	58.3	66.3	64.9	750
Employed part time	14.4	9.5	10.4	
Unemployed and looking	7.6	5.0	5.5	
Unemployed or keeping house	16.7	16.3	16.4	
Other	3.0	2.7	2.8	
Respondent's self-employed status				
Self-employed	13.2	16.7	16.1	1,070
Working for someone	65.8	62.5	63.1	
Working in family business	0.0	0.4	0.4	
Other/unemployed	21.0	20.3	20.5	

whereas other immigrant parents rank their English ability as good (average score = 3.16).

When we compare Nicaraguan parents' adaptation and incorporation with other immigrant parents along economic dimensions, their experiences are generally similar except for income. Table 5.2 presents comparative data about employment status. Most mothers and fathers were employed full time, and most worked for someone else. Few were self-employed or owned businesses.

Nevertheless, Nicaraguan parents are significantly worse off financially than other parents in southern Florida—their average household income of $1,820.90 per month was the lowest among all immigrant groups (on average, all other immigrants earned $2,266.98 per month). Similarly, the probability of earnings above $50,000 or more per year

Figure 5.2. Total Yearly Income for Immigrant Parents

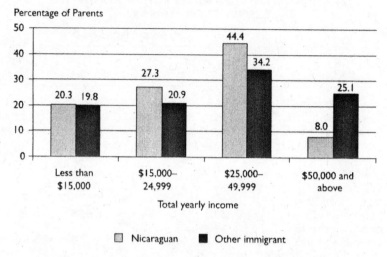

Percentage of Parents

NOTE: The income differences are statistically significant using a chi-square test p-value ≤ .05.

was one-third that of other immigrants (see Figure 5.2). Some of this may be a function of recent arrival. Nevertheless, the educational background and middle-class extraction of Nicaraguans contrasts with their modest achievements in the United States. Their relatively greater dissatisfaction with their new lives is also evident from the survey data. Only 40 percent of the Nicaraguan parents were satisfied with their earnings as compared with 53 percent of immigrant parents of other nationalities.

Nicaraguans are also less likely to have received support from local or federal institutions to alleviate their vulnerability and insecurity. Table 5.3 reflects parents' perceptions about their fragile situation. Most Nicaraguan parents receive little or no assistance from government and charitable organizations.

The absence of legal status had a major impact on Nicaraguan employment prospects, receipt of help from state and nongovernment institutions, and capacity to prosper. In many cases it was a powerful leveling force, neutralizing experience and education. Such was the case of Pedro and Carmen Zúñiga. Since their arrival in 1987, they had lived in the same shabby apartment in Little Havana, unable to move to a better neighborhood for lack of means. Pedro had been born into an afflu-

TABLE 5.3   ADAPTATION AND INCORPORATION
OF NICARAGUAN AND OTHER SOUTHERN
FLORIDA PARENTS: ASSISTANCE RECEIVED
DURING FIRST YEAR IN THE UNITED STATES

Parent's Characteristics

	Nicaraguan	Other	Total	Sample Size
Received assistance during first year[1]				
None	96.8	84.2	86.4	1,080
From government	2.6	12.6	10.8	
From charity	0.5	3.3	2.8	
Contact with agencies or government				
None	54.3	59.7	58.7	1,052
Helpful	36.7	33.4	34.0	
Not helpful	9.0	6.8	7.2	

[1]Significant differences between Nicaraguans and others (chi-square p-value $\leq .05$).

ent family that owned a food processing plant. He had studied chemistry at the University of Managua. One of his prized possessions was a certificate of his former position as a full-time instructor in the Department of Engineering at the same institution. With such a background, he never doubted his ability to succeed abroad. In 1995 he was working as a chemist in a pharmaceutical company, but he had been unable to achieve legal residency. Tormented by regular notices of imminent deportation, he explained his predicament in the following way:

> I am in charge of quality control. I develop formulas and analytical methods at the laboratory, and I supervise the production of medications as well, but my situation is paradoxical, contradictory. I have the credentials to advance in this country. On the other hand, they are shutting all doors for my advancement. I am being blocked.

In addition to obstructed occupational mobility, Zúñiga felt that his uncertain legal status had had a deleterious effect on the family's income:

> [Because I have only an expired work permit] I get paid less than I should. I earn $10 an hour at most. Also, I do the work of three different professionals [quality control, development, and production] but I have no benefits or medical insurance. . . . The company takes advantage of my situation and I have no choice.

TABLE 5.4   PERCEPTIONS OF INCORPORATION
AMONG NICARAGUAN AND OTHER SOUTHERN
FLORIDA PARENTS

Parent's Characteristics

	Nicaraguan (%)	Other (%)	Total (%)	Sample Size
Discrimination experience				
Never	70.0	69.2	69.3	1,071
Rarely	11.0	9.8	10.0	
Occasionally	9.5	14.7	13.8	
Often	9.5	6.3	6.8	
Compared with other people of other races, views opportunities for advancement as . . .				
Less	29.4	16.1	18.4	846
Same	64.4	79.3	76.7	
More	6.2	4.6	4.8	
White Americans consider themselves . . .				
Superior	58.4	58.3	58.3	1,063
Equal	18.9	19.2	19.2	
Don't know or depends	22.6	22.4	22.5	

Such anecdotal claims of discrimination are reflected in our larger sample of Nicaraguan parents. Tables 5.4 and 5.5 show results for perceptions of discrimination from outside the Nicaraguan community and perceptions of social support from within it. In general, Nicaraguan parents' discernment of prejudice was not significantly higher than for other immigrants. Nevertheless, they were more likely to view their opportunities for advancement as diminished by comparison with other groups. Perhaps more significant are the perceptions of reduced solidarity in the Nicaraguan community. By comparison with other groups, Nicaraguan parents were significantly more likely to state that their conationals are "not at all" or "only a little helpful," even when living in the same neighborhood. Similar views are typical of groups besieged by poverty and marginality.[5]

In Miami the dire conditions surrounding Nicaraguans contrast with those that facilitated Cuban adaptation to American society. Compar-

TABLE 5.5   ADAPTATION AND INCORPORATION
OF NICARAGUAN AND OTHER SOUTHERN
FLORIDA PARENTS: SOCIAL SUPPORT

	Parent's Characteristics			
	Nicaraguan (%)	Other (%)	Total (%)	Sample Size
How much do people from respondent's country help each other in the U.S.?[1]				
Not at all	16.0	12.3	13.0	1,046
A little	47.3	20.9	25.6	
Somewhat	23.4	29.2	28.2	
A lot	13.3	37.5	33.2	
People from respondent's country who live in the neighborhood do not help[1]				
True	35.0	14.2	17.8	1,037
False	35.5	57.4	53.5	
Don't know	29.5	28.4	28.6	
People from respondent's country have not been economically successful[1]				
True	29.5	10.0	13.5	1,070
False	63.2	79.7	76.7	
Don't know	7.4	10.3	9.8	

[1]Significant differences between Nicaraguans and others (chi-square p-value $\leq$ .05).

isons heightened the sting of injury. Cubans had been able to form a moral community not solely on the basis of their opposition to communism but also as a result of external support to their collective self-definition. Such backing was manifested in terms of government policy but also by way of positive local responses to the Cuban plight. The interaction between external validation and collective narratives reinforced a sense of common intent.

The opposite occurred among Nicaraguans. Without rhetorical elements to strengthen internal cohesion, they atomized. Yet the structural causes of their fragmentation remained concealed by cultural accounts: "Those poor unfortunate people," said Roberto Tijerino, a Nicaraguan professional, about his compatriots, "we who are luckier or richer have not helped them because, you see, Nicaraguans are very individualistic; solidarity is not our strength."

Lack of solidarity extended beyond group boundaries. According to Pedro Zúñiga, the situation was upsetting because "when Cubans arrive in rafts, they automatically receive their residency." Carmen, his wife, agreed. She had been trying to upgrade her degree as a pharmacist and to learn English at Miami-Dade Community College, but she felt that her treatment was unfair:

> I have to pay for all my courses [and they're not cheap]. Yet a classmate of mine who is Cuban and came in a raft a few weeks ago receives government assistance, and that includes an allowance for books and transportation.

Without symbolic and material resources to ease their settlement, Nicaraguan parents were ill equipped to offer their children the advantages they had contemplated before the diaspora. It is to this question that we now turn.

What Was the Impact on Children?

Despite their vulnerable circumstances, Nicaraguan parents strove to safeguard their offspring and instill in them a sense of national self-regard. Their involvement in their children's lives and their efforts to foster national pride may be reflections of their poor reception in the United States or recent arrival. Nevertheless, their behavior is a significant departure from that of other immigrant parents. Table 5.6 shows findings about parental attitudes and practices in that respect. The first row compares parents' assessment of the weight they assign to children's knowledge about their home country. More than parents in any other group, the vast majority of Nicaraguans believed it is important to know about the homeland. Although they were less inclined to volunteer at schools—probably because of limited linguistic ability—they were more likely than other immigrant parents to know their children's friends' names and their friends' parents' names. We take that as an indication of Nicaraguans' dogged involvement in their children's lives.

Yet the absence of legal residency, and the ensuing fracture of the collective self-definition, had more than a passing effect on the capacity of parents to bolster credibility in the eyes of their own children. Carmen Zúñiga's most serious concern was that her son, Pedro Jr., who was already in the tenth grade and would soon be old enough to go to

TABLE 5.6   PARENTAL ATTITUDES AND
PRACTICES TOWARD CHILDREN

	Mother's Characteristics		Father's Characteristics	
	Nicaraguan	Other	Nicaraguan	Other
Is it important for respondent's child to know about respondent's country?[1]				
A little	1.5%	6.1%	3.4%	7.6%
Somewhat	3.8%	13.5%	6.9%	14.5%
A lot	94.7%	80.4%	89.7%	77.9%
Does respondent ever work as vol. at child's school?[1]				
Yes	31.5	57.0	34.5	61.9
Number of child's friends' names known[1]				
Mean	13.7	10.9	15.3	13.6
(std. dev.)	(21.6)	(16.0)	(23.4)	(19.9)
Number of child's friends' parent's names known				
Mean	10.2	8.0	12.4	10.3
(std. dev.)	(20.0)	(12.8)	(23.9)	(17.3)
SAMPLE SIZE	N = 132	N = 620	N = 58	N = 259

[1]Significant differences between Nicaraguans and others (chi-square p-value ≤ .05).

college, would be stopped dead in his tracks. Like his parents, he had no legal papers. For that reason, the mother's hopes were dim:

> I encourage him to do better than us. A professional career in Nicaragua was expensive but we invested in it; then we lost all because of the political situation. Here we are nothing; our degrees are not recognized. Time is passing and [my son] should be able to get a summer job but he can't because of his undocumented situation.

Pedro Jr., who had been a child of 10 when the family first came to Miami in 1987, had his own anxieties. He didn't believe his parents

TABLE 5.7   LANGUAGE AND EDUCATIONAL ADAPTATION AMONG NICARAGUAN AND OTHER IMMIGRANT STUDENTS IN SOUTHERN FLORIDA

	1992 Outcomes		1996 Outcomes	
	Nicaraguan	Other	Nicaraguan	Other
Language ability				
Bilingual	40.6%[1]	33.0%	47.4%[1]	37.9%
English dominant	27.8%[1]	49.9%	29.7%[1]	50.0%
Foreign lang. dom.	15.8%[1]	4.9%	8.3%[1]	2.7%
Limited bilingual	15.8%[1]	12.2%	14.7%[1]	9.3%
Language preference				
Prefers English	74.4%[1]	80.0%	89.1%[1]	93.4%
Academic achievement				
Math test score[2]	58.6	60.0	—	—
(std. dev)	(25.6)	(27.6)		
Reading test score[2]	39.4[1]	46.7	—	—
(std. dev.)	(23.8)	(24.6)		
Mean GPA	2.4	2.4	2.3	2.3
(std. dev.)	(0.9)	(0.9)	(0.8)	(0.9)
Dropped out 1992–1996	—	—	8.7%	8.9%
SAMPLE SIZE				
Only those reinterviewed in 1996	N = 266	N = 1959	N = 266	N = 1959

[1]Significant differences between Nicaraguans and Others (chi-square p-value $\leq$ .05)
[2]National percentiles in Stanford Achievement Test.
NOTE: Percent distributions within columns (except where noted).

had the ability to improve the family's position significantly. And neither did he think they understood how difficult it was to succeed in the kind of school he attended. There were 36 students in his classroom and noise all the time. Teachers ignored disruptive students. He had the impression that they simply didn't care.

Pedro's experience was typical of Nicaraguan youngsters. Table 5.7 compares Nicaraguan students with other immigrant students in terms of language ability, language preference, and academic achievement. We compare results across the two years in which interviews were conducted for this study.

Nicaraguan students were more likely to report strong bilingual abilities than their counterparts in other national groups and that tendency

Figure 5.3.   Ethnic Identification among Immigrant Students, 1992–1996

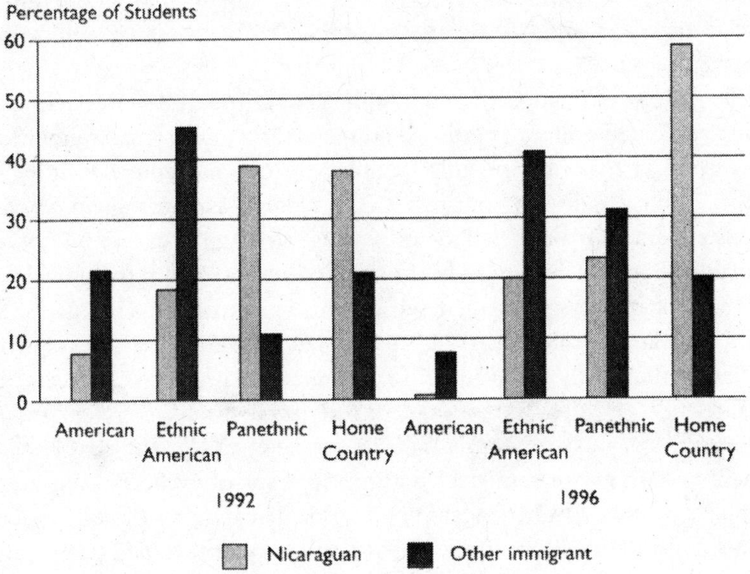

Percentage of Students

augmented over time. On the other hand, they were less likely than other youngsters to prefer English. Although their math abilities are no different from those of other immigrant students, they perform significantly worse on standardized reading tests. Other than these distinctions, Nicaraguan students appeared to exhibit few differences in academic achievement compared to other immigrant students in southern Florida.

Ethnic identity formation is an important aspect of immigrant adaptation and incorporation. Again, the Nicaraguan experience and expressions of ethnic identity formation are unique among the immigrant groups. In Figure 5.3 we compare ethnic identification for Nicaraguan students and other immigrant students across time. At first, Nicaraguan children showed an inclination to define themselves as Hispanic, a panethnic category. With the passage of time, however, they showed an increased propensity to identify with their home country. This finding is remarkable, and we give it full consideration later in this chapter. Here it will suffice to say that studies of immigration consistently have shown that increased length of residence in the United States tends to usher American or hyphenated American identities (Kazal 1995; Lieberson 1980; Simons 1901). Among Nicaraguan children the opposite is true: An inclination to identify with their home country has grown over time.

To gain a better understanding of the change in self-definition among Nicaraguan children, we regressed ethnic identity and a small number of predictive factors in 1996 upon similar factors and ethnic identity in 1992. Table 5.8 displays our results. To identify as Nicaraguan or Hispanic significantly predicted identifying as Nicaraguan in 1996. In other words, the trend was twofold: Those who identified with the homeland in the first place retained that self-definition, but those who identified with the larger category of Hispanic later reverted to Nicaraguan. Whether the family received help from relatives was also significant in that respect. Children in families that received assistance from kin members were less likely to think of themselves solely as Nicaraguan in 1996. These variations are consistent with perceptions of exclusion and weak support from kin and friendship networks. They are also in correspondence with the positive effect of 1992 grade point average (GPA) and parent's employment upon Nicaraguan identity. We give fuller attention to these issues in the next section.

To better understand patterns of academic achievement among Nicaraguan students, we also examined the significant factors influencing GPAs in 1996 (see Table 5.9). Gender stands out as a significant variable. On the whole, girls ranked higher than boys. Fathers' educational attainment and the child's bilingual ability were important factors improving GPAs in 1996. Finally, families who received help from relatives during the first year of residence had children whose GPAs were significantly higher in 1996 than those of Nicaraguans who had received little or no assistance.

Other aspects of adaptation and assimilation, which might be related to ethnic identity formation, are perceptions and experiences of discrimination. Here, Nicaraguan students stand out relative to other immigrant students. Perceptions of discrimination were much stronger among Nicaraguans than among youngsters in other groups. In 1992, 51.33 percent of Nicaraguan students experienced discrimination compared with 44.79 percent among the other immigrant students in the sample. By 1996, however, this difference diminished, and more than half of all of immigrant students experienced discrimination. The bite of prejudice is strongly felt in schools where daily interaction teaches

TABLE 5.8 SIGNIFICANT INFLUENCES
UPON NICARAGUAN STUDENTS' ETHNIC
IDENTITY IN 1996

Ethnic Identity in 1996

	Nicaraguan	Hispanic	Other
Ethnic identity in 1992			
Nicaraguan	66.7%	14.0%	19.3%
Hispanic	58.2%	24.3%	17.5%
Other	36.5%	31.7%	31.7%
Family received help from relatives during first year in U.S.			
Yes	49.1%	32.2%	18.6%
No	57.3%	19.4%	23.3%
GPA in 1992			
Mean	2.5	2.4	2.3
(std. dev.)	(0.8)	(0.9)	(1.0)
At least one parent employed full time in 1992			
Yes	57.9%	21.5%	20.6%
No	46.4%	25.0%	28.6%

NOTE: (N = 238). These factors were identified through the estimation of a multinomial logistic regression equation that also included the following variables: gender, age, strong bilingual ability, language preference, discrimination experience (yes/no), whether the student's friendship network includes Nicaraguans, father's educational achievement (college or more vs. less than college, and year of arrival (pre-1980 versus 1980s).

immigrant children their place in the new society (Matute-Bianchi 1986). According to 17-year-old Pedro Zúñiga Jr.:

> Different people treat you different; they discriminate you because of the way you talk, the way you do things. They make fun of you; they call you stupid, Indian! Most of all Cubans look down on Nicaraguans. It bothers me but I try to ignore it.

Perceptions of discrimination often correlate with a lackluster performance in school. This was true for Pedro, whose disquiet was compounded by low academic achievement. As in the case of other Nicaraguan children, his hopes were high but his grades were slipping. Table 5.8, discussed previously, shows that Nicaraguan students scored significantly below students in other groups on reading tests when they

TABLE 5.9   SIGNIFICANT FACTORS
INFLUENCING NICARAGUAN STUDENTS'
GPA IN 1996

	GPA in 1996	
	Mean	Standard Deviation
Gender		
Boy	2.1	0.9
Girl	2.5	0.7
Father's education		
College or more	2.4	0.8
Less than college	2.2	0.7
Language ability		
Bilingual	2.4	0.8
English dominant	2.4	0.9
Spanish dominant	2.3	0.7
Limited bilingual	1.9	0.7
Family received help during first year in United States		
Yes	2.5	0.8
No	2.3	0.8
Nicaraguan Boys ($N = 128$)		
Language ability		
Bilingual	2.4	0.8
English dominant	2.1	1.0
Spanish dominant	2.0	0.8
Limited bilingual	1.5	0.6
Nicaraguan Girls ($N = 138$)		
Father's education		
College or more	2.6	0.7
Less than college	2.3	0.7
Language used with friends		
Spanish	2.4	0.7
English	2.7	0.8

NOTE: Significant factors were determined through an ordinary least-squares regression model that also included the following factors measured in 1992: age, whether friends were Nicaraguan, ethnic identity, discrimination experience, year of arrival, father's education, and father's current employment status (models for boys and girls run separately, excluding gender).

were first interviewed. Even more frustrating for many children was the breach between their experience and that of their parents (Adams, Gullotta, and Montemayor 1992). Pedro felt that his mother and father demanded too much but were in no position to offer assistance:

> [My parents] say I don't do enough homework. They don't understand that some teachers don't give you homework. Then I get a C and they tell me it's bad; all I hear is bad! Bad! Bad! I was getting good grades but then I got an F in English because I can't understand the teacher. I want to ask the right questions but, like, I don't know how to ask. My parents can't help me either. . . . I try but they don't appreciate it.

Pedro's experience was typical of a new generation, characterized by temporal and physical distance from the values and standards that had led their seniors to migrate yet unable to gain a foothold on the new social terrain. To see Pedro in the same room with his parents was to witness the external effects of intergenerational decline. Despite their troubles, the Zúñigas dressed formally, in a middle-class style, and spoke both English and Spanish articulately. Pedro Jr. donned the normative attire of inner-city youngsters and spoke neither English nor Spanish fluently. He had spent too much of his life in the United States to remember his mother tongue. Trapped in a Hispanic neighborhood, he had been unable to master English. His was the worst of both worlds.

The distance between immigrant parents and their children is magnified by other factors. Especially troubling is the case of women unable to control and discipline teenagers because they lack adequate linguistic skills. Although Spanish is the language spoken in most Nicaraguan households, children use English to communicate with each other and with their friends (Portes and Hao 1998). In adolescence, they often wield that language to separate from their parents and oust them from their lives. Remedios Acuña described a common experience when saying, "I try to keep an eye on Lourdes, my daughter. She's fourteen and almost a woman. She spends hours on the phone but I can't understand most of what she says. She's leaving me out!" Feelings of exclusion are compounded when children must stand for their parents in the public realm. This role reversal of sorts, which blurs the distinctions between adults and minors, is especially galling. When Mrs. Acuña was summoned by the principal of her daughter's school to discuss the girl's repeated absences, she had to rely on Lourdes for translation. Originally unaware of her daughter's trespasses, she was not sure afterwards whether the principal's words (or hers) had been rendered accurately.

An illegal status and limited linguistic ability can further debilitate parents' influence and children's commitment to school. Even youngsters with high ambitions have felt the temptation to work to assist their families. Such was the case of 15-year-old Roger Lacayo, who applied for legal residency to qualify for a summer job and save for college. His appeal was rejected. Although he was an excellent student who aspired to become a psychologist, Roger frequently considered dropping out of school:

> [I think about it] a lot because . . . I feel guilty that my parents have to struggle so much; if I got a job, even an illegal one, I could help them. For us [Nicaraguans in the United States], education is a dream.

Although they speak highly of their adopted country as a place of opportunity and freedom, Nicaraguan parents believe that the character of elementary and secondary education is inferior in the United States and that the spirit of community is weak by comparison with that of their country of origin. An emphasis on material consumption competes, often successfully, with their attempts at instilling in children a sense of discipline and scholastic ambition. Carmen Zúñiga complained that

> [youngsters] don't go to school to study but to model the latest fashions. They demand expensive shoes even when their parents can't afford them. It's all competition. If a kid brings a beeper to school, everybody wants one.

When immigrants belong in social networks characterized by low levels of internal differentiation and when they confront a hostile reception, their authority is eroded further (Fernández-Kelly 1995). According to Dolores Rivas, from Masaya, Nicaragua:

> If people . . . study, they can become anything they want, anything! But there is too much freedom in the United States. My son was bumming around with a bunch of friends, like in a gang, you know. He . . . ended up in jail. But why should that surprise me? The quality of education is very poor and there are all kinds of discipline problems in schools.

Even more telling was the case of Maura Maldonado, a divorced woman who had lived in the United States since 1976. She did not speak English well, partly because she had always worked in garment factories where everyone else spoke Spanish. In 1993, she was making disproportionate mortgage payments for a run-down house in Little

Havana.[6] In her living room, cluttered with bundles of fabric, a grandson, recently arrived from Masaya, was sewing T-shirts.

Mrs. Maldonado said she had a firm belief in education. Therefore, she worried about her daughter, Julliette, who was planning to marry at 17. There was little hope that she would finish high school. Unknown to her mother was that Julliette had been pregnant for three months. Four of Mrs. Maldonado's six children had serious troubles. One was in jail for attempted car theft. These had been harsh blows for Mrs. Maldonado, who thought of herself as a failure. Julliette had similar feelings. Marriage was her chance "to get away." For almost two years, she had worked long shifts at a fast food restaurant for $4.25 an hour. Her top resentment was her mother's expectation that she use all her earnings to help support the family.

The perceptions of mother and daughter were strikingly different. Mrs. Maldonado said she wanted Julliette to stay in school and achieve. Julliette felt she was expected to work long hours and make a substantial contribution to the family income. The older woman thus suffered from a credibility gap caused by the breach between her values and the need to improve her precarious economic situation. Her faith in learning did not seem believable to her daughter, who felt torn by her mother's mixed messages. Similarly, Julliette's decision to have a child expressed a conviction that, having worked to support the family since the age of 16 and having known her boyfriend even longer, it was time for her to be recognized as an adult. Such ideas are common among impoverished adolescents as shown, most dramatically, by the experience of African-American youngsters in urban ghettos. Aware that schools in their neighborhoods do not provide them with skills that can be parlayed into decent jobs, many turn to their bodies in search of empowerment (Fernández-Kelly 1995). Making a substantial contribution to the support of a family, whatever the means; having a child; and living independently are interpreted as proof of maturity. Most of the time, those behaviors parallel the abandonment of educational aspirations.

Intergenerational gaps in perceptions and experience frequently yield feelings of nostalgia. As parents gain a better understanding of the dangers surrounding their children, their longing for the country left behind increases. When asked whether she would have preferred to raise her children in Nicaragua, Norma González answered in the affirmative:

Things are simpler [in Nicaragua]; parents enjoy more authority and it is easier to move about. Here children, especially boys, want to be independent too soon. We try to deal with our children intelligently. We know that we can't give them many of the material things their friends have but we try to get them some, hoping they won't go looking for them by selling drugs or joining gangs.

Yet probable outcomes—academic deficiency, school abandonment, premature participation in the labor force, and involvement in illegal activities—are not inevitable. Among the forces that can neutralize preponderant trends are English proficiency, legal residency, and a home in a good neighborhood. Nelson Tijerino and his family were a case in point. Nicaraguans who had obtained legal status in 1983, they lived in Miami's Coral Park, a well-appointed subdivision. Nelson's father, Roberto, had a bachelor's degree from the University of Managua and worked in the import-export department of a cruise company. The Tijerinos shared a three-bedroom house with other relatives with whom they pooled expenses. They made a smaller mortgage payment than Maura Maldonado for a property of superior quality.

Mr. Tijerino was very satisfied with his son's school, and he had no problems getting respect from him. He was confident that Nelson would finish college. The father's and the son's perceptions were on a par with those of Cubans living in similar circumstances. Nelson liked to be with his family better than with friends. He spoke glowingly about how close he was to his father. Perhaps more tellingly, he had a hopeful image of himself as a Nicaraguan American: "Nicaraguan because I like the food, American because this is my country."

In choosing how to define himself, Nelson was not alone. The ways in which Nicaraguan children are rethinking their position in American society is the subject of the next section.

How Is Identity Changing across Generations?

Immigrants repeatedly engage in purposeful acts to signify their intended character and the way they differ from other groups. A common feature among first-generation immigrants, including Nicaraguans, is that they hold the image of the urban underclass as a pivotal referent to delineate their own place in the new society. They do not perceive inner-city blacks as the disaffected children and grandchildren of internal migrants from the American South but as the very antithesis of their own immigrant condition (Fernández-Kelly 1994; Massey 1993). While new arrivals view themselves as industrious, individualistic, and self-reliant, they see poor blacks as lazy, dependent, and contentious. As a result, social distress is seen as the effect of values and behaviors inimical to those that immigrants expect to deploy in their own pursuit of success. A typical, albeit complex, opinion of American blacks was held by Antonia Miranda:

> They have been discriminated but now they like that situation because it allows them to receive special benefits from the government. We would never think to ask. They don't even have to work but they have lots of children. . . . Maybe they have aspirations like us but they don't have the same spunk. . . . I pity them for their ignorance but sometimes I wish I was black so that I knew the language and could improve my situation.

Across generations, the picture shifts: Many Nicaraguan children do not think of black and Latino youngsters living in tough neighborhoods as a vantage point for self-differentiation. Some do precisely the opposite; they see them as the architects of a new adversarial culture to be emulated. Through interactions with them in schools, parks, and other public spaces, they learn a distinct meaning of being American. This makes for high drama. Whether immigrant children shun or embrace the purported culture of the ghetto has a measurable impact upon their potential for economic and social advancement.

In the hazardous geometry of race, class, and ethnicity, outcomes vary in surprising ways. At 16, Richard Pérez had given up hopes of becoming an American. He was an indifferent student, a self-described "freak" who did not want to follow the rules:

> My parents, they want me to fit in but, like, who ever said you had to be American to have a life? We are here but we don't belong, right? So we should be proud to be Nicaraguan—create our own world, our own rules. . . . Like blacks, we are victims, minorities . . . but (blacks) know how to kick ass, stand up for themselves, and they don't answer to nobody.

Richard backed that characterization by his way of dress, a deliberate imitation of ghetto cool, and by his tastes in music. Rap artists were his favorite. His preferences and demeanor pointed to a larger process: the incorporation of Nicaraguan youth into the most vulnerable segments of urban America (Portes 1995).

The narratives excerpted previously illustrate the triangular relationship between social processes, material resources, and self-definition. Collective identity emerges as both cause and effect from that triangular interaction. In other words, although material circumstances lead to the formation of distinctive identities, these are not mechanical products but relatively autonomous forces that can buttress behavioral outcomes. The downward pressures caused by impeded assimilation consistently lead to ethnic self-definitions. Those, in turn—as in the case of Richard Pérez—can justify a disappointing academic performance or become an instrument for protection and resistance.

There are other ways, however, to negotiate the vicissitudes of life in an unfriendly environment. Claiming membership in a category of people larger than one's own group is one of them (Portes and MacLeod 1996). That is what many Nicaraguan children attempted to do when describing themselves as Hispanic. It was a way to symbolically associate with Cubans, who constitute the mainstream in Miami and with whom they share linguistic and cultural similarities. Youngsters who expected to succeed in the United States experienced a particularly strong dissociative push away from their own national group. The empirical data presented in the previous sections reflects that trend; students with better educational prospects and greater social supports were more likely, and increasingly over time, to identify as Hispanic or as Nicaraguan American.

That was the case of 16-year old Elsie Rivas. She avoided discrimination by shifting between a Hispanic and a Nicaraguan self-definition at school and at the supermarket where she worked. She didn't like the way Nicaraguans spoke because

> They are vulgar, ignorant.... When I am with my Cuban friends I can speak to them normally but some Nicaraguans make me feel ashamed and I am tempted to deny my nationality; they make all of us look bad because of the way they express themselves, with all the bad words and the cussing.

In other words, Nicaraguan children confronted a forked path. Those unable to negotiate a successful adjustment into American society were increasingly emphasizing Nicaraguan identity as part of an emerging minority status. This entailed a shift from national to ethnic self-definitions. Nicaraguan children facing auspicious perspectives did otherwise; they increasingly identified with the country where they had lived most of their lives or found respite in the panethnic category of Hispanic.

In that respect, Alicia Rivas, Elsie's younger sister, held the definitive view. She did not care for invidious distinctions. Sometimes she thought of herself as Hispanic; at other times she preferred Nicaraguan American. It didn't really matter to her because, as she said, "My parents came from Nicaragua but I am really American, more American than those born in this country. Here is where I grew up and here is where I am going to stay."

And so it was one way or another.

Conclusion

The perceptions of immigrants and their children about themselves and other groups are not always accurate. What matters, however, is that those perceptions are an integral part of a social process that will eventually yield what Bellah et al. (1985) call "communities of memory." In their journey, the immigrant children of today are already forging tomorrow's ethnic identities. Through contact, friction, and negotiation, immigrant children are gradually moving into distinct sectors of the larger society. Collective self-definitions will improve or worsen depending on the opportunities available to them.

Damaged or buoyant group identities do not emerge in a vacuum; they are mediated by such mechanisms as legal status, schools, and the ability of parents to shield their children from leveling pressures wielded by institutions and the market economy. How youngsters define themselves often depends on whether they and their parents have successfully resisted those pressures.

Finally, we have stressed the fluid nature of group identity. Self-definitions can act either to augment or deflect stigma depending on circumstances. Among Nicaraguans, the panethnic category *Hispanic* presented sundry possibilities that ranged from affinity with to estrangement from the larger society. When confronting negative stereotypes about their national provenance, it served as an umbrella offering proximity to a larger group without stigma. By contrast, *Nicaraguan,* originally a national designation, has experienced a crucial shift in meaning—it is, increasingly, an ethnic label demonstrating, once again, that there is nothing static about group identity. In the reflux of hope and despair, defensiveness and compliance, resistance and accommodation, collective self-definitions emerge both as the imprimatur of structural factors and as the manifestation of human agency butting heads against those structures.

Notes

The authors gratefully acknowledge the research contribution of Cesar Rosado, doctoral student in sociology at Princeton University. An earlier draft of this paper benefited from discussion at the Seminar on Ethnicity and the New Second Generation, Princeton University, June 19–20, 1998.

1. Estimates vary. The 1990 U.S. Census Bureau reports 74,244 Nicaraguans living in Dade County. Community organizations argue that there are over

250,000. The Planning Department of metropolitan Dade County places the figure at a conservative 90,000. The Statistical Yearbooks of the Immigration and Naturalization Service, the most reliable source, report approximately 280,000 Nicaraguans in the United States. Of these, approximately 50 percent live in Dade County (Cordova 1999).

2. This and other direct quotations in this chapter are taken from a series of 42 interviews conducted by the first author in Miami during 1995–1996 as part of the Children of Immigrants Longitudinal Study (CILS). The names of individuals are pseudonyms.

3. Data come from the Nicaraguan Florida respondents in CILS and from a series of in-depth interviews with 20 youngsters and their parents. The original sample consisted of 340 students interviewed for the first time in 1992. Two hundred and eighty-one of those respondents were reinterviewed in 1995. Thus, the level of attrition between the first and second dates was 18.5 percent, one of the lowest among the ethnic groups represented in the data file. There are only minor differences between students who were successfully interviewed in the two dates and those who were lost after 1992.

4. For a classic account of the importance and functions of social networks, see Granovetter 1990.

5. For a dramatic illustration of this phenomenon among immigrants from El Salvador, see Menjívar 1999.

6. Isolation is another factor marking the Nicaraguan experience. Many families ended up living in areas where resources are costly but of reduced quality. Seeking linguistic and cultural similarities, migrants gravitate toward neighborhoods where conationals reside. Although they offer some initial advantages, those neighborhoods tend to entrap them.

References

Adams, Gerald R., Thomas P. Gullotta, and Raymond Montemayor, eds. 1992. *Adolescent identity formation.* Newbury Park, Calif.: Sage Publications.

Bellah, Robert N., R. Madsen, W. M. Sullivan, A. Swidler, and S. M. Tipton. 1985. *Habits of the heart: Individualism and commitment in American life.* Berkeley: University of California Press.

Cordova, Carlos and Raquel Pinderhughes. 1999. "Central and South Americans in the United States." In *A Nation of Peoples: A Sourcebook on America's Multicultural Heritage,* edited by Elliot Barkin, Westport, CT: Greewood Press.

Fernández-Kelly, Patricia. 1994. Divided fates: Immigrant children in a restructured economy. *International Migration Review* 28 (4), pp. 662.

——. 1995. Towanda's triumph: Social and cultural capital in the transition to adulthood in the urban ghetto. *International Journal of Urban and Regional Research* 18 (1), pp. 89–111.

Granovetter, Mark. 1990. "The old and the new economic sociology: A history and an agenda." In *Beyond the marketplace*, edited by R. Friedland and A. F. Robertson. New York: Aldine de Gruyter.

Kazal, Russell. 1995. Revisiting assimilation: The rise, fall and reappraisal of a concept in American ethnic history. *American Historical Review* 100, no. 2 (April), pp. 437–471.

Lieberson, Stanley. 1980. *A piece of the pie: Blacks and white immigrants since 1880.* Berkeley: University of California Press.

Massey, Douglas S. 1993. Latinos, poverty, and the underclass: A new agenda for research. *Hispanic Journal of Behavioral Sciences* 15 (4), pp. 449–475.

Matute-Bianchi, M. G. 1986. Ethnic identities and patterns of school success and failure among Mexican-descent and Japanese-American students in a California high school: An ethnographic analysis. *American Journal of Education* 95 (2), pp. 233–255.

Menjívar, Cecilia. 2000. *Fragmented Ties: Salvadoran Immigrant Networks in America.* Berkeley: University of California Press.

Ogbu, John U. 1991. "Immigrant and involuntary minorities in comparative perspective." In *Minority status and schooling: A comparative study of immigrant and involuntary minorities,* edited by Margaret A. Gibson and John U. Ogbu. New York: Garland.

Portes, Alejandro. 1995. "Children of immigrants: Segmented assimilation and its determinants." In *The economic sociology of immigration: Essays on networks, ethnicity, and entrepreneurship,* edited by Alejandro Portes. New York: Russell Sage Foundation.

Portes, Alejandro, and Lingxin Hao. 1998. E pluribus unum: Bilingualism and loss of language in the second generation. *Sociology of Education* 71 (October), pp. 269–294.

Portes, Alejandro, and Dag MacLeod. 1996. What shall I call myself? Hispanic identity formation in the second generation. *Ethnic and Racial Studies* 19, no. 3 (July), pp. 524–547.

Portes, Alejandro, and Rubén G. Rumbaut. 1996. *Immigrant America: A portrait.* Berkeley: University of California Press.

Portes, Alejandro, and M. Zhou. 1993. The new second generation: Segmented assimilation and its variants. *Annals of the American Academy of Political and Social Science* 530 (November), pp. 74–96.

Simons, S. 1901. Social assimilation. *American Journal of Sociology* 6 (4), pp, 790–822.

U.S. Immigration and Naturalization Service. 1993. *Statistical yearbook of the Immigration and Naturalization Service.* Washington, D.C.: U.S. Government Printing Office.

Chapter 6

THE PARADOX OF ASSIMILATION
Children of Filipino Immigrants in San Diego

Yen Le Espiritu and Diane L. Wolf

Filipinos constitute the largest Asian-origin immigrant group in California and in the United States; their post-1965 migration to the United States is the second largest only after the Mexican migration. Despite these numbers, Filipino Americans remain a remarkably understudied and overlooked group both in U.S. culture and in academic research. Some speculate that Filipinos are neglected by academics in part because they blend in so easily to the U.S. landscape, particularly those who arrived after 1965, due to their largely urban, professional, and middle-class backgrounds and lifestyles. Indeed, coming from a former U.S. colony, Filipino immigrants tend to be proficient in English and have long been exposed to U.S. lifestyles, cultural practices, and consumption patterns, so much so that before "the Filipino . . . sets foot on the U.S. continent—she, her body, and sensibility—has been prepared by the thoroughly Americanized culture of the homeland" (San Juan 1991: 118). Despite and perhaps because of this ability to blend in, it is imperative that we better understand this group of immigrants.

Drawing on quantitative data from the longitudinal CILS study and qualitative data we have collected in our own research,[1] this paper examines the adaptive trajectories of the children of Filipino immigrants in San Diego, California, by focusing on their patterns of academic achievement and ambition, ethnic identity shifts, and psychological well-being. The Filipino case is paradoxical. On the one hand, the socioeconomic data indicate that Filipino immigrants and their children are relatively successful, acculturated, and assimilated. On the other hand, the data on ethnic self-identities and emotional well-being suggest a concurrent countertrend: First, a significant proportion of young Filipinos reject the assimilative identity *American,* and second, they register relatively lower self-esteem and higher depression than other immigrant groups. We argue that these findings raise significant questions about the conception of assimilation as a linear process—one that leads to increasing identificational assimilation and to improvements in immigrant outcomes over time and generation in the United States (Rumbaut 1997).

Our chapter begins with the broader historical context of Filipino immigration to the United States, to California, and to the research site, San Diego; followed by a delineation of the socioeconomic status of the Filipino CILS sample and the academic achievements and ambitions of young Filipinos. We then examine what it means to grow up as children of Filipino immigrants in San Diego by focusing on shifts in ethnic identity and perceptions of discrimination, the quality of family relationships, and emotional well-being. From our analysis, it is clear that race and gender mark most aspects of young Filipino lives and constitute crucial axes along which children of Filipino immigrants must be understood.

The Context of Filipino Migrations

Unlike European or other Asian groups, Filipinos come from a homeland that was once a U.S. colony. Therefore, the Filipino-American history of immigration and settlement can best be understood within the context of the colonial and postcolonial association between the Philippines and the United States. In 1898, following the Spanish-American War, the United States assumed colonial rule of the Philippines, thereby extending its so-called Manifest Destiny to the Pacific. The U.S. occupation affected all segments of Philippine society (Agoncillo and Guerrero 1970: 303–342). Beside creating strong military and business connections between the two countries, this colonial heritage produced a pervasive cultural Americanization of the population, exhorting Filipinos to regard American culture, society, values, political systems, and way of life as superior to their own (Pomeroy 1974: 171; Cariño

1987). Perhaps most importantly, U.S. colonizers revamped Philippine educational institutions and curricula using the American system as their model and English as the language of instruction. Filipino historian Renato Constantino (1994: 39) contends that the colonial educational system was an instrument of assimilation or Americanization because it "de-Filipinize(d) the youth, taught them to regard American culture as superior to any other, and American society as the model *par excellence* for Philippine society." Infected with colonial culture and with grand illusions about the United States, Filipinos soon started to migrate to what they had been taught to think of as the land of opportunity and fair play.

Like other Asian immigrants, pre–World War II Filipinos were an indispensable labor force that helped to build the American West and Hawaii. After U.S. immigration laws had barred the entry of Chinese in 1882 and Japanese laborers in 1908,[2] Filipinos became the favored source of labor because of their legal status as U.S. nationals (Vallangca 1977). As nationals, Filipinos could migrate freely to the United States; the Philippines thus became "the only available source of permanent labor supply" to fill the labor shortage created by the exclusion of other Asians (Dorita 1975: 40). In Hawaii, Filipinos toiled in the islands' sugar plantations; along the Pacific Coast, especially in California, most flocked to agriculture, forming the backbone of the migratory labor force that moved with the harvests (Chan 1990: 37). During the late 1920s and 1930s, as the Filipino population along the Pacific Coast grew and as the Great Depression engulfed the nation, white resentment against Filipino laborers intensified. To enable the government to restrict the number of Filipino immigrants, their status as U.S. nationals had to be changed. In 1934, yielding to anti-Filipino forces, the U.S. Congress passed the Tydings-McDuffie Independence Act, granting the Philippines eventual independence, declaring Filipinos to be aliens, and cutting Filipino immigration to a trickle of 50 persons a year (Melendy 1977: 27–28, 40–44).

Among the few who were exempted from this immigration restriction were Filipinos who served in the U.S. armed forces, especially in the U.S. Navy. Soon after the United States acquired the Philippines from Spain in 1898, its navy began actively to recruit Filipinos. Prior to and during World War I, the U.S. Navy allowed Filipino enlistees to serve in a range of occupational ratings. However, after the war, the naval authorities issued a new ruling restricting Filipinos, even those with a college education, to the ratings of officers' stewards and mess attendants (Lawcock 1975: 473).[3] In the early 1970s, responding to the demands of the Civil Rights movement and a senatorial investigation on the use of stewards in the military, the U.S. Navy amended its policies to grant Filipino nationals the right to enter any occupational rating (Espiritu 1995: 16). These navy-related immigrants form a distinct and significant segment of the Filipino-American community. In U.S. cities that have large naval facilities, such as San Diego, one can find sizable Filipino communities made up largely of navy families.

The 1965 Immigration Act abolished the national-origins quotas and permitted entry primarily on the basis of family reunification or occupational characteristics, dramatically increasing the number of immigrants from Asia. In the 20 years following passage of the 1965 Act, about 40 percent of the legal immigration to the United States came from Asia (Bouvier and Gardner 1986). The Philippines has been the largest source, with Filipinos comprising nearly one-quarter of the total Asian immigration. From 1961 to 1965, fewer than 16,000 Filipinos immigrated to the United States; from 1981 to 1985, this increased to more than 221,000. Since 1979, more than 40,000 Filipino immigrants have been admitted annually, making the Philippines the second-largest source of immigration to this country after Mexico (Cariño et al. 1990: 2). The 1990 U.S. Census of population counted close to 1.5 million Filipinos in the United States, 50 percent of whom resided in California.

Frustrated by scarce or inappropriate employment opportunities (and also by overpopulation and deteriorating political conditions) and influenced by images of U.S. abundance peddled by the educational system, the media, and relatives and friends already in the United States, many well-educated Filipinos seized the opportunity provided by the 1965 act to emigrate.[4] The push from the Philippines was also political. Declaring martial law in 1972, President Marcos prorogued the legislatures, controlled the media, suspended the writ of habeas corpus, and arrested many of his alleged political opponents (Berry 1989: 168). During the Marcos era, an estimated 300,000 Filipinos emigrated from the Philippines to the United States (Steinberg 1990: 129–130).

Since the 1960s, the Philippines has sent the largest number of professional immigrants to the United States (Rumbaut 1991). Due to the shortage of medical personnel in this country, particularly in the inner cities and in rural areas, doctors, nurses, and other health-related practitioners are overrepresented among the recent Filipino immigrants. Just as the early Filipino immigrants were recruited for farm labor, by the 1970s recent medical graduates in the Philippines were recruited to work in U.S. hospitals, nursing homes, and health organizations (Pido 1986: 85). In fact, the Philippines is the largest supplier of health professionals to the United States, sending nearly 25,000 nurses to this country between 1966 and 1985 and another 10,000 between 1989 and 1991 (Ong and Azores 1994: 154). Indeed, many of the nursing programs in the Philippines are oriented toward supplying the U.S. nursing labor market (Ong and Azores 1994). Once in the United States, however, strict licensing procedures and racial discrimination have forced many Filipino medical professionals to work as nurses' aides and laboratory assistants or in jobs that were totally unrelated to their knowledge and expertise (Takaki 1989: 434–436).

Not all of the contemporary immigrants from the Philippines are professionals, however. Instead, the dual goals of the 1965 Immigration Act—to facilitate family reunification and to admit workers needed by the U.S. economy—have produced two distinct chains of emigration from the Philippines: one comprising the relatives of Filipinos who had immigrated to the United States prior to 1965 and one of highly trained immigrants who entered during the late 1960s and early 1970s. During the period from 1966 to 1975, about the same proportion of Filipino immigrants (subject to numerical limitation) came under the occupational preference categories as under the family preference categories. However, in the 1976–1988 period, the proportion of occupational preference immigrants dropped to 19 to 20 percent, while the proportion of family preference immigrants rose to about 80 percent—the result of tightening entry requirements for professional immigrants in the mid-1970s and their subsequent reliance on family reunification categories to enter the United States (Cariño et al. 1990: 11–12). Because new immigrants tend to be of similar socioeconomic backgrounds as their sponsors, the earliest family reunification immigrants represented a continuation of the unskilled and semiskilled Filipino labor that had emigrated before 1965. In contrast, professional immigrants originate from the middle to upper social, economic, and educational sectors of Philippine society, and they, in turn, sponsor relatives who possess the same backgrounds (Liu, Ong, and Rosenstein 1991). As a result of these two distinct chains of emigration from the Philippines, the contemporary Filipino-American community is more diverse than it had been in the past in terms of class.

San Diego County is the third-largest U.S. destination of contemporary Filipino immigrants (Rumbaut 1991: 220). In 1990, numbering close to 96,000, Filipinos were the county's largest Asian-American group, comprising approximately 50 percent of this population. As in

TABLE 6.1   FILIPINO POPULATION IN THE
UNITED STATES, CALIFORNIA, AND SAN DIEGO,
1910–1990

Year	United States	California	San Diego
1910	2,767	5	—
1920	26,634	2,674	48
1930	108,260	30,470	394
1940	98,535	31,408	799
1950	122,707	40,424	na
1960	181,614	67,134	5,123
1970	336,731	135,248	15,069
1980	774,652	358,378	48,658
1990	1,406,770	733,941	95,945

SOURCE: Up to 1950, the data are from Melendy (1977), whose sources include the annual reports of the U.S. Immigration and the U.S. Census of Population and Housing for each area. Melendy's records for San Diego through 1950 were for the city itself; the numbers from 1960 to 1990
are those for San Diego County.

other parts of the U.S. mainland, the majority of the first group of Filipinos in San Diego were laborers. While the farm workers concentrated in the agricultural communities of El Centro and Escondido, the
urban laborers lived and worked in downtown hotels and restaurants.
Although numerically small (see Table 6.1), the prewar Filipino community was vibrant. Barred from renting or purchasing homes outside
of the business district, most Filipinos lived in the downtown section of
the city. There, around Market Street, Filipinos ran small restaurants,
pool and gambling tables, and sponsored dances and other cultural
events. Rizal Day—a yearly observance in honor of Philippine national
hero Dr. Jose Rizal—was the most celebrated festivity, drawing several
hundred Filipinos from all over the county (Castillo-Tsuchida 1979).

San Diego—the site of the largest U.S. naval base station and the
navy's primary West Coast training facility—has been a prominent area
of settlement for Filipino navy men and their families since the early
1900s. In the 1940s and 1950s, the majority of the Filipino families in
San Diego were navy related. Reflecting this navy dominance, a pioneer
Filipino organization in San Diego was the Fleet Reserve Association,
and the first community center was the Filipino American Veterans
Hall (Espiritu 1995). The navy presence continues to be prominent
today. Indeed, Rumbaut (1991: 220) reported that during 1978–1985,
more than 51 percent of the 12,500 Filipino babies born in the San
Diego metropolitan area were delivered at the U.S. Naval Hospital.

As in other Filipino communities along the Pacific Coast, the San Diego community experienced a dramatic growth in the 25 years following passage of the 1965 Immigration Act. New immigration contributed greatly to the tripling of the county's Filipino-American population in the 1970–1980 period and to another doubling of the population between 1980 and 1990 (see Table 6.1). Many post-1965 Filipinos have also come to San Diego as professionals—most conspicuously as nurses. The arrival of the new immigrants—and the resultant class divisions— has made it more difficult for San Diego's Filipinos to maintain the closeness once shared by the smaller group (Espiritu 1995: 24–25).

Socioeconomic Status, Educational Achievement, and Ambition

The CILS Filipino sample mirrors the larger post-1965 Filipino immigration to the United States in that a sizable proportion of respondents are college-educated professionals who ended up in the U.S. middle class. However, what is striking about the Filipino case is that the women have higher educational attainment, often higher occupational status, and concurrent higher earnings than the men (Wong and Hirschman 1983; Woo, 1985). Of the students sampled for CILS,[5] 30 percent of their fathers but almost 50 percent of their mothers had at least a college degree or more; indeed, very few parents had less than a high school degree. The proportions of parents in white-collar occupations matches closely their educational attainment, with almost 60 percent of the mothers but only about 40 percent of the fathers in white-collar positions. These data are even more intriguing in light of the fact that Filipino fathers in the sample were more likely to be U.S. born—and thus more acculturated—than mothers (16.8 percent and 2.5 percent, respectively).

Reflecting the prominent role that the U.S. Navy plays in the immigration of Filipino men, over 50 percent of the 1992 CILS respondents indicated that their fathers worked for or were retired from the U.S. Navy. These jobs ranged from service and blue collar to white collar. While the Navy employs many Filipino fathers, Filipina mothers are clustered in medically related professions as nurses, health technicians, nursing attendants, or the like as well as in accounting. In 1992, close to a quarter of the CILS respondents indicated that their mothers worked in the field of health care; of these, about half were registered nurses.[6] Finally, Table 6.2 indicates that 42.5 percent of the fathers but only 28.1 percent of the mothers

TABLE 6.2   FAMILY SOCIOECONOMIC STATUS
OF CHILDREN OF FILIPINO IMMIGRANTS IN
SAN DIEGO, CALIFORNIA

	Father (%)	Mother (%)
College graduate	29.9	47.4
High school graduate	26.0	17.9
In labor force	74.3	77.4
White collar	40.0	57.9
Blue collar & low wage service	42.5	28.1
Family Economy		
Class position at T1 (1992)		
Wealthy	3.4	
Middle class	85.0	
Working class	11.0	
Poor	0.3	
Family owns home at T2 (1995)	73.0	
Family's economic situation (since 3 years ago)		
Better	43.0	
Worse	18.4	
Same	38.1	

were in either blue-collar or low-wage service jobs, reminding us that not all Filipinos are middle-class professionals. It is also interesting to note that a slightly higher percentage of mothers are in the labor force compared with fathers, another feature of Filipino immigrants more generally.

Although clearly not every Filipino in the labor force is in a white-collar or upper-blue-collar occupation, the majority of the Filipino youth surveyed lived in middle-class households, the result of having both parents in the labor force. Almost 75 percent of the CILS sample come from families that own their home, a strong indicator of middle-class status. At T1 (1992), 85 percent of the sample categorized their families as "middle class," and another 3 percent stated that they were wealthy; in contrast, just 11 percent of the sample described their families as "working class," and less than 0.5 percent stated that they were poor. Although these figures may underreport less well-off economic conditions, they fit with the general 1990 census figures showing that Filipinos in California had the lowest proportion living below the poverty line—5.8 percent—compared with all other Asian groups (Oliver et al. 1995: 3–32). Finally, when asked to compare their economic situation in 1995 (T2) to that at T1, 80

TABLE 6.3   EDUCATIONAL ACHIEVEMENTS,
ASPIRATIONS, AND EXPECTATIONS OF CHILDREN
OF FILIPINO IMMIGRANTS IN SAN DIEGO,
CALIFORNIA, BY GENDER, IN 1992 (T1)
AND 1995 (T2)

	Male	Female		
GPA (average)				
T1	2.71	3.16		
T2	2.62	3.10		
T2 GPAs (N = 716)				
Under 2.0	16.2	5.3		
> 2.0 and < 3.0	42.3	28.9		
> 3.0	39.6	62.7		

	Educational Desires at T2[1]		Educational Realities at T2[2]	
	Males	Females	Males	Females
Community college	9.2	8.7	24.2	22.4
SDSU	24.2	14.8	23.1	18.8
UCSD	16.4	28.6	11.7	16.2
Other, CA	16.9	19.9	7.8	9.8
Other, not CA	6.1	7.8	1.9	3.1
Military/vocational	5.0	1.4	3.3	1.1
No plans	22.2	18.8	28.1	28.6

[1]The question was, "What college do you want to attend?"
[2]The question was, "What college do you think you'll attend, realistically?"

percent of the CILS sample felt that it was the same or better, suggesting a perpetuation of middle-class status at the very least.

As would be expected from a group of young Asian Americans coming from solid middle-class backgrounds with fairly well educated parents, most Filipino Americans plan to seek higher education after high school (Kao 1995). Again, what is interesting about the Filipino CILS data is the gender pattern: Filipina females had higher educational achievements and aspirations than did males. Filipino parents also reported higher educational expectations of daughters than of sons. However, while young Filipinas generally had higher grades and educational aspirations than did Filipino males, they also tended to curtail their aspirations much more so than did boys.

As demonstrated in Table 6.3, girls' grades were higher than boys' grades at both T1 and T2, with an average GPA of 3.16 for girls at T1 and 3.10 at T2, compared with 2.71 for boys at T1 and 2.62 at T2.[7] Indeed, when GPAs are broken down at T2, almost 60 percent of the males had less than a 3.0 GPA, while more than 60 percent of Filipinas carried above a 3.0 GPA. Girls' performances on standardized reading and math tests at T1 also exceeded boys' scores. In CILS data not presented here, over time, females consistently felt more strongly than boys about the importance of achieving good grades. This difference is reflected in their study habits. Filipina girls spent more time studying and watched less television than did Filipino boys in both time periods. At T2, when grades are more important for qualifying for college, girls exceeded boys in only one category of watching television—the "less than one hour per day" grouping.[8]

The CILS data indicate that young Filipinos have high educational aspirations. As seen in Table 6.4, a higher proportion of young Filipinas expected to attain an advanced degree compared with Filipino males. Table 6.4 also shows that parents' educational aspirations for their children were positively related to their own educational attainment, with most parents hoping that their children would complete college at the very least. Interestingly, parents had higher aspirations for their daughters than for their sons. A higher proportion of parents of daughters hoped their child would attain an advanced degree compared with the parents of sons (68.1 percent and 59.9 percent, respectively). The highest aspirations for daughters came from college-educated mothers: While 72 percent of college-educated mothers hoped that their son would obtain a graduate degree, 86 percent of college-educated mothers hoped their daughter would do the same. Indeed, even parents without college degrees had very high expectations for their daughters' education.

These differences, however, can be linked with the respondents' desired occupations and the occupations that parents hope their child will pursue. Those (predominantly males) hoping to become engineers do not need more than a B.S. to obtain a job in their field. In contrast, those (predominantly females) seeking medical or teaching careers do need advanced education and training. At T2, the occupations that drew the largest numbers of male respondents were engineering (25 percent), medical practice (18 percent), nursing/physical therapy (15.5 percent), business (11 percent), and computing (11 percent); for females, they were medical practice (29 percent), nursing/physical therapy (29 percent), business (13 percent), and teaching (9 percent). In other words, one-third of the males but two-thirds of the females as-

TABLE 6.4   EDUCATIONAL ASPIRATIONS OF
CHILDREN OF FILIPINO IMMIGRANTS AND OF
THEIR PARENTS, BY GENDER, IN 1995 (T2)

	Male	Female
Children's aspirations		
% Less than advanced degree	61.8	49
% Advanced degree	38.2	51
Parents' aspirations		
Less than advanced degree	40.1	31.9
Advanced degree	59.9	68.1

Parents' Aspirations for Children Achieving an
Advanced Degree, by Parental Educational Attainment[1]

	Male	Female
Father's education		
High school degree	64.1	80.7
College degree	68.8	79.6
Mother's education		
High school degree	59.9	79.3
College degree	72.3	86.0

[1]These numbers do not add up to 100 percent because parental aspirations for children attaining a college degree only are omitted. Thus, the difference between each number and 100 is the percentage of fathers or mothers in that educational category who hope their son or daughter will achieve a college degree only.

pired for an occupation in medicine, either as a physician, nurse, or physical therapist—many of which require an advanced degree.

In terms of the type of college they would like to attend, Filipinas again aspired higher than Filipino males of the same age. Almost 30 percent of the girls wished to attend the University of California at San Diego (UCSD), compared with 16 percent of the boys. Proportionally fewer females set their sights on San Diego State University (SDSU) (by 10 percent), but about the same proportion of males and females were aiming for a local community college. And more females than males hoped to attend a college elsewhere in California or outside of California altogether. Finally, about 19 percent of the females and 22 percent of the boys had "no plans" at age 17 when asked about their hopes and desires.

The data become disturbing when we compare students' desires and hopes with what they "realistically" believe will happen. At T2, the community college category grew for both sexes by over 250 percent, while the UCSD option declined more substantially for females (43 percent) than for males (28 percent). The options of attending a college outside of San Diego also dropped markedly as both sexes admitted the unlikelihood of going far from home. Finally, what is also disconcerting is that the "no plans" category swelled up to almost one-third of the entire sample when "reality" set in, increasing by one-third the numbers of females and by one-quarter the numbers of males who chose this category. Together, these data suggest that while Filipinas may have higher aspirations than their male counterparts, the lack of feasibility of their plans, for whatever reasons, hits them harder and forces more of them to aim lower than do males. This setting of sights lower than is necessary, especially in light of their high academic achievements, may actually thwart possibilities of upward mobility.

Interviews with young Filipino Americans confirm the importance of gender in their lives. Many second-generation Filipinas resent what they see as gender inequity in their families: the fact that their immigrant parents regularly place far more restrictions on their autonomy, mobility, and personal decision than on their brothers' (Espiritu 2001). The restrictions on girls' movement sometimes spill over to the realms of academia, possibly affecting their educational trajectories. The high school teachers and counselors Wolf (1997) interviewed reported that some Filipino parents pursued contradictory tactics with their daughter's education by pushing them to excel in high school but then "pulling the emergency brake" when they contemplated college by expecting them to stay at home, even if it meant going to a less competitive college.

Ethnicity: Identity, Language, and Race

The socioeconomic data just discussed suggest that most Filipino Americans have achieved economic assimilation. This section examines the assumption that upward social mobility is linked to sociocultural similarity by focusing on ethnic self-identity and language preference— two key indices of cultural assimilation. An assimilationist perspective would predict that over time and generation, immigrants and their children will move in the direction of both increasing identificational assimilation (i.e., as an unhyphenated American) and increasing linguistic assimilation (i.e., anglicization) (Rumbaut 1997). However, the available data suggest a more dynamic and complex pattern of cultural adaptation: While most Filipino Americans self-identified by national origin, most also preferred English to their parents' native language. Race also shapes the identity of these young Filipinos as they struggled between their belief in the American dream and their experience with racial discrimination.

Reactive Ethnic Consciousness

The CILS data indicate that ethnic self-identities vary significantly over time—but not in the direction predicted by the linear assimilation perspective. As indicated in Table 6.5 (which records changes in ethnic self-identity from T1 to T2), in 1992, the majority of the Filipino students in the sample (59 percent) selected a hyphenated Filipino-American identification, and about one-third (31 percent) identified as Filipino. In very few cases (about 5 percent) did respondents choose the unhyphenated category of American.[9] In sum, in 1992, close to 90 percent of the Filipino respondents ethnically self-identified as Filipino. By 1995, even more Filipino students (92 percent) in the sample self-identified with their or their parents' immigrant origins. However, the proportion of those who selected Filipino and Filipino American reversed to 55 percent and 37 percent, respectively. Thus from T1 to T2, the most significant increase by far was in the proportions choosing Filipino as their immigrant or national-origin identity. Furthermore, an overwhelming 80 percent of those who identified as Filipino at T1 kept that identity by T2, and 75 percent who identified as Filipino at T2 reported that their ethnic self-identity is "very important" to them—a testament to the strength and stability of this unassimilated identity. In comparison, about half of those who identified as Filipino American at T1 kept that identity by T2; the other half shifted to the unhyphenated Filipino label. Of the 34 individuals who identified themselves as American at T1, only about 15 percent of them did so again by T2; a significant percentage (38.2 percent) shifted to the Filipino-American identity, and another 29.4 percent shifted to the Filipino identity. These results indicate that for the Filipinos in the CILS sample, ethnic change over time has not gravitated toward an assimilative or American national identity (e.g., American) but rather toward an immigrant or national-origin identity.

In a qualitative study of Filipino Americans in San Diego County, Espiritu (2001) also found that most Filipinos rejected the assimilative American identity. Instead, they equated *American* with *white* and often used these two terms interchangeably. For example,
who is married to a white American referred to her husband

TABLE 6.5 ETHNIC SELF IDENTITY AMONG CHILDREN OF FILIPINO IMMIGRANTS IN SAN DIEGO, CALIFORNIA, T1 AND T2 CROSS-TABULATION

Ethnic Self-Identity (T2)

Ethnic self-identity (T1)	American	Filipino American	Filipino	Black	Asian	Mixed/ other	Total
American		5 14.7%	13 38.2%	10 29.4%		6 17.6%	34 100%
Filipino American	6 1.4%	200 47.2%	206 48.6%		4 .9%	8 1.9%	424 100%
Filipino		40 17.9%	178 79.8%		1 .4%	4 1.8%	223 100%
Black				1 25.0%	1 25.0%	2 50.0%	4 100%
Asian		1 100.0%					1 100.0%
Mixed/other	8 26.7%	1 3.3%	1 3.3%	3 10.0%	17 56.7%		30 100.0%
TOTAL	11 1.5%	262 36.6%	396 55.3%	2 .3%	8 1.1%	37 5.2%	716 100%

TABLE 6.6 PERCEPTIONS OF DISCRIMINATION,
PERCEPTIONS OF AMERICAN SOCIETY, AND
LANGUAGE PREFERENCE AND PROFICIENCY
AMONG FILIPINO CHILDREN OF IMMIGRANTS IN
SAN DIEGO IN 1992 (T1) AND 1995 (T2)

	T1 (%)	T2 (%)
Discrimination		
There is racial discrimination in U.S.	83.0	87.0
Has experienced being discriminated against	63.5	69.0
Expects discrimination regardless of merit	38.2	44.2
Perceptions of U.S.		
Believes U.S. is best country to live in	62.5	75.7
Prefers American ways	51.8	53.5
Language		
Prefers English	88.3	96.1
Speaks English "very well"	85.9	88.4
Reads English "very well"	87.2	88.4
Speaks Filipino language "very well"	12.3	10.6
Reads Filipino language "very well"	9.4	8.3

can but to her African-American and Filipino-American brothers-in-law as black and Filipino, respectively. This practice reflects the racialized history of Filipinos and other Asians in the United States. Historically, U.S. immigration exclusion acts, naturalization laws, and national culture have simultaneously marked Asians as the inassimilable aliens and whites as the quintessential Americans (Lowe 1996). Excluded from the collective memory of who constitutes a "real" American, Asians in the United States, even as citizens, are expected to remain the "foreigner within"—the non-American. In the case of Filipinos, emigrants from a former U.S. colony, their formation as racialized minorities does not begin in the United States but rather in the homeland already affected by U.S. economic, social, and cultural influences (Lowe 1996: 8). Cognizant of the enduring significance of race, a Filipino man who has lived in the United States for 30 years explained why he still does not identify himself as American: "I don't see myself just as an American because I cannot hide the fact that my skin is brown. To me, American means white" (Espiritu 2001).

The growing ethnic awareness among Filipino youth in the sample corresponded with an increase in their experiences and expectations of race and ethnic discrimination. As indicated in Table 6.6, close to 90 percent of Filipinos in the sample at T2 agreed that there is racial discrimination and much conflict between races in the United States. The majority—about two-thirds—related that they had experienced racial and ethnic discrimination. They also reported more such experiences of rejection or unfair treatment against themselves as they grew older. In 1992, 63.5 percent had already experienced direct discrimination against themselves; in 1995, 69 percent had. The proportion of respondents who expected that people would discriminate against them also increased from 38.2 percent at T1 to 44.2 percent at T2. This increase in perception of discrimination may be a response to the growing anti-immigrant sentiment embodied in the passage of Proposition 187 in California in November 1994. The politics of Proposition 187 was such that those with immigrant origins were forced to confront their backgrounds and identities even if they were legal immigrants who had successfully assimilated into the U.S. economy thus far. Given their experiences with and perceptions of ethnic/racial exclusion and rejection, it is not surprising that the majority of Filipino respondents did not self-identify as American.

It is important to note that Filipino parents were less likely than their children to report that they had experienced racial discrimination (40 percent compared to 69 percent). Yet parents clearly perceived the social distance that separates Filipino and white Americans. For example, over 70 percent believed that white Americans consider themselves superior to Filipinos, 30 percent thought that their child would experience opposition if he or she wanted to join a club of white Americans, and about 20 percent feared that their child would face resistance if he or she wanted to move in a white American neighborhood or marry a white American.

Among young Filipinos suffering discrimination, their own race or nationality was the overwhelming force perceived to account for that unfair treatment (66.8 percent of boys and 73.3 percent of girls). In-depth interviews with second-generation Filipinos in San Diego County corroborate these findings: Many of those interviewed reported that they had been verbally and/or physically harassed by others for their perceived racial differences (Espiritu 1994). These racial incidents constitute key events in the ethnic experiences of these Filipino Americans, a background against which they interpret subsequent incidents and reevaluate their assigned place in U.S. society (see Essed 1991). The CILS data also indicate that such experiences of discrimination tend to be associated over time with the development of a more pessimistic stance about their chances to reduce ethnic and racial discrimination through higher educational achievement (Rumbaut 1994). For example, when asked to agree or disagree with the statement, "No matter how much education I get, people will still discriminate against me," 38 percent of the Filipinos in the CILS sample agreed in 1992; a few years later, this proportion increased to about 44 percent. The enduring presence of racism in the lives of young Filipino Americans indicates that "a European–non-European distinction remains a central division in [U.S.] society" (Lieberson and Waters 1988: 248). This division—as manifested in institutional discrimination and personal prejudice—shapes not only the life outcomes but also the eventual identities of immigrants of color and their descendants.

The growth of a reactive ethnic consciousness is also reflected in the friendship patterns of children of Filipino immigrants. At T1, close to 70 percent indicated that many or most of their friends were from abroad, and about 90 percent reported that they had Filipino friends. At T2, about 60 percent said that many or most of their close friends' parents were foreign born. Again, their social networks closely resembled those of their parents: Over 70 percent of the parents surveyed reported that they socialized mainly with other Filipinos, and about half stated that most of their neighbors were Filipinos. However, Filipino youngsters were much more likely than their parents to have friends from diverse racial/ethnic groups. Over 40 percent of young Filipinos reported having other Asian (other than Filipino) friends; about a quarter had Latino friends, and 18 percent had white friends. In comparison, less than 7 percent of their parents reported that they socialized mainly with Asian, Latino, or white Americans. Reflecting the social distance between Filipino and black Americans, less than 4 percent of both Filipino children and parents befriended black Americans.

A logistic regression analysis of the two most salient ethnic identity variables—Filipino identity and Filipino-American identity as of T2—allows us to identify which of the observed predictors had the strongest effect on ethnic identity. As a whole, nativity had the strongest influence on the type of identity selected. In other words, respondents who were born in the Philippines and whose parents were also born in the Philippines were significantly more likely to identify as Filipino; conversely, those who were born in the United States and who had one U.S-born parent were much more likely to identify as Filipino American. Citizenship status is also significantly associated with ethnic self-identification, with noncitizens more likely to call themselves Filipino and citizens more likely to adopt the Filipino-American label. These findings are in keeping with responses from the entire CILS sample at

T1 (Rumbaut 1994). Parental nativity looms importantly in children's ethnic self-identification in that if at least one parent was U.S. born, then respondents were less likely to identify as Filipino; again, conversely, respondents with one U.S.-born parent tended to gravitate toward a hyphenated identity. Indeed, this is likely the case in the many marriages of Filipino servicemen with U.S.-born wives.

Parental ethnic identification at T1 had weak but nonetheless significant effects on children's identity—if parents identified as Filipino at T1, their children were more likely to identify as Filipino as well at T2. Conversely, if parents identified as Filipino American at T1, children were more likely to identify as the same at T2. Finally, having both parents of the same national origin—namely, Filipino—had a significant effect, again weakly, on the respondent's propensity to identify as Filipino. It is very interesting that perceptions of discrimination washed out with regard to respondents' ethnic identification.

Assimilative Trends

The data on ethnic identity shifts, experiences of discrimination, and friendship patterns just described all point to the rapid growth of a reactive ethnic consciousness among young Filipino Americans in San Diego. However, there is also a concurrent countertrend in the direction of assimilation. Despite their growing awareness of racial discrimination and ethnic inequality and their inclination to socialize mainly with other Filipinos and immigrants, many Filipinos in the sample continued to believe in the American dream—in the promise of equal opportunities for all. Over 50 percent agreed with the statement that "nonwhites have as many opportunities to get ahead economically as whites in the United States." Even more tellingly, as seen in Table 6.6, nearly 63 percent of these students agreed in the 1992 survey that "there is no better country to live in than the United States," and that positive appraisal grew to 76 percent in 1995. Also, at both T1 and T2, more than half of the sample preferred American ways of doing things all or most of the time. This belief in the promise of equal opportunity and the rousing endorsement of the United States—even in the face of racism—testifies to the enduring power of the ideology of the United States as the land of opportunity, fair play, and abundance.

More importantly, on the issue of language preference, Filipino children of immigrants are unequivocally moving toward monolingual English. Even as they self-identified by national origin, an overwhelming majority preferred English to their parents' native tongue. Although over 90 percent of the Filipino sample reported speaking a language other than English at home, they were not fluent in this language. As seen in Table 6.6, only about 1 in 10 indicated that they spoke a Filipino language "very well," and even fewer could read it "very well." In contrast, nearly 9 out of 10 Filipinos reported speaking and reading English "very well." Indeed, Filipinos were the most linguistically assimilated of all the CILS groups surveyed, with 96.1 percent of the respondents preferring English by T2.

The rapid transition toward monolingual English—experienced by all groups in the CILS sample—reflects in part the hostility toward bilingualism and the clamor for "English only" in many parts of the United States. Given this context, many Filipino immigrant parents and their children strive to perfect their English—to speak it properly and accent free. A Filipino immigrant who left the Philippines as a teenager explained why he worked so hard to improve his English: "When we arrived in San Diego . . . I was ridiculed because [of] my accent. . . . I knew that if I wanted to succeed in this country, I had to find a way to improve the way I speak English" (Espiritu 1995: 172–73). In fact, it is not unusual to find ads in Filipino newspapers from private teachers offering to help English-speaking Filipinos lose their accent. In great part, owing to the legacy of U.S. colonialism in the Philippines, over 97 percent of the Filipino parents surveyed for the CILS reported that they speak, understand, read, and write English well or very well. Because they are proficient in English, Filipino parents may be less compelled to teach their children the Filipino language. As a Filipino immigrant parent explained, "We don't teach the children Tagalog because we're comfortable in English also. English comes out almost automatically when we speak to them. Even the grandparents speak English" (Espiritu 1994: 257).

Along the same lines, CILS data suggest that there is a lack of active cultural socialization—the deliberate teaching and practicing of the languages, traditions, and history of the Philippines—in Filipino-American homes. Although close to three-quarters of the parents surveyed stated that it is very important for their child to know about the Philippines, over half (57 percent) reported that they seldom talked to their child about the Philippines, and close to three-quarters (72 percent) admitted that their family seldom celebrated special days connected with the Philippines. A Filipino American tells of the "cultural void" in his family:

> Not much was going on at my house. Nothing. It wasn't made explicit that Filipino culture is something that we should retain, that we should hold on to, as something that's valuable. There wasn't that much sense that we should keep the language. So you don't really get taught, you know. And I found that to be a real common experience among Filipinos my age. Our parents don't realize that we don't know anything about the old country: who was the first president, when was independence day, who was Jose Rizal? (Espiritu 1994: 258)

This perceived lack of cultural transmission in Filipino-American homes can be attributed in part to the parents' long work hours and/or to the pressure that force immigrants to assimilate the mainstream culture. As a Filipina American stated, "We don't celebrate these holidays because growing up in my neighborhood, white-washed suburbia, we just couldn't" (Espiritu 1994: 259).

The quantitative and qualitative data on Filipino Americans just described indicate that ethnic identification is, in fact, a more dynamic and complex social phenomenon than has been predicted by either the pluralist or assimilationist model. On the one hand, the data show that the majority of second-generation Filipino Americans self-identify by national origin and socialize mainly with other Filipinos. These data seemingly support the pluralist position that expects immigrants and their descendants to remain as distinct national communities. On the other hand, the data also indicate that many Filipino Americans overwhelmingly favor life in the United States and prefer English to their parents' native language—a seemingly assimilationist stance. Together, these data challenge the position that identity is bipolar—meaning that one gravitates toward either the pole of nativism or the pole of assimilation. As the data indicate, most Filipino Americans maintain a strong Filipino and Filipino-American identity and network *and* conform to the forces of acculturation and assimilation.

Psychosocial Well-Being and the Process of Adaptation

The cultural assimilation issues just discussed—ethnic identity shifts, language shifts, and perceptions of discrimination—involve highly subjective and emotional processes. In this section, then, we will examine the psychological well-being of young Filipino children of immigrants

TABLE 6.7   SELF-ESTEEM AND DEPRESSION
BY GENDER

	Male	Female	Total
Self-esteem (scale of 1–4)			
T1	3.31	3.18	3.25
T2	3.37	3.27	3.32
Depression (scale of 1–4)			
T1	1.54	1.82	1.68
T2	1.59	1.86	1.72
Percent depressed, by categories (T2)[1]			
Low (< 1.5)	44.8	27.5	36.2
Medium (1.5 < 2.0)	29.5	32.5	31.0
High (> 2.0)	25.6	40.1	32.8
Depression score by level of parent-child conflict (T2)			
Low conflict	1.46	1.72	1.58
Medium conflict	1.83	1.93	1.88
High conflict	1.77	2.36	2.12
Self-esteem score by level of parent-child conflict (T2)			
Low conflict	3.47	3.42	3.44
Medium conflict	3.20	3.21	3.20
High conflict	3.15	2.75	2.91

[1]Figures are column percentages.

by examining two key cognitive and affective dimensions of psychosocial adaptation: self-esteem and depression. Although the kind of educational achievement and English language fluency experienced by Filipino young people is typically associated with positive self-esteem and psychological well-being, Rumbaut (1994) found that among all the different nationalities in CILS, only the Filipinos (and Vietnamese) reflect statistically significantly lower self-esteem scores and higher depression scores, net of other factors particularly among the females. Given the comparative socioeconomic advantages of the Filipino population, these findings are surprising and suggestive of "assimilation and its discontents" (Rumbaut 1997).

As seen in Table 6.7, during both times surveyed, females had consistently lower self-esteem and higher depression scores than did males.[10] A test of means from data at both T1 and T2 confirms that gender differences in depression scores and self-esteem scores are highly significant.[11] In data on self-esteem scores not presented here, across all categories (low, medium, and high self-esteem), females consistently registered lower than males. However, girls' overall self-esteem rose more than did males' self-esteem between ages 14 and 17, thus substantially narrowing the gap between males and females. For example, the 12 percent gender gap in the high self-esteem category at T1 closes to only 4 percent by T2. Despite overall lower self-esteem, this shift in females over time is a very positive one, particularly in light of the generally lower self-esteem experienced by young women of the same age group in the larger society.

Depression scores by gender demonstrate that both males and females register slightly higher scores at T2 than at T1, with females again having consistently higher scores. In Table 6.7, depression scores at T2 are broken down further, demonstrating that the majority of males cluster in the low category while the majority of females cluster in the high category. When these data are compared with T1 data (not shown here), we see a different trend from the shifts in self-esteem just discussed. While the difference between male and female self-esteem narrowed considerably over time, a substantial gender gap is maintained in depression scores: The 19 percent gap between males and females in the category of high depression in T1 declined little over time, and by T2 there was still a considerable difference of 14.5 percent.

Finally, GPA is inversely related to depression and positively related to self-esteem. In other words, the lower the GPA, the more likely the Filipino child of immigrants is to have lower self-esteem and higher depression. GPA is also inversely related to family conflict. For some young people, problems at home may overwhelm their ability to study, concentrate, and do well at school; with others, not doing well at school could be at the root of some family conflict and their resultant depression.

The CILS data are all the more troubling in view of the recent reports by the federal Center for Disease Control and Prevention (CDC), based on surveys of teen risk behavior among San Diego public high school students, that found a high proportion of Filipina female students reporting suicidal ideation (45.6 percent) and suicidal attempts (23.3 percent) in the year preceding the survey—the highest levels of any major ethnic group surveyed. Although Filipino males did not receive the same kind of media attention as did Filipinas (Lau 1995), 29.4 percent of them had suicidal thoughts, and 12 percent of them had attempted suicide in the preceding year, the latter rate being close to double that of all other males surveyed. Thus, these relatively high rates of depression and low self-esteem, particularly among Filipinas, need serious attention since they have often translated into emotional despair.

In Wolf's focus groups with Filipino children of immigrants attending the University of California, she found that 6 of the 22 students interviewed (27 percent), all female, admitted to having had suicidal ideation and that some had attempted suicide, while others referred to suicidal attempts by siblings. Most mentioned the intense pressure they felt from parents to succeed and that they felt unseen and unheard. Furthermore, students felt unable to discuss their distress with parents for fear of sanctions. Discussing these problems outside the family—for example, with a friend or counselor—was not considered an option due to the possibility of "gossip," which would bring shame on the family. In sum, the little data that exist on this issue point to a relatively troubling profile of psychological well-being in a context of relative middle-class success and assimilation, suggestive of an achievement paradox (Rumbaut 1999). Further exploration of these emotional worlds constitutes one of the main foci in our current collaborative and comparative project on Filipino and Vietnamese children of immigrants.

Given the oft-hostile outside world, many immigrants and their children look to the family to sustain and support them (Glenn 1986: 193). The data demonstrate that an overwhelming majority of young Filipinos in the CILS sample lived with their two biological parents in an intact family. In both T1 and T2, 80 percent of the samples lived in a family setting with both parents, while less than 10 percent lived in a stepfamily and less than 10 percent lived with only one parent.[12] This low level of family disruption compared with U.S. averages may not necessarily reflect more harmonious marriages but instead Filipino ideologies of family cohesion, unity and loyalty, a Catholic aversion to divorce, and perhaps a greater need to cohere to the smaller family unit due to the absence of the wider family network. It is important to note that while the prevalence of intact biological nuclear families among Asians is often used as an indicator of family cohesion and perhaps as the basis of "family values," such measures may obfuscate problematic contradictions and conflict.

Like other immigrant groups, Filipino American women and men identify the family (sa pamilya) as a tremendous source of cultural pride (di Leonardo 1984; Kibria 1993). In focus groups with Filipino children of immigrants in Northern California, Wolf (1997: 461) was struck by the "strong, spontaneous and emotional statements about family as the center of what it means to be Filipino." Similarly, in a study of Filipino-American families in San Diego County, Espiritu (2001) found that most Filipinos believed themselves to be superior to white Americans because they are more family oriented and more willing to sacrifice for one another. However, this ideology of family cohesion contrasted with many of the same subjects' experiences of pressure and conflict emanating from that same group.

In the CILS data, the ideology of the family as an important primary group is expressed as well but is not necessarily matched by the actual practice or feelings of family cohesion and consensus. Importantly, female respondents appear to experience more conflict and contradiction than male respondents. At T2, while almost two-thirds of the sample felt strongly that family togetherness is always or often important, only about half lived in families in which family members feel close, and not quite 40 percent were in families that enjoy spending time together. In other words, while the great majority of the respondents indicated that the ideology of family togetherness and cohesion is extremely important to them, few actually experienced this cohesion in their family life.

In many of their responses to the questions on family togetherness, a majority of females expressed more distance from the family and less desire to spend time together than did the males. This gender difference is corroborated by the family cohesion scale, which is based on three variables concerning the degree to which the respondent thinks family togetherness is important, whether the respondent's family likes to spend time together, and whether they feel close. The average score of the family cohesion scale at T2 was 3.62 for males and 3.48 for females. This difference could be attributed to more family conflict experienced by daughters than by sons due to stronger attempts to control female behavior and sexuality. Females also experienced more family conflict than did males. At T1, about 30 percent of the females, compared with 21 percent of the males, clashed with parents all or most of the time. At T2, proportionally more females than males argued about conflicting goals with their parents. These findings suggest that more males are in concert with parental goals than are females. In our current project, we examine in more depth the complex web of family relations by eliciting the perspectives of children of Filipino and Vietnamese immigrants and their parents.

Finally, we turn our focus to a least-squares regression analysis of both measures of psychosocial well-being—self-esteem and depression—at T2 when the respondents were 17. Parent-child conflict emerges as the strongest predictor of both self-esteem and depression: the higher the parent-child conflict, the lower the self-esteem and the higher the level of depression. It is likely that in most cases, this high level of conflict is affecting young people's senses of self, particularly in light of the importance of family ideology for these young people and in Filipino culture; it could also be the reverse in that those who are depressed and apathetic may experience more pressure from parents. Gender, or being female, was the second-strongest factor predicting depression, which is not surprising given the strong gender differences that persisted over time in the depression variable. Interestingly, at T1, gender also constituted the second-strongest predictor of self-esteem but at T2 moved to being the fifth most important factor.

English proficiency was the second most important variable in predicting self-esteem, meaning that the better the respondent's English, the higher his or her self-esteem, although it was not significant in predicting depression. However, related to English proficiency, GPA had the third-strongest effect in predicting both self-esteem and depression. For the depression variable, GPA had a moderate and negative effect, meaning that lower grades were able to explain a higher level of depression. These patterns simply strengthen the bivariate patterns we have discussed earlier in terms of the interrelationships between psychological well-being, family conflict, and doing well at school. Rumbaut (1999) also found that variables that signify English language proficiency and educational achievements, what he termed "competence in role performance," had strong and significant effects in predicting self-esteem in the entire CILS sample.

Foreign language proficiency had a positive and strong effect at T2 in that the more Tagalog (or other Filipino language) they knew, the higher their self-esteem. This suggests that maintaining a strong ethnic identity helped young Filipino children of immigrants have a stronger and more solid sense of self. However, as with English language proficiency, foreign language proficiency again was not significant in predicting depression. At T1, experiencing discrimination was the third-strongest variable in explaining depression but was no longer significant at T2. In other words, young people may have initially internalized racial discrimination, but over time, as their own ethnic identity solidified and they became more conscious of their Filipino identity as a group, they internalized discrimination to a lesser extent. In his multivariate analysis of all the CILS groups, Rumbaut (1999) found that discrimination and other related variables that create the "experience of perceived danger and lack of control over threatening life events" were also significant in predicting depression.

At T2, having one parent who was born in the U.S. or was a naturalized citizen was significant but had weak effects on positive self-esteem. At T1, however, having a Filipino or Filipino-American identity was significant but had negative but weak effects on predicting self-esteem. All identity variables wash out by T2 in predicting self-esteem.

Conclusion

What is it like to grow up Filipino in San Diego as the child of immigrants? These data point to several interesting and seemingly contradictory patterns. First, as predicted by the pluralist model, second-generation Filipinos, like others in the CILS sample, move toward an ethnic rather than an American identity over time. But they also conform to the forces of assimilation because they believe in the American dream and prefer English to their parents' native language. These data suggest that ethnic identification is a more dynamic and complex social process than has been predicted by either the assimilationist or pluralist perspectives. Second, young Filipinas have higher educational aspirations, higher grades, and more academic demands on them from parents than do Filipino males. Filipinas appear to work harder and achieve more success in school, striving higher than males and reproducing gendered patterns that exist among their parents. Unfortunately, the data also suggest that despite these ambitions, Filipinas also end up accepting less and aiming downwards. Rapid acculturation does not necessarily lead to conventionally anticipated outcomes.

Third, psychologically, Filipinas experience more family conflict, more depression, and lower self-esteem than do their male counterparts. Indeed, as has been pointed out elsewhere (Rumbaut 1994; Wolf 1997; Espiritu 2001), their psychological indicators are unexpectedly dramatic, particularly in light of the seeming ease and success that they and their families have had in assimilating into U.S. society and their solidly middle-class status compared with other groups in the CILS sample. Several possible explanations are suggested. One is that Filipino parents' middle-class status allows them to tighten their controls over their children, since they are already part of the system as opposed to being marginalized by it compared with other immigrant groups. Another possibility is that our notion of assimilation is flawed in that it suggests more ease and integration than what may be occurring for some. Speaking English and owning one's home do tell us about economic integration but not about socioemotional matters. In other words, such measures cannot and do not elucidate the *process and meaning* of assimilation for those who live and experience it. Thus, our analysis underscores that rather than navigating a path toward a sense of ease and belonging, the process of assimilation is a complex one, ripe with contradictions and disrupture. Indeed, this case and our current comparative qualitative research on Filipino and Vietnamese children of immigrants encourage a critical rethinking of the notion of assimilation in and of itself.

Notes

First and foremost, we wish to fully acknowledge the depths of our gratitude to Rubén Rumbaut. Without his labor-intensive and wise statistical acumen, advice, and support, we would not have been able to write this paper. We also thank Alejandro Portes for his important input and support. We are grateful to all our colleagues on the CILS project for their useful feedback. We wish to thank each other for maintaining a good sense of humor as well as meeting deadlines during this transnational endeavor. Finally, we wish to acknowledge little Gabriel Espiritu, born during the gestation of this paper; another second-generation child for whom, like those in our paper, we hope the future is bright.

1. This includes in-depth interviews with more than 100 Filipinos in San Diego (Espiritu 1995) as well as interviews with high school counselors and teachers in Vallejo, California, and with University of California–Davis students concerning family cohesion, conflict, and self esteem (Wolf 1997).

2. The Chinese Exclusion Law of 1882 suspended immigration of Chinese laborers for 10 years. Chinese exclusion was extended for another 10 years in 1892 and 1902 and was made indefinite in 1904. In 1907 Japan and the United States reached a "Gentlemen's Agreement" whereby Japan stopped issuing passports to laborers desiring to immigrate to the United States.

3. In 1970, of the 16,669 Filipinos in the U.S. Navy, 80 per-cent were in the steward rating (Ingram 1970). A college-educated Filipino described the indignity he felt in steward school: "At the school, we were taught how to cook and bake, how to set the table, and how to position the silverware, and the glass and the cup. They basically taught us the job of a waitress. Personally, I was so insulted. I was almost a chemical engineer, and I came to the United States just to become a steward" (Espiritu 1995: 108).

4. Since the 1960s, the Philippines has had an oversupply of educated citizens. With U.S. aid, the Philippines underwent an educational boom in the decades following World War II. In 1970, 25 percent of the college-age population in the Philippines were enrolled in colleges and universities. In its ratio of enrollment in higher education per 100,000 population, the Philippines ranked second only to the United States among the world's nations.

5. Reflecting long-established migration histories, the vast majority of the CILS Filipino sample—75 percent—were either born in the United States or arrived before the age of five, meaning that much if not all of their socialization

occurred while in the United States and all of their schooling took place there. Of the 808 Filipino youth first surveyed, over half were born in the United States, 20 percent came to the United States between infancy and five years old, and another quarter came to the United States after the age of five years.

6. The other health care occupations include dietician, health record technician, physician, practical nurse, health technician, dental assistant, nursing attendant, orderly, and dental-medical technician.

7. ANOVA test of means of GPA between males and females at T1 demonstrates significance at the .000 level ($p < .0001$) at T1 and also at T2.

8. Wolf's interviews (1997) with teachers and counselors at two high schools in northern California pointed to similar patterns: Filipina daughters of immigrants were more highly motivated to succeed academically than were Filipino males and achieved excellent grades in addition to impressive extracurricular participation. Indeed, at both high schools, Filipinos constituted about one-quarter of the school population, and Filipinas were consistently the valedictorians and salutatorians.

9. While almost none (only one case) identified ethnically as Asian, when asked about their *race* at T2, an overwhelming 61 percent selected Asian, suggesting that they perceived Asian to be a racial rather than an ethnic identity.

10. CILS used the Rosenberg Self-Esteem measure, which consists of 10 questions, and the Center for Epidemiological Studies Short-Form Depression (CES-D) measure, which consists of four items that query about the respondent's feelings during the past week.

11. ANOVA test of means at T1 demonstrated that depression scores were significant at the .000 level ($p < .0001$); at T2, depression scores were significant at the .000 level ($p < .0001$). Self-esteem scores were significant at the .000 level at T1 ($p < .0001$) and at T2 ($p < .014$).

12. Of all the groups surveyed for CILS, the highest proportion living with grandparents is found in the Filipino sample. At T1, 16 percent had one grandparent living with them, and another 7 percent had two. This had decreased by T2 to 12 percent with one grandparent and 4 percent with two. However, compared with other groups in the CILS surveys, this means that a higher proportion of the Filipino youth have had longer and closer exposure to their grandparents' views and are, therefore, exposed to multiple generational perspectives on life in the Philippines and in the United States.

References

Agoncillo, Teodoro A., and Milagros C. Guerrero. 1970. *History of the Filipino people.* Quezon City: R. P. Garcia.

Berry, William E., Jr. 1989. *U.S. bases in the Philippines: The evolution of a special relationship.* Boulder, Colo.: Westview Press.

Bouvier, Leon, and Robert Gardner. 1986. Immigration to the U.S.: The unfinished story. *Population Bulletin* 41, pp. 1–50.

Cariño, Benjamin V. 1987. "The Philippines and southeast Asia: Historical roots and contemporary linkages." In *Pacific bridges: The new immigrants from Asia and the Pacific Islands,* edited by James T. Fawcett and Benjamin V. Cariño. Staten Island, N. Y.: Center for Migration Studies.

Cariño, Benjamin V., James T. Fawcett, Robert W. Gardner, and Fred Arnold. 1990. *The new Filipino immigrants to the United States: Increasing diversity and change.* Honolulu: East-West Center.

Castillo-Tsuchida, Adelaida. 1979. *Filipino migrants in San Diego, 1900–1946.* San Diego: San Diego Society, Title Insurance and Trust Collection.

Chan, Sucheng. 1990. *Asian Americans: An interpretive history.* Boston: Twayne.

Constantino, Renato. 1994. Identity and consciousness: The Philippine experience. Paper presented at the Eighth World Sociology Congress, Toronto, Canada.

di Leonardo, Micaela. 1984. *The varieties of ethnic experience: Kinship, class and gender among California Italian Americans.* Ithaca: Cornell University Press.

Dorita, Mary. 1975. *Filipino immigration to Hawaii.* San Francisco: R&E Research Associates.

Espiritu, Yen Le. 1994. The intersection of race, ethnicity, and class: The multiple identities of second-generation Filipinos. *Identities* 1 (2–3), pp. 1–25.

———. 1995. *Filipino American lives.* Philadelphia: Temple University Press.

———. 2001. "We don't sleep around like white girls do": Family, gender, and culture in Filipino American lives. *Signs* 26 (2), pp. 415–440.

Essed, Philomena. 1991. *Understanding everyday racism.* Newbury Park, Calif.: Sage.

Glenn, Evelyn Nakano. 1986. *Issei, nisei, war bride: Three generations of Japanese-American women at domestic service.* Philadelphia: Temple University Press.

Ingram, Timothy. 1970. The floating plantation. *Washington Monthly* (October), pp. 17–20.

Kao, Grace. 1995. Asian Americans as model minorities? A look at the academic performance of immigrant youth. *Social Science Quarterly* 76 (Fall), pp. 1–19.

Kibria, Nazli. 1993. *Family tightrope: The changing lives of Vietnamese Americans.* Princeton: Princeton University Press.

Lau, Angela. 1995. Filipino girls think suicide at number one rate. *San Diego Union-Tribune,* February 11, p. A-1.

Lawcock, Larry Arden. 1975. Filipino students in the United States and the Philippine independence movement: 1900–1935. Ph.D. diss., University of California–Berkeley.

Lieberson, Stanley, and Mary C. Waters. 1988. *From many strands: Ethnic and racial groups in contemporary America.* New York: Russell Sage Foundation.

Liu, John M., Paul M. Ong, and Carolyn Rosenstein. 1991. Dual chain migration: Post-1965 Filipino immigration to the United States. *International Migration Review* 25 (3), pp. 487–513.

Lowe, Lisa. 1996. *Immigrant acts: On Asian American cultural politics.* Durham, N.C.: Duke University Press.

Melendy, Brett. 1977. *Asians in America: Filipinos, Koreans, and East Indians.* Boston: Twayne.

Oliver, J. Eric, Frederick Gey, Jon Stiles, and Henry Brady. 1995. *Pacific Rim states Asian demographic data book.* Oakland: Office of the President, University of California.

Ong, Paul, and Tania Azores. 1994. "The migration and incorporation of Filipino nurses." In *The new Asian immigration,* edited by Paul Ong, Edna Bonacich, and Lucie Cheng. Philadelphia: Temple University Press.

Pido, Antonio J. A. 1986. *The Pilipinos in America: Macro/micro dimensions of immigration and integration.* Staten Island, N.Y.: Center for Migration Studies.

Pomeroy, William J. 1974. "The Philippines: A case history of neocolonialism." In *Remaking Asia: Essays on the American Use of Power,* edited by Mark Selden. New York: Pantheon Books.

Rumbaut, Rubén G. 1991. "Passages to America: Perspectives on the new immigration." In *America at Century's End,* edited by Alan Wolfe. Berkeley and Los Angeles: University of California Press.

———. 1994. The crucible within: Ethnic identity, self-esteem, and segmented assimilation among children of immigrants. *International Migration Review* 28 (4), pp. 748–794.

———. 1997. "Assimilation and its Discontents: Between Rhetoric and Reality." *International Migration Review,* 31, 4: 923–960.

———. 1997 "Ties that bind: Immigration and immigrant families in the United States." In *Immigration and the family: Research and policy on U.S. immigrants,* edited by Alan Booth, Ann C. Crouter, and Nancy Landale. Mahwah, N.J.: Lawrence Erlbaum Associates.

———. 1999. "Passages to adulthood: The adaptation of children of immigrants in Southern California." In *Children of immigrants: Health, adjustment, and public assistance,* edited by Donald J. Hernández. Washington, DC: National Academy Press.

Sánchez, George. 1993. *Becoming Mexican American: Ethnicity, culture, and identity in Chicano Los Angeles, 1900–1945.* New York: Oxford University Press.

San Juan, E., Jr. 1991. Mapping the boundaries: The Filipino writer in the U.S.A. *The Journal of Ethnic Studies* 19 (1), pp. 117–131.

Steinberg, David Joel. 1990. *The Philippines: A singular and a plural place.* Boulder, Colo.: Westview Press.

Takaki, Ronald. 1989. *Strangers from a different shore.* Boston: Little, Brown.

Vallangca, Caridad Concepción. 1977. *The second wave: Pinoy and Pinay, 1945–1965.* San Francisco: Strawberry Hill Press.

Wolf, Diane L. 1997. Family secrets: Transnational struggles among children of Filipino immigrants. *Sociological Perspectives* 40 (3), pp. 457–482.

Wong, Morrison G., and Charles Hirschman. 1983. Labor force participation and socioeconomic attainment of Asian American women. *Sociological Perspectives* 26, pp. 423–446.

Woo, Deborah. 1985. The socioeconomic status of Asian American women in the labor force: An alternative view. *Sociological Perspectives* 28, pp. 307–338.

Chapter 7

STRADDLING DIFFERENT WORLDS
The Acculturation of Vietnamese Refugee Children

Min Zhou

The Vietnamese are the largest of the refugee groups to have settled in the United States since the mid-1970s. The emergence of this new ethnic group in the American scene, along with approximately half a million other southeast Asians, is primarily the result of U.S. military involvement in the region. The story of Vietnamese Americans is one of very rapid growth, from a population of insignificant size in the early 1970s to one that numbered over 615,000 by 1990, when it made up almost 10 percent of the nation's Asian-American population. Even this figure understates the true size of the Vietnamese-origin population, since it excludes no fewer than 200,000 Sino-Vietnamese (ethnic Chinese) who fled Vietnam and arrived in the United States as part of the larger refugee outflow from southeast Asia (Rumbaut 1995). The children of Vietnamese refugees are thus the newest of the new second generation. As of 1990, 52 percent of all Vietnamese-American children under 18 years of age were U.S. born, 27 percent arrived in the United States prior to the age of 5, 17 percent arrived between the ages of 5 and 12, and only 4 percent arrived as adolescents.

For many Vietnamese refugees, the journey to America and their adjustment to the new land was extremely hard. With the exception of the relatively small elite group evacuated at the fall of Saigon, most of the refugees lacked education, job skills, and measurable economic resources. They also suffered from the trauma of war and flight and from the severe emotional distress that they experienced at refugee camps. Once arrived in the United States, they were powerless to decide where and when they would be resettled, with almost all of the refugees starting their American life on public assistance.

Growing up in America has been difficult for the children of the refugees as well. The parents' low socioeconomic status makes it difficult for the children to succeed, even though both parents and children desperately want to get ahead. The environment in which the children find themselves further limits the chances: Too many live in neighborhoods that are poor and socially isolated, where local schools do not function well and the streets are beset by violence and drugs.

To all these difficulties are added the generic problems of second-generation acculturation, aggravated by the troubles associated with coming of age in an era far more materialistic and individualistic than those encountered by immigrant children in years gone by. Today's second generation often finds itself straddling different worlds and receiving conflicting signals. At home, they hear that they must work hard and do well in school to move up; on the street they learn a different lesson, that of rebellion against authority and rejection of the goals of achievement. Today's popular culture, brought to the immigrants through the television screen, exposes children to the lifestyles and consumption standards of American society, raising their expectations well beyond those entertained by their parents. As a result, the children are not as willing as their parents to work at low-paying, low-status jobs, but at the same time, many may not have the education, skills, or opportunities to do better. This mismatch between rising aspirations and shrinking opportunities can either lead to "second-generation decline" (Gans 1992) or provoke "second-generation revolt" (Perlmann and Waldinger 1997).

So do immigrant children manage to traverse the difficult social terrain they encounter? Or do they fall into one of the many traps that afflict young people—especially those of socioeconomically disadvantaged or minority background—in contemporary America? This chapter inquires into these questions through the prism of Vietnamese-American adolescents in San Diego. I seek to explore the complex, multidimensional process of acculturation, as understood and experienced by these children and as captured by the San Diego portion of the Children of Immigrants Longitudinal Survey (CILS).[1] Before delving into the specific case study, I first furnish a historical account of why the

Vietnamese fled their country, how they resettled in the United States, and how resettlement affected the adjustment of the second generation.

The Settlement of Vietnamese Refugees in the United States

The Vietnamese arrived under circumstances quite different from those encountered by today's typical legal immigrant.[2] Unlike most other contemporary immigrants, the Vietnamese were pushed out of their homeland, forced to leave without adequate preparation and with little control over their final destinations. Many of them had minimum formal education, few marketable skills, little English language proficiency, and scant knowledge of the ways of an advanced society—assets that would ease the passage into America. They also lacked a preexisting ethnic community that could help out with assistance of varying sorts. Instead, they had to initially depend almost entirely upon the government and individual or institutional sponsors to determine where they would resettle.

The Flight from Vietnam

The initial flight from Vietnam was touched off by the withdrawal of American troops from Vietnam and by rumors and fears in the face of an uncertain future. Given the bitterness of the war in Vietnam; the suddenness of South Vietnam's defeat in the Spring of 1975; and rumors about the Hanoi government's intention to execute all former South Vietnamese civil servants, policemen, and other officials as well as all those who had served the Americans in any capacity, many people left the country, by sea, land, and air.

Before 1977, a total of 130,000 refugees fled Vietnam. This initial wave of refugees were mostly members of the elite and the middle class who either had access to the evacuation arranged by the American military or could afford their own means of flight. After the airlift at the fall of Saigon, thousands of refugees fled Vietnam by boat from the end of 1975 to 1978. But the phrase "boat people" came into common usage as a result of the flood of refugees casting off from Vietnam in overcrowded, leaky boats at the end of the 1970s and the beginning of the 1980s. By 1979, an estimated 400,000 refugees, known as the "second wave" of flight, escaped Vietnam in boats for Thailand, Malaysia, Indonesia, and Singapore (Caplan, Choy, and Whitmore 1989; Tran

1991; Roberts 1978). This mass exodus was disproportionately made up of ethnic minorities, particularly the Sino-Vietnamese.

It seems relatively easy for most Americans to understand why many South Vietnamese fled the country immediately following the fall of Saigon. But it is more difficult to grasp why the refugees kept fleeing for so many years after the Vietnam War ended, especially considering that the Hanoi government did not plunge the South into a bloodbath as so many had feared. As Carl L. Bankston and I argued in *Growing up American* (1998), several reasons account for the lengthy flow of refugees from Vietnam. First, political repression continued to make life difficult for those individuals who were detained at or released from education camps as well as for their family members. Second, economic hardships, exacerbated by natural disasters and poor harvests in the years following the war, created a widespread sense of hopelessness. Third, incessant warfare with neighboring countries further drained Vietnam's resources for capital investment and development. These severe adversarial conditions, triggering the second and third exodus of Vietnamese boat people in the late 1970s and early 1980s, continued to send thousands of refugees on the rugged journey to a better life.

Once the early refugee waves established communities in the United States, leakage of information from America to Vietnam provided impetus for a continuing outward flow. Upon resettlement in the United States and other Western countries, many Vietnamese refugees rebuilt overseas networks with families and friends. Letters frequently moved between the receiving countries and Vietnam, providing relatives in the homeland with an intricate knowledge of the changing refugee policies and procedures of resettlement countries.

Since the mid-1990s, however, immigration from Vietnam has begun to assume a different shape. Though a substantial proportion continues to be admitted as refugees, an increasing number have been entering the United States as family-sponsored immigrants, a flow that will surely grow in years to come. As the refugee influx ebbs, family reunification can be expected to dominate Vietnamese immigration into the next century.

The Resettlement in the United States

Unlike most regular immigrants, who are sponsored either by close families or by U.S. employers and can make decisions as to where to settle in the United States, refugees are often sponsored by the government or voluntary agencies of the receiving country and cannot choose their destinations. In the case of the Vietnamese and other southeast Asian refugees who did not have established ethnic communities in the United States, the U.S. government resettlement agencies, known as voluntary agencies (VOLAGs),[3] almost entirely decided where the refugees would settle. Initially, the United States admitted Vietnamese refugees as a response to a special emergency rather than as part of an ongoing process of resettlement. Thus, the official resettlement policy aimed at dispersing southeast Asian refugees to minimize the impact on local receiving communities and to integrate refugees into the American economy and society as quickly as possible.

The early resettlement attempts to scatter refugees around the nation led this new ethnic group to establish a presence even in those Midwestern and mountain states least populated by recent immigrants. However, as time went by, distinctive Vietnamese concentrations emerged, through secondary migration, in large metropolitan areas that were the most popular destinations for many recent immigrants of varying nationalities. Geographically, the Vietnamese were highly concentrated in California. As of 1990, almost half of America's Vietnamese population lived in California (up from 27 percent in 1980). Within California, the Vietnamese also clustered in just a few metropolitan areas with the state, with over 70 percent living in just four metropolitan areas—Anaheim–Santa Ana, Los Angeles–Long Beach, San Jose, and San Diego.

Another chief goal of resettlement was to help refugees achieve economic independence as quickly as possible. Integrating refugees into American society required the development of a comprehensive program of support and preparation. Generous government aid ensured a basic level of well-being until the refugees became self-sufficient. Many Vietnamese refugees started their American life at the bottom of the socioeconomic ladder, a fact reflected in their high rates of labor force nonparticipation, unemployment, poverty, and dependence on public assistance. In fact almost all of them began on welfare. The three cash assistance programs most commonly utilized by Vietnamese refugees were Aid to Families with Dependent Children (AFDC), Supplementary Security Income (SSI), and Refugee Cash Assistance (RCA). The first two programs were forms of public assistance, or welfare, available to U.S. citizens. AFDC was for low-income families with children, and SSI was for the elderly or disabled poor. Refugees not eligible for either of these forms of assistance generally received RCA during their first 6 to 18 months and were also able to apply for food stamps.

While early official policies toward Vietnamese refugees were generally sympathetic, the American public was ambivalent. As early as 1975, at the time of the initial entry of the Vietnamese, a Gallup poll indicated that a majority of Americans preferred that the Vietnamese be kept out of the United States (Kelly 1986). Many Americans felt that such culturally different people would create additional difficulties for acculturation, and some saw the Vietnamese as new economic competitors as well as reminders of an unpleasant war. In the late 1970s, Americans at lower socioeconomic levels, those most likely to have to compete with the new arrivals for jobs, were found to show significantly higher levels of prejudice than individuals of higher socioeconomic status against the Vietnamese (Cotter and Cotter 1979). The entry of Vietnamese people into the fishing industry of the Gulf Coast in the late 1970s and early 1980s provoked resentment from native-born fishermen who felt threatened by the competition (Starr 1985). Prejudice against the Vietnamese resulted in some incidents of violence. In 1983, for example, a Vietnamese high school student in Davis, California, was taunted by a group of white high school students and then stabbed to death. In 1989, in Raleigh, North Carolina, a Chinese American who was mistaken for a Vietnamese was beaten to death by men who were angry over the Vietnam War. In 1990, in Houston, a young Vietnamese American was stomped to death by skinheads. These were, of course, exceptional occurrences, but they could represent the most extreme manifestations of an incomplete acceptance of the Vietnamese by American popular opinion.

Adaptation to U.S. Society

Despite severe exit conditions—the traumatic flight combined with poor human capital and economic resources—and unfavorable contexts of reception—a lack of preexisting community ties, high levels of dependency, and an ambivalent and sometimes hostile public—Vietnamese refugees have made progress into American society after a decade or so of adjustment. Even with a continuously large refugee influx, the 1990 census data showed a number of quite striking improvements over the pattern observed 10 years earlier (see Table 7.1). The English proficiency rate was 38.6 percent, up from 26.6 percent in 1980 (and exceeding the level attained by the U.S. foreign-born population overall). The

TABLE 7.1   SELECTED SOCIOECONOMIC
CHARACTERISTICS OF VIETNAMESE-
AMERICAN POPULATION: UNITED STATES
VERSUS SAN DIEGO[1]

	United States		San Diego	
	1980	1990	1980	1990
English proficiency				
Speaking English well or very well (%)	26.6	38.6	27.4	38.1
Education (%)[2]				
Less than high school	37.8	39.2	36.5	43.3
High school graduate	22.5	17.9	18.9	15.5
Some college	27.1	26.0	31.1	28.0
College graduate	12.6	16.9	13.5	13.2
Labor force (%)[3]				
Male	65.7	71.9	52.8	75.2
Female	49.7	56.2	47.2	52.3
Self-employment (%)[3]	2.8	6.5	—	—
Median household income ($)	15,800	33,500	15,045	30,200
Home ownership (%)	37.0	48.5	32.1	43.2
Poverty (%)	28.0	25.3	22.1	27.2
Public assistance (%)	8.8	8.0	12.9	11.1
Number of cases (5% sample)	12,508	27,806	396	957

SOURCE: U.S. Bureau of the Census, 1980, 1990.
[1]Data weighted.
[2]Aged 25+.
[3]Aged 16+.

proportion of college graduates among adults aged 25 and over was
16.9 percent, up from 12.6 percent. Labor force participation rate
among males aged 16 or over was 71.9 percent, up from 65.7 percent in
1980. And ethnic entrepreneurship burgeoned at 6.5 percent as compared with 2.8 percent in 1980. As their human capital and labor force
status steadily improved, so, too, did their economic well-being. By
1990, the median household income of the Vietnamese stood at
$33,500, above the average of $30,000 for all American households;
home ownership was 49 percent, up from 37 percent in 1980; and the
poverty rate stood at 25 percent, down from 28 percent in 1980 but still
substantially higher than the national average. San Diego's Vietnamese
population generally revealed a similar pattern, with two notable excep-

tions: During the 1980s, levels of educational attainment slightly declined and the poverty rate substantially increased, with both changes likely to have been affected by the continuous influx of low-skilled refugees into the metropolitan area as well as by the exodus of more affluent Vietnamese to Santa Ana and San Jose (Rumbaut and Ima 1988). Notwithstanding improvement, the Vietnamese still lagged behind their American counterparts socioeconomically.

Progress was also noticeable among the 1.5 and second generation growing up in America. As of 1990, Vietnamese adolescents were less likely than their American peers to drop out of high school, and Vietnamese young adults were more likely than their American peers to attend college. For example, in the Los Angeles metropolitan region, the dropout rate among U.S.-born Vietnamese aged 16–19 was 5 percent compared with 8 percent among whites; the high school dropout rate among U.S.-born Vietnamese adults aged 18–24 was 9 percent, compared with 11 percent among whites; and the college attendance rate among U.S.-born Vietnamese was 50 percent, compared with 38 percent among whites (Cheng and Yang 1996). These trends, should they continue, foreshadow this group's catching up to and eventually surpassing the U.S. educational norm. However, the socioeconomic circumstances in which most Vietnamese children find themselves are still greatly disadvantaged, comparable only to those encountered by children of the most underprivileged native minority group. If Vietnamese children are to succeed, first in school and then in their careers, they cannot depend on the class resources of their families, limited as they are.

Though the record mainly highlights progress, one can also find troubling trends. The 1990 census data revealed that Vietnamese adolescents were disproportionately more likely than their other Asian counterparts to be institutionalized, constituting a quarter of all Asian institutionalized adolescents, though in absolute numbers relatively few of them were confined to correctional institutions of various sorts.[4] In terms of rates of institutionalization, Vietnamese adolescents ranked second among racial/ethnic groups (210 per 100,000), after blacks (695 per 100,000) and higher than all other Asian groups (93 per 100,000). Noticeably, this phenomenon was a problem of youth: While the rate of institutionalization for all Vietnamese was 140 per 100,000, the rate for minors under 18 was 210 per 100,000. This contrast took on an additional meaning in that while institutionalized Vietnamese adults were almost all foreign born, the delinquent youths were the products either of refugee flight (as many were unaccompanied minors) or of the U.S.

experience (Rumbaut and Ima 1988; Zhou and Bankston 1998). The evolving Vietnamese youth delinquency problems are so real and sometimes life threatening that they have become the number one concern in Vietnamese communities across the nation. A 1994 *Los Angeles Times* poll showed that the greatest number of Vietnamese in southern California named crime, street violence, and gangs as their chief community problems (*Los Angeles Times* 1994). The bifurcated trends suggest that although acculturation pressures put many Vietnamese on the road to success, they lead others to go astray, for reasons to be explored in greater detail shortly.

The Impacts of Refugee Resettlement on Children

Young people old enough to remember flight and resettlement continue to be haunted by the traumas of sudden exile. The younger ones or those born in the United States might be free of horrific memories of life in Vietnam, of the flight from the ancestral land, or of life in refugee camps. But they are still deeply affected by family histories and stereotypes about their ethnicity in the host country. The abrupt nature of the move from Vietnam to America means that life in Vietnam is still an immediate reality, even for young people whose entire lives have been spent in the United States.

The unique circumstances of refugee resettlement exact a heavy toll on the children. As mentioned previously, the movement of refugees is involuntary, lacking adequate preparation, control over final destinations, and a long-term orientation toward settlement, making it a process qualitatively different from that experienced by regular immigrants. Dislocation and disorientation of the parent generation combined with disadvantaged socioeconomic status have affected children's adjustment in several key aspects. At home, the children of refugees are often caught in a role reversal due to the social and economic isolation of parents. As children increasingly adopt the role of family spokespersons, parental authority declines, which further intensifies generational conflicts. The issue of conformity to or rebellion against parental authority and homeland cultural ways is probably one that is faced by most young people with immigrant parents. But for Vietnamese children, the fact that their parents are not simply immigrants but refugees adds a unique dimension to their outlooks on life. Hardship in Vietnam and the process of exile have become a central family myth, a shared story that shapes understanding, behavior, and identity formation. The difficulties suffered in

Vietnam and in the movement from Vietnam to America have given Vietnamese children a strong sense of their own identity. The traumas of repression and the pains of exile are not just individual biographical episodes but defining experiences for a whole people. Some young people, born or raised in the United States, may reject or react against these experiences, but they still grow up with them as ever-present parts of their own lives. Thus, one of the greatest challenges facing second-generation, or 1.5-generation, Vietnamese Americans is whether they will respect their family histories and conform to parental expectations or reject them.

At the neighborhood level, the impact of the parents' social and economic marginality on the children is profound. Most adult refugees came here with little preparation for beginning life in the new country. Although their labor force participation increases and economic dependence decreases over time, the Vietnamese are still heavily concentrated in minimum wage occupations and still disproportionately rely on public assistance to survive. The young people, keenly aware that they belong to a group that is marginal to American society, will sometimes admit to feelings of discomfort toward the relatively low-status jobs performed by their parents and dependence on public assistance. These young people are not simply agonized by the embarrassment of welfare dependency and the negative view of their parents. They have also suffered from real hardships: Their families provide them with limited resources, and they frequently live in low-income communities subject to adversarial influences of social isolation and poverty.

Vietnamese Adolescents in San Diego

San Diego has been a major resettlement center for Vietnamese refugees since 1975. Part of the reason is the location of Camp Pendleton, one of the four military camps to which the 1975 refugees were evacuated from Vietnam (Rumbaut 1989). As of 1990, the metropolitan area ranked the sixth-largest metropolitan area for Vietnamese settlement in the United States, following Anaheim–Santa Ana; Los Angeles–Long Beach; San Jose; Houston; and Washington, D.C. Of the Vietnamese residing in this metropolitan area, 81 percent were concentrated in the central city, making up the fourth-largest racial/ethnic minority group following Mexicans, blacks, and Filipinos. Of the 15 census tracts where Vietnamese were overrepresented (at least 5 percent), 12 of them had a high concentration of immigrants (ranging from 30 percent to 44 percent); 7 of them had an extremely high poverty rate (over 25 percent), and 4 had a poverty rate above the national average (16 percent to 24 percent). The Vietnamese initially clustered in a neighborhood called Linda Vista ("LV," which was later referred to as "Little Vietnam"), just north of Highway 8. During the 1980s, a much larger Vietnamese enclave took shape in East San Diego south of Highway 8, but the more resourceful Vietnamese moved north to Mira Mesa and further north to Rancho Peñasquitos (Rumbaut and Ima 1988).

In San Diego, CILS workers interviewed 363 Vietnamese eighth and ninth graders whose median age was 14 in 1992 (T1) and 304 of the same group in 1995 (T2), who had then become high school juniors or seniors. About 48 percent of these respondents were female; 15 percent were U.S. born, 46 percent were 1.75ers (the foreign born arriving before age 6), and 39 percent were 1.5ers (the foreign born arriving after age 6). Like many immigrant children arriving in the city of San Diego, Vietnamese adolescents tend to live in minority-concentrated neighborhoods and go to schools that have a majority of minority students from low-income families. The sample shows that at the neighborhood level, most the Vietnamese families lived in mixed neighborhoods that contained at least 40 percent immigrants and over half nonwhites. Over 60 percent of the Vietnamese adolescents were in schools where white students were the numerical minority; 49 percent were enrolled in inner-city schools; and 48 percent were in schools where over half of the students were qualified for receiving subsidized lunch, an indicator of poverty. The average size of the schools was 1,447, though the size of many inner-city schools in San Diego varied from year to year. One of the inner-city schools included in the survey provides an illustrative example. In 1992, Hoover High School had an enrollment of a little over 2,000 students, of whom 16 percent were white, 17 percent were black, 33 percent were Latino, and 34 percent were Asian. About 66 percent of the students were so poor that they qualified for free school lunches. In 1998, a *Los Angeles Times* article showed that of Hoover High School's 1,900 students, only about 5 percent were white; that 20 percent were black, roughly 50 percent were Latino, and 20 percent were Asian; and that the majority of students qualified for free school lunches (Woo 1998).

Also, like other immigrant children in school, Vietnamese adolescents were relatively isolated in their own co-ethnic circle. The majority (65 percent to 79 percent) of them reported having at least some friends from Asia or Vietnam, compared with only 5 percent who reported having friends from Europe or Canada and 2 percent who reported having friends from native-born minority groups. About 16 percent reported having Latino friends. Moreover, 66 percent of the Vietnamese spoke Vietnamese with their friends in school, and less than 30 percent spoke English with friends.

These patterns bear significant sociological implications on acculturation. Living in underprivileged inner-city neighborhoods, in particular, immigrant children attend schools where they meet native-born peers, many of whom have little hope for the future and have developed an oppositional outlook toward the mainstream society. They also meet foreign-born peers of other national origins, many of whom came from recent immigrant families with few socioeconomic resources and were exposed to American culture mainly through the media and TV screen. Such contact is likely to alter the pattern of acculturation, leading immigrant children to adopt goals and aspirations different from those of the mainstream middle class and of their own parents. How these children negotiate and navigate around their immediate social environment between neighborhood and home shapes their identity and acculturation experience. Next, I take a close look at the Vietnamese adolescents in San Diego from the CILS data to examine the complex process of acculturation and the particular ways by which acculturation affects children's adjustment.

Acculturation and Its Variants

The classical assimilationist perspective conceptualizes acculturation as a linear and progressively irreversible but sometimes bumpy process that leads to the reduction of cultural heterogeneity and convergence in patterns of language, thinking, feeling, and behavior. Although Gordon's is a multidimensional typology of assimilation (1964), the ideology behind this conceptualization is the normative expectation that diverse immigrant groups from underprivileged backgrounds should eventually abandon their old ways of life and become completely "melted" into the mainstream culture as indistinguishable nonethnics, or "Americans," through residential integration and occupational achievement in a sequence of succeeding generations. Thus, models measuring acculturation often operate under the assumption that there is a natural process by which diverse immigrant-ethnic groups come to share a common culture and gain equal access to the opportunity structure of society; that this process consists of gradually deserting old cultural and behavioral patterns in favor of new ones; and that, once set in motion, this process moves inevitably and irreversibly toward cultural homogeneity (Park 1928; Warner and Srole 1945).

From the assimilationist standpoint, distinctive ethnic traits such as native languages, ethnic identity, ethnic institutions, and ethnic social relations may be sources of disadvantages. These disadvantages negatively affect acculturation, but the effects are greatly reduced in each of the successive generations, since native-born generations adopt English as the primary means of communication and become more and more similar to the earlier American population in language use, outlook, and behavior. Although complete acculturation to the dominant American culture may not ensure all immigrants full social participation in the host society, immigrants must free themselves from their old cultures to begin rising up from marginal positions (Gordon 1964). How acculturation is conceptualized has been a central theme of inquiry among students of immigration. As acculturation intrinsically interacts with dynamic social environments in which it takes place, the process often entails multiple dimensions with segmented outcomes (Portes and Zhou 1993). In the following pages, I focus on examining several key measures of acculturation and delineating patterns of acculturation among the children of Vietnamese refugees using the CILS data.

Language Adaptation and De-Ethnicization

Two changes in particular denote acculturation: the first occurring when immigrants or their descendents abandon the native tongue in favor of English, and the second transpiring when they identify themselves in new ways, either linking home and host countries or dropping the home country link altogether. Assimilation models predict that language shifts and identificational changes will both be positively affected by time. Put somewhat more formally, the longer the U.S. residency, the more complete the switching from foreign language use to English monolingualism and the more likely that self-categorization will take the form of a nonhyphenated American identity.

To what extent does the experience of Vietnamese adolescents approximate the assimilationist prediction? The CILS data allow for a closer examination. On language proficiency, the CILS data include a set of survey items inquiring about a respondent's ability to speak, under-

TABLE 7.2   LANGUAGE ADAPTATION
AMONG VIETNAMESE ADOLESCENTS

	T1 (%)	T2 (%)
English proficiency		
Ability to speak English very well	51.2	53.9
Ability to understand English very well	50.0	53.9
Ability to read English very well	47.1	49.7
Ability to write English very well	46.8	41.8
Mother-tongue proficiency		
Ability to speak parental language very well	41.4	33.6
Ability to understand parental language very well	42.8	37.5
Ability to read parental language very well	17.1	14.1
Ability to write parental language very well	15.7	11.2
Language use		
English monolingual	6.9	7.4
Fluent bilingual	29.2	22.3
Preference to speak English	51.8	74.3
N	363	304

SOURCE: CILS 1992, 1995.

stand, read, and write English as well as his or her mother tongue. The response scales range from "very well," "well," and "not well" to "very little." From these language proficiency items, I have constructed three new variables: English monolingualism (coded 1 for those who reported speaking English only), fluent bilingualism (coded 1 for those reporting speaking, understanding, reading, and writing English very well while at the same time speaking and understanding Vietnamese well), and preference to speak English (code 1 for those selecting English as the language they prefer to speak most of the time). In terms of identity, the CILS survey included an open-ended question asking respondents to identify which ethnic- or national-origin category they use to identify themselves. Using this information, I have constructed an ethnic identity variable by collapsing all possible answers into five categories: Vietnamese, Vietnamese American, Asian American, Other, or American.

Table 7.2 shows the patterns of language adaptation among Vietnamese adolescents in San Diego at T1 and T2. The data indicate a general tendency of convergence toward English corresponding with a divergence from Vietnamese. The change in language proficiency conforms to what is predicted by assimilationist models—English language proficiency increases over time with decreasing proficiency in

TABLE 7.3   ETHNIC IDENTITY AMONG
VIETNAMESE ADOLESCENTS

	T1 (%)	T2 (%)
Ethnic identity		
Vietnamese	44.1	52.6
Vietnamese American	46.3	31.6
Asian American	.3	14.1
Other	6.6	1.3
American	2.7	.4
Ethnic resilience		
Viewing one's chosen identity as very important		58.6
Vietnamese		69.4
Vietnamese-American		47.9
Asian-American		44.2
Other		50.0
American		0
N	363	304

SOURCE: CILS 1992, 1995.

one's mother tongue. The trend in language use also reveals a similar pattern, though not as clear cut. English monolingualism, representing only a small fraction of the group, increased only slightly, but fluent bilingualism decreased quite significantly, with more adolescents preferring to speak English as of T2.

While language adaptation seems to be linear and straightforward, de-ethnicization appears to be a more complex process. Patterns of self-reported ethnic identity among Vietnamese adolescents shifted over time, but that shift was by no means linear. As shown in Table 7.3, in 1992, 44.1 percent of respondents identified themselves ubiquitously as Vietnamese; another 46.3 percent, as Vietnamese Americans; almost none, as Asian Americans; and only a few (less than 3 percent), as Americans. Three years later, the modal category became the national-origin category, with over half of the respondents (52.6 percent) identifying as Vietnamese. The proportion identified as Vietnamese American dropped to 31.6 percent, the proportion identified as Asian American increased substantially to 14.1 percent, and the proportion identified as American dropped to almost 0 (only 1 case). The varied patterns of ethnic identification do not appear to be associated with gender and generational status.[5] With gender and generational status controlled, the self-reported identity associated with national origin or one with a hyphen is still the dominant category. These findings complicate the prospect of acculturation.

What is more interesting about this identify shift is that among those who identified themselves as Vietnamese at T1 (127 out of 304), 63 percent (83) retained that identification while 21 percent (27) switched to considering themselves Vietnamese American by T2. In contrast, among those who identified themselves as American (10 out of 304) at T1, all had switched to either Vietnamese or Vietnamese American or Asian American by T2. Comparatively, among those who identified themselves as Vietnamese American (146 out of 304) at T1, 39 percent (57) remained so identified while 46 percent (67) dropped the hyphen by T2. Patterns of identity shifts are multidirectional.

It may be argued that self-reported identity among adolescents should not be treated as a reliable measure of ethnic resilience because teenagers' identity formation is influenced not simply by acculturation but also by the process of growing up as adolescents. To what extent do these adolescents take their chosen ethnicity seriously? The respondents in CILS were asked another question immediately after they had chosen their identities: "How important is this identity to you?" Possible responses were "not important," "somewhat important," and "very important." As shown at the bottom rows of Table 7.3, 58.6 percent of all respondents viewed their chosen identities as very important. Among those who identified themselves as Vietnamese, almost 70 percent regarded this ethnic choice as very important, compared with 50 percent or less among those choosing other identities. This finding may not exclude the possibility of adolescent identity swing. However, given that fact that more adolescents shifted their identities back to the unhyphenated ethnic category (their parents' ethnicity) than the other way around, the chosen national-origin identity was both real and seriously taken, indicating a strong ethnic resilience among Vietnamese adolescents. Here, the linear prediction of an ideal "ethnic-turned-American" scenario did not seem to fit well with the Vietnamese. The Vietnamese adolescents' experience was definitely not de-ethnicization but rather ethnic resilience. This reverse pattern challenges the traditional notion of acculturation.

Perception, Feelings, and Expectation of Discrimination

At another dimension, acculturation may be measured by an individual's perception, feelings, and expectation of social acceptance or treatment by the host society. The assimilationist models assume a unified host society to which immigrants are expected to conform and attribute new immigrants' uneasiness, anxiety, and discomfort with the host society and their perception and feelings of discrimination to the lack of exposure and initial disadvantages. Over time, immigrants, especially their children, are expected to experience greater ease and comfort with American life as they become an indistinguishable part of the host society. For example, upon arrival, immigrants tend to cluster in ethnic enclaves for emotional and instrumental supports provided by co-ethnics or ethnic institutions because they are structurally and culturally barred from participation in the larger society. As they overcome disadvantages associated with the cultural lag or the lack of human capital, they will face fewer entry barriers. Likewise, their perception of the host society will be increasingly favorable as they become an integral part of that society.

Stratification models provide contrary hypotheses. Because American society is stratified by class and race, perceptions, feelings, and expectations of social acceptance or treatment are inevitably shaped by the system of stratification. Often times, members of the first generation are eager to embrace the American ideals of individual freedom and equal opportunity. Upon arrival, they are busy trying to rebuild their lives in the new land or are simply striving for survival and tend to view their own initial disadvantages or downward mobility as temporary and surmountable. Thus, the less acculturated are less likely to be affected, at least psychologically, by the negative effects of racial/ethnic stratification. As they become more acculturated, their perception of the host society will necessarily be molded by the social or racial strata of which they have become a part. While the less acculturated first-generation members may be slow in adopting the same sense of entitlement and deprivation as the native born, their children, with a birth right and a high degree of acculturation, tend to be more likely than their parent generation to see things through a racial/ethnic lens and thus more likely to attribute certain life and work experiences to factors associated with racial or ethnic group memberships.

Table 7.4 explores this possibility with regard to perceived, felt, and expected discrimination and makes comparisons between children and their parents. Perception of discrimination was measured by two survey items in the CILS. Children and parents were asked similar questions but in a somewhat different way. Children were asked whether they agree with the following two statements: "There is racial discrimination in economic opportunities in the U.S." and "Americans generally

TABLE 7.4   PERCEPTIONS, FEELINGS, AND
EXPECTATIONS OF DISCRIMINATION:
VIETNAMESE ADOLESCENTS VERSUS PARENTS

	Child		Parent
	T1 (%)	T2 (%)	T2 (%)
Perception of discrimination			
Racial discrimination in economic opportunities: Agree a lot	31.6	30.9	1.6[1]
Americans feel superior to foreigners: Agree a lot	27.9	35.9	52.9[2]
Feeling of discrimination			
Had been discriminated against: Yes	65.5	72.4	27.0
Felt discriminated by teachers: Yes	17.5	29.3	
Felt discriminated by students: Yes	38.4	41.4	
Felt discriminated by counselors: Yes	6.0	13.8	
Felt discriminated by whites: Yes	25.1	36.2	
Felt discriminated by Latinos: Yes	7.6	18.8	
Felt discriminated by blacks: Yes	25.7	25.7	
Expectation of discrimination			
Expected discrimination no matter what	35.0	37.3	8.2[3]
Primary reason for discrimination			
Race/Ethnicity/Nationality	59.6	61.1	16.3
N	363	304	251

SOURCE: CILS 1992, 1995.
    [1]Parents responding "a little less" to the question about opportunities for economic advancement as compared with other racial/ethnic/national-origin groups.
    [2]Parents responding "superior" to the question about how white Americans consider themselves.
    [3]Parents responding "yes" to one of the three questions about expected discrimination against their children.

feel superior to foreigners." Possible answers ranged from "agree a lot," "agree a little," and "disagree a little" to "disagree a lot." Parents were asked two comparable questions: "Compared to people of other races or nationalities, you view opportunities for your own job advancement as: a lot less, a little less, same as others, a little more, or a lot more" and "In general, you think that white Americans consider themselves: superior, equal, or inferior."

As shown in the upper part of Table 7.4, the overall perceptions about racial discrimination and native or white superiority were substantial. Almost a third of Vietnamese adolescents held pessimistic views on overall racial discrimination in economic opportunities, and the decreases in reporting from T1 to T2 were insignificant. Comparatively, parents held a more optimistic view. Though measures in the parental survey were not exactly the same as those in the children's survey, less than 2 percent of the parents viewed their own economic opportunities as "a lot less" than people of other race or national origins. In terms of the perceived superiority of Americans, however, children and parents varied widely but the reverse: About a third of the children at T2 thought that Americans felt that they were better than foreigners, up significantly from T1 (27.9 percent), while over half of the parents thought that white Americans considered themselves superior. One possible explanation for the parent-child disparity in perception is that parents may have formed stereotypical preconceptions about white superiority before migration, whereas children's perception may be based more on their actual exposure than preconceptions.

The middle part of Table 7.4 reports feelings of discrimination. Children were asked a straightforward question: "Have you ever felt discriminated against?" Parents were asked a similar question: "Do you feel that you have been discriminated against?" Answers to both questions were a simple yes or no. As shown, the feeling of discrimination varied widely between children and parents. Children were over twice as likely as their parents to report that they had felt discrimination, and such reporting increased over time. Among children, there were specific measures on how they felt about discrimination by various groups. Noticeably, there was a significant increase over time in their reporting on all groups except for African-American students. It is noteworthy that the proportions reporting discrimination by counselors and by Latinos increased over 100 percent, which should not be taken lightly despite the overall low proportions. School counselors usually work closely with students at a more intimate and less threatening basis than teachers. The significant increase in feelings about counselor discrimination are suggestive of serious problems in the way in which schools treat Vietnamese students. Likewise, the significant increase in Latino discrimination may suggest that intergroup tensions are being built up and accumulated among students in school, since most of the Vietnamese students attend schools where Latino students are overconcentrated.

The lower part of Table 7.4 examines expected discrimination. Respondents were asked whether they thought the statement "No matter how much education I get, people will still discriminate against me" was "very true," "partly true," "not very true," or "not true at all." Over a third of the respondents considered the statement very true or partly true, and there was a modest increase over time. There were no directly comparable questions in the parental survey, but parents were asked three yes-no questions about expected discrimination against their children by white Americans: (1) "My child will experience opposition if he/she joins a club of white Americans," (2) "My child will experience opposition if he/she moves into a white American neighborhood," and (3) "My child will experience opposition if he/she marries a white American." About 8 percent responded affirmatively to the first and third statement, and only 2 percent answered yes to the second statement. Here, the differences in parent-child views were significantly large. Finally, children and parents differed in attribution; children were much more likely than their parents to single out race, ethnicity, or nationality as the primary reason for discrimination.

Of course, these findings are by no means conclusive. It is not uncommon for adolescents, native born and immigrant alike, to constantly change or adjust their perception about the world as they experience the pain and tensions of growing up. However, the consistency in reporting patterns over time among adolescents and the persistent gaps between parents and children in their perceptions, feelings, and expectations of discrimination are beyond the mere agonizing experience of adolescence.

Generational Dissonance and Consonance

Conflict between immigrant parents and their U.S.-born or -raised children is a perennial theme in the study of immigrant adaptation. Members of the second generation want to fit in. Because their frame of reference is shaped by the lessons learned from their American peers, from the television screen, and from other forms of mass media, this process of fitting in also means that the children want more than their parents do. Parents, in contrast, tend to focus on survival as well as economic mobility. More importantly, they retain a dual frame of reference in which the norms of the home society, not the host society, provide the benchmark against which to assess their accomplishments. These differences provide the flash points for the conflict between immigrant children and their parents. In the children's eyes, the parents are traditional minded and old fashioned, holding tightly to "old world" values, norms, and behavioral patterns, which inhibit assimilation. In the parents' eyes, the children are too attracted by American culture and its negative influences.

Differing life experiences between children and parents inevitably widen the generational gap, leading to intense bicultural conflicts that push children and parents into separate social worlds. However, it may be simplistic to assume that the parent generation is reluctant to let go of old-country traditions and ties and that the younger generation is eager to discard and sever them. For many of today's new immigrants, acculturation began before arrival in the United States, thanks to the influence exercised by American media in their homelands and, in the Vietnamese case, a direct American presence (Rumbaut 1997 and 1999a). Hence, immigrant parents and children will inevitably share certain experiences in acculturation while differing in many others.

The generational gap between immigrant adolescents' world and their parents' world is best captured by what Portes and Rumbaut conceptualize as "generational dissonance and generational consonance" (Portes and Rumbaut 1996). *Generational consonance* occurs when parents and children both remain unacculturated or both acculturate at the same rate or both agree on selective acculturation. *Generational dissonance* occurs when children neither correspond to levels of parental acculturation nor conform to parental guidance, leading to role reversal and parent-child conflicts. Past studies of earlier European immigrant family life have shown intense generational dissonance in the family over host-society and homeland interests (Brown 1994; Child 1943; Covello 1972). However, other studies have also found that generational conflicts within immigrant families do not necessarily frustrate successful adaptation to a host society. In fact, many immigrant families today consciously modify and adapt their own values, such as the emphasis on education, to make them more congruent with the host society than with the homeland, laying the foundation for generational consonance (Schulz 1983; Sung 1987; Zhou and Bankston 1998).

Whether or not generational conflicts lead to negative adaptational outcomes depends largely on the class status of the family as well as that of the community. Today's new second generation comes from diverse socioeconomic backgrounds. Children from middle-class families may not like their parents' ways of pushing them to do as the parents expect, but these children are shielded with a comfortable safety net to counter negative cultural influences and are unlikely to reject the expectations of the community in which they live, which dovetail with their familial expectations. Children from poor families, in contrast, lack such a safety net and often encounter in their neighborhoods a gap between familial goals and those prevailing in their local social environment, which are often marginal to and sometimes even at odds with the larger society. Under this situation, rejecting familial goals on the part of the children can cause stagnation or downward mobility.

Worlds Apart: Generational Dissonance

At what point do children and parents diverge? Language is undoubtedly the foremost point of divergence. Parents' lack of English proficiency not only jeopardizes their own social mobility but also creates intense generational tensions. For example, parents who are unable to speak English well will in many respects become dependent on their children for daily contact with the outside world, hence putting the children who act as interpreters and translators on behalf of the parents in an authoritative position. Such role reversal usually leads to weakening parental control. Meanwhile, the children are anxious that they may never become "American" because of these duties and intrinsic family and ethnic ties (Zhou 1997a, 1997b; Zhou and Bankston 1998).

Here I examine two aspects of language dissonance: the language proficiency gap and fluent bilingualism. As discussed previously, fluent bilingualism is operationalized in terms of the fluency in speaking, understanding, reading, and writing English and fluency in speaking and understanding one's mother tongue. This measure is designed to capture the extent to which children and parents maintain fluid and regular communication, assuming that continued native language retention would allow parents to maintain effective control over children.

While children are far more likely to acquire English language proficiency than their parents and to do so at a more rapid rate, the degree of divergence from parents may vary from one dimension to another. For example, Vietnamese children are more than 10 times as likely as their parents to speak, understand, read, or write English very well. This substantial language gap can be viewed as a potential risk for immigrant families, where parents may feel a loss of control over their children and children may develop resentment their parents' broken or accented English. It can also be a potential risk, causing the children to sever ties with ethnic institutions that give meaning and directions to the lives of the parent generation (Habenstein 1998). Nonetheless, language dissonance is not just an intergenerational problem; it is also a problem among members of the younger generation. Over 70 percent of Vietnamese adolescents use the Vietnamese language frequently with

Figure 7.1.   Key Points of Divergence: Children versus Parents, 1995

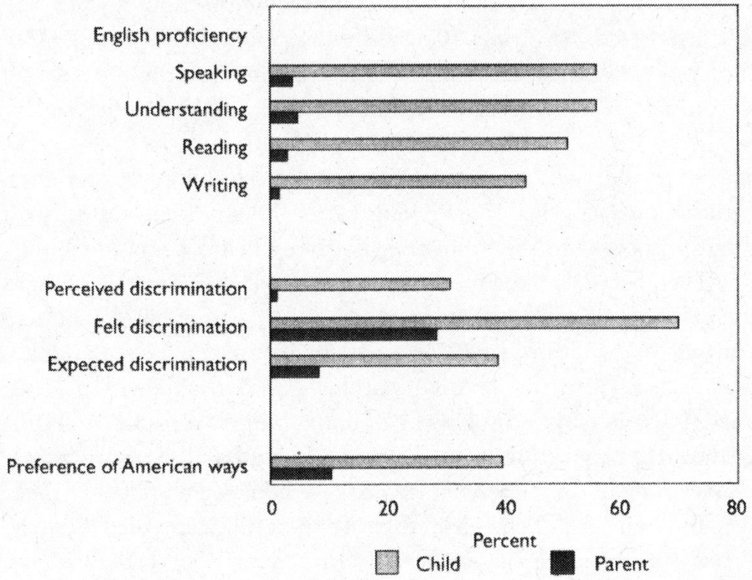

SOURCE: CILS 1995.

their friends in school, and among those whose self-reported identity is Vietnamese, over 70 percent are limited bilinguals.

Another point of divergence lies in perceptions, feelings, and experiences of American society. Immigrant children and their parents tend to perceive their host society and their relationships with it from different angles. In terms of perceived discrimination in economic opportunities, felt discrimination, and expected discrimination, there are significant generational gaps (see also Table 7.4). Take felt discrimination, for example: Children are almost three times as likely as their parents to report feeling of discrimination, not to mention the much wider gaps in perceived and expected discrimination. And children are three times as likely as their parents to prefer American ways most of the time. Figure 7.1 depicts the aspects and degree of divergence.

It should be noted that generational dissonance occurs when children acculturate more quickly than parents and parents lose the ability to exercise guidance, developments that lead to intensified parent-child conflicts, role reversal, and ultimately the loss of parental authority (Portes and Rumbaut 1996). As we all know, children will almost always acculturate more swiftly, and this form of generational dissonance is assumed to start soon after children enter school and to become exacerbated over time (Covello 1972; Habenstein 1998). The question has to do with whether and when the difference in the pace of acculturation leads to intense intergenerational conflicts and the loss of parental control.

Figure 7.2 addresses to what extent Vietnamese children experience intergenerational conflicts by looking at the longitudinal patterns of children's responses to the following six survey items: being in trouble with parents, being disliked by parents, parent's lack of interest in their children, being embarrassed by parents' ways, parent-child conflict, and parent-child split on American ways. As Figure 7.3 shows, about a quarter of the adolescents reported that they got in trouble with parents because of disagreements in the way of doing things "most of or all the time," but this proportion is not particularly high and did not change much over time. A small percentage of these adolescents felt that their parents did not like them—less than 10 percent responded "partly true" or "very true" to the statement "My parents don't like me" in 1992—and that increased only 2 percent in 1995. Relatively more adolescents (about 30 percent) responded "partly true" or "very true" to the statement "My parents are usually not interested in what I say" in 1992, but that percentage remained the same in 1995. A quarter of the adolescents initially reported that they were embarrassed by their parents' ways, and that proportion fell to 18 percent in 1995.

Parent-child conflict and parent-child split on American ways are two reconstructed measures for generational dissonance that take into account both the children's and their parents' views. *Parent-child conflict* refers specifically to the situation where the children feel embarrassed by parents' ways and at the same time get in trouble with parents because of disagreements over how things should be done or when the children think that their parents either did not like them or were uninterested in what they say. As shown, the proportion of those reporting conflicts was low, and there was not much change from 1992 to 1995. *Parent-child split on American ways* refers to the situation where the children prefer American ways when their parents dislike them. Here, parent-child split on American ways was moderate (less than 30 percent) and remained similar over time. Overall, these findings imply a relatively low level of generational dissonance among Vietnamese adolescents. Put in somewhat different terms, the generations did not always agree, but the range of disagreement was relatively modest and

Figure 7.2.   Generational Dissonance: 1992 and 1995

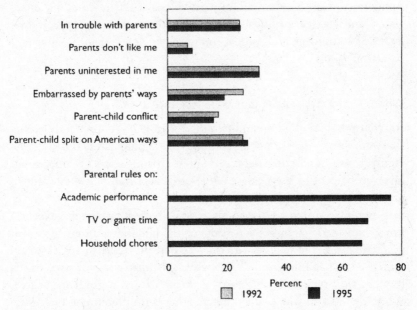

SOURCE: CILS 1992, 1995.

did not appear to eventuate in sharp conflict. Not surprisingly, then, the survey also shows that parents maintained relatively strong control. About two-thirds of the parents reported that they had specific rules about academic performance (that is, about maintaining a certain GPA and doing homework), watching television or playing video games, and household chores. It would appear that these rules are also successfully enforced, given the relatively low levels of parent-child conflict, as just noted previously.

Thus, generational dissonance need not always cause a loss of parental control. In this case, parents and children differed in linguistic habits, in perceptions of discrimination, and in preference for American ways, yet parental authority appeared unchallenged. That this disagreement did not eventuate in conflict, I suggest, results from the structure of social relations within the family and the immigrant community, which, in turn, prevents the displacement of parental authority so often found in immigrant communities. As I have shown elsewhere, when immigrant parents and children maintain ties to a tightly knit ethnic community, they are likely to share similar experiences with other parents and children and to receive consistent support and control from the community. The ethnic community provides a space for co-ethnic interaction and creates a buffer zone to ease the tension between individual self-fulfillment and family commitment (Zhou 1998; Zhou and Bankston 1998).

Worlds Connected: Generational Consonance

At what point do children and parents converge? Children and parents share common educational aspirations and similar familial beliefs. As Figure 7.3 shows, both generations aim high with respect to education: Over 90 percent of Vietnamese adolescents reported that they want to attain at least a bachelor's degree, an answer echoed by 87 percent of their parents. Moreover, the children actually maintain higher expectations than their parents: 68 percent of the children wanted to earn a graduate degree, compared with only 16 percent of their parents. Interestingly, the children didn't perceive this disparity, as two-thirds thought that their parents expected them to earn a graduate degree. While we have no way of knowing whether this difference is an artifact of the survey or reflects some real generational divergence, it may not matter: The crucial point is not so much the correctness of the children's perception as the relationship between those perceptions—whether right or wrong—and their own expectations. In short, the children aspired to those goals that they perceived their parents to hold.

Parents and children also intersect on the home front. Family cohesion and familism have been central in the lives of Vietnamese Americans. Many parents fear that as children become increasingly acculturated, they may be losing their children and that the level of familism may decline. The 1995 CILS data contain three relevant questions on family cohesion and three on familism. *Family cohesion* refers to the attitude and feeling toward family, reflected in the responses to the following statements: "Family members (often or always) like to spend free time with each other," "Family members (often or always) feel very close to each other," and "Family togetherness is (often or always) very important." *Familism* concerns the family ideology about duties and obligations, indicated by agreements or disagreements with the following statements: "If someone has the chance to help a person get a job, it is always better to choose a relative rather than a friend"; "When someone has a serious problem, only relatives can help"; and "The person who helps you the most with homework is a family member (parents or siblings)."

Figure 7.3.   Generational Consonance: 1995

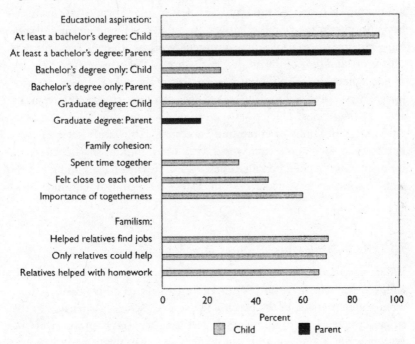

SOURCE: CILS 1995.

Since the CILS data do not contain parallel information on the earlier survey, I cannot make a longitudinal comparison. Figure 7.3 shows a considerably high level of family cohesion: 35 percent reported that family members often or always liked to spend free time with each other, 47 percent reported that family members often or always felt close to each other, and 60 percent reported that family togetherness was often or always very important. Familism is even more compelling: 71 percent agreed that they would give preference to a relative over a friend as regarded offering help in finding jobs, 70 percent agreed that only relatives could help with serious problems, and 67 percent agreed that the person who helped the most with homework was either a parent or a sibling.

So far, I have shown the variants of acculturation and the dynamics of intergenerational relations. How immigrant children are related to American society is largely contingent upon particular patterns of language use; ethnic identification; perceptions, feelings, and expectations of daily experiences; and various forms of social relations in and out of the family. At the societal level, it involves cross-cultural exposure and intergroup relations. At the family level, it involves bicultural socialization and intergenerational relations. At either level, immigrant children must constantly straddle these different worlds—that of their adolescent peers and that of the adults. In the process of growing up, they are unlike other American adolescents, who simply fight between an adolescent world and an adult world. They also have to struggle to make sense of the inconsistencies between two separate adult worlds: that of the immigrant family or community and that of the larger society. Even within their own adolescent world, they often find inconsistencies centering around hyphenated identities. Next, I focus on examining the effects of some of these acculturation issues on the adjustment outcomes.

The Effects of Acculturation

What constitutes successful adjustment? Recent studies of immigrant children have focused on several key measures of adjustment: self-esteem and depression at the psychological level, school suspension at the behavioral level, and educational performance and aspiration at the academic level (Portes and Rumbaut 1996; Rumbaut 1997, 1999a, 1999b; Zhou and Bankston 1998). Accordingly, I examine five reconstructed variables in the CILS indicating different levels of adjustment. Self-esteem is a composite measure from 10 survey items developed by Rosenberg (1979) with a scale ranging from 1 to 4, and depression is a composite measure from four survey items ranging from 1 to 4 (see Appendix 7.1 for details; also see Rumbaut 1999b). Average GPA is a continuous variable ranging from 0 to 5. Number of school suspension varies from 0 to 6. Educational aspiration is categorized into a dummy variable coded 1 for those who expect to earn a graduate degree and 0 otherwise. Table 7.5 provides descriptive information on the these dependent variables. Over a third of Vietnamese adolescents reported low self-esteem, and almost a third reported high depression. Over time, both self-esteem and depression increased modestly. More than half of the Vietnamese had above-average GPAs. About 80 percent had never been suspended from school during the study period. Educational aspiration was strong at both T1 and T2, and the increase was significant.

How are the various acculturation measures—ethnic identity, language use, felt discrimination, generational dissonance, and generational consonance—related to Vietnamese adolescents' adjustment? To

TABLE 7.5   SELF-ESTEEM, DEPRESSION,
SCHOOL SUSPENSION, AVERAGE GPA,
AND EDUCATIONAL ASPIRATION

Adaptation Measures	T1	T2
Average self-esteem score (ranged 1 to 4)	3.1	3.1
Low, > 3.0 (%)	37.4	35.5
Medium, 3.0 to 3.5 (%)	40.8	38.9
High, < 3.5 (%)	21.8	25.6
Average depression score (ranged 1 to 4)	1.7	1.7
Low, > 1.5 (%)	42.1	38.5
Medium, 1.5 to 1.99 (%)	27.6	27.0
High, < 1.99 (%)	30.3	34.5
Average GPA (ranged 1 to 5)	—	3.0
Low, > 2 (%)	—	11.8
Average, 2 to 3.0 (%)	—	31.6
Above average, < 3.0 (%)	—	56.6
Average school suspension (ranged 0 to 6)	—	.4
Never (%)	—	80.6
Once (%)	—	8.2
More than once (%)	—	11.2
Educational aspiration (%)		
Less than high school	12.5	8.2
College degree	27.7	24.0
Graduate degree	59.8	67.8
N	304	304

SOURCE: CILS 1992, 1995.

examine the effects of acculturation, I use ordinary least-squared (OLS) regression models (and a logistic regression model for educational aspiration). I include eight key independent variables in my multivariate analyses. These are ethnic identity (coded 1 for those who identified themselves as Vietnamese or Vietnamese American and regarded this identity as very important), fluent bilingualism (coded 1), English monolingualism (coded 1), felt discrimination (a composite measure ranging from 0 to 7), parent-child conflict (coded 1 if adolescents felt embarrassed by parents' ways and at the same time often got in trouble with parents or thought that their parents either did not like them or were uninterested in what they said), parent-child split on American ways (coded 1 if children preferred American ways when their parents disliked American ways), parent-child agreement in educational achievement (coded 1 for those whose educational aspiration matched that of their parents), and family cohesion (a composite measure ranging from 0 to 15). My multivariate analyses also control for gender (code 1 as female), length of U.S. residence (coded 1 for those who arrived in the United States less than five years previously), parental education (coded 1 as for having either parent with a high school education or more), and attendance at an inner-city school (coded 1). The number of hours spent studying daily is included as an additional control in the model predicting GPA. Appendix 7.2 provides detailed information on the operationalization of these independent and control variables.

Based on the findings in the previous sections, I hypothesize that ethnic identity, fluent bilingualism, and generational consonance positively influence outcomes, while English monolingualism, felt discrimination, and generational dissonance negatively influence outcomes. Figure 7.4 provides OLS or logistic regression models predicting five adjustment outcomes. To ease interpretation, I have converted logit coefficients to odds ratios (see Appendix 7.3): Values greater than 1 indicate a positive relationship between any independent variable and the relevant outcome variable, and values less than 1 denote a negative relationship. The black solid bars signal significant effects, while gray solid bars indicate effects that do not reach statistical significance. Since space precludes detailed discussion of the individual coefficients, I simply summarize some of the most important findings. First, fluent bilingualism significantly boosted self-esteem, reduced depression, and raised educational aspiration, supporting existing research about the importance of maintaining communication with parents in immigrant families (Bankston and Zhou 1995; Rumbaut 1994). Second, Vietnamese or Vietnamese-American identity taken as very important by the adolescents significantly influenced self-esteem but did not yield noticeable effects on other outcomes. Third, felt discrimination significantly increased depression but also raised educational aspiration. Fourth, neither of the two generational dissonance measures had significant effects, though they both point to expected directions. However, parent-child conflict significantly raised rather than reduced educational aspiration. Finally, the effects of both measures of generational consonance are in the expected directions: Parent-child agreement in educational achievement significantly affected outcomes at emotional, behavioral, and academic levels, while family cohesion significantly affected the adolescents only at the emotional level.

Figure 7.4. OLS or Logic Regression Models Predicting Self-Esteem, Depression, School Suspension, GPA, and Educational Aspiration

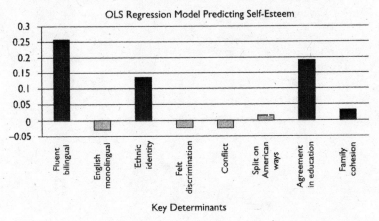

OLS Regression Model Predicting Self-Esteem

Key Determinants

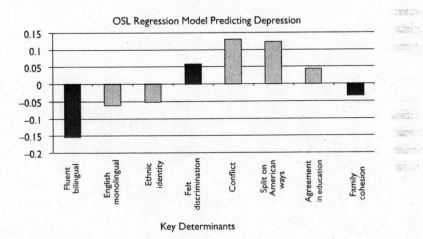

OSL Regression Model Predicting Depression

Key Determinants

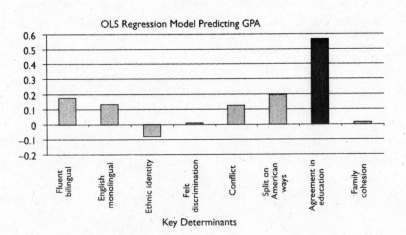

OLS Regression Model Predicting GPA

Key Determinants

Figure 7.4   (*continued*)

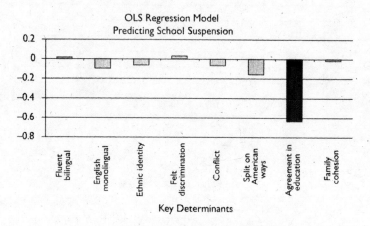

OLS Regression Model
Predicting School Suspension

Key Determinants

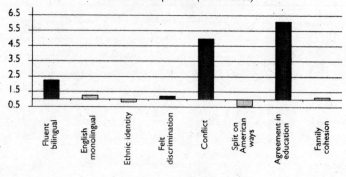

Logistic Model Predicting
Educational Aspiration (Odds Ratios)

Key Determinants

SOURCE: CILS 1995.
NOTE: Black solid bars, $p < .05$ (two-tailed test). Gray solid bars indicate
statistical insignificance.

Conclusion

For the children of refugees and immigrants, the adaptation to American society involves constant struggles: learning to speak a language different from the one spoken at home, developing one's own identity, going to school, meeting societal expectations, and ultimately fitting in. In contrast to their parents, these children are unlikely to use their parents' homeland standards to assess their process in the new land. Instead, they consciously develop and modify their own coping strategies to become acculturated and incorporated in American society. Inevitably, the children straddle different social worlds. While they often experience conflict with their parents, the children also find ample room for agreement. Thus, this study of acculturation among Vietnamese adolescents in San Diego suggests that acculturation takes a multidimensional form.

Though generalization at this point may be premature, here I only summarize some of the most important themes that have emerged from this study and speculate about their implications. First, immigrant adolescents experience much faster linguistic adaptation than their parents, with the language gap between English proficiency and native language proficiency widening with time. While acquiring English proficiency is undoubtedly crucial, maintaining fluent bilingualism is equally important and sometimes even more beneficial. As shown in the analysis, English monolingualism does not have any significant effects on outcomes, but fluent bilingualism significantly raises self-esteem, reduces depression, and increases educational aspiration. This effect implies that fluency in the mother tongue can help maintain effective parent-child communication and thus effective parent control in non-English-speaking immigrant families.

Second, immigrant adolescents do not have a single answer to what is meant by becoming "American" or becoming "ethnic." As they become more mature and extend their span of life lived in the United States, they are more likely to choose an identity affiliated either with their ancestral homeland or with a hyphenated ethnicity, rather than abandoning their Vietnamese identity. This reverse trend of identity switching and ethnic resilience is not unique to the Vietnamese. In fact, it has found to be the model form among children of the new immigrants, many of whom are the subjects of study for this book. More importantly, ethnic resilience does not prove disadvantageous but rather boosts self-esteem. Today, many immigrant adolescents may acquire an American identity by becoming indistinguishable from their peers in the established American mainstream, as predicted by the assimilation theory. But presently, the adoption of an American identity takes on a deeper meaning: It includes rather than excludes an ethnic component. Successful adaptation of the second generation depends on the extent to which those born or reared in the United States continue to hold a distinctive ethnic identity and on the extent to which this distinctive identity provides resources in meeting the challenges of American life.

Third, the immigrant family is the site of control and tension while also serving as a source of social support. The children may experience generational dissonance and consonance simultaneously, and conflicts in the home may not uniformly lead to undesirable outcomes. In the case of the Vietnamese, generational dissonance, in terms of parent-child conflict and parent-child split on American ways, did not have observable negative effects on adaptation, except that it significantly increased educational aspiration. In contrast, generational consonance, as indicated by parent-child agreement on educational achievement and family cohesion, served as the single most important determinant for successful adaptation. Of course, young people whose families hold high expectations for them, have strict rules about proper behavior, and stress hard work are likely to perform well in school, but that does not necessarily preclude exceptions—some may still perform poorly, especially when they have close ties to youths from disadvantaged native minorities (Portes and Stepick 1993). Thus, it seems unlikely that parent-child conflict or parent-child disagreement on American ways results in uniform outcomes.

In sum, acculturation involves multiple dimensions as well as multiple directions. The varied patterns of acculturation pose a challenge to the linear thinking of the assimilationist perspective. With different linkages to a multicomplexity of social contexts, these patterns will directly affect children's psychological well-being, school performance, and academic aspiration, which have significant bearing on their career prospects and life chances. However, maintaining ties to the world of immigrant parents may not constitute a distinct disadvantage. Generational or bicultural conflicts, however tense they may be, may differ at the level of perception from the level of actual experience among immigrant adolescents. Not all "old world" ways are obsolete; some of them may actually facilitate adaptation. Thus, additive or selective acculturation, rather than subtractive or indiscriminant acculturation, may become the normative path to social mobility.

APPENDIX 7.1 OPERATIONALIZATION AND DISTRIBUTION OF THE DEPENDENT VARIABLES: SELF-ESTEEM, DEPRESSION, SCHOOL SUSPENSION, GPA, AND EDUCATIONAL ASPIRATION

Adaptation Measures	T1 (%)	T2 (%)
Self-esteem		
I am a person of worth: Agree a lot	54.1	56.3
I have a number of good qualities: Agree a lot	52.0	60.5
I feel I am a failure: Disagree a lot	49.9	48.4
I do things as well as most others: Agree a lot	60.7	58.2
I do not have much to be proud of: Disagree a lot	44.8	46.7
I take a positive attitude toward myself: Agree a lot	45.0	44.1
I am satisfied with myself: Agree a lot	43.2	38.8
I wish I had more respect for myself: Disagree a lot	22.3	30.9
I certainly feel useless at times: Disagree a lot	20.3	18.1
At times I think I am no good at all: Disagree a lot	30.3	33.9
Depression		
I felt sad: Most of the time	13.1	21.7
I could not get going: Most of the time	17.0	19.4
I did not feel like eating: Most of the time	10.7	9.5
I felt depressed: Most of the time	19.9	16.4
GPA (mean)		3.1
School suspensions since Time 1 (mean)		.41
Educational aspiration (mean)		.68

SOURCE: CILS 1992, 1995.

APPENDIX 7.2   VARIABLES INCLUDED IN REGRESSION MODELS

Variable	Mean	Standard Deviation	Minimum	Maximum	N	Label
Dependent variables						
Self-esteem	3.15	.52	1.00	4.00	301	Self-esteem
Depression	1.70	.64	1.00	4.00	303	Depression
GPA	3.07	.91	.00	4.80	304	GPA
Suspension	.41	1.01	0	6	304	N of school suspensions
Educational aspiration	.68	.47	.00	1.00	304	Coded 1 as graduate degree
Independent variables						
Ethnic identity	.52	.50	.00	1.00	304	Coded 1 as Vietnamese or Vietnamese American and regarding this identity as very important
Fluent bilingualism	.27	.44	.00	1.00	304	Coded 1 as fluent bilingual
English monolingualism	.08	.26	.00	1.00	304	Coded 1 as English monolingual
Felt discrimination	2.37	2.03	.00	7.00	304	Felt discrimination
Family cohesion	10.19	3.01	3.00	15.00	304	Family cohesion
Agreement in education	.85	.36	.00	1.00	304	Coded 1 as parent-child agreement in education
Parent-child conflict	.11	.31	.00	1.00	304	Coded 1 as parent-child conflict
Parent-child split on American ways	.29	.45	.00	1.00	304	Coded 1 as parent-child disagreement in American ways
Control variables						
Female	.48	.50	.00	1.00	304	Coded 1 as female
Recency of arrival	.17	.38	.00	1.00	304	Coded 1 as recent arrivals
Parental education	.34	.47	.00	1.00	304	Coded 1 as parents with high school education or more
Inner-city schools	.48	.50	.00	1.00	304	Coded 1 as inner-city schools
Study hours	3.38	1.55	1	6	304	Hours spent studying daily

SOURCE: CILS 1992, 1995.

APPENDIX 7.3 OLS OR LOGISTIC REGRESSION MODELS PREDICTING
SELF-ESTEEM, DEPRESSION, SCHOOL SUSPENSION, AVERAGE GPA, AND
EDUCATIONAL ASPIRATION

Dependent Variables	Self-Esteem	Depression	GPA	School Suspension	Educational Aspiration
Language use					
Fluent bilingual	.257***	-.153*	.176	.016	.818*
English monolingual	-.028	-.061	.133	-.096	.211
Ethnic identity	.135**	-.051	-.078	-.059	-.181
Felt discrimination	-.022	.058***	.006	.025	.162**
Generational dissonance					
Parent-child conflict	-.023	.130	.123	-.066	1.598***
Parent-child split on American ways	.015	.123	.193	-.154	-.501
Generational consonance					
Agreement in education	.189**	.043	.565***	-.633***	1.802***
Family cohesion	.031***	-.033***	.013	-.014	.053
Control variables					
Study hours	—	—	.108***	—	—
Gender (female)	-.091	.170**	.387***	-.515***	.678**
Recency of arrival	-.243***	.237**	.144	-.338**	-.321
Parent's education	-.028	.075	.100	-.087	.279
Inner city	.026	-.039	-.182	-.030	-.458
Constant	2.663***	1.747***	1.837***	1.468***	-1.855***
R^2	.170	.112	.225	.170	—
N	301	303	304	304	304

SOURCE: CILS 1995.
***$p < .01$; **$p < .05$; *$p < .10$ (two-tailed test).

Notes

The author would like to thank Alejandro Portes, Rubén G. Rumbaut, Roger Waldinger, and Sara Curran for their helpful comments. She also thanks Vincent Fu, Rebecca Kim, and Diana Lee for their research assistance.

1. The San Diego portion of the CILS data includes a total of 363 Vietnamese adolescents from Wave I (1992) and 304 from Wave II (1995, about 16 percent attrition). Wave II also includes a parental survey with 251 Vietnamese parent interviews, about 83 percent of the student interviews at T2.

2. This section was rewritten partially from Chapter 1 of *Growing Up American* (Zhou and Bankston 1998). The chapter provides a more detailed account.

3. VOLAGs were working mainly under government contracts to oversee refugee resettlement and in most cases decided refugees destinations. The largest VOLAG was the U.S. Catholic Conference, which had the task of finding sponsors, individuals, or groups who would assume financial and personal responsibility for refugee families for up to two years (Lanphier 1983; Montero 1979).

4. Although there is no breakdown of types of institutions by detailed race categories, census data provide total numbers of institutionalized juveniles in the detailed race categories.

5. The correlation between ethnic identity and gender is not significant. While ethnic identity is significantly associated with generational status at the .05 level, the overconcentration of those in the category of Vietnamese or of Vietnamese American remains substantial across generations.

References

Bankston, Carl L. III, and Min Zhou. 1995. Effects of minority-language literacy on the academic achievement of Vietnamese youth in New Orleans. *Sociology of Education* 68 (January), pp. 1–17.

Brown, Mary E. 1994. "Parents and children: Fundamental questions about immigrant family life." In *Immigrant America: European ethnicity in the United States*, edited by Timothy Walch. New York: Garland.

Caplan, Nathan, Marcella H. Choy, and John K. Whitmore. 1989. *The boat people and achievement in America: A study of family life, hard work, and cultural values.* Ann Arbor: University of Michigan Press.

Cheng, Lucie and Philip Q. Yang. 1996. "Asians: The 'model minority' reconstructed." In *Ethnic Los Angeles*, edited by Roger Waldinger and Mehdi Bozorgmehr. New York: Russell Sage Foundation.

Child, Irving L. 1943. *Italian or American? The second generation in conflict.* New Haven: Yale University Press.

Cotter, Barbara S., and Patrick R. Cotter. 1979. "American attitudes toward Indochinese refugees: The influence of region." In *Proceedings of the First Annual Conference on Indochinese Refugees*, compiled by G. Harry Stopp

Jr. and Nguyen Manh Hung. Fairfax, Va.: Citizens Applied Research Institute of George Mason University.

Covello, Leonard. 1972. *The social background of the Italo-American school child*. Totowa, N.J.: Rowman & Littlefield.

Gans, Herbert J. 1992. Second-generation decline: Scenarios for the economic and ethnic futures of the post-1965 American immigrants. *Ethnic and Racial Studies* 15 (2), pp. 173–192.

Gordon, Milton. 1964. *Assimilation in American life*. New York: Oxford University Press.

Habenstein, Robert W. 1998. "The 'then and now' overview of the immigrant family in America." In *Ethnic families in America: Patterns and variations*, edited by Charles H. Mindel, Robert W. Habenstein, and Roosevelt Wright, Jr. 4th ed. Englewood Cliffs, N.J.: Prentice Hall.

Kelly, Gail Paradise. 1986. Coping with America: Refugees from Vietnam, Cambodia, and Laos in the 1970s and 1980s. *Annals of the American Academy of Political Social Science* 487 (September), pp. 138–149.

Lanphier, C. Michael. 1983. "Dilemmas of decentralization: Refugee sponsorship and service in Canada and the United States." In *The southeast Asian environment*, edited by Douglas R. Webster. Ottawa, Ont.: University of Ottawa Press.

Los Angeles Times. 1994. *Los Angeles Times* poll: Vietnamese in southern California. Archive number USLAT94-331. Storrs, Conn.: The Roper Center for Public Opinion Research.

Montero, Darrel. 1979. Vietnamese Americans: Patterns of resettlement and socioeconomic adaptation in the United States. Boulder, Colo.: Westview Press.

Park, Robert E. 1928. Human migration and the marginal man. *American Journal of Sociology* 33 (6), pp. 881–893.

Perlmann, Joel, and Roger Waldinger. 1997. Second generation decline? Immigrant children past and present—a reconsideration. *International Migration Review* 31 (4), pp. 893–922.

Portes, Alejandro, and Rubén G. Rumbaut. 1996. *Immigrant America: A portrait*. 2d ed. Berkeley: University of California Press.

Portes, Alejandro, and Alex Stepick. 1993. *City on the edge: The transformation of Miami*. Berkeley: University of California Press.

Portes, Alejandro, and Min Zhou. 1993. The new second generation: Segmented assimilation and its variants among post-1965 immigrant youth. *Annals of the American Academy of Political and Social Science* 530 (November), pp. 74–98.

Roberts, S. V. 1978. Boat people brave adversity to see new lives in U.S. *New York Times*, December 18, p. B8

Rosenberg, Morris. 1979. *Conceiving the self*. New York: Basic Books.

Rumbaut, Rubén G. 1989. "Portraits, patterns, and predictors of the refugee adaptation process: Results and reflections from the IHARP panel study." In *Refugees as immigrants: Cambodians, Laotians, and Vietnamese in America*, edited by David W. Haines. Totowa, N.J.: Rowman & Littlefield.

————. 1994. The crucible within: Ethnic identity, self-esteem, and segmented assimilation among children of immigrants. *International Migration Review* 28 (4), pp. 748–794.

————. 1995. "Vietnamese, Laotian, and Cambodian Americans." In *Asian Americans: Contemporary trends and issues,* edited by Pyong Gap Min. Thousand Oaks, Calif.: Sage Publications.

————. 1997. "Ties that bind: Immigration and immigrant families in the United States." In *Immigration and the family: Research and policy on U.S. immigrants,* edited by Alan Booth, Ann C. Crouter, and Nancy Landale. Hillsdale, N.J.: Lawrence Erlbaum Associates.

————. 1999a. "Assimilation and its discontents: Ironies and paradoxes." In *Rhw Handbook of International Migration: The American Experience,* edited by Charles Hirschman, Josh De Wind, and Philip Kasinitz. New York: Russell Sage Foundation.

————. 1999b. "Passages to adulthood: The adaptation of children of immigrants in southern California." In *Children of immigrants: Health, adjustment, and public assistance,* edited by Donald J. Hernandez. Washington, D.C.: National Academy of Sciences Press.

Rumbaut, Rubén G., and Kenji Ima. 1988. "Twelve case histories." In *The adaptation of Southeast Asian refugee youth: A comparative study.* Washington, D.C.: U.S. Office of Refugee Resettlement.

Schulz, Nancy. 1983. *Voyagers in the land: A report on unaccompanied southeast Asian refugee children, New York City, 1983.* Washington, D.C.: U.S. Catholic Conference, Migration and Refugee Services.

Starr, Paul D. 1985. Community structure and Vietnamese refugee adaptation: The significance of context. *International Migration Review* 16 (3), pp. 595–613.

Sung, Betty Lee. 1987. *The adjustment experience of Chinese immigrant children in New York City.* Staten Island, N.Y.: Center for Migration Studies.

Tran, Thanh V. 1991. Sponsorship and employment status among Indochinese refugees in the United States. *International Migration Review* 25 (3), pp. 536–550.

U.S. Bureau of the Census. 1980. *Census of population and housing, 1980.* Public-use microdata samples, machine-readable files, 5% sample. Washington, D.C.: U.S. Government Printing Office.

————. 1990. *Census of population and housing, 1990.* Public-use microdata sample, machine-readable files, 5% sample. Washington, D.C.: U.S. Government Printing Office.

Warner, W. Lloyd, and Leo Srole. 1945. *The social systems of American ethnic groups.* New Haven, Conn.: Yale University Press.

Woo, Elaine. 1998. Seeking causes and solutions at seven California campuses, lower standards, money, changing student body are the challenges. *Los Angeles Times,* May 17, 1998.

Zhou, Min. 1997a. Growing up American: The challenge confronting immigrant children and children of immigrants. *Annual Review of Sociology* 23, pp. 3–95.

———. 1997b. "Social capital in Chinatown: The role of community-based organizations and families in the adaptation of the younger generation." In *Beyond black and white: New voices, new faces in the United States schools,* edited by Lois Weis and Maxine S. Seller. Albany: State University of New York Press.

———. 1998. 'Parachute kids' in southern California: The educational experience of Chinese children in transnational families. *Educational Policy* 12 (6), pp. 682–704.

Zhou, Min, and Carl L. Bankston III. 1998. *Growing up American: The adaptation of Vietnamese adolescents in the United States.* New York: Russell Sage Foundation.

Chapter 8

SHIFTING IDENTITIES
AND INTERGENERATIONAL CONFLICT
Growing up Haitian in Miami

Alex Stepick, Carol Dutton Stepick, Emmanuel Eugene,
Deborah Teed, and Yves Labissiere

Emmanuel, a graduate research assistant, had passed out a survey on school violence to a class at King High School, which is predominantly Haitian. One open-ended question asked students to indicate their racial or ethnic identity. A number of students asked Emmanuel, who is Haitian himself, to explain what the question meant, a query that he and other researchers working on the same project frequently receive when they ask adolescents in Miami for their ethnic identity. Emmanuel decided to explain to the entire class that racial or ethnic identity meant "how you view yourself, if you are Haitian, African American, black, or whatever." Seemingly satisfied, the students set about filling in the questionnaire. One student who is black, however, was soon walking through the rows, looking over other students' shoulders at their answers. When this student turned in his questionnaire, Emmanuel noticed that he had not indicated his racial or ethnic identity. One-on-one, Emmanuel asked him why he had avoided that question. He replied in perfect unaccented American adolescent English, "Okay, okay, I'm going to answer the question." He retrieved the questionnaire and filled in "white."

A perplexed Emmanuel queried, "Surely, you don't see yourself as white, do you?"

The student responded, "I know I'm not white, but I don't want to reveal my identity."

"Well, where were you born?"

"The United States."

"Where were your parents born?"

"In Haiti, but I am ashamed to say that."

A few months later, at a high school a couple of miles away that has proportionally fewer Haitians and serves a population that is more working and middle class, one of the Haitian teachers of English as a Second Language (ESOL) organized a Haitian Flag Day celebration. About 1,000 kids poured into the auditorium. Most attending the celebration were recent arrivals, still enrolled in ESOL classes. Many who filled the school auditorium were dressed in Haiti's national colors of red and blue or in T-shirts emblazoned with *Quis Queya* (the aboriginal name for the island that Haiti shares with the Dominican Republic) or in stereotypical peasant garb (blue denim and straw hats). To open the program, one young man with a distinct Haitian accent welcomed everybody with the standard Haitian greeting, *"Sak pase?"* (What's happening?). In unison, the crowd roared the standard response, *"N'ap boule!"* (We're burning/rolling!). The loudspeakers then blared the Haitian national anthem as flag bearers and dancers paraded down the center and side aisles. The program consisted primarily of native Haitian folk dances and music, most performed solely by young women in red and blue costumes. The dance steps were derived primarily from Haiti's religious heritage of Vodoun. By American standards the movements are suggestive, pelvically oriented with many thrusts. The crowd loved it, jumping up out of their seats and stabbing the Haitian flags in the air.

Teachers visibly displayed their dismay, frowning their disapproval from the edges of the auditorium as if they were prison guards waiting for a riot. A week earlier, another high school had erupted in violence while protesting the school's administration. Although Haitian Flag Day was about celebration and not protest, the barely controlled boisterous energy alarmed the administrators. The vice principal cut the assembly short by announcing that there were rules that had to be followed and that the students had to respect them and act accordingly. She never exactly said what rules were in danger of being broken, leaving some with the impression that having fun and being proud of being a Haitian might be against the rules.

The truncated celebration of Haitian Flag Day and the student who was ashamed of his Haitian roots reflect a continuing, consuming struggle for Haitian youth in southern Florida. The struggle over iden-

tity and how they should present themselves and their culture defines
what the youth themselves view as the most critical aspects of their
lives. The cultural dissonance between Haitian youth and Haitian
adults, between Haitian youth and school personnel, and between
Haitian youth and other southern Florida youth becomes more important to Haitian students than their grades, test scores, or for some even
going on to college. The struggle affects all Haitian youth, regardless of
their parents' background, their neighborhood, or their school.

Theoretical Framework

Haitians present an academic and identity paradox. Along with many
other immigrant students, Haitian youth have high educational aspirations, and they spend considerable effort in school. Their educational
outcomes, however, are not as high as for most other immigrant students. While some individual Haitian students do indeed excel, many
more regress toward the relatively low mean of academic achievement
typical of students attending inner-city schools in low-income neighborhoods.

The identity crisis highlighted in the introductory examples emerged
from our ethnographic work as well as the CILS data as the most potent empirical fact for the Haitian second generation. This fact, however, did not emerge sui generis. Rather, Haitian youths' identity crisis
is linked to a set of causes and a separate set of consequences. The theoretical framework we use to interpret why the identity crisis emerges
and what consequences it has derives specifically from the importance
we attribute to the context of reception and parental human capital as
contributing causes to a Haitian youth identity crisis. Cultural dissonance primarily includes parent-child conflict and youths' alienation
from their home-country culture in association with the youths' identity crisis, and diminished academic achievement is a consequence.

The paradox of high aspirations and low achievement among many
Haitian students has numerous contributing causes, but we argue that
the most important is the negative context of reception encountered by
Haitians in southern Florida. *Context of reception* includes government
policies toward a particular immigrant group, local labor market conditions, and local social relationships (Portes and Rumbaut 1996: 84).

Government policies can range from an open-arms welcome that
could include not only the provision of legal status but also the provi-

sion of benefits to the rejection of arrivals as illegal immigrants and even massive efforts to repatriate. Historically, for example, those fleeing communism have been welcomed with legal status and other benefits (Hein 1993; Lennox 1993; Loescher and Scanlan 1986; Stepick 1992; Teitelbaum and Weiner 1995; Zolberg 1988; Zucker and Zucker 1987). Many other immigrant flows have been labeled as undocumented and denied legal status, the right to work legally, and other benefits.

Local labor market conditions refers to the availability of jobs that accept or might even prefer immigrant workers versus a labor market that scorns a particular immigrant group. Some local labor markets, such as that of southern California, have developed a preference and even dependence on immigrant labor, thus making it relatively easy for new immigrants to find work (Portes and Bach 1985). On the other hand, other local labor markets have not recently received large flows of immigrants and do not have many niches for immigrants (Lamphere, Stepick, and Grenier 1994).

The concept of local social relationships includes and expands upon Portes and Rumbaut's concept of the co-ethnic community (1996). Co-ethnic communities can assist new immigrants by providing preferred access to resources. Earlier-arriving immigrants can help newcomers find housing, jobs, and access to other services much more quickly than the new immigrants might have been able to do on their own (Portes and Stepick 1993). Co-ethnic immigrant communities that have little internal solidarity, low integration into the local labor market, and are relatively poor, however, may be able to assist new arrivals only in relatively limited ways (Portes and Stepick 1993).

Apart from co-ethnic community, local social relationships include the public perception in a local area of particular immigrant groups. Public perception can range from seeing immigrants as positive contributors to society to seeing them as a drain on resources that might also bring disease or other negative consequences. Local public perception is usually congruent with government policies, but it is more pervasive in that it is not just immigrants' interactions with government officials but also with the much broader population. Groups that have a negative image are likely to encounter prejudice in looking for housing, finding jobs, and seeking services, regardless of their legal immigration status.

Characteristics of the immigrants themselves also affect how the second generation adapts. Human capital, that is, education and work experience, affects immigrant adaptation, and specifically the human capital of parents affects the educational outcomes of children (Pearlman 1995; Portes and Rumbaut 1993; Schultz 1993). Children whose parents have high educational levels are much more likely to do well in school themselves (Lanasa and Potter 1984; MacLeod 1995; Wharton 1986). Thus, immigrant children whose parents may have never had the opportunity for much education in their home country are challenged in the U.S. educational system (Fuligni 1997). Their parents, for example, are less likely to be able to help them with homework or to advise them on how to study or what courses to take.

In communities where the first-generation immigrants have a negative context of reception and low levels of human capital, the second generation is more likely to experience cultural dissonance. A negative context of reception and low levels of human capital impede assimilation of the first generation, who will not have easy access, for example, to learning English either on the job or in English language classes. The second generation, on the other hand, acculturates more readily. Through attending American schools, watching American television, and being in peer communities with native-born Americans, the second generation invariably Americanizes.

While the first-generation immigrant parents typically desire some Americanization for their children, Americanization frequently produces parent-child conflict as second-generation children learn and emphasize values and behaviors that conflict with those of their parents. Second-generation children, for example, may express American "freedom" in their willingness to ignore parental authority and to dress in American styles that can be both more expensive and sexually provocative than immigrant parents find acceptable. Second-generation immigrant children may also use their greater knowledge of American culture as a tool against their less-informed parents. They may say that a grade of F means "fine" or that physical discipline against them will bring the police and cause the parents to be thrown in jail.

This alienation of second-generation children from their parents has been called *cultural dissonance*, that is, a situation in which parents and children possess dissonant cultural views of appropriate ideas and behavior (Portes and Rumbaut 1996). It includes children not conforming to parental guidance and a potential role reversal between parents and children as children claim better knowledge about the host culture and society. Accordingly, cultural dissonance frequently results in intensified parent-child conflict. This dissonance may be measured in differences in language knowledge between parents and children and especially in parent-child conflict. It also can be manifest in social psychological out-comes that include youths' ethnic identity self-labeling, perceptions of discrimination, lower self-esteem, and elevated depression. Diminished second-generation educational achievement is an important consequence of cultural dissonance and the associated social psychological variables.

Figure 8.1 summarizes the links between the causes and conse-quences of Haitian youths' identity crisis with the components of con-text of reception and parental human capital as causes; cultural disso-nance, self-esteem, and depression as intermediary social psychological variables; and academic achievement as a consequence. The remainder of this chapter empirically develops these relationships, in which an ex-tremely negative context of reception and low parental human capital combine to produce cultural dissonance and negative social psycholog-ical outcomes and, in turn, transform high educational aspirations into relatively low achievement. More specifically, we argue that in response to prejudice, many Haitian students develop an ambivalence about their cultural roots, including both an alienation from their parents' na-tive language and conflict with and frequently alienation from their parents. First we establish the historical and demographic background of Haitians in southern Florida, including their negative reception as re-flected in the extraordinary prejudice and discrimination they have con-fronted. We then demonstrate how this negative reception has pro-duced profound ambivalence over their identities and an associated strained relationship with their parents. The substantive portion of the chapter concludes with a multivariate analysis of the Haitian students' academic achievement. We conclude that the forces of prejudice and discrimination, combined with low parental human capital, diminish the academic achievement of Haitian students. The result is an ethnic effect that elevated individual (such as hours studying) and family char-acteristics (such as socioeconomic status [SES]) cannot overcome.

This paper relies upon two sources of data: the CILS data set and our own qualitative fieldwork among Haitian high school students in three Miami–Dade County high schools. For our analysis of the CILS data, we have classified as Haitian any respondent who had either a Haitian-born mother or a Haitian-born father. With this definition, the CILS data contains 181 respondents. If only children with Haitian-born fa-thers are counted as Haitian, CILS has a sample of 152 Haitian respon-dents. If only children with a Haitian-born mother are counted as Haitian, CILS has 177 Haitians. Of the respondents with Haitian-born mothers, 23 reported having anglophone West Indian fathers.

Figure 8.1.   Haitian Youths' Identity Crisis

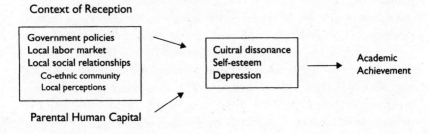

Context of Reception

Government policies
Local labor market
Local social relationships
  Co-ethnic community
  Local perceptions

Cuitral dissonance
Self-esteem
Depression

Academic
Achievement

Parental Human Capital

Stepick and Stepick have been working in Miami's Haitian community for over 15 years. They began research among Haitian high school
students in 1989 (Stepick et al. 1990). In the Fall of 1995, they began a
longitudinal, qualitative project, *The Academic Orientation of Immigrant and Native Minorities,* in four Miami–Dade County public high
schools.[1] Research began with cohorts of 300 students then entering
high school. We focused not only on Haitians but also on English-
speaking West Indians, Nicaraguans, Cubans, Mexicans, and African
Americans in four different high schools. Using participant observation
and intensive interviewing, we sat in high school classes and hung out
with students between classes and after school. We interviewed not
only students but also teachers, counselors, and administrators, along
with students' parents. We also replicated the CILS student and
parental interviews with our total sample, most of whom finished the
eleventh grade when this chapter was written. A few of the ethnographic examples and many of the analytic themes also come from earlier research most extensively reported in Stepick (1998) and Portes and
Stepick (1993).

Context of Reception

Haitians are Miami's, and more generally southern Florida's, largest
black immigrant group. Because the U.S. Census has had such a difficult time counting Haitians, it is impossible to know precisely how
many there are either in southern Florida or in the rest of the United
States. Miami–Dade County by the late 1990s had probably 125,000
Haitians, with another 25,000 to 30,000 in adjacent Broward
County. The 1990 U.S. Census counted nearly 300,000 people in the

entire United States who acknowledged their primary ancestry to be Haitian. At least in Miami–Dade County, however, the U.S. Census missed as many as 50 percent of some neighborhoods' residents (Stepick and Stepick 1992). Adjusting for the undercount, the most generous estimate would be approximately 450,000 Haitians residing in the United States in 1990.[2] The population undoubtedly grew during the 1990s. The U.S. Haitian population is overwhelmingly concentrated in two states, New York[3] and Florida, with about 150,000 in each. Massachusetts, primarily Boston, has a significant concentration, with around 30,000 Haitian residents. The remaining population of Haitians in continental North America is spread thinly throughout many U.S. states and Canada.

In the 1960s and earlier, Haitian immigrants encountered the problems and difficulties typical for any new immigrant group and perhaps more so because they were "triple minorities," that is, not only were they foreigners but they also spoke a language that no one else spoke (Haitian Creole) and were black (Bryce-LaPorte 1993). Nevertheless, the U.S. Immigration and Naturalization Service (INS) authorities have seldom pursued illegal Haitian immigrants in the northeastern or Midwestern United States, and neither until very recently have Haitians in those regions received much public attention.

During the late 1970s and early 1980s, Haitians entered U.S. media consciousness as boatloads of seemingly desperately poor and pathetic people washed onto southern Florida's shores (Boswell 1983; Miller 1984). The first detected Haitian refugee boat arrived in Florida in September 1963. When they requested political asylum, the INS summarily rejected their claims and dispatched the boatload back to Haiti. The second detected boat did not appear until 1973, and it was not until 1977 that Haitians began arriving regularly. Since then, the U.S. government has conducted a resolute campaign to keep Haitian refugees from coming to Florida.

The U.S. government claimed they were economic refugees, no different from Mexicans clandestinely crossing the U.S.-Mexican border in Texas and California. Haitian advocates asserted that the so-called boat people were genuine political refugees fleeing persecution and even probable death. The distinction between political refugees and economic immigrants has animated both the government efforts to exclude Haitians and advocates' struggles for Haitian arrivals to remain in the U.S. (Stepick 1982a). During the 1970s and 1980s, no other immigrant group suffered more U.S. government prejudice and discrimination than

Haitians. The U.S. Coast Guard has attempted to intercept boats of Haitians before they left Haitian waters, undocumented Haitians who made it to U.S. shores have been disproportionately incarcerated, and no other national group has had such a high disapproval rating for political asylum requests. Repeatedly, local southern Florida and national officials have identified Haitians as a health threat: In the late 1970s, tuberculosis was allegedly endemic among Haitians; in the early 1980s, the Centers for Disease Control (CDC) identified Haitians as one of the primary groups at risk for AIDS, along with homosexuals, hemophiliacs, and intravenous drug abusers. In spite of the removal of Haitians from that list, in the late 1980s the U.S. Food and Drug Administration (FDA) officially refused to accept the donation of blood from individuals of Haitian descent. The FDA's fears proved baseless, and the decision was eventually reversed but only after it had a profound impact, especially on Haitian professionals and college students who thought they had escaped the stigma of being Haitian.

The largest concentration of Haitians in southern Florida is in the Little Haiti section of the City of Miami. Through the 1980s and 1990s, working-class Haitians spread north from Little Haiti through the Miami suburbs and adjacent municipalities in Broward County to the north. There is also an increasingly large middle class of Haitians who generally live in the suburbs of Miami-Dade and Broward counties, away from Little Haiti. Since the mid-1980s, a secondary migration of many middle-class Haitians from the northeastern United States has increasingly settled in the greater Miami area. These Haitians or their parents had earlier bypassed Miami because of its legacy of Southern segregation. The secondary migrants tended to be more educated and contributed to an emerging Haitian middle class, while increasing numbers of professionals, entrepreneurs, and others of middle-class origins also migrated to southern Florida directly from Haiti.

Labor Market Incorporation

In the early 1980s, the first surveys of recently arrived Haitian immigrants to southern Florida revealed extraordinarily high unemployment. As many as 80 percent of females and nearly 50 percent of males claimed to be unemployed and looking for work (Stepick 1982b; Stepick 1984b). The tuberculosis and AIDS hysteria hit Haitians hard after they encountered some labor market success, particularly in hotels and restaurants that predictably feared hiring workers who allegedly carried communicable diseases. In spite of both health scares proving false, they still damaged Haitians' labor market incorporation.

Haitians turned to informal sector work in great numbers. Most commonly, they engaged in tasks such as dressmaking and tailoring, door-to-door and flea market commerce, food preparation, child care, transportation, and the provision of semiskilled services in such areas as construction work, auto repair, and electronic repair (Stepick 1984a; Stepick 1988). These survival strategies, which provided very low incomes, were not considered real jobs by Haitians who waited for opportunities in the formal labor market. As fears of disease subsided, Haitians gradually incorporated themselves into the local economy, primarily in unskilled, low-wage positions. Haitians are now common in "back of the house" positions in hotels and restaurants such as chambermaids, food preparers, and busboys, in other words, in jobs that do not entail much face-to-face interaction with customers (Stepick et al. 1994).

While a Haitian professional and middle-class community is emerging in southern Florida, the majority of Haitians have relatively low human capital. Southern Florida's Haitians do have higher levels of education than their typical compatriots back home in the Western Hemisphere's least-developed nation (Stepick and Portes 1986), but by U.S. standards and compared with other southern Florida immigrants, their educational background is low. As Table 8.1 indicates, over 60 percent of fathers and nearly two-thirds of mothers of the CILS Haitian parents did not graduate from high school.

Given these low levels of education, it is not surprising that a comparatively high percentage of Haitian parents are unemployed or working in the service sector, that relatively few are managers or administrators, and that comparatively few are even in clerical positions. Haitians' SES, as summarized in a standardized composite measure in Table 8.1, is far below the mean for the CILS sample. Similarly, it is not surprising that over 80 percent reported an annual family income of less than $25,000, compared with slightly under 40 percent for the remainder of the CILS families. Accordingly, fewer Haitian parents believed they could afford to pay for a college education for their children, and nearly three-fourths were unwilling to go into debt for their children's college education. One surprising finding is that a higher proportion of Haitians than the rest of the CILS sample reported owning their own homes, rather than renting or sharing quarters. This reveals primarily how Haitians elect to spend their money and reflects that in spite of difficult labor market incorpora-

TABLE 8.1   HAITIAN VERSUS
OTHER CILS PARENTS

	Haitian Parents (%)	Other CILS Florida Parents (%)
Father not a high school graduate	60.2	36.0
Mother not a high school graduate	67.5	29.6
Unemployed	8.6	4.8
Self-employed	5.2	22.2
Service sector	26.8	9.6
Manager, administrator	3.6	9.8
Clerical	8.9	22.3
Family income less than $25K	81.9	39.1
Can pay for child's college	19.5	34.7
Not willing to go into debt for child's education	73.6	30.7
Single parent, T1[1]	29.7	22.8
Single parent, T2[1]	27.0	21.6
Own home, T1	67.0	61.5
Own home, T2	80.5	68.6
SES Standardized index	−.1535[2]	.1313

NOTE: All significant at .01 level except own home T1 and T2.
[1]In this and subsequent tables, T1 refers to the first survey and T2 refers to the follow-up survey.
[2]These numbers reflect a standardized SES index that has a mean of 0. Thus, Haitian parents on average are below the mean, while the rest of the CILS' parents are above the mean.

tion and correspondingly low economic standing, Haitians are rooted and committed to remaining in southern Florida.

Local Social Relationships

Rosina, a high school student born in the Bahamas of Haitian parents, asserted, "It's one thing I don't like about American people, they're always pickin' on Haitians. Like, any time, like, two Americans get into, like, an argument or somethin' like, I mean the curse word they use is 'Haitian' . . . it's some type of curse word." Guerda, who stated that Haitian slurs upset her, claimed with outrage that an African American had just accused a Haitian of eating cat for lunch. "I mean, I'm proud of my country [Haiti] and I will never deny it."[4]

In the early 1980s, when Haitians first started entering the high school closest to Little Haiti in significant numbers, conflict episodically convulsed the school, forcing administrators to close it temporarily a number of times. Students severely ridiculed and beat up anyone Haitian looking or who spoke Creole or accented English. African American students mocked newly arrived Haitian boys for playing soccer instead of football and basketball, a greater sin to many African American students than not wearing deodorant or "dressing funny."

In spite of the best intentions, occasionally teachers and administrators reinforced the negative stereotypes of Haitians in the ways they treated them. For example, in January 1986 about 35 newly arrived Haitian students required a separate classroom, but the administration had already assigned all existing space in the extremely overcrowded school. The only available space was a partially enclosed outdoor area designed for equipment storage. One wall was a roll-up section of chain link. The new arrivals remained in this space all day, each day. As word of this room spread through the school, it acquired a nickname, "Krome North," a reference to the INS detention center in the Everglades on the farthest edge of Miami.

Yet prejudice against Haitians was far more blatant outside the school. During the 1986 soccer quarter-finals, King High School played a prestigious private school. The King team consisted solely of Haitian immigrant students. Throughout the game, the players and the coaches from the private school taunted the King players by ridiculing their accents and skin color. A year later a similar thing happened when King played a public school with a mixed Cuban-American and Anglo student body. When rain began to fall, some of the Haitian parents in the stands made makeshift umbrellas from sticks and fronds. The Latinos on the other side went wild and jeered rudely, shouting racial slurs and mockingly pretending to be gorillas.[5]

By 1992 and the first CILS survey of eighth and ninth graders, Haitians were no longer new to local schools. Yet both the legacy and fact of prejudice and discrimination persisted both in the first (1992, T1) and the follow-up (1995, T2) surveys. As Table 8.2 demonstrates, Haitians, along with West Indians (the other black immigrant group in the sample), reported perceiving, expecting, and experiencing more discrimination than the other CILS students. Moreover, the likelihood of experiencing discrimination and the view that it will persist regardless of one's education increased as the children became older.

This conclusion is further substantiated by multivariate analysis. The CILS survey contained numerous questions relevant to perceived discrimination: whether one believes discrimination exists regardless of economic opportunities; if one has ever experienced discrimination;

TABLE 8.2   DISCRIMINATION

	Haitians	West Indians	Other CILS Respondents
Ever felt discrimination, T1	62.8	66.5	43.5
Ever felt discrimination, T2	73.5	74.8	53.3
Discrimination from students, T1	70.3	56.6	55.1
Discrimination from students, T2	63.0	51.3	46.6
Agrees a lot that racial discrimination exists in U.S., T1 (%)	50.8	53.8	41.1
Agrees a lot that racial discrimination exists in U.S., T2 (%)	47.1	57.5	32.7
People will still discriminate regardless of education, T1 (% agreeing very true or partly true)	48.9	53.1	21.7
People will still discriminate regardless of education, T2 (% agreeing very true or partly true)	63.7	54.7	24.5

and, if so, from whom (teachers, counselors, students, whites, blacks, or Latinos). The set of questions centered on discrimination was asked in both the first (T1) and the second (T2) surveys. We conducted a series of stepwise regression analyses using each of these along with a combined index (one for T1 and another for T2) as dependent variables. For independent variables, we stepped sets of variables. The first set consisted of variables reflecting race, since racial discrimination is the most prevalent form in the United States. We specifically examined whether the respondent was Haitian, West Indian, or a black immigrant (i.e., either Haitian or West Indian); whether one used a racial label in self-identity; and the percentage of black students in the school the respondent attended. The second set of variables was designed to control for demographic characteristics since we hypothesized that age and experience in the United States could affect immigrants' perceptions of discrimination. This set included gender, age, length of time in the United States, and whether one was a U.S. citizen or not. The third set included SES indicators, as we hypothesized that those with higher SES may have less experience with discrimination. This set included the

TABLE 8.3   LOGISTIC DETERMINANTS
OF DISCRIMINATION AT T2[1]

	Full CILS Sample[2]	Haitian Sample
Black immigrant[3]	1.223**[2]	
	(.17)	
Parents' SES, T1[1]	−.1825*	−.5128
	(.08)	(.30)
Time in U.S.	−.0865	−.5837
	(.06)	(.24)
English skills, T1[4]	−.1051	−.8169
	(.16)	(−.68)
Foreign language skills, T1[5]	−.0553	.2838
	(.063)	(.27)
Gender	−.5628	.1186
	(.10)	(.42)
Percent black students, T1[6]	.0064	−.0075
	(.002)	(.01)
Constant	.37	4.33
Chi square (degrees of freedom)	173.6**	10.322

*Significant at .05 level.
**Significant at .001 level.
[1]Parents' SES is a standardized index that combines mother's and father's occupational prestige, income, and home ownership.
[2]Logistic beta coefficients with standard errors in parentheses.
[3]Black immigrant was scored 1 for Haitian and West Indians and 0 otherwise.
[4]English is an index of four items: ability to understand, speak, read, and write in English. Each was rated by the respondent on a 1–4 scale. Ratings of parental English come from the parental survey where the responding parent rated his or her own English and that of his or her spouse.
[5]Foreign language is an index of two items, the ability to understand and speak the language, each rated on a 1–4 scale.
[6]Percent of students at respondent's school who are reported as black by school district.

father's and mother's SES indices and prestige scores as well as the SES and prestige scores of the respondent's desired occupation. The final set of variables reflected acculturation. Here standard assimilation theory would predict that the more assimilated immigrants would experience less discrimination. This set included English language ability, foreign language ability, language spoken at home, and parents' English abilities. We first analyzed the entire CILS sample for southern Florida. We then separated out the Haitian CILS students and analyzed them separately.

Table 8.3 reports the regression analyses for perceptions of discrimination. We performed stepwise regression first for the entire

CILS sample and then for the Haitian subsample. For the entire CILS sample, the most significant predictor of discrimination was the dichotomous variable "black immigrant." Haitians and West Indians were categorized as black immigrants. Everyone else was categorized as not a black immigrant. For the entire CILS sample, knowledge of English, knowledge of a foreign language, length of time in the United States, gender, or the percentage of black students at the respondent's school did not significantly affect perceptions of discrimination.

For the Haitian subsample, we eliminated the variable "black immigrant" since the entire subsample was defined as such. No variables were significant. Although Table 8.3 reports only the results for perceptions of discrimination regardless of education for T2, testing the other independent variables yielded the same results. Whatever experiences may have occurred between T1 and T2 did not alter the determinants of discrimination. All that mattered across the entire sample and at both points in time was whether one was black or not.

Cultural Dissonance

The discrimination perceived and actually confronted by Haitians produces profound cultural dissonance, which is manifest in youth rapidly covering up their home culture, consequent parent-child conflict, low self-esteem, high depression, and shifting self-identity. Table 8.4 indicates that the reported English language ability of the Haitian students was statistically equal to that of the other CILS southern Florida students (an index of 3.79 versus 3.83 at T1). Similarly, their English language ability reportedly improved from T1 to T2 (to 3.86 for Haitians and 3.88 for the remainder of the CILS sample). In contrast, Haitian parents claimed less knowledge of English (2.67 versus 3.10 for other CILS parents), and Haitian students claimed less knowledge of a foreign language (which would be Haitian Creole) than the remainder of the southern Florida CILS sample (2.34 T1 and 2.43 T2 versus 2.85 T1 and 2.94 T2 for the rest of the CILS sample).[6] Thus, there was apparently a larger gap in language knowledge between Haitian children and parents than existed for the rest of the CILS sample. Haitian students knew English significantly better than their parents (3.86 T2 versus 2.67) and claimed to not know their native language as well as other CILS students.

TABLE 8.4   LANGUAGE ABILITY

	Haitian Students and Parents	Other CILS Students and Parents
Student's English skills, T1	3.79	3.83
Student's English skills, T2	3.86	3.88
Student's foreign language skills, T1	2.34***	2.85
Student's foreign language skills, T2	2.43***	2.94
Parent's English skills	2.67**	3.10
Parent's spouse English skills	2.70*	3.00

*Significant at .05 level.
**Significant difference at .005 level.
***Significant difference at .001 level.
NOTE: This analysis excludes respondents who had either a West Indian mother or West Indian father.

We emphasize that the Haitian students did not claim to know Creole well, as opposed to us having an objective measure of their really not knowing it. The CILS's measures of language are all self-reported. Respondents were asked to rate their language skills on a 1–4 scale for understanding, speaking, reading, and writing English and a foreign language. We have never witnessed a Haitian child who did not understand his or her parents' Creole. In short, we believe the Haitian students were underestimating their Haitian Creole language abilities. The ethnographic example at the beginning of this chapter in which the student attempted to hide his Haitian roots is hardly unique. We have previously reported on numerous cases of Haitian students covering up their identity (Portes and Stepick 1993; Stepick 1996; Stepick 1998; Stepick et al. 1990). We interpret the students' claimed ignorance of Creole as a reflection of cultural dissonance, an effort by the students to distance themselves from their roots.

Table 8.5 provides further evidence that many Haitian students do not wish to reveal their cultural roots. The table compares the parents' claim as to which language was spoken in the home with what students said was spoken in the home. At T1, in 39.8 percent of the Haitian cases, the parents claimed a foreign language, namely, Creole, was spoken at home, while their children claimed English was spoken there. In contrast, in barely over 10 percent of cases did parents of non-Haitian CILS students claim that a foreign language was spoken

TABLE 8.5   LANGUAGE CONSISTENCY
BETWEEN STUDENTS AND PARENTS

	Haitians		*Others*	
	English	Foreign	English	Foreign
Language spoken at home according to parents	14.4%	86.6%	16.1%	83.9%
Language spoken at home according to children				
English[1]	69.2%	39.8%	60.5%	10.1%
Foreign[1]	40.6%	59.4%	32.5%	89.9%
TOTALS	100.0%	100.0%	100.0%	100.0%
N	26	61	428	608

[1]Numbers in these rows are percentages of the particular column. Thus, the 39.8 percent in the first column of the row labeled Foreign reflects that in the households where the parents claimed a foreign language was spoken, 39.8 percent of the students in those households claimed that English was spoken.

at home and their children claimed that English was spoken. In short, Haitian students were significantly more likely to deny that a foreign language was spoken at home and correspondingly more likely to claim their parents spoke English when in fact their parents did not speak English at home.

The differences in reported language ability reflect broader alienation of the Haitian students from their parents and the culture their parents represent. As Table 8.6 demonstrates, Haitian youth felt their families were just as important as other CILS students did because there were no significant differences in the measures of familism between the two groups either at T1 or T2. However, Haitians were statistically significantly more embarrassed by their parents than other CILS students. Although this embarrassment declined from T1 to T2, Haitians still maintained higher levels of embarrassment than the other immigrant youth. Accordingly, compared with other CILS students, Haitian youth reported higher levels of parent-child conflict, and these levels rose from T1 to T2. Ethnographic examples reveal the bases of this conflict.

Robert's mother is on the phone in tears, not knowing how to cope with the cultural conflicts she faces. She claims her son does not have sufficient interest in school and believes he may be getting into trouble. She is willing to pay for a private school, but her son wants to continue

TABLE 8.6   FAMILY RELATIONS

	Haitians	Other CILS Respondents
Familism, T1[1]	1.78	1.79
Familism, T2	1.87	1.81
Embarrassed by parents, T1[2]	.25***	.15
Embarrassed by parents, T2[2]	.15***	.10
Parent-child conflict, T1[3]	1.90***	1.65
Parent-child conflict, T2[3]	1.97***	1.61
Parent-child conflict, T2 (4-item scale)	2.09***	1.76
Self-esteem, T1[4]	3.43	3.39
Self-esteem, T2	3.44	3.52
Depression, T1[5]	1.75*	1.64
Depression, T2	1.81**	1.75

*Significant at .05 level.
**Significant at .01.
***Significant at .001.
[1]Mean of a 3-item scale reflecting youth's commitment to family. Each item scored 1 to 4 (Rumbaut 1994). While Haitian youth demonstrated a slight rise in familism, they were not statistically significantly different from other CILS youth.
[2]Mean of a 3-item scale regarding beliefs about the commitment to family. Each item was scored 1 to 4 (Cuellar, Harris, and Jasso 1980; Vega et al. 1986).
[3]Mean of a 3-item scale reflecting conflict or disagreements with parents. Fourth item added for T2. Each item scored 1 to 4.
[4]Rosenberg Self-Esteem scale, with 10 items each scored 1 to 4.
[5]Center for Epidemiological Studies Short-Term Depression Scale (CES-D), with 4 items scored 1 to 4.

at the public high school. She wants to force him to go to the private school, but fears her son's response. She confides:

> I feel caught up between two forces. On the one hand, I have to prevent the police from coming to my doorstep, which means that I need to help my son so that he does not engage in criminal activities. On the other hand, I have to prevent HRS [Human and Rehabilitative Services, now called the Department of Children and Families] from coming to my doorstep. This is a really difficult situation for me.

If this mother punishes her son harshly by not only enrolling him in the private school but also probably beating him, as she would in Haiti, she could face charges of child abuse. If she protects him from the police for his petty misdemeanors, she risks facing the police herself while avoiding Florida's Department of Children and Families. Police and social workers have numerous examples of children shouting, "I'll call the authorities and charge you with child abuse if you hit me!" as parents get ready to strike them. When police arrive, they face a dilemma. They have received multicultural training and know that the parent is attempting to exercise authority according to Haitian standards. The police do not want to undermine the parents' authority. They sympathize with the Haitian parents' concern that if the parents cannot control their offspring, the children will fall prey to the vices of gangs, violence, drugs, and crime. The police also must enforce U.S. law, and Haitian parental disciplinary standards frequently exceed its bounds (Stepick 1998).

Haitian parents commonly assert that American culture puts children at risk and can lead them to fail in school and in life. For example, Mme. Durand, the mother of a Haitian teen, believes that the American system inadvertently encourages children to engage in untimely sexual activities. She especially targeted assistance given teenage mothers when she stated, "I am glad they are cutting assistance now. They [the girls] will be more careful." Mme. Durand complains that America gives too much freedom to children after they turn eighteen. Mme. Durand and her husband both argue that many Haitian families have difficulty maintaining parental authority because of the permissiveness of the American system. Her opinion is that "children here think they are adults when they turn eighteen. I thank God my eighteen-year-old son is still living with me."

Mme. Durand's comments reveal that conflict can be more severe for girls than for boys. Marie, for example, is an English Honors student who is also an excellent gospel singer, as is her father, who is well known in that field. Marie appeared to embody the ideal immigrant adolescent, an outstanding student, close to her parents and deeply involved in church activities. But then she showed signs of assimilation—she acquired an African-American boyfriend. In her parents' eyes, the boyfriend and especially the fact that he was African American meant she was no longer serious about her education. Haitian girls are not supposed to express interest in boys until they have finished school. Her parents suspended all her privileges. Not only could she not see or talk to the boy, but she was not allowed to watch television or even go to church, a restriction that devastated Marie. On top of that, her academic future was also jeopardized. Marie had wanted to attend the local public university, Florida International University; major in occupational therapy; and pursue a health career like her mother, who is a registered nurse. But her mother now refused to provide Marie with the income tax information she needed to complete her financial aid application. Debbie, the research assistant who had come to know Marie, visited the home. Debbie indicated that Marie was no longer seeing the boy and that the deadline for financial aid applications was rapidly approaching. Marie's mother refused to believe Debbie. Instead, she insisted that if Marie was not serious about college, if she instead wanted to fool around with boys and get herself in trouble, then she, her mother, was not willing to pay for college.

A few weeks later, Marie's grandmother, who had recently arrived from Haiti and who spoke no English, answered the phone. The call was for Marie from a girlfriend who spoke unaccented English. The grandmother, aware of Marie's mother's concerns, believed the phone call was from the African-American boyfriend. That evening Marie's father, hearing the grandmother's version, became so enraged that he bit his daughter, breaking the skin.

Marie left home that evening to stay with her boyfriend. She called the police who, in turn, asked the State Department of Children and Families to investigate. Meanwhile, Marie has moved in with the family of one of her girl friends, a Latina, and her parents continue to condemn her. Not only could Marie not obtain the income tax information she needed for the financial aid application, but also her mother refused to give her her immigration resident alien card, which Marie would need to get a job. Perhaps not surprisingly, Marie's grades have dropped dramatically. From her parents' point of view, Marie defied the first rule of the parent-child relationship—she failed to acknowledge her parents' absolute right to determine her behavior.

Marie's case is extreme but far from unique. Table 8.7 displays gender differences in family relations and associated psychological correlates. Parental conflict for female youth increased from T1 to T2 and was significantly higher than that for boys at T2. Our ethnographic work has revealed numerous examples similar to Marie's conflict over dating and gender relations. The ethnography also reveals the sincere, genuine concern that parents have for their children. For Americans, many Haitian parents react extremely to control and discipline their children with occasionally tragic results. In Haiti, when similar conflicts occur, a relative or godparent or even part of a whole village is likely to reinforce or mediate the parent's authority. In the United States, without those traditional support systems, parent-child disagreement or open conflict is more likely to result in extreme alienation.

The students themselves are ambivalent on this issue. In a class discussion on the differences between the United States and Haiti, one girl spoke right up with a look of disgust:

TABLE 8.7   HAITIAN GENDER
DIFFERENCES IN FAMILY RELATIONS

	Females	Males
Familism, T1	1.68[1]	1.96
Familism, T2	1.80	1.99
Embarrassed by parents, T1	.25	.25
Embarrassed by parents, T2	.15	.15
Parent-child conflict, T1	1.87	1.94
Parent-child conflict, T2	2.03[1]	1.86
Parent-child conflict, T2 (4-item scale)	2.15	1.96
Self-esteem, T1	3.35	3.33
Self-esteem, T2	3.43	3.44
Depression, T1	1.79	1.69
Depression, T2	1.91[1]	1.61

[1]Significant at .05 level.

> All the kissing and touching in public. You would never do that back in Haiti. Here people are always kissing, even at school in the hallways.

Louis, a recent arrival, also deplores the permissiveness of American culture, saying

> I don't like the fact that the American culture gives children so much power over their parents. The parents' authority is undermined. They can't tell their children what to do. They are in trouble when the police come.

But he adds,

> Haitian parents don't talk to their children. Children don't feel comfortable with their parents. When they have a problem, they can't talk about it with their parents. There is no respect for children. In the parents' view, children never say something good.

Alan, who has been in the United States for two years, concurs, "Haitian parents are not friends with their children. That can lead the children to do bad things."

Suzanne, felt her mother treated her "like a little child too much." When asked if her mother was behaving like a Haitian or an American regarding parental control, she replied,

> Like a Haitian. She thinks like a Haitian in the old days. To her, a girl should start dating at twenty-one. This creates a lot of conflict between me and her. I am eighteen. She doesn't think I should be dating. We argue. When boys call me at home, she doesn't like that.

But Suzanne herself is caught between two cultural models that define the adolescent years quite differently: as childhood in Haiti and as emergent adulthood in America. Suzanne sees it this way:

> Children have too much freedom in the American culture. Way too much. They take advantage of it. In the Haitian culture, I think children have too little freedom. You can't do nothing. Like in the Haitian culture, they have been living in school and church. They don't let you go out with your friends.

Suzanne looks forward to college perhaps in Chicago, to "going away from [her] parents, having an experience on [her] own, and living by [her]self."

Some Haitian adolescent children actually perceive their parents' child-rearing practices as potentially leading to downward segmentary assimilation. Marcelene, born in the United States of Haitian parents, asserts, "Their authoritarian way drives you away from them. You can't talk to them. This can lead you to do bad stuff."

These ethnographic examples and the survey reflect that Haitian youth may be in conflict with their parents but that they still feel that family is important. Table 8.6, which reports the mean levels of an index of familism, confirms that Haitian youth valued families as much as other CILS youth. Thus, conflict does not reflect a diminution of one's feelings for family but an intensification of negative ways of relating. Children such as Marie, Robert, and the others quoted previously all experience high conflict with their parents. Yet they all still care very much about their parents, and they all recognize how important family is to them.

At the same time, Haitian community leaders and the police do indeed report an increase in "bad stuff" by Haitians, namely, use of drugs, participation in gangs, and involvement in crime. The survey also reveals that over time Haitian youth pay psychologically, so by T2 they had lower self-esteem and higher depression than other CILS students. While depression remained relatively constant over time for other CILS students, it increased dramatically for Haitian females as they grew older, but parental restrictions remained unchanged or even became tighter.[7]

Shifting Identity

Feelings of embarrassment about one's parents, alienation from one's cultural roots, and increases in depression all combine to create shifting self-identification for Haitian youth. The episodes that began this chapter reflect profound variation in Haitian adolescents' identity, from shameful cover-ups to proud flag-waving. Yet the variation does not simply reflect a unilineal evolution from the pride of the early arrivals to the shame or resentment of the more assimilated. Changes in the labels of individual ethnic identity do indeed occur, but they are not unilineal or even unidimensional at any point. Individuals may begin as "pure Haitians" and then assimilate to American culture. As well, the assimilation may be only in particular contexts. An adolescent may be Haitian among trusted friends and family and American among strangers. The label he or she uses to describe him- or herself may similarly fluctuate both through time and across contexts.

When we began our ethnographic fieldwork with a cohort of ninth graders, the same age as the CILS cohort, most of the Haitian students had little or even no idea of the concept of racial or ethnic identity. They conceived of themselves first as individuals. They knew that their parents were from Haiti, and some of the students had also been born there. They also had learned that in the United States others would perceive and frequently label them as black. Identity critically affects their lives, but they often are uncertain what label best fits them. In a fundamental, profound, and, probably to most social scientists, surprising sense, Haitian adolescents in southern Florida do not know who they are ethnically or at least how they should label themselves. Identity is important, but they do not always know what label fits. Within the subculture of American adolescence, most of the kids self-identify with labels relative to their peers. Like teens everywhere they are jocks, nerds, snobs, cool, or out-of-it before they are Haitian, Haitian American, or black. The younger the child, the less aware they are of external, non-peer-generated ethnic labels. At T_1, the labels probably did not mean as much to the respondents as at T_2. As they grew older, they became both more aware and more sophisticated in their adoption and potential instrumental use of ethnic labels.

Table 8.8, which reports the percentages of Haitian adolescents who chose particular ethnic labels at T_1 and T_2, reveals that while behavior may be more Americanized, the primary trend in labels was toward more national, less-assimilated ethnic identities. The plurality of Haitian respondents at both T_1 (39.4 percent) and T_2 (43.8 percent) announced a hyphenated identity, perhaps not unexpected for the children of immigrants. However, shifts between T_1 and T_2 contradicted the presumptions of unilineal assimilation that immigrants become

TABLE 8.8 HAITIAN ADOLESCENT ETHNIC SELF-IDENTITY, T1 AND T2 CROSS-TABULATION

| | Ethnic Self-Identity at T1 | | | | | |
	American	Hyphenated	Haitian	African American	Mixed, other	Percent, T1
Ethnic self identity at T2						
American	0	0	0	0	0	13.9
Hyphenated	63.2	51.9	28.6	53.3	0	39.4
Haitian	10.5	31.5	59.5	20.0	57.1	30.7
African American	10.5	1.9	2.4	13.3	0	10.9
Mixed, other	15.8	14.8	9.5	13.3	42.9	5.1
Overall percent, T2	0	43.8	37.2	4.4	14.6	
N	19	54	42	15	7	

NOTE: Numbers in table are column percentages. They reflect the percentage of Haitian CILS students who chose the column label at T1 and the row label at T2. Thus, of the students who chose the American label at T1, 63.2 percent of them chose a hyphenated label at T2.

more Americanized with time. First, while 13.9 percent identified themselves as American at T1 (one of whom claimed to be white American, as in the separate story that began this chapter), absolutely no one claimed to be American at T2. Most of those who had labeled themselves as American at T1 shifted to Haitian American at T2. A significant percentage (31.4 percent) of those who identified as Haitian American at T1 shifted to what appears to be an even more unassimilated label by identifying themselves simply as Haitian, dropping the hyphenated American part of their identity. Somewhat similarly, most who had identified themselves as African American at T1 also shifted to the hyphenated Haitian-American identity (53.3 percent). In general, the movement is away from assimilated identities, away from American or African American, and toward Haitian American or simply Haitian.

There is, nevertheless, a concurrent countertrend. Table 8.8 indicated that 28.6 percent of those who labeled themselves as simply Haitian at T1 shifted to a hyphenated identity at T2. These Haitian adolescents thus appear more in line with traditional assimilation theory, which predicts a movement away from national identity toward a more assimilated, in this case hyphenated, identity. Statistical analysis did not reveal any clear pattern that differentiates those who were claiming more assimilated labels from those going in the opposite direction. Most likely, the change simply reflects emerging but still shallow attachment to ethnic identity.

Analysis not presented here indicates that Haitian adolescents at T1 and T2 who attended predominantly black schools were somewhat more likely to label themselves as either Haitian Americans or Haitians and correspondingly less likely to call themselves African Americans or mixed. Conversely, those Haitians attending predominantly nonblack schools (which in Miami are usually predominantly Hispanic) were slightly more likely to adopt a mixed or African American label.

This finding, summarized in Figure 8.2, appears to contradict earlier research on segmentary assimilation that claimed that immigrant youth who could be classified as similar to native minorities (e.g., black immigrants and African Americans) and who lived in inner-city, minority neighborhoods could assimilate to the opposite subculture of inner-city, minority youth (Portes and Zhou 1993). Such youth would assume the behavior of African Americans, walking the walk and talking the talk (Portes and Stepick 1993; Stepick 1998). Haitian leaders in Miami during the early 1990s feared that they were losing Haitian youth to the inner-city, oppositional youth culture (Stepick and Stepick

Figure 8.2.   Patterns of Ethnic Self-Identification

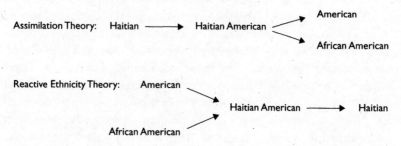

SOURCE: Adapted from Alejandro Portes, "Children of Immigrants: Segmented Assimilation and Its Determinants," in *The Economic Sociology of Immigration* (New York: Russell Sage Foundation, 1995), 261.

1994). But in the CILS data only a small number of Haitians claimed an African-American identity label, and that almost disappeared as it shrank by two-thirds between T1 and T2. Moreover, those in predominantly black schools were even slightly *less* likely to claim an African-American identity.

By limiting the enquiry into ethnic identity to self-labeling, the struggles embodied in identity formation are not revealed in the survey data. Even as most Haitian adolescents appear to be moving away from American identity labels, their behavior reflects Americanization that alienates them from their parents and other first-generation Haitian immigrants, as reflected in both ethnographic and survey findings.

Determining Academic Achievement

Both Haitian students and their parents have high and stable educational aspirations. As demonstrated in Table 8.9, more than two-thirds of the Haitian students and over one-half of their parents expected the Haitian students to achieve graduate degrees. While slightly fewer students had such high aspiration at T2, the decline was small. Parents had lower expectations than their children, but even they expected most of their children to obtain advanced degrees.

Haitian students' academic achievement, however, did not match their aspirations. As demonstrated in Table 8.9, overall CILS students experienced declining GPAs and declining standardized math scores

TABLE 8.9 ACADEMIC ASPIRATIONS AND ACHIEVEMENT

	Haitians		Other Southern Florida CILS Students	
	T1	T2	T1	T2
Students expect to finish college only	23.8	20.4	22.8	21.4
Students expect to obtain graduate degree	71.3	67.2	71.4	71.8
Parents expect children to finish college only		26.7		27.5
Parents expect children to obtain graduate degree		51.2		46.5
GPA (males and females)				
Males	1.95 (65)	1.84 (65)	2.23 (1,241)	2.13 (974)
Females	2.46 (112)	2.29 (88)	2.44 (1,318)	2.36 (1,061)
Reading percentile (males and females)				
Males	26.57 (52)	31.50 (36)	45.88 (1,054)	50.58 (504)
Females	32.51 (96)	31.58 (52)	45.13 (1,159)	49.32 (525)
Math percentile (males and females)				
Males	43.12 (52)	39.94 (36)	58.49 (1,049)	54.15 (542)
Females	45.94 (96)	33.81 (52)	58.10 (1,168)	47.94 (552)

from T1 to T2, but the Haitian females' GPAs and math scores declined more than those of the other CILS students. Standardized reading test scores increased for both Haitian and other CILS students, as would be expected for populations in which for many English is a second language. While Haitian (and non-Haitian) females did have higher GPAs and reading scores at both T1 and T2 and higher math scores at T1 than Haitian males, the significant decline between T1 and T2 in GPA and math achievement for Haitian females further suggests that the processes of adaptation were especially trying for Haitian females. While all immigrant females' math scores declined during high school, those of Haitian females dropped more than the rest of the CILS's sample. At T1, Haitian females' math scores were even above Haitian males, but they dropped nearly 30 percent (from 45.94 to 33.81) at T2.

Multivariate analyses of the determinants of GPA, reported in Table 8.10, confirm that gender was the most important factor in academic achievement. We conducted forced-entry stepwise regression with GPA at T1 and T2 as the dependent variables. Table 8.10 reports the results for T2. T1 results are not reported here since they substantively duplicated the T2 results. We first entered individual-level variables: gender, length of time in the United States, and hours studying and watching television, along with knowledge of English and Haitian Creole. For the second step, we entered social psychological variables at T1 of parent-child conflict, family composition, self-esteem, and depression. The third step incorporated SES variables at T1 of owning a home, father's socioeconomic index, mother's socioeconomic index, and whether both parents were working. The final step entered peer environmental variables, specifically whether the respondent had friends who had dropped out of high school or were going to college; the percentage of black students at the respondent's school at T1; and indices of the school's atmosphere, specifically levels of crime and violence. We ordered the steps according to what the literature indicates is the order of importance for determinants of academic achievement. We selected these particular variables because both our ethnographic work and simple correlations of the CILS data indicated that they were important. Whenever possible, we used T1 variables to predict GPA at T2 in order to establish the appropriate causal order. In other words, for example, aspirations at T1 can be conceived of as raising GPA at T2, whereas aspirations at T2 could be either the cause or consequence

TABLE 8.10   DETERMINANTS OF GPA T2

	Model 1[1]	Model 2	Model 3	Model 4
Individual characteristics				
Gender	.220* (2.14)	.227* (2.28)	.242* (2.40)	.184 (1.70)
Hours watching TV, T1	-.289 (-2.81)	-.243* (-.334)	-.234* (-2.20)	-.232* (-2.04)
Aspirations, T1	.217* (2.03)	.156 (1.46)	.148 (1.33)	.119 (1.03)
English language skills, T1	.214* (2.02)	.127 (1.16)	.121 (1.08)	.112 (.98)
Social psychological		NS	NS	NS
SES background			NS	NS
Peers environmental				NS
Constant	-.120	.115	.154	1.38
Adjusted R^2	.166	.218	.213	.204

*Significant at .05 level.
**Significant at .01.
***Significant at .001.
[1]Standardized OLS coefficients. *T* values in parentheses.
"NS" = None significant

of GPA at T_2. The only cases where we used T_2 variables for predicting GPA at T_2 were when we had only T_2 measures. These were limited to the indices of the school's atmosphere. Simple correlations indicated that gender, hours spent studying, parent-child conflict, self-esteem, and having friends who dropped out versus friends going to college had the highest simple-order correlations with GPA. Multivariate analysis, however, washed out the effects of the social psychological and SES characteristics, peer environment variables, and nearly all the individual variables.

Gender was significant in three out of the four models, and hours watching television was significant in two out of four. Except in the full model, girls had higher GPAs. Also, watching more television tended to be associated with lower GPAs. More surprising were the variables not significant at all or not consistently significant. Because so many variables were not significant, they are excluded from Table 8.10, but they are worth mentioning. It did not matter how long a student had been in the United States. Those born in the United States were just as likely to have the same levels of academic achievement as those who had arrived only five years ago. Similarly, it barely mattered how much English one knew. Only in the first model, which included just individual-level variables, did better English predict higher GPAs. Once social psychological variables were introduced, the effects of English on GPA were washed out. Similarly, high aspirations were associated with higher GPAs when only individual-level variables were included, but the effects of aspirations disappeared with the introduction of social psychological variables.

While the social psychological variables diminished the importance of the individual variables, none of them proved individually significant. Similarly, neither the SES variables nor any of the peer environmental variables were significant.

Overall, the multivariate analysis reveals how unimportant individual, socioeconomic, family, social psychological, or peer environmental variation within the Haitian community is. Most Haitian students had high aspirations, so those with higher aspirations performed no better. Since nearly all Haitian students have had some trouble in their relationships with their parents, there was little variance in the parent-child conflict measures; those with slightly better relations still did not demonstrate higher academic achievement. Most Haitians had a relatively low SES, so a slightly higher status did not improve the chances of attaining a higher GPA.

Conclusion

The pain and shame of being a Haitian in Miami constantly assail second-generation Haitian youth in southern Florida. Numerous youth cover up their roots as in the example at the beginning of this chapter where the young man examined what everyone else was calling themselves and then claimed that he was white. For those who claim to be or are labeled as Haitians, prejudice and discrimination commonly confront them. It may come from teachers and school administrators who fear that Haitian dancing may cause a riot, as in the second example of this chapter's introduction, or it can come from fellow students who demean boat people or even from parents who disgracefully mocked Haitian students and parents as in the example of the soccer match. It remains a sadly consistent story that we have been witnessing and documenting among first- and second-generation southern Florida Haitians for nearly 20 years. Only West Indians report comparable levels of discrimination, reflecting the continuing importance of race in America and the peculiar circumstances of being a black immigrant.

Perceptions of discrimination, cultural dissonance, and shifting ethnic self-identity leap out ethnographically. Haitians, along with West Indians, perceived discrimination far more than other CILS students. They were more likely to claim they did not know their native language, although ethnographic data indicate they did indeed understand and speak Haitian Creole. And they reported higher and increasing levels of parent-child conflict. Ethnographically, the parent-child conflict was frequently interpreted by both children and parents as a struggle over Americanization. Children commonly laid claim to American adolescent expressions of individualism that include independence from one's parents' dictums. The battles can be particularly trying for adolescent females over whom traditional Haitian families exercise nearly absolute control, especially concerning expressions of sexuality.

The survey data *appear* to contradict this ethnographic reality. According to the survey, Haitian youth were moving away from American identities toward more Haitian ones. Between T1 and T2, those who had self-identified as Americans completely changed their minds, moving toward the hyphenated Haitian-American identity. Similarly, most of those who had claimed an African or black American identity also moved toward a hyphenated Haitian-American identity. Moreover, a significant number of those who claimed a hyphenated Haitian-American identity at T1 moved to a purely national Haitian identity at

T2. The direction of the shifts in labels contradicts classical assimilation theory, which predicts exactly the opposite drift, toward more American identities with time. Something more complicated is happening.

The comparison of the survey and ethnographic data reveals a critical disjuncture between labels and behavior. While the labels were becoming less assimilated, the children's behavior was undoubtedly more Americanized. The children did dress and act more American, and in the case of the Haitians, specifically more African American. Their parents perceived, emphasized, and lamented the shift. From the children's perspective, however, the continuing discrimination they confronted, the limited protection of becoming a cover-up, gradually awakened the recognition that they were not identical to African Americans or mainstream Americans, that they were partly Haitian though certainly different from the kind of Haitian their parents were. Hence, the label of Haitian American began to feel more comfortable as they moved through adolescence.

The extraordinarily negative context of reception confronted by Haitians, along with the relatively low levels of parental human capital, sets in motion the intense dynamic of Haitian youths' identity struggle. While all adolescents struggle with their identities and all immigrants shoulder an added burden of conflicting home country versus U.S. identities, Haitians encounter a much more hostile world. Unlike most Cuban immigrants and southeast Asian refugees, Haitians never have been welcomed by the U.S. government. Unlike most Mexican immigrants, there are no economic niches awaiting them. Unlike West Indians, they neither speak English nor have cultural elements, for example, reggae music, that are admired by the host society. While their parents are well off compared to Haitians back home in Haiti, by U.S. standards adult Haitian immigrants in southern Florida have exceptionally low levels of human capital. They are not prepared for the local labor market, and they have struggled greatly to integrate into it. Similarly, Haitian parents have little experience with formal education, especially in English, and can provide little help for their children's studies. All of these factors conspire against Haitian youth. All Haitian youth, regardless of socioeconomic background and neighborhood, encounter prejudice and resentment.

Similarly, the consequences of Haitian identity struggles are shared by virtually all Haitian youth. Analysis of academic achievement revealed that variation between Haitians and other CILS ethnic groups was probably more important than variation among Haitians, with the significant exception of gender. While a few Haitian youth did excel academically, overall Haitians had the lowest levels of academic achievement, and achievement appeared to decline as students advanced through high school. Few of the standard predictors make much difference in their achievement. Haitian girls academically outperformed Haitian boys, but their academic accomplishments diminished between T1 and T2. As with the broader CILS sample, spending more hours studying improved GPA, but when controlling for other factors, its impact diminished. Indeed, once other variables entered into the multiple regression analysis, no other variables had a significant impact—not individual traits (such as aspirations or length of time in the United States), not social relationships (such as parent-child conflict), not social psychological variables (such as self-esteem or depression), not socioeconomic background, not peer or environmental variables. The most significant impact is the most diffuse, pervasive one, the negative context of reception. Being a black immigrant in southern Florida, and especially from a group negatively and unfairly stereotyped, affects Haitian students much more than their individual efforts or characteristics can usually overcome.

Haitian youth in southern Florida are undergoing powerful transformations. Their identities shift on multiple levels simultaneously. As they move toward adopting less-assimilated labels, their behavior reflects more Americanization, particularly African-American styles. While they struggle to express their Haitian culture, they confront both prejudice against Haitians and American racism. As they continue to care about their family, they have increased conflict with their parents. As they persist with elevated educational aspirations, their educational achievement is declining. Haitians are becoming American, but in a specifically black ethnic fashion. They are likely to be perceived and treated as African Americans, subject to the prejudice and discrimination that characterizes American society. Their educational achievement indicates that a few of them are likely to move into the middle class while the remainder remain working class. Yet internally they are likely to remain aware of their Haitian heritage. How that Haitian heritage will be expressed and cherished remains to be seen.

Notes

1. Funding was provided by NSF SBR-9511515, the Andrew Mellon Foundation, and the Carnegie Corporation. Alex Stepick is the principal inves-

tigator; Carol Dutton Stepick is the director of field research; and Emmanuel Eugene and Deborah Teed are graduate research assistants who have worked specifically with Haitian adolescents.

2. Approximately, 30,000 more Haitians reside in Canada, most of whom are in Quebec, primarily Montreal. Adding the U.S. and Canadian figures together and adjusting for the undercount produces a total population estimate of Canadian and U.S. Haitians of close to 500,000 in 1990. No one knows for sure, however, how accurate this estimate is.

3. New York contained the first concentration of Haitians in the United States. They settled there in the wake of Francois "Papa Doc" Duvalier's dictatorship and associated increased U.S. involvement in Haiti in the early 1960s. Through the 1960s and early 1970s, Haitian immigrants bypassed Miami, which still suffered from the remnants of Southern segregation. Although racism was certainly more prevalent throughout the United States and in Canada than in Haiti, it was less severe and did not have legal sanction in the northern parts of the United States and Canada. A large Haitian community emerged in New York City (Buchanan 1979a; Buchanan 1979b; Buchanan 1980; Buchanan 1983; Charles 1992; Glick-Schiller 1977; Glick-Schiller et al. 1987; Glick-Schiller and Fouron 1990; Keely et al. 1978; Laguerre 1984), along with smaller communities in Chicago (Woldemikael 1989; Woldemikael 1985), Boston (Saint-Louis 1988), and Montreal (Dejean 1980).

4. The ethnographic material in these paragraphs appeared earlier in Stepick 1998 and was gathered primarily by Peggy Nolan. We use pseudonyms for the adolescents and the schools.

5. Negative stereotyping of Haitians is hardly new or peculiar to Haitian refugees to the United States (McCormick 1996). The anthropologist Sidney Mintz (1974: 267) remarked that "few countries in modern times have received as bad press at the hands of foreign observers as Haiti." The medical doctor and anthropologist Paul Farmer (1994: 45) maintains, "At worst, journalistic writing about Haiti distorts events and processes in predictable ways, helping to perpetuate a series of particularly potent myths about Haiti and Haitians." Robert Lawless (1992: xiii) devoted an entire book to the subject, *Haiti's Bad Press,* in which he writes, "Few people would disagree with the statement that favorable reports about Haiti are as rare as positive declarations on the nutritional value of cannibalism or the healing power of black magic."

6. The survey included four questions designed to assess ability to understand, speak, read, and write a foreign language. Each question had a 1–4 scale. Haitian Creole, however, has only recently become a written language, and thus few Haitian students or parents have had an opportunity to read or write the language. Thus, combining the four items into one scale would prejudice the results against Haitians knowing their native language. Therefore, for the purposes of this chapter, we used only the ability to understand and to speak as measured of foreign language knowledge to compare Haitians and other CILS respondents. We also excluded from this particular analysis respondents who claimed either a West Indian mother or West Indian father since English should have been one of the languages of the household.

7. Self-esteem was also significantly correlated with parent-child conflict, but Haitians' self-esteem was more similar to the rest of the CILS sample, except for T2, when it was significantly lower.

References

Boswell, Thomas D. 1983. In the eye of the storm: The context of Haitian migration to Miami, Florida. *Southeastern Geographer* 23 (November), pp. 57–77.

Bryce-LaPorte, Roy Simón. 1993. Voluntary immigration and continuing encounters between blacks: The post-quincentenary challenge. *Annals, AAPS* 530 (November), pp. 28–41.

Buchanan, Susan. 1979a. Haitian women in New York City. *Migration Today* 7 (4), pp. 19–25, 39.

———. 1979b. Language identity: Haitians in New York City. *International Migration Review* 13 (2), pp. 298–313.

———. 1980. Scattered seeds: The meaning of migration for Haitians in New York City. Ph.D. diss., New York University.

Buchanan, Susan Huelsebusch. 1983. The cultural meaning of social class for Haitians in New York City. *Ethnic Groups* 5 (July), pp. 7–30.

Charles, Carolle. 1992. "Transnationalism in the construct of Haitian migrants' racial categories of identity in New York City." In *Towards a transnational perspective on migration: Race, class, ethnicity and nationalism reconsidered,* edited by N. Glick-Schiller, L. Basch, and C. Blanc-Szanton. New York: New York Academy of Sciences.

Cuellar, José, L. C. Harris, and R. Jasso. 1980. An acculturation scale for Mexican normal and clinical populations. *Hispanic Journal of Behavioral Sciences* 2 (3), pp. 199–217.

Dejean, Paul. 1980. *The Haitians in Quebec.* Ottawa, Ont.: The Tecumseh Press.

Farmer, Paul. 1994. *The uses of Haiti.* Monrode, Maine: Common Courage Press.

Fuligni, Andrew J. 1997. The academic achievement of adolescents from immigrant families: The roles of family background, attitudes, and behavior. *Child Development* 68, no. 2 (April), pp. 351–363.

Glick-Schiller, Nina. 1977. "Ethnic groups are made, not born: The Haitian immigrant and American politics." In *Ethnic encounters,* edited by G. Hicks and P. E. Leis. North Scituate, Mass.: Duxbury Press.

Glick-Schiller, Nina, Josh DeWind, Marie-Lucie Brutus, Carolle Charles, Georges Fouron, and Antoine Thomas. 1987. "All in the same boat? Unity and diversity in Haitian organizing in New York." In *Caribbean life in New York City: Sociocultural dimensions,* edited by C. Sutton and E. Chaney. New York: Center for Migration Studies.

Glick-Schiller, Nina, and Georges Fouron. 1990. Everywhere we go we are in danger: Ti Manno and the emergence of a Haitian transnational identity. *American Ethnologist* 17 (2), pp. 329–347.

Hein, Jeremy. 1993. Refugees, immigrants, and the state. *Annual Review of Sociology* 19, pp. 43–59.

Keely, Charles B., Patricia Ewell, Austin T. Fragomen Jr., and Silvano M. Tomasi. 1978. *Profiles of undocumented aliens in New York City: Haitians and Dominicans.* Staten Island, N.Y.: Center for Migration Studies.

Laguerre, Michel S. 1984. *American odyssey: Haitians in New York City.* Ithaca, N.Y.: Cornell University Press.

Lamphere, Louise, Alex Stepick, and Guillermo Grenier, eds. 1994. *Newcomers in the workplace: Immigrants and the restructuring of the U.S. economy.* Philadelphia, Penn.: Temple University Press.

Lanasa, Philip J. III, and Jane Hopkins Potter. 1984. Building a bridge to span the minority-majority achievement gap. Conference paper, Durham, N.C.

Lawless Robert. 1992. *Haiti's bad press.* New York: Schenkmann Press.

Lennox, Malissia. 1993. Refugees, racism, and reparations: A critique of the United States' Haitian immigration policy. *Stanford Law Review* 45, no. 3 (February), pp. 687–724.

Loescher, Gilbert, and John A. Scanlan. 1986. *Calculated kindness: Refugees and America's half-open door, 1945 to the present.* New York: The Free Press.

MacLeod Jay. 1995. *Ain't no makin' it: Aspirations and attainment in a low-income neighborhood.* 2d ed. Boulder, Colo.: Westview Press.

McCormick, Clare. 1996. *An incomplete picture: Images of Haitians and Haitian Americans in* The Miami Herald. Miami: Florida International University.

Miller, Jake C. 1984. *The plight of Haitian refugees.* New York: Praeger.

Mintz, Sidney W. 1974. *Caribbean transformations.* Baltimore, Md.: Johns Hopkins University Press.

Pearlman, Michael. 1995. The role of socioeconomic status in adolescent literature. *Adolescence* 30 (Spring), pp. 223–231.

Portes, Alejandro, and Robert L. Bach. 1985. *Latin journey: Cuban and Mexican immigrants in the United States.* Berkeley: University of California Press.

Portes, Alejandro, and Rubén G. Rumbaut. 1993. The educational progress of children of immigrants. Release no. 2 of the project "Children of immigrants, the adaptation process of the second generation." Unpublished paper. Baltimore, Md.: Department of Sociology, Johns Hopkins University.

———. 1996. *Immigrant America: A portrait.* Berkeley: University of California Press.

Portes, Alejandro, and Alex Stepick. 1993. *City on the edge: The transformation of Miami.* Berkeley: University of California Press.

Portes, Alejandro, and Min Zhou. 1993. The new second generation: Segmented assimilation and its variants. *Annals of the American Academy of Political and Social Sciences* 530 (November), pp. 74–95.

Rumbaut, Rubén G. 1994. The crucible within: Ethnic identity, self-esteem and segmented assimilation among children of immigrants. *International Migration Review* 28 (4), pp. 748–94.

Saint-Louis, L. 1988. *Migration evolves: The political economy of network process and form in Haiti, the U.S., and Canada.* Boston: PhD dissertation at Boston University.

Schultz, Geoffrey F. 1993. Socioeconomic advantage and achievement motivation: Important mediators of academic performance in minority children in
urban schools. *The Urban Review* 25 (September), pp. 221–232.

Stepick, Alex. 1982a. Haitian boat people: A study in the conflicting forces
shaping U.S. immigration policy. *Law and Contemporary Problems, Duke
University Law Journal* 45, no. 2 (Spring), pp. 163–196.

Stepick, Alex, with Tom Brott, Dan Clapp, Donna Cook, and Jockesta Megie.
1982b. "Haitians in Miami: An assessment of their background and potential." Department of Sociology and Anthropology, Miami: Florida International University.

Stepick, A. 1984a. The Haitian informal sector in Miami. Paper presented at
The Urban Informal Sector: Recent Trends in Research and Theory. Baltimore, Md.: Department of Sociology, Johns Hopkins University.

———. 1984b. Haitians released from Krome: Their prospects for adaptation
and integration in south Florida. Miami: Latin American and Caribbean
Center, Florida International University.

———. 1988. "Miami's two informal sectors." In *The informal sector in developing and developed countries,* edited by Alejandro Portes, M. Castells, and
L. Benton. Baltimore, MD: Johns Hopkins University Press.

———. 1992. "Unintended consequences: Haitian refugees and destabilizing
Duvalier." In *U.S. foreign affairs and immigration policy,* edited by C.
Mitchell. Philadelphia: Pennsylvania State University Press.

———. 1996. "Pride, prejudice, and poverty: Economic, social, political, and
cultural capital among Haitians in Miami." In *Immigrants and immigration
policy: Individual skills, family ties, and group identities,* edited by H. O.
Duleep and P. V. Wunnava. Greenwich, Conn.: JAI Press.

———. 1998. *Pride against prejudice: Haitians in the United States.* Edited by
N. Fonder, New Immigrants Series. Boston: Allyn & Bacon.

Stepick, Alex, Max J. Castro, Marvin Dunn, and Guillermo Grenier. 1990.
*Changing relations among newcomers and established residents: The case of
Miami.* Final report to the board of the Changing Relations Project. New
York: Ford Foundation.

Stepick, Alex, Guillermo Grenier, Hafidh Hafidh, and Sue Chafee. 1994. "The
view from the back of the house." In *Newcomers in the workplace,* edited by
L. Lamphere, G. Grenier, and Alex Stepick. Philadelphia: Temple University.

Stepick, Alex, and Alejandro Portes. 1986. Flight into despair: A profile of recent Haitian refugees in south Florida. *International Migration Review* 20,
no. 2 (Spring/Summer), pp. 329–350.

Stepick, Alex, and Carol Dutton Stepick. 1992. Alternative enumeration of
Haitians in Miami, Florida. U.S. Bureau of the Census. Final report for joint
statistical agreement 90–108.

Stepick, Alex, and Carol Dutton Stepick. 1994. Preliminary Haitian needs' assessment: Report to the City of Miami. Miami: Immigration and Ethnicity
Institute, Florida International University.

Teitelbaum, Michael S., and Myron Weiner, eds. 1995. Threatened people,
threatened borders: World migration and U.S. policy. New York: W. W.
Norton.

Vega, William A., Thomas Patterson, James Sallis, Philip Nader, Catherine Atkins, and Ian Abramson. 1986. Cohesion and adaptability in Mexican-American and Anglo families. *Journal of Marriage and the Family* 48 (November), pp. 857–867.

Wharton, Clifton R. 1986. The future of the black community: Human capital, family aspirations, and individual motivation. *Review of Black Political Economy* 14 (4), pp. 9–16.

Woldemikael, Tekle Mariam. 1985. Opportunity versus constraint: Haitian immigrants and racial ascription. *Migration Today* 13 (4), pp. 7–12.

———. 1989. *Becoming black American: Haitians and American institutions in Evanston, Illinois.* New York: AMS Press.

Zolberg, A. 1988. The roots of American refugee policy. *Social Research* 55 (4), pp. 649–678.

Zucker, Norman L., and Naomi Flink Zucker. 1987. *The guarded gate: The reality of American refugee policy.* San Diego: Harcourt Brace Jovanovich.

Chapter 9

FADE TO BLACK?

The Children of West Indian Immigrants
in Southern Florida

Philip Kasinitz, Juan Battle, and Inés Miyares

> Jamaica has no room for millionaires. For anyone who wants to become
> a millionaire, we have five flights a day to Miami.
>
> **Jamaican Prime Minister Michael Manley, 1975,**
> **quoted in Darrell E. Levi, *Michael Manley* (1982: 157).[1]**

> JIM: Yuh ride on the luxury bus, Gloria? Dem nice eh?
>
> GLORIA: Not the one I ride to Liberty City. I sit down on the tough seat and watch the fancy tall buildings with the white people get lower and lower, till dem reach shack with black people and I was in the heart of the ghetto.
>
> JIM: Gloria, you sure it is America you go? . . .
>
> JIM: Is a high price we pay for that visa.
>
> GLORIA: I don't think it worth the price, Jim. Is two America. White America, Black America. Which one you going to?
>
> **Trevor Rhone, *Two Can Play* (1986: 47)**

The previous quotes illustrate the contradictory meanings that the United States in general, and southern Florida in particular, have for the peoples of the English-speaking Caribbean.[2] On the one hand, Florida is a golden land. As seen in videos and the images picked up by the satellite dishes now omnipresent in even the most modest West Indian villages, Florida is a consumer's paradise where North American material wealth coexists with a tropical climate. It is a place where those whose ambition (others might say greed) was too big for the constraints of the Democratic Socialist experiment of Manley's Jamaica could become, if not millionaires, at least affluent enough to live in a style impossible back home. At the same time for West Indians, that economic prosperity comes at a price: the price of leaving nations in which they are members of the majority race and joining the ranks of the United States' most consistently oppressed racial minority. Thus, in Rhone's play, Gloria, who has briefly sojourned as an undocumented immigrant in Miami, warns her husband of the flaws in his emigration scheme. In the United States, she tells him, a racial identity of which he is now barely aware will become a central fact in his life.

The second generation feels these contradictions acutely, perhaps even more acutely than their immigrant parents. Their racial socialization took place in the United States, and they have little or no direct experience of societies in which people of African descent are the majority. Many have had the advantage of growing up in middle-class families. West Indian households have incomes higher on average than those of other southern Florida residents. Yet despite middle-class incomes, racial segregation means that the children of West Indian immigrants often live in neighborhoods segregated from whites and better-off Latinos. Many have grown up in areas of high crime and economic disinvestment and have attended problematic schools. Ironically, the very advantages that facilitated their parents' entrance into the growing white-collar and service sector labor force of the 1970s and 1980s—the English language, relatively high degrees of education, a tradition of female labor force participation, and the post–Civil Rights movement opening up of opportunities for blacks, particularly in the public sector—have also discouraged the formation of an ethnic enclave of the type so important in the upward mobility of other recent immigrants to greater Miami (Portes and Bach 1985). Thus, while ghettoized residentially (and therefore in terms of access to many public services), the children of West Indian immigrants have neither the disadvantages nor the advantages of economic concentration.

Speaking English from birth and often hard to distinguish from African Americans in appearance, these young people are also, in the words of Roy Bryce-LaPorte (1972), "invisible" as immigrants or as ethnics. This, no doubt, eases some of the tensions of acculturation. Yet, as it may be speeding assimilation into a black community which is itself "lost in the fray" (Portes and Stepick 1993: 176) of southern Florida's recent ethnic history, such rapid and easy acculturation may be a decidedly mixed blessing.

Race, Identity, and the Second Generation

Until recently, most academic work on the possible trajectories of the children of the post-1960 immigrants has been, of necessity, speculative. Nevertheless, since the early 1990s several highly influential models have been proposed. Herbert Gans's "second generation decline" scenario (1992) predicts that those second-generation immigrants who are restricted by a lack of economic opportunities and racial discrimination to poor inner-city schools, bad jobs, and shrinking economic niches will experience downward mobility relative to their immigrant parents. In this case, Gans argues that substantial acculturation may take place without much structural assimilation. This is particularly likely for those children of immigrants for whom becoming American means, in effect, becoming black American. Clearly, if assimilation means joining the street culture of the urban ghetto, becoming American can be every immigrant parent's worst nightmare! Gans hypothesizes that the children of immigrants will refuse to accept many of the jobs that their parents hold and will thus experience downward mobility. The other possibility he cites is that the children of immigrants will refuse to become American and stay tied to their parents' ethnic community. Thus, Gans (1992: 173–174) turns traditional, straight-line assimilation theory on its head: "The people who have secured an economically viable ethnic niche are acculturating less than did the European 2nd and 3rd generation and those without such a niche are escaping condemnation to dead-end immigrant and other jobs mainly by becoming very poor and persistently jobless Americans."[3]

Portes and Zhou (1993) make a similar argument in their article on segmented assimilation, perhaps the most influential theoretical formulation among those studying the contemporary second generation. The segmented assimilation model describes the various outcomes of different groups of second-generation youth and argues that the mode of incorporation for the first generation gives the second generation access to different types of opportunities and social networks as well as differing amounts of cultural and social capital. Those who are socially closest to American minorities, such as West Indians, may adopt an oppositional, reactive ethnicity. Those groups who come with strong ethnic networks, access to capital, and fewer ties to U.S. minorities experience a linear ethnicity that creates networks of social ties and may provide access to job opportunities while reinforcing parental authority and values. Thus, Portes and Zhou (1993) argue that those groups that most effectively *resist* acculturation may end up with better opportunities for second-generation upward mobility.[4]

This theme has been further elaborated and amplified in the recent work of Rubén Rumbaut (1995, 1997). Acculturation, Rumbaut notes, may in many ways prove a hindrance to upward mobility and in some cases may impact negatively on the quality of life and even the physical well-being of contemporary immigrants and their children. Similarly, Zhou and Bankston's work (1998) on Vietnamese youth in New Orleans makes a case for the preservation of ethnic social capital, at times even at the expense of acquiring connections with the host society. This begs the question of what will happen in those groups, such as West Indians, who do not, or cannot, maintain an economic ethnic enclave but whose racial identity may prevent assimilation into the mainstream middle class.

When compared with other contemporary immigrants, West Indians and their children stand out in two crucial respects: ease of acculturation and race. On the one hand, becoming American is a shorter journey for them than for most other immigrants. They arrive as native speakers of English. They come from homelands thoroughly penetrated by U.S. mass media and in which the tourist trade has led to considerable exposure to Americans in person. They also come from tiny nations where a large portion of the population emigrates to the United States and where emigration has been a normal and expected part of the adult life experience for a very long time. Thus, many have considerable knowledge of the United States from friends and family members before arrival and ready made social networks once they are here. On the other hand, the overwhelming majority of West Indian immigrants are considered black by North American standards[5] even if they might not be considered so according to the racial constructions of their nations of origin.[6] Therefore, becoming American means becoming a *black* American, with all that this has historically entailed.

There has now been considerable research on how West Indian immigrants and their children react to this situation. Comparing different cohorts of first-generation immigrants, Kasinitz (1992) argues that the racial structure of the United States discouraged the formation of a distinct ethnic identity earlier in the century, whereas for more recent immigrants the American context provides considerably more social space for ethnic differentiation within the African-American population.

Foner's comparative study (1985) of Jamaicans in New York and London also points to the importance of context and how the presence of the African-American community in the United States shapes Jamaican attempts to maintain ethnic distinctiveness in a way their cousins in Britain do not. Vickerman's study (1998) of first-generation immigrant men further expands on this theme by pointing out under which circumstances West Indian immigrants to the United States feel compelled to distance themselves from African Americans and under which circumstances (mainly, ironically, encounters with whites and thus exposure to racism) they identify with African Americans in a form of reactive solidarity. Finally Waters (1999), studying the children of immigrants, points to three possible paths for the West Indian second generation. Some choose an "ethnic" response in which young people assert a Caribbean-American identity and distance themselves from African Americans. Yet this attempt may prove futile if whites do not recognize the difference or if parents lack the material resources to effectively shield second-generation youth from the influence of the street. Others exhibit an "American"—that is, *African* American—response, in which they assimilate into the culture around them. This scenario is often accompanied by considerable conflict with parents. Finally, some assert an immigrant identity in which the young people stress their national origins and emphasize their own or their parent's early experiences in the "home" country.

It is important, however, to avoid applying the segmented assimilation model too mechanistically. Neither African-American or West Indian cultures are monolithic. There is a considerable African-American middle class, and when it embraces new immigrants (as, for example, the fraternal organizations of black professionals and the alumni groups of historically black colleges have sometimes done), it can be a considerable resource for upward mobility. On the other hand, West Indian immigration is diverse. Among the model minority of immigrant "strivers" are plenty of "rude boys" and "sufferers" from the slums of Kingston and Port of Spain. The English-speaking Caribbean has produced a considerable oppositional culture of its own, one that has been a major influence on U.S. black street culture, particularly in southern Florida.

Further, the conditions that hinder incorporation and upward mobility in one arena may promote it in another. Residential segregation, for example, while disadvantageous in many respects, can be an advantage in attaining political representation as it creates electoral districts where even relatively small groups constitute a local plurality. This is particularly true when an immigrant group such as West Indians can be (and routinely is) categorized as part of a domestic minority for purposes of the Voting Rights Act. In New York, West Indian immigrants now hold several seats in the city council and the state assembly. English-speaking West Indians have been slower to mobilize politically in southern Florida, although in 1998 several Haitians challenged African Americans for seats in the state legislature and on local school boards, causing tensions between black immigrants and black natives (Viburn 1998).

New York City has long been the primary U.S. destination for West Indian migrants, and today they constitute the city's largest immigrant group. However, in recent years southern Florida has emerged as the second-largest and fastest-growing anglophone Caribbean settlement in the United States. In 1990 Florida was home to 22 percent of Jamaican Americans (the largest single national group of anglophone Caribbean immigrants), up from 13 percent in 1980. During the same decade New York's portion of the Jamaican-American population dropped from 54 to 44 percent.

Black Immigrants in Southern Florida

Given southern Florida's proximity to the Caribbean, it is not surprising that black immigrants have been a presence in the region since the mid-nineteenth century. A sizable Bahamian community grew up in early Key West, where historic "Bahamian Houses" in the older parts of town are still highly prized. In 1885 the Florida State census numbered 40 blacks (including "mulattoes") among the 332 souls in Dade County. Of these, 12 were Bahamian and 6 were from other parts of the West Indies. By the early 1890s a Bahamian community had started to grow up in Coconut Grove (Lavender 1996).

This community and other black Caribbean settlements made considerable efforts to maintain a distinct ethnic identity as Dade and Broward counties grew during the early twentieth century. Yet the stark facts of racial segregation eventually overwhelmed them. Miami was incorporated in 1896—the year of *Plessy* v. *Ferguson.* Early-twentieth-century Miami was an atypical Southern city in many respects: A place full of newcomers, entrepreneurs, and speculators, it lacked a significant antebellum past or a traditional planter elite, and its large Jewish population sometimes made it seem like the southernmost borough of New York. Yet in terms of race relations, Miami was an almost pure-type Jim Crow town. The races were physically separated, and the walled ghetto closest to downtown was literally called "Colored Town" (later genteelly changed to "Overtown," although no one forgot the original meaning). Schools, beaches, and even golf courses were segregated, separate and highly unequal (George 1986; Mohl 1987; Dunn 1992).

Ironically blacks, both Caribbean and African American, played a significant role in the incorporation of Miami. Florida law required a minimum of 300 voters for a city charter. Numbering only 243, Miami's adult white citizens briefly enfranchised 181 blacks. Having served their purpose by voting overwhelmingly for incorporation, blacks were then promptly disenfranchised and would not have a meaningful voice in Miami politics for the next half century (Lavender 1996). Jim Crow social and economic segregation was backed up by violence. As the black population of Dade County grew from just under 1,200 in 1900 to nearly 30,000 in 1930,[7] an active Ku Klux Klan and other white vigilantes used beatings, bombings, and lynchings to maintain racial order with the vocal support of the local press. Black immigrants were particular targets of this intimidation, as Dunn notes: "Local whites impressed upon them appropriate southern 'Negro' behavior standards. In 1910, a Miami municipal court judge, John Grambling, congratulated the Miami police for changing the attitudes of 'Nassau Negroes' who 'upon their arrival here considered themselves the social equal of white people.'"

No matter how much black immigrants may have wanted to maintain distance from the growing African-American population, the lack of white recognition as a distinct group, combined with the fact that black immigrants shared schools and neighborhoods with black natives, eventually obscured such differences.

Black immigration to the United States slowed to a trickle during the depression and was further curtailed by the 1952 McCarran Walter Act (Reimers 1985). When large-scale West Indian migration to the United States resumed in the 1960s, it was not initially centered on southern Florida. Segregation made the region unattractive to black immigrants, and even after the Civil Rights movement, middle-class black economic gains were slower in coming to Miami than to other parts of the South. However, by the late 1970s middle-class black progress and a growing economy, plus other attractions—including, not incidentally, the climate—made Dade and Broward counties more attractive to West Indians, both those coming directly from the Caribbean and those coming from other parts of the United States. By the late 1980s a leader of the New York's Jamaica Progressive League would note that "people used to believe they were going back ... They would work hard in New York, save their money and retire to Jamaica. Now they save their money and retire to Miami" (Kasinitz 1992: 118).

While retirees helped start the move to southern Florida, younger immigrants and their children soon joined them. By 1990 (see Table 9.1), Dade County was home to 53,676 anglophone West Indian immigrants (not including their U.S.-born children), who constituted 11.5 percent of the adult black population.

While many, particularly new arrivals, settled in Miami's increasingly impoverished traditional black ghettos, others went directly to the suburbs. By 1990, 32,208 anglophone West Indians had settled in Broward County, where they constituted 8.7 percent of black adults. A few moved into white neighborhoods, although when they did, those neighborhoods seldom stayed white for long: In the CILS data, only 13.3 percent of West Indian parents interviewed reported that most of their neighbors were white, and only 7.9 percent said that most were Hispanic. In the majority of cases, the anglophone Caribbean parents of the CILS sample reported living in mixed neighborhoods—but this probably indicates a mix of African American and Afro Caribbean. As the index of residential dissimilarity in Table 9.2 shows, Dade County West Indians were highly segregated from non-Hispanic whites and even more segregated from Cubans. West Indians are somewhat less segregated in suburban Broward although still more likely to live in black neighborhoods than not.

In general, the anglophone Caribbean population is widely distributed in both counties. There is no dominant West Indian residential neighborhood as there is in New York, and neither is there an ethnic commercial center: no Little Jamaica to parallel Little Havana or Little Haiti (although since the mid-1990s a largely middle-class West Indian concentration in Lauderhill in Broward County has in some ways started to resemble one). For the most part, West Indians live where other blacks live. There are large concentrations in the traditional black ghettos north of downtown Miami (Overtown and Liberty City) and the western part of Fort Lauderdale and the adjacent unincorporated areas.

TABLE 9.1   WEST INDIAN–BORN POPULATIONS
OF DADE AND BROWARD COUNTIES, FLORIDA

	Dade	Broward
West Indian born (including Jamaican)	53,676	32,208
Jamaican born	34,308	23,424
West Indian born as a percentage of the total black population	8.5%	6.8%
West Indian born as a percentage of the adult black population	11.5%	8.7%

SOURCE: U.S. Bureau of the Census 1990a.

TABLE 9.2   INDEX OF RESIDENTIAL
DISSIMILARITY BETWEEN WEST INDIANS AND
CUBANS AND NON-HISPANIC WHITES, DADE
AND BROWARD COUNTIES, FLORIDA

	West Indian/Cuban	West Indian/Non-Hispanic White
Dade	.797	.663
Broward	.554	.558

SOURCE: U.S. Bureau of the Census 1990b.
NOTE: This index of dissimilarity measures residential proximity between groups by census tract. It is scored on a scale of 0 to 1; the higher the coefficient, the greater the degree of segregation (that is, 0 indicates identical residential patterns and 1 indicates complete dissimilarity in residential patterns). For a description of the index, see Plane and Rogerson, 1994.

Economically, the West Indian community in southern Florida has done relatively well. As Table 9.3 shows, the 1989 median household income for West Indians was $37,500 in Dade County and $36,255 in Broward County, in both cases higher than for non–West Indian residents as well as for many other immigrant groups. Home ownership was particularly high: 70 percent in Dade County and 64.2 percent in Broward County.[8] Male labor force participation was higher than average in both counties, but it is female labor force participation—72.1 percent in Dade County and 78.4 percent in Broward County—that was particularly striking. This high rate of labor force participation among both men and women probably accounts for the relatively high *household* incomes.[9] The rate of public assistance participation was also low among the group, something the parents of

TABLE 9.3 SOCIOECONOMIC CHARACTERISTICS OF THE WEST INDIAN–BORN POPULATIONS OF DADE AND BROWARD COUNTIES

	Dade		Broward	
	West Indian	Non–West Indian	West Indian	Non–West Indian
Median family income	34,984	29,180	31,620	32,200
Median household income	37,500	31,000	36,255	35,000
Percent home ownership	70.0	59.0	64.2	72.7
Percent female labor force participation	72.1	55.6	78.4	51.9
Percent male labor force participation	75.6	75.0	87.8	69.9
Percent self-employed	10.3	8.6	4.9	9.2
Percent public sector	11.3	9.6	9.3	8.4
Percent received public assistance	3.3	6.0	5.2	2.3
Percent in poverty	13.7	16.7	13.5	8.5
Percent 200% above poverty line	64.2	69.8	73.4	76.6
Percent college graduates	10.6	19.0	9.7	19.7
Percent professionals	17.7	17.2	14.6	18.9
Percent in industry of employment				
Agriculture and mining	1.4	0.8	0.0	1.1
Construction	4.6	4.6	3.4	5.4
Manufacturing	3.3	9.8	8.2	7.3
Transportation	7.7	7.1	8.6	5.5
Wholesale trade	4.4	4.2	2.2	3.3
Retail trade	14.4	13.3	17.5	14.2
Finance, insurance, and real estate	8.5	6.0	7.1	7.1
Professional services	22.1	15.6	28.0	15.2
Personal services	6.7	4.0	1.5	2.8

SOURCE: 1990 U.S. Census, Public Use Micro Sample (PUMS).

Figure 9.1.   Parent SES Index for Selected Ethnic Groups, Southern Florida CILS Sample ($N = 2,597$)

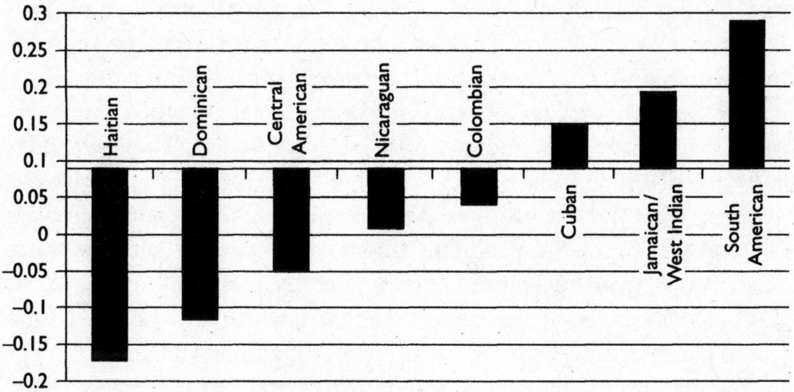

NOTE: Axis crosses at overall sample mean.

the CILS respondents point to with considerable pride.[10] Their poverty rate was lower than that of non–West Indians in Dade County. It was slightly higher than that of non–West Indians in Broward County, but this is not surprising as they are concentrated in the most urban parts of a county that includes many wealthy suburbs.

As Table 9.3 also shows, the West Indians in both counties were highly represented in professional services (which includes nursing and other health-related services) and retail trade. In Dade County, they are notably underrepresented in manufacturing. On the other hand, self-employment, so often the immigrant route to upward mobility, is low for Broward County West Indians, and while it is slightly higher than the rate for all non–West Indians in Dade County, it is still modest compared with that of most other immigrant groups. Among the parents of the West Indian CILS respondents, self-employment was 9.7 percent, far lower than the almost 17 percent in the overall southern Florida CILS sample.[11]

Like the general West Indian population of greater Miami, the parents of the CILS respondents are relatively well off. Using a standardized composite index socioeconomic status (SES) that measures mother's and father's education, occupational prestige, and home ownership, Figure 9.1 shows West Indians to have the highest SES of any major immigrant group in the Miami CILS sample except South Americans. Indeed, it is noteworthy than in terms of SES, the anglophone Caribbean group is closer to Cubans and South Americans than to Haitians and Dominicans. Of those CILS parents who reported household incomes, 60 percent earned over $25,000 a year; 26 percent, over 50,000 per year. Of those who reported an occupation, 23 percent were clerical workers; 13 percent, service workers; 17 percent, professionals; 11 percent, managers or administrators; and 4 percent, school teachers. They have generally avoided blue-collar work: Less than 3 percent were operatives or laborers. West Indians also *perceive* themselves as successful. Seventy-seven percent of the West Indian CILS parents disagreed with the statement "People from my country have *not* been economically successful in the United States," a higher percentage than any of the southern Florida groups except for the astounding 94.5 percent among Cubans.

West Indians exhibit strong job networks and "ethnic niches," particularly among women in the health care industry. In some cases, this may reflect premigration occupations, but for others it is a response to perceptions of opportunities for training and employment here. For example, one mother of a CILS respondent had been a teacher in Jamaica, but seeing the "disrespect" with which students treated teachers in the United States, she quickly dismissed the idea of teaching here. After a short time working in light manufacturing, she found a job in retailing, which she held for many years while studying to obtain credentials to move on to a more professional position. After a false start in a shady business school offering training for bank teller jobs that never materialized, a fellow immigrant steered her toward the nursing program at a local community college. After many years of part-time study and full-time work, she eventually received her nursing certificate and, shortly thereafter, a nursing job, also with the aid of a fellow immigrant.

It is worth noting, however, that white-collar service sector and public sector niches such as health care require education credentials as well as social capital. The safety-net effect of the ethnic enclave for the less educationally successful seen in some other groups may thus be lacking. Further, while these niches are no doubt beneficial to the group, they provide few opportunities for capital accumulation compared with self-employment. Obviously, even the most skilled and highly networked nurses do not start their own hospitals! Although concentration in the service sector has provided access to some of the fastest-growing sectors of the economy, it provided few of the entrepreneurial opportunities usually associated with ethnic economies.

TABLE 9.4   SELECTED CHARACTERISTICS
AND RESPONSES FOR THE PARENTS OF WEST
INDIAN SOUTHERN FLORIDA CILS SAMPLE
RESPONDENTS

Pecent college graduate	20.0
Percent self-employed	9.7
Percent who	
Expect child to graduate college	80.8
Have rules about child doing homework	99.2
Have rules about maintaining a certain GPA	100.0
Percent who say the statement "People from my country have not been successful in the United States" is	
True	6.9
False	76.9
Don't know	16.2

The relatively modest rate of business ownership among an otherwise upwardly mobile group may also, to some degree, reflect the emphasis that the group places on education and a longstanding cultural preference for educational rather than entrepreneurial routes of mobility that is often seen in the West Indies.[12] Among the CILS parents, college graduation rates were 20 percent, but perhaps more important are the high educational aspirations they have for their children. As Table 9.4 shows, 80.8 percent expect their children to graduate from college, the highest percentage of any of the major southern Florida groups, including Cubans. Virtually all reported having rules concerning homework. As one CILS parent explains:

> Most Jamaicans, the ones who mean themselves and their kids good, they are like this: education takes a priority. So if you give them a toy, it has to be an educational toy. Homework is a priority.

Can such high aspirations be translated into reality? The parents of many of the CILS respondents certainly try. From the in-depth interviews we hear reports of families organized around schoolwork, with elaborate rules and strict supervision. Many clearly see the embattled family as a bulwark against the all-too-familiar dangers of the street. Yet the group's high labor force participation, particularly its high female labor force participation, also means that many second-generation youths are on their own much of the time, even in two-parent families.

Interestingly, 69 percent of the West Indian CILS respondents agreed with the statement that the "American way of life weakens the family." Only 45 percent live with both biological parents, and 31 percent were living with a single parent at the time of the initial, junior high school survey. There are no doubt many reasons for this. Female-headed households are more common in the West Indies than in many of the homelands of most other CILS parents, and female economic independence is an often-noted feature of West Indian life.[13] West Indians are also one of the few groups in which more women migrate than men. It is not unusual for single and even married women to initially migrate alone, leaving behind husbands and children, who often join them years later. Such a situation can clearly try even the best marriage. And, of course, to the extent that female labor force participation allows women to exit bad marriages, the high rate of marital breakup need not necessarily be a bad thing. Still, as we will see later, West Indian CILS respondents from two-parent households have markedly better academic outcomes, making the high number a of single-parent families a cause for concern.

During the 1970s and 1980s, the labor market characteristics of West Indian community—high female labor force participation and high rates of high school graduation—were well suited to the demands of the changing southern Florida economy and the changing opportunity structure for better-educated blacks. Despite the large number of noncitizens among them, West Indians, like African Americans, are *more* likely than other Dade and Broward residents to work in the public sector (where educational credentials are often essential). This means that for the second generation, educational success is crucial for replicating their parents' social status.

Although Caribbean blacks have not generally created residential enclaves in southern Florida, they have become a more pronounced cultural presence. Trinidadians have organized a popular Carnival celebration in Miami, and Caribbean performers are now frequently seen in venues throughout the area. Cultural groups work to bring West Indian dance and theater to Miami audiences, and Jamaican television can now been seen on cable in Dade and Broward counties. Yet despite these attempts to maintain a distinct immigrant identity, race still often obscures ethnicity in the public lives of Miami's black immigrants. This is even more true of English-speaking West Indians than for Haitians, for whom language and arguably a more exotic (to North American eyes) culture serve to reinforce ethnic distinctiveness. For English-speaking West Indians, the line between themselves and African Americans has a "now you see it, now you don't" quality. This is particularly evident in the way the mass media frames racial and ethnic conflicts. In a region where politics is often portrayed as a conflict between immigrants and blacks, black immigrants are more often as not seen as black, their immigrant status remaining largely invisible. Everyone remembers the fact that William Lozano, the policeman whose killing of a black motorcyclist and his passenger touched off the 1989 riot, was a Colombian immigrant. No recounting of these events would seem complete without this fact. It is far less often remembered that the motorcycle driver, Clement Lloyd, was also an immigrant from the West Indies.

Fading to Black? The Invisible Second Generation

Where does this leave the children of West Indian immigrants? Will they conform to their parent's high educational expectations and replicate their relative economic prosperity? Or will incorporation into black America set the stage for second-generation decline—or perhaps a merger with a growing black middle class? Is an increased identification with African Americans associated, as either cause or effect, with taking up an oppositional cultural stance and thus with a decline in school performance?

As Rumbaut (1996, 1997) has noted, the change in ethnic self-identification for many groups between the two CILS surveys reflects both historical changes (such as when Mexican-American respondents took up a more nationalist identity in the wake of Proposition 187) and social psychological changes in identity between early and late adolescence. Clearly, any findings about changing identity during adolescence also must be interpreted with some caution: *All* adolescents change aspects of their identities during those years. Nevertheless, it is striking that there was a significant increase in the preference for racial self-description—that is, as black or African American as opposed to simply American or hyphenated American—between the initial, junior high school CILS survey and senior high school follow-up survey. For many in this group, growing up and having contacts outside the parental household meant increased contact with, and perhaps acceptance of, North American racial categories. This is consistent with Waters's ob-

Figure 9.2.   Change in Racial Identification, West Indian Southern Florida
CILS Sample

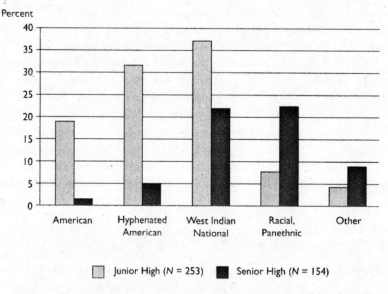

NOTES: Examples of West Indian national identities are Jamaican, Trinidadian,
etc. Examples of Racial, Panethnic identities are black, African American, etc. The
probability of reported differences across all categories being due to chance is less
than 1 in 1,000.

servation (1999) that among West Indian youth, ethnic identity is the
least stable. Over time it tends to polarize between racial identification
with African Americans and nationalist association with the parents'
countries of origin (see Figure 9.2). "Racialization" is, in this respect, a
form of assimilation.

There is an interesting exception to this trend. Like other West Indians, Jamaicans, the largest national group of anglophone Caribbean respondents, were far less likely to choose a hyphenated or unhyphenated
American identity on the senior high school survey than they had been
in junior high. Yet unlike other West Indians, Jamaicans were more
likely to prefer a national identity, that is, to call themselves Jamaicans
(see Figure 9.3). Indeed, this is one of the very few items on the survey
for which there was any significant difference between Jamaicans and
other West Indians. This is, however, not that surprising. Although its
population is only about 2.5 million, Jamaica is still more than twice as
populous as any of the other anglophone Caribbean nations. It has

Figure 9.3. Change in Racial Identification for Jamaicans Southern Florida CILS Sample

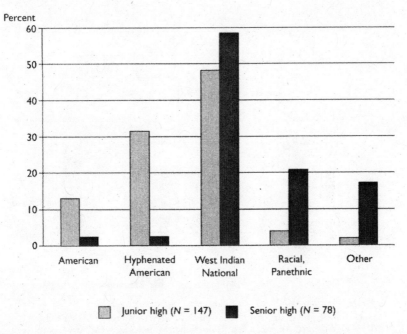

NOTES: Examples of West Indian national identities are Jamaican, Trinidadian, etc. Examples of Racial, Panethnic identities are black, African American, etc. The probability of reported differences across all categories being due to chance is less than 1 in 1,000.

been independent longer than any, except Trinidad and Tobago, and in many ways has a more distinct national identity. Perhaps more important in this context, reggae and dance hall music and the cultural images that accompany them have given Jamaica a much clearer image in international youth culture than other Commonwealth Caribbean nations. Indeed, West Indians from other countries are often presumed to be Jamaican, and in some African American circles the word *Jamaican* is used to refer all West Indian youth.[14]

Consistent with the notion of racial identification as a form of assimilation, we see in Figure 9.4 that the preference for a racial self-identification (as black or African American) on the second survey was far more common among the true second generation—that is, among those born in the United States—than in the 1.5 generation. On the

Figure 9.4.   Percent Racial versus Nonracial Identification by Length of Time in the United States, West Indian CILS Follow-Up Sample ($N = 154$)

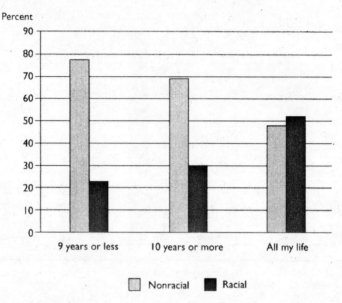

NOTES: Respondent self-identifies as black or African American rather than as American, Hyphenated American (e.g., Trinidadian-American), a national group (e.g., Jamaican, Trinadadian, etc.), or Other.

The probability of reported differences across all categories being due to chance is less than 1 in 100.

other hand, we were surprised to find that racial identification was *not* related to having personally been the victim of direct discrimination, although this may only be because the experience of discrimination was so common in the group (see Table 9.4). And neither, as Table 9.5 shows, was there any significant relationship between asserting a racial identity and level of self-esteem,[15] reported symptoms of depression,[16] inner-city versus suburban residence, or parental SES. And, also to our surprise, racial identity had no significant relationship with grade point average (GPA). Thus, we cannot assume that a more racial sense of self necessarily indicates the embrace of an oppositional identity or even identification with African Americans. Indeed, both African-American and Afro-Caribbean culture are replete with positive images of blackness, and being in touch with some aspects of the parental culture—Garveyism, Pan-Africanism, Rastafarianism, and so on—might lead to

TABLE 9.5   COMPARISON OF SCORES FOR RACIAL SELF-IDENTIFICATION VERSUS NONRACIAL SELF-IDENTIFICATION IN SENIOR HIGH FOR THE WEST INDIAN SOUTHERN FLORIDA CILS SAMPLE

	Racial Self-Identification	Nonracial Self-Identification
Self-esteem in senior high	3.50	3.50
Depression in senior high	1.71	1.74
Parental SES in senior high	.17	.28
GPA in senior high	2.49	2.48
Percent white in senior high	18.22	27.38
Percent hispanic in senior high*	37.31	24.47
Percent black in senior high**	42.43	45.40
Discrimination[1]	22.4%	75.8%
Nondiscrimination	77.6%	24.2%
	100.0%	100.0%
Inner-city school in junior high[2]	52.5%	47.4%
Suburban school in junior high	47.5%	52.6%
	100.0%	100.0%

*The probability of reported differences being due to chance in less than 1 in 100.
**The probability of reported differences being due to chance is less than 1 in 1,000.
[1]Chi-square test showed no statistically significant relationship between racial self-identification and discrimination.
[2]Chi-square test showed no statistically significant relationship between racial self-identification and location of school.

a racial as well a national sense of identity. Our findings probably indicate, however, that by the end of senior high school a significant portion of the respondents had come to see race as a key factor—be it positive or negative—in determining where they stood in American society. Racial identification *was* related to the racial composition of the respondent's school, but in a complicated and perhaps distinctly Miami way. West Indians who self-identified in racial terms (i.e., as black or African American) generally attended schools with a lower proportion of whites than those who did not. By contrast, those who reported a racial identity attended schools with a higher proportion of Hispanics, which we suspect reflects the hardening racial cleavages between black and Latino youth.

Whether or not West Indian youth see themselves as blacks, there is reason to believe that they believe that others see them as such. On the senior high school survey, 75.3 percent of all West Indian respondents reported having been the victims of discrimination, a higher percentage than any of the other southern Florida groups. Once again we should interpret this finding with some caution. It is worth noting that 53.3 percent of all of the non–West Indian and Haitian respondents also reported being the victims of discrimination. Nevertheless, it is striking that the experience of discrimination almost perfectly reflects social and phenotypical proximity to African Americans. West Indians were the most likely to report having been discriminated against, followed closely by Haitians, then by Dominicans, and lastly by the other Latino groups.[17]

The perception of discrimination is not, however, simply a matter of living among African Americans and coming to share their worldviews. Indeed, there was no relationship between the racial composition of the respondent's school and having experienced discrimination. Discrimination was significantly related to parental SES: the higher the parental SES, the more likely respondents were to perceive themselves as victims of discrimination: The mean score on the standardized SES scale for respondents to the senior high school survey who reported having been the victim of discrimination was 2.89, as opposed to only 0.98 for those who had not experienced discrimination.[18] This may reflect the higher expectations of racial fairness among more middle-class respondents. On the other hand, parental SES may also be serving as a proxy for contact with whites (and Latinos). Presumably better-off young people are more likely to travel through white neighborhoods, to shop in nonghetto stores, to use public spaces in downtown locations, and to meet whites (and better-off Latinos) on the job and in social settings. Each of these settings is an opportunity to experience discrimination.

Neither the pervasive perception of discrimination nor the increased identification with African Americans in late adolescence seems to have damaged the striving spirit of most of the West Indian youth. As Table 9.6 shows, in junior high school West Indian boys were significantly more likely to exhibit signs of depression than other male respondents, while West Indian girls exhibited lower depression levels. Yet both of these relationships had disappeared by the time of the follow-up survey. Overall West Indian self-esteem scores were significantly higher than those of other respondents on the first survey, once again the result of much higher self esteem of the part of the girls (boy's scores were identical to those of other male respondents). The positive mental health outcomes for West Indian girls may reflect the anglophone Caribbean's

TABLE 9.6   COMPARING WEST INDIAN RESPONDENTS WITH OTHER RESPONDENTS IN THE SOUTHERN FLORIDA CILS SAMPLE

	West Indians		Other Southern Florida	
	Junior High	Senior High	Junior High	Senior High
Depression mean score	1.60	1.70	1.64	1.64
Male	1.69**[1]	1.55	1.47	1.51
Female	1.68*[2]	1.77	1.80	1.76
N (males and females)	249	186	2,555	2,014
Self-esteem mean score	3.47**[3]	3.53	3.38	3.51
Male	3.43	3.52	3.43	3.54
Female	3.49**[4]	3.54	3.34	3.49
N (males and females)	248	185	2,560	2,017

*The probability of reported differences being due to chance in less than 1 in 100.

**The probability of reported differences being due to chance is less than 1 in 1,000.

[1]West Indian males in junior high report statistically significantly higher levels of depression than other males in the southern Florida sample.

[2]West Indian females in junior high report statistically significantly lower levels of depression than other females in the southern Florida sample.

[3]Overall, West Indians in junior high report higher self-esteem than the other respondents in the sample.

[4]West Indian females in junior high report statistically significantly higher levels of self-esteem than other females in the southern Florida sample.

traditions of relative gender equality. West Indian female self-esteem scores remained higher than those of the rest of the southern Florida sample in senior high, although the relationship was no longer statistically significant.

The Gateway to the Future: Betting on Education

Given the mode of incorporation and the structural location of southern Florida's West Indian immigrants, educational success will be crucial in shaping the life chances of their children. The group has no ethnic enclave to fall back on, and as many West Indian youths increasingly identify with African Americans (and see themselves as victims of discrimination), they may well be coming to share the opportunity structure of the African-American community. As the immigrant generation is disproportionately concentrated in white-collar and service sector occupa-

Figure 9.5.   Grade Point Average in Junior High and Senior High for Selected Ethnic Groups, Southern Florida CILS Sample (N = 2,736)

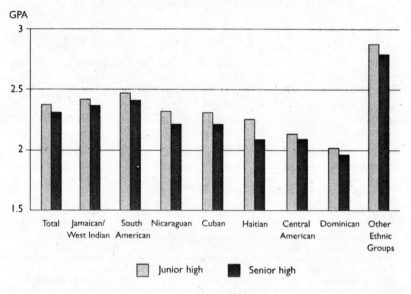

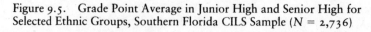

tions, their children can only make use of parental social capital if they acquire those educational credentials. Further, those jobs held by their parents that do not require extensive educational credentials are, by and large, in the lower-paid parts of the service sector: sales, personal service, child care, elder care, and so on. These jobs often require a great deal of face-to-face interaction with whites as well as a certain amount of frankly servile behavior. To the extent that acculturated Caribbean youths—highly aware of discrimination—start to see themselves (and to be seen by whites) as similar to African Americans, they may be reluctant to take these jobs, and whites may be reluctant to offer them.

On the whole, the educational outcomes exhibited by the CILS respondents present a mixed but generally positive picture. Given the middle-class nature of much of the West Indian sample and the fact that they are the only CILS southern Florida immigrant group whose parents generally arrived in the country speaking English, it should not be surprising that the group's median GPA ranked third highest among the groups, behind only South Americans and the largely European and Asian "Other" category (see Figure 9.5). Like all other groups, median

GPAs dropped between junior and senior high school but not significantly.

Examining the bivariate relationships between various measures of educational success and the group's characteristics, we can get an idea of where educational success is, and is not, occurring.[19] Not surprisingly, we see in Table 9.7 that higher SES was consistently correlated with higher educational outcomes, as was home ownership. Girls consistently had higher GPAs than did boys. More troubling is the fact that being born in the United States generally led to lower educational outcomes, although the relationship was only significant for GPA in junior high. (The fact that many relationships seen on the junior high survey were no longer statistically significant in senior high may simply reflect the lower number of respondents in the second survey.) Identification as black or African American (i.e., racial self-identification) was also consistently correlated with lower scores, but in no case was the relationship significant. Interestingly, the perception of having experienced discrimination was consistently correlated with slightly *better* educational outcomes. However, given the association between the perception of discrimination and higher SES, this may merely be a proxy for class.

School characteristics, however, tell a more striking story, one that, given the lack of control many West Indian parents have over the neighborhood and school contexts in which the second generation finds itself, may be of particular importance. In Table 9.7 we see that school poverty, measured here by the percentage of the student body eligible for the federally subsidized lunch program, was significantly associated with lower math and reading scores. The percentage of black students in the school was also associated with negative outcomes, although the relationship was only significant for GPA on the junior high survey. The percentage of whites was generally associated with higher scores, while the percentage of Hispanics had little effect. In general, the picture here is one of the negative impact of poor, predominantly black, and generally inner-city schools.

As the model in Table 9.8 indicates, school poverty continued to be a predictor of lower scores, even after individual characteristics, including parental SES, were taken into account. It had a significant effect on GPA as well as reading and math scores in junior high, as seen in Table 9.9, and approached significance for GPA in senior high. Being born in the United States was also generally a predictor of lower outcomes, although it was only significant for GPA. Not surprisingly, parental SES

TABLE 9.7   BIVARIATE RELATIONSHIPS BETWEEN DEMOGRAPHIC VARIABLES
AND SELECTED EDUCATIONAL OUTCOMES FOR THE WEST INDIAN SOUTHERN
FLORIDA CILS SAMPLE

	GPA in Junior High	Math Score in Junior High	Reading Score in Junior High	GPA in Senior High
Demographics				
Females (t)	2.51**	52.8	43.8	2.47**
Males	2.17**	56.8	47.2	2.10**
Born in the United States (t)	2.26*	51.0	43.3	2.22
Not born in the United States	2.50*	57.1	48.6	2.44
SES (r)	.196**	.284**	.204***	.213**
Own home in junior high (t)	2.48	60.8***	49.5*.	2.45*
Don't own home in junior high	2.26	41.9***	39.5**	2.18*
Own home in senior high (t)				2.55**
Don't own home in senior high				2.18**
Respondent lives with				
Biological parents (t)	2.69***	64.9***	49.6	2.63***
Not biological parents	2.13***	42.8***	42.3	2.09***
Stepparent (t)	2.02**	40.5**	41.0	2.00**
Not stepparent	2.47**	56.3**	46.9	2.41**
One parent (t)	2.19**	44.4**	44.9	2.12**
Not one parent	2.48**	58.6**	46.6	2.44**
Other parental configuration (t)	2.02***	44.4***	31.0***	1.92**
Not other parental configuration	2.35**	57.8***	44.9***	2.25***

Student attitudes and perceptions				
Parent-child conflict in junior high (r)	−.225*	−.034	−.041	−.200*
Parent-child conflict in senior high (r)				−.162**
Discriminated against (t)	2.54	57.6	46.9	2.51
Not discriminated against	2.38	55.9	41.6	2.31
Racial self-identification at junior high (t)	2.30	51.1	35.6	2.21
Nonracial self-identification at junior high	2.40	54.4	47.0	2.35
Racial self-identification at senior high (t)	2.48	56.1	43.7	2.49
Nonracial self-identification at senior high	2.56	57.8	46.5	2.48
Depression score at junior high (r)	−.218*	−.093	−.013	−.157*
Depression score at senior high (r)	−.170	−.091	−.002	−.149**
Friend abroad (r)	.127	.088	.083	.122
School characteristics				
Percent black students (r)	−.174**	−.296	−.245	−.127
Percent white students (r)	.095	.193**	.260*	.052
Percent Hispanic students (r)	.117	.149	.033	.097
Friend abroad (r)	.127	.088	.083	.122
School poverty (r) (+)	−.097	−.271***	−.197*	−.086

*The probability of reported differences being due to chance is less than 5 in 100.
**The probability of reported differences being due to chance is less than 1 in 100.
***The probability of reported differences being due to chance is less than 1 in 1,000.
(r) Pearson's correlations.
(t) T-tests.
(+) Portion of school eligible for the federally subsidized lunch program.

TABLE 9.8   UNSTANDARDIZED REGRESSION
COEFFICIENTS FOR SELECTED EDUCATIONAL
OUTCOMES FOR WEST INDIAN STUDENTS IN THE
SOUTHERN FLORIDA CILS SAMPLE (STANDARD
ERRORS IN PARENTHESES)

	Model I GPA in Junior High	Model II GPA in Senior High[1]
Female	.248* (.122)	.258* (.129)
Parental configuration[1]		
Stepfamily	−.469** (.175)	−.311 (.202)
Single parent	−.346** (.135)	−.318* (.143)
Other family configuration	.313 (.362)	−.346 (.222)
Born in the United States	−.311** (.121)	−.285* (.126)
Racial self-identification	.244 (.240)	.235 (.249)
Parents' SES index	.186 (.121)	.248* (.122)
School poverty	−.007** (.002)	−.004 (.002)
Discriminated against	.078 (.134)	−.156 (.141)
Hours per day spent on homework	.060 (.041)	.055 (.043)
Hours per day spent watching TV	−.056 (.034)	−.066 (.036)
Self-esteem score	.510*** (.129)	.371** (.132)
Constant	1.089* (.516)	1.382* (.544)
Adjusted R^2	.279	.195

*The probability of reported differences being due to chance is less than 5 in 100.
**The probability of reported differences being due to chance is less than 1 in 100.
***The probability of reported differences being due to chance is less than 1 in 1,000.
[1]Parental configuration and self-esteem were measured in senior high.

and hours doing homework continued to be predictors of higher out-comes, as was high self-esteem. Interestingly, hours watching television had little effect. Racial self-identification was not a significant predictor of educational outcomes. This is not surprising, however, as asserting a black or African-American identity was closely associated both with being born in the United States, which generally lowered educational outcomes, and higher SES, which generally raised them!

The picture that emerges, then, is one of families struggling to maintain school performance, often in an environment that can have the opposite effect. It is thus interesting that there was a strong relationship between GPA and family configuration for West Indian students. Only 45 percent of West Indian respondents were living with both biological parents at the time of the first survey, a much lower percentage than for

TABLE 9.9   UNSTANDARDIZED REGRESSION
COEFFICIENTS FOR SELECTED EDUCATIONAL
OUTCOMES FOR WEST INDIAN STUDENTS IN THE
SOUTH FLORIDA CILS SAMPLE IN JUNIOR HIGH
(STANDARD ERRORS IN PARENTHESES)

	Model I Reading	Model II Math
Female	1.93 (4.23)	–2.66 (4.80)
Parental configuration		
Stepfamily	–5.30 (6.42)	–16.77* (7.29)
Single parent	–1.72 (4.56)	–15.71** (5.18)
Other family configuration	–3.57 (13.93)	–19.28 (15.82)
Born in the United States	–2.67 (4.20)	–5.159 (4.77)
Racial self-identification	–1.11 (7.77)	9.07 (8.83)
Parents' SES index	5.26 (3.99)	8.411 (4.53)
School poverty	–.253** (.087)	–.284** (.099)
Discriminated against	3.99 (4.88)	–.05 (5.54)
Hours per day spent on homework	3.28* (1.45)	3.70* (1.62)
Hours per day spent watching TV	–1.20 (1.22)	–.03 (1.38)
Self-esteem score	8.92* (4.39)	1.43 (5.00)
Constant	17.20 (17.71)	61.90** (20.11)
Adjusted R^2	.123	.195

*The probability of reported differences being due to chance is less than 5 in 100.
**The probability of reported differences being due to chance is less than 1 in 100.
***The probability of reported differences being due to chance is less than 1 in 1,000.

most immigrant groups and closer to the figures for African Americans. Thirty-one percent were being raised by single parents (usually mothers), and 19 percent were in stepfamilies. The GPAs of students in single-parent families were significantly lower, even when controlling for SES. This is striking since previous research using national data sets, such as the National Educational Longitudinal Study, has consistently found that once SES is controlled for, differences in GPA across various family types disappear for largely native-born samples of whites, blacks, and Latinos (Battle 1997, 1998). In this respect, West Indians seem more like other immigrants than other blacks.[20]

Why is having two-parent families more important in the educational outcomes for this group than for the general population? While the data do not allow us to explore this much further, we can speculate that families with two parents probably have stronger network ties (having more adult contacts) and may be more able to re-create an ethnic environment within the home, relying less on public facilities. This would be consistent with Waters's finding (1999) that West Indian parents attempt to keep the influences of the streets at bay by pushing children toward private, usually ethnic activities and associations but that this strategy is most effective for those with superior resources, including time, which for single mothers is in notoriously short supply. The high rate of West Indian female labor force participation clearly is central to the group's relative economic prosperity. Yet it is hard to pass on social or cultural capital to children with whom one spends little time. For single parents it may sometimes prove impossible. The children of single parents are also probably more reliant on the schools and other public facilities, a cause for concern given the negative effects of the impoverished schools and neighborhoods in which many West Indians find themselves.

Conclusion

More than for any other immigrant group in greater Miami, the future life chances of the children of anglophone Caribbean immigrants will probably be shaped by race rather than ethnicity. Although about half the group strongly asserts a nation-of-origin identity (more among the Jamaican subgroup), the fact that racial identity is stronger among the second generation than the 1.5 generation and the group's keen perception of itself as the victim of discrimination, combined with the lack of a distinctly West Indian residential or economic enclave, points to a growing, if predictably ambivalent, identification with the broader African-American community.

This need not necessarily lead to downward assimilation. In terms of household income, the children of anglophone Caribbean immigrants are among the best off of southern Florida's second generation. As the black middle class has grown, many anglophone Caribbean immigrants have taken advantage of new opportunities for economic upward mobility and residential suburbanization. Despite some distinct ethnic niches, West Indian opportunities are, by and large, where African-American middle-class opportunities are, in white-collar and upper-level service sector employment and not in the entrepreneurial activity so important for most other immigrant groups.

For many second-generation West Indians, residential racial segregation remains an important obstacle not just to better housing but also to access to public services, quality education, and perhaps even equal treatment from the police. Perhaps more than for any other group in the CILS sample, schooling will play a crucial role in the future of the West Indian second generation. The success of English-speaking West Indians in inserting themselves in the mainstream service sector has put them in positions where the use of ethnic connections and networks is highly contingent on educational credentials. Knowing many nurses, physical therapists, or midlevel white-collar financial service workers will be of little use to second-generation youth if they do not have the college degrees that such positions require. For those who are kept in dangerous neighborhoods and forced to attend inferior schools because of racial segregation, fewer such college degrees will probably be forthcoming. Given the correlation between high school grades and two-parent families among this group, the large number of single-parent households is cause for particular concern. The struggle against the pernicious effects of the street is one few single parents can win.

It is also probable that second-generation West Indian youth will be reluctant to take the jobs that the less well off of their parents now hold: home attendants, domestic workers, or drivers and security guards. Many will no doubt conform to high parental expectations and benefit from parental ethnic characteristics and networks, and thus not have to! Yet without a viable ethnic enclave to serve either as a springboard or a safety net, the future of a West Indian middle class is ultimately linked to that of the larger African-American middle class, into which it is, for better or for worse, rapidly merging. For those who can take advantage of educational opportunities, southern Florida may indeed be a golden land, despite the continued awareness of racial discrimination that the West Indian middle class shares with its African-American counterparts. Those who cannot are in danger of living out Gans's second-generation decline scenario.

Notes

1. Manley's remark, made at a bi-election rally in Montego Bay, was widely quoted in Jamaica at the time. Manley would later insist that it had been taken out of context and his meaning distorted. See also Kaufman 1983.

2. This chapter deals with anglophone Caribbean immigrants as a group, in effect recombining the 12 so-called Caricom nations that until the early

1960s made up the British West Indies. While these nations all have distinct individual characteristics, their common histories and continuing common institutions (such as the University of the West Indies and the West Indies Cricket Team), as well as the common settlement patterns, economic niches, and high intermarriage rates of the region's immigrants in the United States, generally make for a single ethnic group within North American society. See Kasinitz 1992. In the CILS sample, Jamaicans, the largest West Indian national group, constituted 45 percent of the total anglophone West Indian population (approximately their proportion of the anglophone Caribbean population nationwide), making them the only group with sufficient numbers to be analyzed separately. There are a few statistically significant differences between Jamaicans and other West Indians, and thus in this chapter *West Indians* includes Jamaicans except where specifically noted. One exception, where Jamaican CILS respondents did look quite different from the other West Indians in the sample, concerns the question of national identity and is discussed later.

3. See also Woldemikael 1989.

4. For a further elaboration, see Zhou 1997. Of course, the notion that for some immigrant groups assimilation into American life might cause social or economic downward mobility—and this is particularly likely for groups at risk of being "assimilated" into extant ethnic and racial minorities—was not new in 1993. Some of the paradoxical effects of assimilation into American life were noted by observers as early as Tocqueville, and the dangers of assimilating into black America are recognized in Reid 1938; Glazer and Moynihan 1963; Kasinitz 1992; Bryce-LaPorte 1972; and other sources. However, by naming the concept of segmented assimilation and laying out its implications in a more systematic way than any previous observers, Portes and Zhou (1993) have been tremendously influential and have inspired a host of fruitful elaborations of this theme.

5. The major exception being West Indians of East Indian descent, principally from Trinidad and Guyana. In New York, where most of these Indo-Caribbean immigrants settle, this subgroup is large enough to have formed its own ethnic community with a distinct ethnic neighborhood (Richmond Hill in Queens) and organizations. In Florida, however, their numbers remain quite small.

6. Many people of mixed blood, for example, considered "brown" or "colored" in Caribbean racial terms, "become" black upon encountering the so-called one-drop rule in the United States. For an interesting fictional depiction of this situation, see Cliff 1987.

7. No figures are available for Broward County before 1920, when 1,572 of the 5,135 residents were black. By 1930 the black population of Broward had risen to 6,687, or 33 percent of the total.

8. That the Broward County figure was lower than the countywide average is not surprising, as West Indians remain concentrated in the most urban parts of the largely suburban county. However, the high figure in mostly urban Dade County is striking.

9. On the tradition of female labor force participation in the West Indies, see Massiah 1989. On West Indian labor force characteristics in New York, see Kasinitz and Vickerman 2001.

10. Qualitative follow-up interviews with a subsample of the CILS parents were conducted around the time of the senior high school interviews by Patricia Fernández-Kelly. References to and quotes from the parents refer to this data.

11. The South Florida CILS parents are remarkably entrepreneurial even compared with their counterparts in San Diego. How much of this difference is attributable to the different composition of the immigration in the two cities and how much to differences in the local economies is an interesting question.

12. See, for example, Austin 1984; Foner 1973.

13. See Mintz 1986; Smith 1961.

14. Indeed, Rasta-influenced Jamaican patois has been taken up by rebellious West Indian youth from other backgrounds and even some African Americans. See Century 1999; Kasinitz 1998.

15. The self-esteem measure used here is the 10-item Rosenberg global self-esteem scale. It is scored in the CILS as the mean of the 10 items, each of which is scored on a 1–4 scale, with 4 being the highest level of self-esteem. For further details on the scale and its use in the CILS, see Rumbaut 1996.

16. The measure of depression used here is a 4-item index drawn from the widely used 20-item Center for Epidemiological Studies Short-Form Depression Scale (CES-D). The respondents were asked how often they had experienced various depressive symptoms during the previous week, with the answers ranging on a scale of 1 ("rarely") to 4 ("most of the time"). For further details on the scale and its use in the CILS, see Rumbaut 1996.

17. All of the Latin American groups in southern Florida clustered between 50 and 55 percent except, tellingly, the Dominicans, the group with the largest proportion of people of African descent, among whom 61.3 percent reported experiencing discrimination.

18. This difference is significant at the .05 level; that is, the probability that it is due to chance is less than 1 in 20.

19. We did not include the senior high school reading and math scores in this analysis. The reason is that in senior high, unlike in junior high, the reading and math tests are optional, and those who take them are highly self-selected.

20. For a study of the impact of ethnic characteristics on academic performance among several recent immigrant groups, not including West Indians, see Portes and MacLeod 1996. This study finds that controlling for SES lessens but does not eliminate significant effects of ethnic characteristics.

References

Austin, Diane. 1984. *Urban life in Kingston, Jamaica: The culture and class ideology of two neighborhoods*. New York: Gordon and Breach Science Publishers.

Battle, Juan. 1997. The impact of divorce on the academic achievement of African American and white grade school students. *Family Perspective* 29 (2), pp. 61–74.

———. 1998. What beats having two parents: Educational outcomes for African American students in single-versus dual parent families. *Journal of Black Studies* 28 (6), pp. 783–801.

Bryce-LaPorte, Roy S. 1972. The experience of invisibility and inequality. *The Journal of Black Studies* 3, no. 1 (September), pp. 29–56.

Century, Douglas. 1999. *Street kingdom: Five years inside the Franklin Avenue Posse.* New York: Wagner.

Cliff, Michelle. 1987. *No telephone to heaven.* New York: Vintage.

Dunn, Marvin. 1992. "Blacks in Miami." In *Miami now! Immigration, ethnicity and social change,* edited by Alex Stepick and Guillermo Grenier. Gainesville: University of Florida.

Foner, Nancy. 1973. *Status and power in rural Jamaica: A study of educational and political change.* New York: Teachers College Press.

———. 1985. Race and color: Jamaican migrants in London and New York City. *International Migration Review* 19, no. 4 (Winter), pp. 708–727.

Gans, Herbert. 1992. Second generation decline: Scenarios for the economic and ethnic futures of the post-1965 American immigrants. *Ethnic and Racial Studies* 15 (2), pp. 173–193.

George, Paul S. 1986. Colored Town: Miami's black community, 1896–1930. *Florida Historical Quarterly* 56 (April), pp. 423–447.

Glazer, Nathan, and Daniel Patrick Moynihan. 1963. *Beyond the melting pot.* Cambridge, Mass.: MIT Press.

Kasinitz, Philip. 1992. *Caribbean New York: Black immigrants and the politics of race.* Ithaca: Cornell University Press.

———. 1998. "Community dramatized, community contested." In *Island sounds in the global city,* edited by Ray Allen and Lois Wilkin. New York: ISAM and Brooklyn College.

Kasinitz, Philip, and Milton Vickerman. 2001. "Ethnic niches and racial traps: Jamaicans in the New York regional economy." In *Transnational Communities in New York City,* edited by Hector Cordero-Guzmán, Ramón Grosfoguel, and Robert Smith.

Kaufman, Michael. 1983. *Jamaica under Manley.* Westport CT: Lawrence and Hill.

Lavender, Abraham D. 1996. "Growth of black communities in Dade and Broward counties." In *Black communities in transition: Voices from south Florida,* edited by Abraham D. Lavender and Adele S. Newson. New York: University Press of America.

Levi, Darrell E. 1982. *Michael Manley: The making of a leader.* Athens: University of Georgia Press.

Massiah, Joycelin. 1989. Women's lives and livelihoods: A view from the Commonwealth Caribbean. *World Development* 17 (July), pp. 965–977.

Mintz, Sidney. 1986. *Caribbean transformations.* Baltimore: Johns Hopkins University Press.

Mohl, Raymond A. 1987. Black immigrants: Bahamians in early 20th century Miami. *Florida Historical Quarterly* 65 (January), pp. 271–297.

Plane, David, and Peter A. Rogerson. 1994. *The analysis of population.* New York: John Wiley & Sons.

Portes, Alejandro, and R. L. Bach. 1985. *Latin journey: Cuban and Mexican immigration in the United States.* Berkeley: University of California.

Portes, Alejandro, and Leif Jensen. 1987. What's an ethnic enclave? The case for conceptual clarity. *American Sociological Review* 52 (6), pp. 768–771.

———. 1989. The enclave and the entrants: Patterns of ethnic enterprise in Miami before and after Mariel. *American Sociological Review* 54 (6), pp. 929–949.

Portes, Alejandro, and Dag MacLeod. 1996. Educational progress of children of immigrants: The role of class, ethnicity and school context. *Sociology of Education* 69 (October), pp. 255–275.

Portes, Alejandro, and Min Zhou. 1993. The new second generation: Segmented assimilation and its variants. *The Annals of the American Academy of Political and Social Science* 530 (November), pp. 74–97.

Portes, Alejandro, and Alex Stepick. 1993. *City on the edge: The transformation of Miami.* Berkeley: University of California Press.

Reid, Ira. 1938. *The Negro immigrant.* New York: Columbia University Press.

Reimers, David. 1985. *Still the golden door: The Third World comes to America.* New York: Columbia University Press.

Rhone, Trevor. 1986. *Two can play* and *School's out.* New York: Longman.

Rumbaut, Rubén G. 1995. "The new Californians." In *California's immigrant children,* edited by Rubén G. Rumbaut and Wayne A. Cornelius. San Diego: Center for U.S.-Mexico Studies, University of California.

———. 1996. The crucible within: Ethnic identity, self-esteem, and segmented assimilation among children of immigrants. In *The new second generation,* edited by Alejandro Portes. New York: Russell Sage Foundation.

———. 1997. Assimilation and its discontents: Between rhetoric and reality. *International Migration Review* 31 (4), pp. 923–960.

Smith, M. G. 1961. *West Indian family structure.* Seattle: University of Washington Press.

U.S. Bureau of the Census. 1990a. *Census of population and housing.* Public-use microdata sample, 1% sample. Washington, D.C.: U.S. Government Printing Office.

———. 1990b. *Census of population and housing.* Summary tape file 3A. CD-ROM.

Viburn, Marjorie. 1998. Caribbean immigrant's political moves stir tensions. *The Wall Street Journal,* June 30.

Vickerman, Milton. 1998. *Crosscurrents: West Indians and race.* New York: Oxford University Press.

Waters, Mary C. 1999. *Black identities: West Indian immigrant dreams and American realities.* Cambridge: Harvard University Press and Russell Sage Foundation.

Woldemikael, T. M. 1989. *Becoming black American: Haitians and American institutions in Evanston. Illinois.* New York: AMS Press.

Zhou, Min. 1997. Segmented assimilation: Issues, controversies and recent research on the new second generation. *International Migration Review* 31 (4), pp. 975–1008.

Zhou, Min, and Carl L. Bankston III. *Growing up Americans: How Vietnamese children adapt to life in the United States.* New York: Russell Sage Foundation.

Chapter 10

CONCLUSION
The Forging of a New America:
Lessons for Theory and Policy

Alejandro Portes and Rubén G. Rumbaut

Assimilation and Pluralism

The two general theories, or metaphors, that for so long have domi-
nated the discourse on the fate of immigrants in America—assimilation
and ethnic pluralism—do not fare very well in light of the evidence in
the preceding chapters. True, supporters of the assimilation perspective
can point to the near-universal adoption of English, the equally rapid
loss of foreign languages, and the widespread shift to American fash-
ions and lifestyles as evidence that the new second generation is indeed
"melting." But against this conclusion rises an equally solid body of evidence pointing to a universal shift from American identities to ethnic
ones, increasing perceptions of discrimination against one's own group,
and an overall reassertion of heritage and cultural distinctness that
bodes ill for predictions of future national homogeneity.

Neither is it the case, according to the findings reported in the preceding chapters, that full assimilation carries with it the promise of educational and future occupational success. Learning English is, of course, a
precondition for such outcomes, but the loss of parental language fluency
drives a wedge within immigrant families, reducing parental guidance
and control at a crucial time in the lives of these adolescents. There is, in
addition, a consistent decline in drive and work effort paralleling accul-

turation and, among some groups at least, the business and professional success of the first generation translates into a more slackened attitude toward academic work, higher rates of school attrition, and greater conflict with still goal-driven parents.

If assimilation theory does not provide a good framework for comprehending this complex set of findings, it would be equally risky to assert that pluralism does so. The rediscovered national identities and cultural origins among today's children of immigrants do not represent linear continuations of what their parents brought along. They are rather a "made-in-the-U.S.A." product born of these children's experiences of growing up American. As such, these reaffirmed ethnicities and perceptions of discrimination are integral parts of the process of acculturation, as it takes place in real life. Second-generation youths who loudly proclaim their Mexicanness or Haitianness often do so in English and with a body language far closer to their American peers than to anything resembling their parents' culture.

Almost 40 years ago, Nathan Glazer and Daniel P. Moynihan summarized their study of descendants of European immigrants and domestic migrants in New York City by stating that the key point about the vaunted melting pot was that "it did not happen" (1970: xcvii). By this, they meant that enduring and important differences characterized the respective ethnic communities and that, contrary to the desires and predictions of assimilationists, they were not at all in a process of dissolution. The other side of the argument, of course, is that the Italians, Jews, Irish, and Puerto Ricans of New York City became something quite different from what their migrant forebears had been. They each became American in their own way as the product of the interaction between what the group brought by way of skills, traditions, and language and what it encountered in the big metropolis. This was the melting pot that *did* happen.

In other cities and with different national origins, the same process is taking place today. Results presented in each of the preceding chapters show how the interaction between immigrant parents' characteristics and contexts of reception plays itself out for different nationalities, forging distinct but undeniably American personalities and outlooks. These findings also make abundantly clear that the process can be quite difficult and yield outcomes at variance with the rosy predictions of a uniform linear ascent. Assimilation to American society undoubtedly takes place, but the key question is to *what sectors* of the society and in what conditions does this shift occur. For it is not the case that a vast host nation receives each immigrant group with the same attitude or bestows on each the same doses of benevolence and assistance.

Segmented Assimilation and Its Types

Findings from the studies presented in this book illustrate how segmented the process of assimilation has become. In some instances, high human capital among immigrant parents combines with a relatively neutral or favorable context of reception to produce rapid mobility into the middle class. These families possess the necessary wherewithal to support an advanced education for their children. At the same time, the very success of achieving a comfortable middle-class lifestyle often leads to conflict between parents bent on maintaining their traditional values and ambitions and their thoroughly acculturated offspring. The case of Filipino immigrants and their children, analyzed in careful detail by Yen Le Espiritu and Diane L. Wolf (Chapter 6), approximates this situation.

In other cases, socioeconomic success depends less on advanced educational credentials in the first generation than on the possession of entrepreneurial skills and a favorable context of reception that facilitates the construction of solidary ethnic communities. Although immigrant parents may not reach advanced professional positions, their success at small business, combined with dense social networks, provides a supportive environment for the educational and occupational advancement of the second generation. In these instances, parental authority is buttressed by co-ethnic ties, leading to a more paced process of acculturation and less social distance between generations. The diverse Cuban enclave in Miami, constructed by the first generations of exiles from the island and analyzed by Lisandro Pérez (Chapter 4), provides a close approximation to this type of assimilation. So does another group of refugees—the Vietnamese—whose positive reception by the U.S. government provided the grounds for the reconstruction of families and communities and the emergence of bounded solidarity. The compelling results for children growing up in the Vietnamese community of San Diego, including their comparatively greater drive to achieve than that found among Cuban-American youth in Miami public schools, are analyzed by Min Zhou (Chapter 7).

A number of immigrant groups combine little professional or entrepreneurial skills with an unfavorable governmental and societal reception. The challenges of adaptation to a foreign environment, considerable to begin with, are magnified by the hostility of the surrounding environment. Poverty is the lot of most immigrants in this situation and, with it, regular exposure to the lifestyles and outlooks of the most downtrodden segments of the native population. Children of these immigrant families seldom have the opportunity to assimilate into middle-class American circles but every opportunity to do so into those of the native poor and the underclass. This occurs at the same time that the economic and social difficulties faced by their families prevent the emergence of well-structured ethnic communities capable of reinforcing parental authority. Downward rather than upward assimilation is a real possibility for children growing up under these conditions.

By far, the most important group among those exposed to these circumstances is the Mexican Americans. As David López and Ricardo D. Stanton-Salazar make clear in Chapter 3, Mexican immigration has been going on for so long as to spawn several "old" second generations. Yet the lot of today's Mexican immigrant children may be even worse than those of their predecessors because of persistent external discrimination, the disappearance of industrial job ladders, and the increasing educational requirements of a technology-driven economy. The size of Mexican immigration dwarfs that of any other national group, while its continuing poverty and adaptive difficulties present a major challenge for the future. The extent to which Mexican-American youths manage to overcome these barriers or, on the contrary, fall further behind will play a central role in the long-term character of their ethnic community and of the cities and states where it concentrates.

However, contrary to some statements in the literature suggesting that the threat of downward assimilation is an exclusively Mexican problem, several of the preceding studies show that other sizable immigrant nationalities are also at risk. They include Nicaraguans, a group whose high original expectations were dashed by an unwelcome official reception and subsequent severe handicaps in the southern Florida labor market. As a consequence, the study by Patricia Fernández-Kelly and Sara Curran (Chapter 5) shows that even professional Nicaraguan families have difficulties guiding their children, as their tenuous legal status translates into precarious employment that leads, in turn, to poor housing and low-quality schools. Despite considerable human capital, Nicaraguans have been unable to reproduce the Cuban pattern of enclave development because they lacked the crucial element of a benevolent and supportive external environment.

The pattern is even more evident in the two predominantly black minorities in the CILS sample. Haitian immigrants in southern Florida have suffered not only from a generally hostile governmental reception but from widespread social and labor market discrimination as well. Combined with the low average human capital of the first generation, this has produced what is arguably the most impoverished immigrant community in the region. As the Stepicks and their associates show in Chapter 8, the process of assimilation of the Haitian second generation inexorably leads into black America, as mainstream society fails to make any distinction between immigrant and native blacks and discriminates against them in equal fashion. Given their poverty, Haitian immigrants seldom join the African-American middle class but instead settle in close proximity to the most downtrodden sectors of the native minority. In Miami's inner-city schools, Haitian-American youths are regularly exposed to patterns of acculturation inimical to educational achievement and upward mobility. Surrounded by a weak ethnic community, only parents and families stand as barriers to socialization into this path.

Jamaican and other West Indian immigrants are subject to similar external discrimination, and as Philip Kasinitz, Juan Battle, and Inés Miyares point out (Chapter 9), they are also in the process of "fading to black." However, in their case, an unfavorable context of reception is partially balanced by the educational and occupational credentials of many parents, their fluent (and distinctly accented) English, and their commitment to preserve their culture and aspirations. Perhaps more than among any other nationality, West Indian assimilation represents a contested terrain where downward pressures stemming from external discrimination are countermanded by the intellectual and material resources of families and their commitment to see their children through.

Paths of Acculturation

Figure 10.1 reproduces the theoretical model that guided our own analysis of general results from the CILS surveys, which is presented in a separate companion volume, *Legacies* (Portes and Rumbaut 2001). Although authors of chapters in the present book were entirely free to analyze the data in their own terms and wrote their chapters independently of our own, it is worth noting that their results are mostly in agreement with the sequences posited by this model. The studies of individual

Figure 10.1. The Process of Segmented Assimilated: A Model

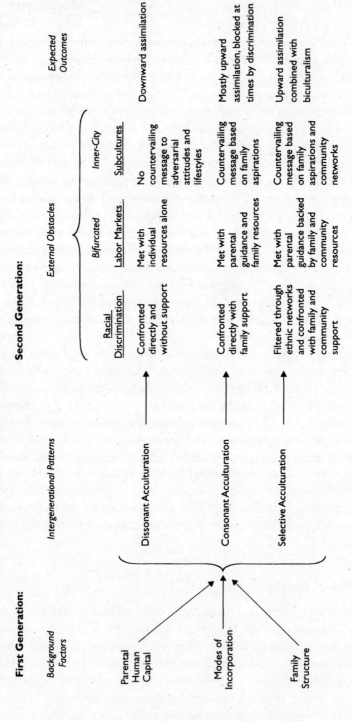

First Generation:

Background Factors	Intergenerational Patterns

Parental Human Capital

Modes of Incorporation

Family Structure

Dissonant Acculturation

Consonant Acculturation

Selective Acculturation

Second Generation:

External Obstacles

Racial Discrimination	Bifurcated Labor Markets	Inner-City Subcultures	Expected Outcomes
Confronted directly and without support	Met with individual resources alone	No countervailing message to adversarial attitudes and lifestyles	Downward assimilation
Confronted directly with family support	Met with parental guidance and family resources	Countervailing message based on family aspirations	Mostly upward assimilation, blocked at times by discrimination
Filtered through ethnic networks and confronted with family and community support	Met with parental guidance backed by family and community resources	Countervailing message based on family aspirations and community networks	Upward assimilation combined with biculturalism

nationalities support the proposition that there is no single assimilation path detectable in the second generation and, moreover, that different outcomes are influenced by the experiences and achievements of the first. The adaptation process registers individual variants and exceptions but, by and large, it follows a predictable sequence where outcomes build on each other, with earlier successes and failures decisively affecting future outlooks, identities, and achievements.

First-generation resettlement is decisively influenced by what immigrants bring with them in the way of skills, experiences, and resources and the environment that receives them. The concept of modes of incorporation (Portes and Rumbaut 1996) was coined to highlight the basic and separate components of this context of reception, consisting of official policy toward specific nationalities; public receptivity, indifference, or rejection toward them; and the character and resources of preexisting co-ethnic communities. Modes of incorporation are important because they can facilitate, alter, or prevent the deployment of individual skills. This is illustrated poignantly by the experience of downwardly mobile Nicaraguan professional families and, in contrast, by that of post-1980 Cuban refugees whose generally modest educational credentials are compensated by the protection of the ethnic enclave (Fernández-Kelly and Curran, Chapter 5; Pérez, Chapter 4, in this volume).

The combination of these initial factors determines the socioeconomic status of immigrant families and the character of the communities that they are able to create. These affect decisively, in turn, relationships between parents and children. The storm and stress of the adolescent years, marked by a growing generational gap, are compounded, in the case of immigrant families, by a contest between two cultures often at odds over values and normative expectations (Rumbaut and Ima 1988; Rumbaut 1991, 1994). As shown by the CILS parental survey, all parents, regardless of nationality, tend to harbor high achievement expectations for their children. They do so, however, within the context of cultures that commonly put much more emphasis on parental authority and children's family obligations than is the rule in the United States.

In earlier publications, we have developed a typology of intergenerational relations in immigrant families to distinguish the principal paths that this cultural confrontation can take (Portes and Rumbaut 1996; Portes and Zhou 1993). *Consonant acculturation* occurs as parents and children learn the language and culture at approximately the same pace and adjust their behavior accordingly. More educated parents and those fluent in English are more likely to come closer to this path, as they are better able to understand and empathize with changes in their children's lives. Among major nationalities in the CILS sample, Filipinos appear most likely to approximate this path because of their high average education, knowledge of English, and relative absence of strong ethnic communities. However, as the study by Espiritu and Wolf points out, this is not entirely the case, as clashes of expectations still occur between parents and children and increasing awareness of racial discrimination brought about by the fast pace of acculturation in this group can lower children's self-esteem and encourage a reactive ethnicity. As these authors note, assimilation is anything but a panacea, even among these comparatively privileged families.

Much more problematic, however, is the opposite situation. *Dissonant acculturation* takes place when children's learning of English and introjection of American cultural outlooks so exceed their parents' as to leave the latter hopelessly behind. This path is marked by sharply higher levels of family conflict and decreasing parental authority because of divergent expectations and children's diminishing regard for their own cultural origins. Parents in this situation often complain that they cannot control their children since their entreaties and attempts at discipline are often ignored. Working-class immigrants and those lacking the support of strong co-ethnic communities are at greater risk of moving along this path because their own poverty reduces the authority of their directives, which are further weakened by lack of external validation. The dramatic accounts of Haitian and Nicaraguan families in the respective chapters of this book provide illustrations of this path. Parents enjoining their youths in Creole or Spanish to abide by the norms of their culture may have little to show for it. Their own unenviable situation stands as a negative model, showing in their children's eyes that such allegiance does not pay.

In between these extremes is a third alternative marked by a paced learning of the host culture along with retention of significant elements of the culture of origin. *Selective acculturation* is commonly associated with fluent bilingualism in the second generation. Bilingualism preserves channels of communication across generations even when parents remain foreign monolinguals. In other situations, partial loss of parental languages is compensated by supportive networks in the immigrant community. In every instance, the key element in selective acculturation is the absorption by second-generation youths of key values and normative expectations from their original culture and concomitant respect for them. While such a path may appear inimical to successful adaptation in the eyes of conventional assimilationists, in fact it can lead to better psychosocial and achievement outcomes because it preserves bonds across immigrant generations and gives children a clear reference point to guide their future lives.

As Zhou's study of the Vietnamese community in San Diego and Pérez's study of the Cuban enclave in Miami show, selective acculturation is commonly grounded on densely knit networks, capable of supporting parents' cultural outlooks and expectations. Pérez notes that fluent bilingualism is far more common among children attending private Cuban schools at the core of the ethnic enclave than among those in assimilation-oriented public schools. Zhou demonstrates that fluent bilingualism, although less common among Vietnamese-Americans, significantly increases self-esteem, reduces depressive symptomatology, and increases educational aspirations.

Barriers to Adaptation

Equipped with the material and moral resources that their families and communities can make available and placed along one or another path of acculturation, second-generation children face the various barriers to successful adaptation created by the host society. Of these, none is more important than discrimination. As noted in our introduction to this volume and elaborated by Leif Jensen in Chapter 2, the new second generation comes overwhelmingly from Latin America, the Caribbean, and Asia, and the majority of its members are considered nonwhite according to American racial norms. The CILS data show a clear gradient in perceptions of racial and ethnic discrimination—from a relatively low level among children of Cuban, Canadian, and European parents to very high levels among the offspring of Haitian and West Indian immigrants.

A key and common finding of the studies of individual nationalities is the progressive ethnicization of self-identities during adolescence. That is, instead of becoming more American with the passage of time, second-generation youths increasingly shift to ethnic- and racial-minority identities, ranging from the panethnic labels into which they are commonly classified (Asian, black, and Hispanic) to a reactive embracing of their parents' nationality. This common trend reflects the influence of external discrimination and growing awareness by children of the place they occupy in American hierarchies of race and social status. But even this pervasive process is modified by the paths of acculturation followed by immigrant families.

Children undergoing dissonant acculturation accompany this identity shift with greater signs of psychological maladjustment, including lower self-esteem and more frequent depression. Filipino Americans, in particular females, provide evidence of this association (Espiritu and Wolf, Chapter 6). By contrast, selective acculturation protects individuals against the psychosocial traumas of external discrimination. Despite their tendency to shift to panethnic identities, Cuban Americans in Miami still possess the highest levels of self-esteem and lowest perceptions of discrimination in the CILS sample (Pérez, Chapter 4). Among the Vietnamese as well, more reassertive national identities are also associated with higher self-esteem and aspirations (Zhou, Chapter 7).

A second barrier to successful second-generation adaptation lies in the presence of alternative behavioral models inimical to educational achievement. The emergence of these oppositional models in the inner city is linked to a long history of racial discrimination and segregation against domestic minorities, analyzed in detail by various authors (Barrera 1979; Massey and Denton 1993; Tienda and Stier 1996; Vigil 1988; Wilson 1987). The key point is that recent immigrants confront these realities as a fait accompli that can derail the achievement of higher educational and occupational status among their offspring. The CILS parental survey shows that immigrant parents combine high ambition for the future with a widespread fear that their children will fall victim to these deviant lifestyles. This fear leads some parents to the extreme of sending their young back home to be educated under the protection of kin and away from American streets (Portes and Rumbaut 2001).

In Chapter 2, Jensen reports that immigrant families tend to disproportionately settle in larger metropolitan areas and, within them, in central cities. An unexpected consequence of this settlement pattern is to put immigrant children in close contact with the cultural models of the inner city. This contact takes place in the streets and in the schools, raising a daily challenge to parental goals and normative expectations. The influence of this encounter is again significantly affected by paths of acculturation. Children ensconced in well-structured communities undergoing selective acculturation tend to be unaffected by oppositional messages and models. As Zhou (Chapter 7) makes clear, this psychological shield is not contingent on parents' socioeconomic status but depends instead on the character of their families and networks. Even poor immigrant communities, such as the Vietnamese in San Diego, can effectively insulate their young provided that they maintain a high level of institutional integration and solidarity. In such cases, the messages that education does not pay and that school conformity is "acting white" are effectively countermanded not by parents but by an entire web of social relations. The opposite is, of course, the case for children undergoing dissonant acculturation. The pervasive influence of drugs and gangs is confronted in isolation as second-generation youths grow progressively distant from their parents. Although this situation does not necessarily guarantee downward assimilation, it places these children at risk, as the study of the Haitian case illustrates (Chapter 8). The cumulative character of immigrant adaptation is nowhere more evident than in those instances where poverty stemming from low human capital leads to settlement in downtrodden urban areas and where weak ethnic communities associated with a negative mode of incorporation deprive immigrants of a vital social resource at a key moment in their children's lives.

The CILS surveys followed students only as far as the end of high school and, hence, provide no information on their occupational lives. It stands to reason, however, that occupational success will be determined by their qualifications and by labor market demand. As members of the new second generation enter adulthood, they confront a labor market in the midst of a momentous transition, taking it away from its old industrial base and toward an information-driven service economy. This transition has spelled the partial end of traditional blue-collar occupational ladders and concentrated labor demand on two sectors: unskilled and low-paid service employment and well-paid non-manual service jobs requiring advanced training (Morales and Bonilla 1993; Sassen 1991; Wilson 1987).

As the studies in this volume show, occupational aspirations among all second-generation groups are consistently high. However, the possibilities of their fulfillment, and with it, the achievement of a middle-class or higher lifestyle vary widely. The cumulative character of the process of adaptation, observed so clearly in these results, leads to the expectation of a significant bifurcation in early occupational attainment, with some individuals and groups gaining access to jobs requiring at least a college degree, while others see their opportunities restricted to manual work little better than that performed by their parents. While first-generation immigrants may have readily accepted such jobs as a ticket to life in America, their offspring are keenly aware of their stigmatized character. Frustration of their lofty aspirations and the prospect of a life spent in dead-end menial work may lead some of these youths to drift into alternative, deviant forms of employment. To the extent that the cumulative disadvantages of a negative mode of incorporation, weak ethnic communities, and dissonant acculturation culminate in labor market abandonment, the nation faces the prospect of a new rainbow underclass where new ethnicities join those already marginalized at the bottom of society. Along with individual and collective success stories, the studies presented in this volume offer reason to believe that this dismal outcome is not unrealistic, at least for some members of the new second generation.

Lessons for Theory

The explanatory model presented in Figure 10.1 can be interpreted as a specific instance and illustration of three broader theoretical notions: path dependence, the role of social capital, and the decisive importance of structural embeddedness in constraining individual action. The concept of path dependence in economics, akin to the sociological concept of cumulative causation (Becker 1963; Portes 1995), refers to the progressive narrowing of options for action brought about by the accumulation of past decisions and events. The creation of ethnic niches in specific sectors of the labor market (Waldinger 1986, 1996; Waters 1999; Wilson 1987) offers a good example. Once a firm has started to meet its labor needs with workers of a particular ethnic origin, the operation of social networks will lead to the identification and hiring of new workers of the same ethnicity to fill new vacancies, leading cumulatively to the effective monopoly of employment opportunities. Managers of such firms find their employment decisions constrained by the operation of this path-dependent process.

In our case, cumulative causation operates as a series of distinct paths where initial characteristics and the reception of newly arrived immigrants facilitate future access of the second generation to key moral and material resources or prevent it. Such access, or lack thereof, in turn determines the probabilities of a successful upward path versus downward assimilation. It is possible, but not likely, that children of impoverished immigrant parents living in inner-city neighborhoods and attending custodial public schools will graduate from an elite college. It is equally possible, but not likely, that children of immigrant professionals or entrepreneurs ensconced in a social environment that promotes bilingualism and selective acculturation will end up in drug gangs and in prison. Path dependence for second-generation children operates as a "funnel" in which opportunities for success appear abundant and open to all at the start but are progressively restricted by the operation of forces rooted in the individual's social context.

Of these, none is more important than family and community networks. *Social capital* is defined as the ability to gain access to needed resources by virtue of membership in social networks and larger social structures (Bourdieu 1985; Portes 1998). From the standpoint of the recipient, resources acquired through social capital have the character of a gift since they are not purchased in the market but obtained freely or on concessionary terms. For second-generation youths, the key resources are those that facilitate access to good neighborhoods and schools, prevent dissonant acculturation, and promote academic achievement. Not surprisingly, offspring of economically advantaged parents can gain ready access to these resources. But those whose parents are poor can also do so through their possession of social capital. The first source of such gifts is the family itself, where intact and extended units have a decisive advantage over single-parent households. Family solidarity can operate to pool the social and economic resources necessary to escape dysfunctional neighborhoods or, barring this, to limit the damage caused by external racism and deviant subcultures.

It is often the case, however, that barriers confronting the second generation prove overwhelming to families, and this is when co-ethnic communities come into play. Bounded solidarity operates as a source of social capital by reinforcing parental authority and expectations for the future. This invaluable resource cannot be purchased in the market but depends instead on the density and strength of networks grounded on a common origin. Children may initially perceive such networks as restrictive, but the effective constraints that they create yield significant benefits in the long run. Social capital is the factor accounting for the paradox that more successful integration to American society does not depend on complete acculturation but rather on selective preservation of immigrant parents' culture and the collective ties that go with it.

The concept of modes of incorporation represents a specific instance of structural embeddedness of individual action. The structures in question are those of the receiving government, society, and preexisting ethnic community. Together, they function to place individuals in different positions at the entry of the funnel of adaptation, determining the extent to which individual skills can be put into play and the level of social capital available to first-generation parents. This perspective is, of course, directly opposed to theories of immigrant assimilation that focus primarily or exclusively on individual human capital. These theories, which have been advanced by some economists (see Borjas 1990, 1999), either neglect the role of contextual forces in determining immigrant adaptation or portray them in superficial ways.

Contrary to such views, the findings from the preceding chapters and from the CILS study in general consistently point to the constraints and opportunities created by the social structures that incorporate newcomers, regardless of the latter's ambition or level of skills. Immigrants with high aspirations and advanced educational credentials can be prevented from putting them to use and placed on a downward assimilation path by the operation of forces over which they have little control. Others with much poorer personal endowments may find themselves in an upward mobility course out of extensive government assistance and strong community support. The concept of structural embeddedness can be envisioned as a second "funnel" of immigrant adaptation, one that does not operate through time, like the one described earlier, but through successive levels of generality. Governmental policies and societal conduct and outlooks operate to mold local structures, including the character of ethnic communities. These, in turn, directly affect individuals, determining the extent to which human capital can be put into play and social capital accessed for normative regulation of the second generation.

Lessons for Policy

On balance, results from the CILS surveys indicate that there is reason for concern about the future of the second generation. While most of these children will adjust well and will readily integrate into the mainstream of society, others are at risk of downward assimilation as an outgrowth of the forces just discussed. An enlightened, proactive policy would seek to reduce the numbers of those so exposed at present rather than confront the problem when it is too late. Unfortunately, there are two reasons not to be overoptimistic about the likelihood of such policies. First, social problems in America are seldom addressed until they have matured into full-blown pathologies. By that standard, the challenges to adaptation of the new second generation do not qualify. Instead, attention focuses on the concentrated poverty, violence, gangs, and drugs, rendering large sectors of American cities nearly uninhabitable. These problems are addressed at present with common disregard for the fact that the downtrodden minorities most directly affected by them are actually the children and grandchildren of former migrants— Southern blacks, Puerto Ricans, and earlier Mexican immigrants. The likelihood that the offspring of today's labor immigrants may follow a similar path and confront the same fate in the future has yet to enter American public consciousness.

Second, the policy positions that have garnered most favor with the American electorate are more likely to promote this dismal outcome rather than prevent it. Nativism, which seeks to reduce immigration to the minimum and isolate those who stay in a position of social inferiority, triggers predictable reactive processes leading to ethnic reassertiveness, withdrawal from normal mobility channels, and hostility toward mainstream institutions. The aftermath of the passage of Proposition 187 in California is only the latest example of the lamentable results of nativist policies and of the explosive divisions that they create (López and Stanton-Salazar, chapter 3 in this volume; Portes and Rumbaut 2001).

Forceful assimilationism does not seek to expel newcomers but to integrate them as quickly as possible into the American mainstream (Unz 1999). English immersion and the rapid loss of foreign languages and cultures promoted by assimilationist policies weaken immigrant parents' authority and help drive a wedge between generations. A common outcome is dissonant acculturation with its sequel of negative effects. The paradox is that, in seeking to make "good Americans" out of the second generation, English immersion and similar programs undermine the single resource that poor immigrant youths have to succeed: namely, the social capital inherent in their families and co-ethnic communities. In the programmatic scenario promoted by forceful assimilationism, schools and immigrant families work at cross-purposes, with negative consequences for both.

Despite the presence of large numbers of professionals and entrepreneurs in today's first generation, the majority of immigrants are still poor workers. The best chance for educational achievement and economic ascent among their children lies in selective acculturation. Unfortunately, this path has no political constituency at present so that its successes are often accomplished against and not with the support of educational and other mainstream institutions. The simplest and most effective proactive policy in support of today's second generation would consist of reversing this drift: backing up immigrant parents and the sense of self-worth and ambition grounded on their cultural past. As a basis for policy, selective acculturation is not the same as multiculturalism, for it does not seek to promote the emergence of quasi-permanent separate collectivities but rather to integrate effectively the new immigrant generations into the ladders of socioeconomic mobility of American society. It does so by helping these children preserve what assimilationism and dissonant acculturation take away from them—a clear sense of their roots, the value of fluency in a second language, and the self-esteem grounded on strong family and community bonds.

References

Barrera, Mario. 1979. *Race and class in the Southwest: A theory of racial inequality.* Notre Dame, Ind.: Notre Dame University Press.

Becker, Howard S. 1963. *Outsiders: Studies in the sociology of deviance.* New York: Free Press.

Borjas, George J. 1990. *Friends or strangers: The impact of immigrants on the U.S. economy.* New York: Basic Books.

———. 1999. *Heaven's door: Immigration policy and the American economy.* Princeton, N.J.: Princeton University Press.

Bourdieu, Pierre. 1985. "The forms of capital." In *Handbook of theory and research for the sociology of education,* edited by J. G. Richardson. New York: Greenwood.

Glazer, Nathan, and Daniel Patrick Moynihan. [1963] 1970. *Beyond the melting pot: The Negroes, Puerto Ricans, Jews, Italians, and Irish of New York City.* Reprint. Cambridge, Mass.: MIT Press.

Massey, Douglas S., and Nancy A. Denton. 1993. *American apartheid: Segregation and the making of the underclass.* Cambridge, Mass.: Harvard University Press.

Morales, Rebecca, and Frank Bonilla, eds. 1993. *Latinos in a changing U.S. economy: Comparative perspectives on growing inequality.* Newbury Park, Calif.: Sage.

Portes, Alejandro. 1995. "Economic sociology and the sociology of immigration: A conceptual overview." In *The economic sociology of immigration: Essays on networks, ethnicity, and entrepreneurship,* edited by Alejandro Portes. New York: Russell Sage Foundation.

———. 1998. Social capital: Its origins and applications in modern sociology. *Annual Review of Sociology* 24, pp. 1–24.

Portes, Alejandro, and Rubén G. Rumbaut. 1996. *Immigrant America: A portrait.* 2d ed. Berkeley: University of California Press.

———. 2001. *Legacies: The story of the immigrant second generation.* Berkeley and New York: University of California Press and Russell Sage Foundation.

Portes, Alejandro, and Min Zhou. 1993. The new second generation: Segmented assimilation and its variants. *Annals of the American Academy of Political and Social Sciences* 530 (November), pp. 74–96.

Rumbaut, Rubén G. 1991. "The agony of exile: A study of the migration and adaptation of Indochinese refugee adults and children." In *Refugee children: Theory, research and practice,* edited by Frederick L. Ahearn Jr. and Jean Athey. Baltimore, Md.: Johns Hopkins University Press.

———. 1994. The crucible within: Ethnic identity, self-esteem, and segmented assimilation among children of immigrants. *International Migration Review* 28, no. 4 (Winter), pp. 748–794.

Rumbaut, Rubén G., and Kenji Ima. 1988. *The adaptation of Southeast Asian refugee youth: A comparative study.* Washington, D.C.: U.S. Office of Refugee Resettlement.

Sassen, Saskia. 1991. *The global city: New York, London, Tokyo.* Princeton, N.J.: Princeton University Press.

Tienda, Marta, and Haya Stier. 1996. "The wages of race: Color and employment opportunity in Chicago's inner city." In *Origins and destinies: Immigration, race, and ethnicity in America,* edited by Silvia Pedraza and Rubén G. Rumbaut. Belmont, Calif.: Wadsworth.

Unz, Ron. 1999. "California and the end of white America." Commentary 108 (November), pp. 17–28.

Vigil, James Diego. 1988. *Barrio gangs: Street life and identity in southern California.* Austin: University of Texas Press.

Waldinger, Roger D. 1986. *Through the eye of the needle: Immigrants and enterprise in the New York garment trade.* New York: New York University Press.

———. 1996. *Still the promised city? African Americans and new immigrants in post-industrial New York.* Cambridge, Mass.: Harvard University Press.

Waters, Mary C. 1999. *Black identities: West Indian immigrant dreams and American realities.* Cambridge and New York: Harvard University Press and Russell Sage Foundation.

Wilson, William Julius. 1987. *The truly disadvantaged: The inner city, the underclass, and public policy.* Chicago: University of Chicago Press.

CONTRIBUTORS

JUAN BATTLE received his Ph.D. in sociology at the University of Michigan and holds a joint position as associate professor at Hunter College and the City University of New York Graduate Center. His fields of study include sexuality, race, social problems, and quantitative research methods, and he has published articles in *African American Research Perspectives* and *Race, Gender & Class*.

SARA CURRAN received her Ph.D. in Sociology from the Univeristy of North Carolina and is assistant professor of sociology at Princeton University. Her areas of research are family demography, migration, and development. She is currently working on a book about the causes and consequences of migration and education decisions for gender and family relations in Thailand.

YEN LE ESPIRITU received her Ph.D. in Sociology from the University of California, Los Angeles, in 1990. She is a professor of ethnic studies at the University of California, San Diego, and a former President of the Asian American Studies Association. Her research focuses on race relations, ethnic identities, gender, and migration. Her most recent book is *Asian American Women and Men: Labor, Laws, and Love*. She is currently completing a manuscript on the transnational and gendered lives of Filipino immigrants in San Diego.

EMMANUEL EUGENE is expected to complete his Ph.D. in Comparative Sociology in the Department of Sociology and Anthropology at Florida International University in 2001. His doctoral dissertation is entitled "Re-Imagining the Nation across National Borders: The Transnational Politics of Migrant and Non-Migrant Haitians Negotiated on Haitian Radio Based in South Florida."

PATRICIA FERNÁNDEZ-KELLY was awarded a doctoral degree in social anthropology from Rutgers University in 1981. She currently holds a joint position at the Princeton University Department of Sociology and Office of Population Research. She has written extensively about international migration and the effects of economic globalization on working women and their families in Mexico and the United States. She is the author of *For We Are Sold, I And My People: Women and Industry in Mexico's Frontier*. With filmmaker Lorraine Gray, she coproduced the Emmy Award–winning documentary *The Global Assembly Line*. She is currently completing a monograph about the recomposition of the Cuban-American working class in Hialeah, Florida.

LEIF JENSEN earned a Ph.D. in Sociology from the University of Wisconsin, Madison. He is professor of rural sociology and demography at Pennsylvania State University. In addition to his studies on immigration, he maintains research interests in poverty, underemployment, household economic strategies, and problems of children and youth in developing countries. He has published articles in *Rural Sociology* and *The Gerontologist*.

PHILIP KASINITZ received a Ph.D. in Sociology from New York University in 1987. He is a professor of sociology at Hunter College and the City University of New York Graduate Center. He is the author of *Caribbean New York: Black Immigrants and the Politics of Race* and co-editor of *The Handbook of International Migration*. He is currently working on a project on second-generation immigrants in the New York metropolitan area. Professor Kasinitz is a former chair of the International Migration Section of the American Sociological Association. In addition to his studies on international migration, he works on urban issues and contemporary American race relations.

YVES LABISSIERE received his Ph.D. from the University of California at Santa Cruz and is assistant professor of psychology and community studies at Portland State University. In 1998–1999, he received a Ford Foundation/National Research Council Minority Postdoctoral Fellowship to work on Haitian identity at the Immigration & Ethnicity Institute at Florida International University.

DAVID E. LÓPEZ received a Ph.D. in Sociology for Harvard University in 1972. He is associate professor of sociology at the University of California, Los Angeles. His recent publications include "Social and Linguistic Aspects of Assimilation Today" in *The Handbook of International Migration* and "Who Does What? California's Emerging Plural Labor Force" in *Organizing Immigrants*. His current research centers on the consequences of ethnic change in California.

INÉS MIYARES is associate professor of geography at Hunter College in New York City, specializing in the geography of recent immigration, refugee resettlement, and Latin American transnationalism. Her work has focused on Hmong, post-Soviet, and Cuban refugees; Salvadorans on temporary protected status; and the social and political geography of Latin American immigrants in the United States. Since 1998, Dr. Miyares has conducted a field school in Peru for undergraduate and graduate students interested in primary research on historical and contemporary Andean societies and on Andean natural environments.

LISANDRO PÉREZ received his Ph.D. from the University of Florida and is associate professor of sociology and director of the Cuban Research Institute at Florida International University in Miami. Pérez currently serves as the editor of *Cuban Studies*. He directed the fieldwork in southern Florida for the T1 and T2 (1992–1996) surveys of the Children of Immigrants Longitudinal Study. He is co-author, with Guillermo Grenier, of the forthcoming *Legacy of Exile: Cubans in the U.S.*

ALEJANDRO PORTES is professor of sociology at Princeton University and director of the Center for Migration and Development at the Woodrow Wilson School of Public Affairs. He has formerly taught at Johns Hopkins University, where he held the John Dewey Chair in Arts and Sciences; Duke University; and the University of Texas–Austin. He served as president of the American Sociological Association in 1998–99, received the Distinguished Career Award from the Section on

International Migration of the American Sociological Association, is a fellow of the American Academy of Arts and Sciences, and was elected to the National Academy of Sciences. His books include *City on the Edge: The Transformation of Miami; The New Second Generation; The Urban Caribbean; Immigrant America: A Portrait;* and *Legacies: The Story of the Immigrant Second Generation* (the last two co-authored with Rubén G. Rumbaut).

RUBÉN G. RUMBAUT is professor of sociology at Michigan State University and the founding chair of the Section on International Migration of the American Sociological Association. During the 1980s he directed the principal studies of the incorporation of refugees from Vietnam, Laos, and Cambodia—including the Indochinese Health and Adaptation Research Project and the Southeast Asian Refugee Youth Study. Since 1991 he has directed, with Alejandro Portes, the Children of Immigrants Longitudinal Study, whose results are scrutinized in this volume. His books include *Immigrant America: A Portrait* and *Legacies: The Story of the Immigrant Second Generation* (both with Portes); *Immigration Research for a New Century: Multidisciplinary Perspectives; Origins and Destinies: Immigration, Race, and Ethnicity in America;* and *California's Immigrant Children: Theory, Research, and Implications for Educational Policy.*

RICARDO D. STANTON-SALAZAR received a Ph.D. in education from Stanford University in 1990. He joined the faculty of the Rossier School of Education at the University of Southern California in the fall of 2000 as an Associate Professor. Interested in exploring new ways of addressing social inequality in society, Stanton-Salazar has examined the social networks and help-seeking experiences of low-income urban Latino adolescents in his research and writing. He has published an article in *Harvard Educational Review* and is the author of *Perilous Webs: The Social Support Networks of Working-Class Mexican-Origin Adolescents.* His main fields of interest are sociology of education, youth culture, race and ethnic relations, and family studies.

ALEX STEPICK received a Ph.D. from the University of California at Irvine. He is director of the Immigration and Ethnicity Institute and professor of anthropology and sociology at Florida International University. He is the author of *Pride Against Prejudice* and co-author with Alejandro Portes of *City on the Edge: The Transformation of Miami.*

CAROL DUTTON STEPICK is the research director of the Immigration and Ethnicity Institute at Florida International University and has conducted research with Haitians over the past 20 years. She was research director for the project "Academic Orientation of Immigrant and Native-Minority Adolescents," which was funded by the National Science Foundation, the Carnegie Corporation, the Andrew Mellon Foundation, and the Spencer Foundation. She is currently research director for the project "Religion, Immigration and Civic Life in Miami," funded by the Pew Charitable Trusts.

DEBORAH DYER TEED received her Ph.D. in Comparative Sociology in the Department of Sociology and Anthropology at Florida International University in Miami. Her doctoral dissertation was entitled "Voices at the Shore: Ethnolinguistic Identity among Haitian Adults and Immigrants."

DIANE L. WOLF received a Ph.D. in Development Sociology from the department of Rural Sociology at Cornell Universiy. She is associate professor of sociology at the University of California, Davis and a former Vice-President of the Pacific Sociological Association. She and Yen Le Espiritu are working on a collaborative project, "Emotional Lives: Children of Vietnamese and Filipino Immigrants," in San Diego. Her other project focuses on postwar family reconstruction among Jewish children who were hidden in the Netherlands during World War II.

MIN ZHOU is professor of sociology and Asian American studies at the University of California, Los Angeles. Her main areas of research are immigration and immigrant adaptation, ethnic and racial relations, Asian Americans, ethnic entrepreneurship and enclave economies, the community, and urban sociology. She is the author of *Chinatown: The Socioeconomic Potential of an Urban Enclave,* co-author of *Growing up American: How Vietnamese Children Adapt to Life in the United States,* and co-editor of *Contemporary Asian America.*

INDEX

Compositor: Impressions Book and Journal Services, Inc.
       Text: Sabon
    Display: Syntax